The FBI and the KKK

The FBI and the KKK

A Critical History

MICHAEL NEWTON

McFarland & Company, Inc., Publishers

Jefferson, North Carolina, and London

The present work is a reprint of the illustrated case bound edition of The FBI and the KKK: A Critical History, *first published in 2005 by McFarland.*

LIBRARY OF CONGRESS CATALOGUING-IN-PUBLICATION DATA

Newton, Michael, 1951–
The FBI and the KKK : a critical history / Michael Newton.
p.   cm.
Includes bibliographical references and index.

ISBN 978-0-7864-4072-6
softcover : 50# alkaline paper ∞

1. United States. Federal Bureau of Investigation — History.
2. Ku Klux Klan (1915–) — History.   I. Title.
HV8144.F43N478   2009   322.4'20973 — dc22   2005025414

British Library cataloguing data are available

Cover photograph ©2009 Digital Vision

Manufactured in the United States of America

*McFarland & Company, Inc., Publishers
Box 611, Jefferson, North Carolina 28640
www.mcfarlandpub.com*

Again, and always, for Heather

Contents

Preface

America's oldest terrorist group and its premier law enforcement agency were organized four decades and 450 miles apart. Both were founded in secrecy and in calculated defiance of Congress. Each was ostensibly created to defend the nation and the U.S. Constitution while protecting citizens from lawlessness, yet both have violated state and federal laws from the beginning, often with impunity. Both cherish a passion for secrecy, defying courts and statutes to preserve clandestine operations. Leaders of both organizations have traditionally championed right-wing causes that include persistent strains of xenophobia, racial and religious bigotry, sexism, homophobia and vigilante "justice." While theoretically at odds since 1922, the two organizations have secretly collaborated in pursuit of common goals and enemies.

At first glance, there appears to be no similarity between the Ku Klux Klan and the Federal Bureau of Investigation. One is a secret society pledged to white supremacy and "racial purity" at any cost, burdened with a 140-year history of brutal crimes; the other is an internationally famous police force, renowned for scientific crime-fighting techniques and sworn to the defense of civil rights as guaranteed by federal law in the United States. Klan members dress in hooded robes or stylized paramilitary garb, while FBI agents favor conservative business suits. Klansmen increasingly perceive themselves as waging "racial holy war" against "ZOG"—the "Zionist Occupation Government" in Washington, D.C.—while FBI agents defend federal authority.

And yet, despite those seemingly irreconcilable dissimilarities, the FBI and KKK share 80 years of parallel history, their sagas often intertwined. Klansmen have praised the FBI as often as they have reviled it. For decades, FBI agents moved reluctantly against the KKK—if they moved at all—and when forced to act decisively in the mid–1960s, their tactics were sometimes as lawless as the Klan's. At the same time, while some Ku Klux Klan factions were infiltrated and harassed, others were organized and led by FBI informants, surviving on covert infusions of federal cash. Even as bureau spokesmen boasted of their "secret war" against the KKK, FBI agents suppressed evidence of violent crimes (including mass murder), thus subverting prosecution of known terrorists, and actively collaborated with Klansmen or Klan-infested police departments to facilitate attacks on minority activists.

Hundreds of books, both popular and scholarly, have told the separate stories of the FBI and the Ku Klux Klan. Before J. Edgar Hoover's death in 1972, even the

FBI's most bitter critics felt obliged to praise the bureau for its legendary role in "breaking up" the mighty 1920s Klan — although, in fact, agents did nothing of the kind. Later FBI excesses, in the violent years of Dixie's "Second Reconstruction," were dismissed by many journalists and civil libertarians as minor sins committed in a worthy cause. Even today, when thousands of incriminating documents have been released under the Freedom of Information Act, discussion of FBI-KKK collaboration is generally relegated to footnote status in broader histories of the American civil rights movement.

The work in hand aims to fill that void in scholarship, collecting for the first time in one volume all the evidence of conflict and collusion between the FBI and Ku Klux Klan, from their first interaction in 1922 to the present day. It is a story as dramatic and distressing as any other in our nation's covert history. The fact that such events, spanning the best part of a century, remain unknown to most Americans is in itself a cautionary tale. If equal justice under law has any meaning in the present day, we all must learn from the mistakes of history and thus avoid their repetition in the future.

Introduction

The Ku Klux Klan and the Federal Bureau of Investigation developed on parallel paths. Both, despite public claims to the contrary, were organized in defiance of congressional authority. Both — again, despite denials from the bureau — restricted active membership to white males through the first half of the twentieth century. Both were pledged, after 1917, to the task of rooting out "Bolsheviks" and "radicals" from American society. In that pursuit, both trampled on the very laws that their respective charters promised to defend.

To understand the convoluted love-hate relationship between the KKK and FBI, we must explore the roots of each and watch them grow. Those roots lie deep in southern soil, and for the Klan they may be traced to the unsettled months after the climax of the Civil War.

BIRTH OF AN EMPIRE (1866–1876)

America's most persistent terrorist group began as a private social club in the spring of 1866. Its founders were six young Confederate veterans residing in Pulaski, Tennessee. All were in their twenties, the well-educated sons of good families. Four were fledgling lawyers, one served as editor of the *Pulaski Citizen,* and a fifth would be elected to the Tennessee state legislature. As described by one years later, they were "hungering and thirsting" for amusement after four long years of war. Their only goal at first was to "have fun, make mischief, and play pranks on the public."[1]

To that end, they organized a secret society. Some of them were college men, familiar with the southern Kuklos Adelphon fraternity, and they chose *ku klux*— a corruption of the Greek word for "circle"— as the name of their club, adding *klan* (spelled with a "k" for uniformity). As founding officers, they made up lofty titles for themselves: Grand Cyclops (president), Grand Magi (vice president), Grand Turk (sergeant-at-arms), Grand Exchequer (treasurer), and Lictor (guardian of the meeting place, or Den). Costumes were left to the individual member's taste, stressing a flair for the ghoulish and bizarre. As for playing pranks, "the public" was primarily confined to superstitious former slaves, whom Klansmen terrorized at will by posing as the ghosts or zombies of Confederate war dead. Almost at once, the Klan lured new initiates and soon expanded from Giles County to surrounding districts.[2]

It arrived at an auspicious time in southern history. Martyred president Abraham Lincoln and his successor, Tennessee Unionist Andrew Johnson, had proposed a simple plan for readmission of the wayward southern states. In order to rejoin the Union, ten percent of each state's white electorate from 1860 was simply required to abolish slavery, repeal secession ordinances, and repudiate any Confederate war debts. Blanket amnesty was granted to any ex–Confederate, except ranking leaders of the late rebel government, who swore an oath of loyalty to the United States. By November 1865, every state except chaotic Texas had complied with those terms. Newly elected senators and representatives stood ready to take their seats on Capitol Hill when Congress reconvened on 4 December 1865.[3]

The Republicans who dominated Congress quickly dashed those hopes. Presidential Reconstruction was too slick and easy for embittered war hawks like Charles Sumner and Thaddeus Stevens, who wanted the Old South to pay for its sins. More to the point, those sins were still ongoing, in the form of "Black Codes" passed by every southern state, which made a public mockery of the Thirteenth Amendment's ban on slavery. Under the Black Codes, freedmen were variously forbidden to own land or weapons, to break labor contracts with white employers or establish any "independent business," to make "insulting gestures" or utter "seditious speeches." South Carolina barred blacks from any occupation except "farmer or house servant." Florida prescribed 39 lashes for blacks who "intruded" on white assemblies or public conveyances, and the same punishment awaited blacks caught publicly smoking cigars in Selma, Alabama. "Stubborn or refractory servants" could be fined $50 under Alabama's Black Code, or "hired out at auction for a period of six months" if unable to pay the fine. Black children over two years old could be torn from their families and "apprenticed" to whites until maturity if their parents failed to teach them white-approved "habits of industry and honesty."[4]

Congressional Republicans, dubbed "radical" by white supremacist southern Democrats, were livid at the South's flagrant defiance. In April 1866 they passed America's first Civil Rights Bill, overriding President Johnson's veto. Two months later, a Fourteenth Amendment to the U.S. Constitution was approved — again over Johnson's veto — to guarantee freedmen full citizenship. President Johnson's third veto was overridden in January 1867 with passage of a law granting the vote to blacks in Washington, D.C.[5]

Southern whites reacted to the news from Washington as they had for generations, with violence directed toward blacks. In May 1866 Memphis police led white rioters on a pogrom that left 46 freedmen and two white Republicans dead, more than 80 blacks wounded, and 90 black homes, 12 schools and four churches burned to the ground. Two months later, New Orleans police led another massacre, killing 34 blacks and wounding more than 200. Throughout Dixie, individual lynchings, murders and assaults upon freedmen increased exponentially.[6]

On 2 March 1867, Congress passed the first of several Reconstruction Acts, dividing the former Confederacy into military districts ruled by Union generals, ordering new elections for state constitutional conventions, and empowering blacks to vote for the first time in Southern history. One month later, the KKK's Pulaski den called a meeting at Nashville's Maxwell House hotel, "coincidentally" synchronized with the state's Democratic convention. The meeting's purpose was declared in secret circulars:

> To reorganize the Klan on a plan corresponding to its size and present purposes; to bind the isolated Dens together; to secure unity of purpose and concert of action; to hedge the members up by such limitations and regulations as are best adapted to restrain them within proper limits; to distribute the authority among prudent men at local centers and exact from them a close supervision of those under their charge.[7]

The Klan's unstated "present purpose" was guerrilla warfare against blacks, Republicans, and any other groups or individuals who jeopardized the vaunted "southern way of life," embodied in the antebellum economic system and the holy creed of white supremacy. To that end, a command structure was formalized including Provinces (counties), Dominions (congressional districts), and Realms (states). Each state would theoretically be ruled by a Grand Dragon, and Dixie at large — now christened the Klan's "Invisible Empire" — would be supervised by an autocratic Grand Wizard. In its new prescript, the Klan vowed to "recognize our relations to the United States Government and acknowledge the supremacy of its laws," while dedicating itself "To the Lovers of Law and Order, Peace and Justice."[8]

The Klan's choice for Grand Wizard clearly demonstrated the gap between stated ideals and practical reality. Nathan Bedford Forrest, 46, was a former slave trader and Confederate cavalry leader, known in equal measure for his daring in combat and gross insubordination (including death threats) to his superiors in uniform. In April 1864 his troops had massacred black prisoners of war at Fort Pillow, Tennessee, their victims including a number of women and children. Controversy persists as to whether Forrest ordered the slaughter or simply lost control of his men, but one telling report describes his tour of the killing ground, pointing out individual corpses and remarking, "They've been in my nigger-yard in Memphis." Appointed Grand Wizard in May 1867, Forrest ensured by his style of command that the reorganized KKK would combine the worst aspects of violence and irresponsibility.[9]

Within a year of the Nashville meeting, Klansmen were found throughout the South, recruitment often coinciding with General Forrest's travels as an itinerant labor contractor. The first dens outside Tennessee were organized in Alabama, where Klansmen competed with rival Knights of the White Camellia (KWC). Both organizations also existed in Arkansas and Louisiana, with reports of overlapping membership. Texas boasted three "chivalrous" orders, including the Klan, KWC, and Knights of the Rising Sun. Florida Klansmen sometimes shed their masks and operated as the Young Men's Democratic Club, and Carolina knights shared vigilante chores with the Constitutional Union Guard. Virginia's Klan was short-lived, fading by the end of 1868, but Kentucky made up the difference, emerging as the only Union state to have an active Reconstruction Klan.[10]

Wherever dens were organized, a racist reign of terror ensued. Tennessee witnessed the first bloodshed by Klansmen under Grand Dragon George Gordon, with Pulaski and Giles County among the state's most lawless districts. Murders were common, and floggings more so; one victim was left crippled after he received 900 lashes on a midnight raid. In Alabama, Congress documented 109 murders committed by Grand Dragon John Morgan's knights, and that number was no doubt conservative. Klansmen burned Greene County's courthouse, followed shortly by three schools for blacks. In Eutaw, Klan rioters killed four blacks and wounded 50 in October 1870. Georgia was worse yet under Grand Dragon (later governor and U.S. senator) John Gordon: in the three-month period from August to October 1868, Klansmen killed 31 persons, shot 43 more, stabbed five, and whipped at least 55, including eight floggings of 300 to 500 lashes apiece. The Klan-led riot at Camilla, in September 1868, left seven blacks dead and more than 30 injured.[11]

Virginia suffered only scattered violence before the Klan dissolved in late 1868, but Arkansas endured a replay of the Civil War in miniature, between Governor Powell Clayton's militia and Klansmen led by Grand Dragon Robert Shaver (or Augustus Garland; reports vary). Columbia County saw ten blacks killed in a three-week period of August 1868, and Lafayette County logged 20 murders in the same month. When Governor Clayton purchased muskets for his troops out of state, Klansmen hijacked the shipment and destroyed them. At Lewisburg, in November 1868, Klansmen destroyed one-third of the town while trying to burn a Republican's store. Louisiana's terror climaxed during the presidential campaign of 1868 with an appalling 1,081 murders, 135 persons shot and wounded, and 507 otherwise assaulted. Florida Klansmen mimicked their Arkansas brethren by stealing muskets from the state militia, appropriating some for their own use. Jackson County was among the South's worst in Reconstruction, its 179 murder victims including two Republican county clerks and the Klan's first Jewish target, liberal merchant Samuel Fleishman. Mississippi Klansmen, under Grand Dragon James George, conducted a vicious campaign against black schools and "carpetbag" teachers. Meridian's riot of March 1871 started in the county courthouse, Klansmen killing the judge and eight black witnesses before they ran amok through the town at large.[12]

In Texas, where Klansmen competed or collaborated with Knights of the White Camellia and Knights of the Rising Sun, near anarchy prevailed throughout Reconstruction. General John Reynolds, commanding Union forces in the Lone Star State, found murders of freedmen "so common as to render it impossible to keep an accurate record of them," and no final tabulation was attempted. Kentucky witnessed as much Ku Klux violence as any state of the old Confederacy, but it was more diverse: In addition to the usual raids on blacks and Republicans, Kentucky Klansmen burned Shaker homes at Bowling Green and devoted much of their time to defending moonshine stills. At Harrodsburg alone, they murdered 25 victims and flogged at least 100. Klansmen got a late start on their raids in North Carolina, but they made up for it in 1869 and 1870, battling Governor William Holden's militia in Caswell and Alamance Counties. More than a hundred members were arrested, but in vain; in 1871, Holden made history as the first American governor to be impeached and removed from office. The terror lasted longest in South Carolina, where the Laurens riot of October 1870 killed 12 Republicans on the eve of state elections. York County was the Klan's strongest bastion, with two-thirds of all white men enlisted; its raiders killed 11 persons and flogged 600, burning down five schools and churches.[13]

Fervent denials notwithstanding, much of the Klan's violence was clearly political. Blacks were targeted more often for voting than for any real or imaginary crimes, and Republican officials of both races were constantly at risk throughout the South. In every state where Klansmen rode, the terrorism had dramatic political impact. Tennessee Republicans saw their margin of victory slashed by 18,000 votes between 1867 and 1868. In Alabama, 2,000 "radical" votes were wiped out in Greene County alone. Louisiana's Republican primary vote of April 1868 was cut in half before November's general election, while the Democratic turnout more than doubled. Terrorists disenfranchised some 3,000 Georgia Republicans in 1868, and Democrats effectively regained control of the state government two years later. Kentucky blacks voted for the first time in 1870 with passage of the Fifteenth Amendment, but renewed Ku Klux raiding soon barred them from the polls.[14]

With southern lawmen either friendly to the KKK or driven into hiding by its mayhem, and state militias frequently outnumbered and outgunned by nightriders, only the federal government remained to curb Klan terrorism. Step one, in March 1870, was the Fifteenth Amendment to the U.S. Constitution, giving the vote to former slaves. To give that pledge teeth, Congress next passed a series of Enforcement Acts. The first, in May 1870, applied stiff penalties to anyone convicted of conspiring to deprive U.S. citizens of suffrage or other civil rights. The second, nine months later, placed federal authorities in charge of voter registration and balloting in congressional elections. Finally, in April 1871, a third bill—popularly dubbed the Ku Klux Act—defined Klan violence as rebellion against the United States, permitting the president to declare martial law in troubled areas.[15]

While southern Democrats denounced the new legislation and denied any need for federal intervention in Dixie, a joint congressional committee opened hearings on the plague of racial violence below the Mason-Dixon Line. The panel interviewed scores of victims and dozens of Klansmen, including Grand Wizard Forrest (who later admitted to friends that he "lied like a gentleman" while testifying under oath). The net result, a 612-page report with 12 volumes of supporting testimony, documented a state of virtual anarchy across the Deep South, from Mississippi through the Carolinas.[16]

Thus doubly armed with facts and legislation, President Ulysses Grant launched his campaign against the Ku Klux Klan. Before the program ran its course, 1,849 terrorists were indicted in South Carolina, 1,180 in North Carolina, 930 in Mississippi, and lesser numbers in four other states. Only South Carolina fell subject to the Ku Klux Act, with martial law briefly imposed on nine of the state's most violent counties. There was a world of difference, though, between arresting Klansmen and convicting them. In Tennessee, where the Klan got its start and committed its earliest crimes, only a single raider was ever convicted. Fourteen Klansmen faced trial in Florida, again with only one conviction. Together, Alabama and Georgia saw 160 Klansmen indicted in 1871, but none had been tried by year's end. A total of 262 Mississippi knights were finally convicted, including 28 who pleaded guilty to murder, but all received suspended prison terms in exchange for promises to quit the Klan. In South Carolina's York County, 57 Klansmen were imprisoned, but 161 of those indicted for serious crimes were never tried. By late 1872, 65 Klansmen were in federal prison and several times that number confined to southern jails, but parole and pardons liberated nearly all of them by 1875.[17]

Grant's war against the KKK was superficially effective in that it dissolved the formal order. Virginia's Klan had dissolved in December 1868, and Wizard Forrest called for general disbandment a month later, but his order was widely ignored. Tennessee knights remained active until spring 1869, and Louisiana's Knights of the White Camellia apparently folded their robes in the summer of that year. Klan leaders in Alabama and Georgia tried to disband their troops in 1869 and 1870, respectively, but raiding continued until federal troops began making arrests. South Carolina was the last hold-out, but most students of the Klan agree that the Invisible Empire formally disbanded in all states sometime between late 1871 and early 1873.[18]

Klansmen without their robes and titles, though, were still Klansmen in spirit — and they still had work to do in several states before the South was finally restored to what the Democratic party called "Home Rule." On Easter Sunday 1873, terrorists in Colfax, Louisiana, burned the courthouse and slaughtered more than 60 blacks. Nine months later, armed Democrats seized power in Texas and abolished Reconstruction there. April 1874 saw the formation of a new, unmasked White League in Louisiana, followed by a massacre of 60 Republicans at Coushatta in August and a *coup d'etat* that toppled the state government in September, leaving 27 dead and 105 wounded in New Orleans. The same bloody season witnessed a mass lynching of 16 Tennessee blacks on 26 August 1874. White terrorists inaugurated the "Mississippi Plan" for political domination in December 1874 with a massacre of 75 Republicans at Vicksburg. Subsequent slaughters at Yazoo City (July 1875) and Clinton (September 1875) paved the way for near-insurrection at November's election, thus restoring the state to "Home Rule" by white supremacists. The presidential campaign of 1876 sparked racist pogroms at Hamburg, Arkansas, and in several South Carolina towns, where former Klansmen were reorganized as Red Shirts; the worst outbreak, at Ellenton in September, claimed 41 lives. November's balloting was marked by violence throughout the South, climaxed by a compromise between Republican Rutherford Hayes and Democratic contender Samuel Tilden. After meeting with a Democratic delegation that included Georgia's late Grand Dragon, Hayes traded Dixie for the White House, ending Reconstruction in exchange for Tilden's concession of defeat. As seen by many Southern whites, the KKK and allied groups had won their battle to "redeem" the prostrate South.[19]

Racism Ascendant (1876–1907)

Congress made a last bid to insure black civil rights two years before the Hayes-Tilden compromise, with passage of another Civil Rights Act in March 1875. It anticipated progress of another century when it declared:

> All persons within the jurisdiction of the United States shall be entitled to the full and equal enjoyment of the accommodations, advantages, facilities, and privileges of inns, public conveyances on land or water, theaters, and other places of public amusement; subject only to the conditions and limitations established by law and applicable alike to citizens of every race and color, regardless of any previous condition of servitude.[20]

Those new rights were, at least in theory, defended by provisions of the various Enforcement Acts passed by Congress in 1870 and 1871. One statute threatened private parties who conspired to abrogate the civil rights of any individual.

> If two or more persons conspire to injure, oppress, threaten, or intimidate any person in any State, Territory, Commonwealth, Possession, or District in the free exercise or enjoyment of any right or privilege secured to him by the Constitution or laws of the United States, or because of his having so exercised the same; or if two or more persons go in disguise on the highway, or on the premises of another, with intent to prevent or hinder his free exercise or enjoyment of any right so secured, they shall be fined under this title or imprisoned not more than ten years, or both.[21]

A second clause specifically addressed abuses practiced by peace officers or others in authority.

> Whoever under color of any law, statute, ordinance, regulation, or custom, willfully subjects any person in any State, Territory, Commonwealth, Possession, or District to the deprivation of any rights, privileges, or immunities secured or protected by the Constitution or laws of the United States, or to different punishments, pains, or penalties, on account of such person being an alien, or by reason of his color, or race, than are prescribed for the punishment of citizens, shall be fined under this title or imprisoned not more than one year, or both.[22]

By the time President Grant signed the Civil Rights Act of 1875, however, the U.S. Supreme Court had already begun whittling away the rights of blacks protected under federal law. The war of attrition began in 1873 with the *Slaughterhouse* cases, declaring that the Fourteenth Amendment protected only federal civil rights, not "civil rights heretofore belonging exclusively to the states." Two years later, in *Minor v. Happersett,* the high court seemingly ignored the Fifteenth Amendment, ruling that the U.S. Constitution conferred suffrage on no one, and that the United States per se had no voters of its own creation. Two cases from 1876 carried the campaign further: in *United States v. Reese et al.,* the court held that while the Fifteenth Amendment barred discrimination in voting, it did not confer a right to vote; *United States v. Cruikshank,* springing from the Colfax massacre of 1873, dismissed the federal convictions of three Louisiana terrorists, permitting federal prosecution only of officials who conspired against free exercise of civil rights. In *Hall v. de Cuir* (1877), the court held that states could not prohibit racial segregation on a common carrier. Six years later, a ruling in the collective *Civil Rights Cases* found the Civil Rights Act of 1875 unconstitutional, its various provisions unenforceable. In 1890's case of *Louisville, New Orleans, and Texas Railroad v. Mississippi,* the court ruled that states could constitutionally require segregation on public conveyances. *Plessy v. Ferguson* affirmed that ruling in 1896, establishing the doctrine of "separate but equal" facilities for different races. *Williams v. Mississippi* accelerated disfranchisement of freedmen in 1898, approving Mississippi's literacy tests and "understanding" rules that stripped blacks of their right to vote. As late as 1903, the court's decision in *James v. Bowman* confirmed that federal legislation attempting to ban private or official interference with the right to vote was unconstitutional.[23]

With a green light from the White House and the Supreme Court, Southern states wasted no time in legislating white supremacy, the several legislatures grinding out a paper avalanche of "Jim Crow" segregation ordinances. Railroads were first on the list, beginning in Tennessee (1881), soon followed by Florida (1887); Mississippi (1888); Texas (1889); Louisiana (1890); Alabama, Arkansas, Kentucky and Georgia (all in 1891); South Carolina (1898); North Carolina (1900); Maryland (1904); and Oklahoma (1907). Streetcars were next, proceeding with North Carolina and Virginia (1901); Louisiana (1902); Arkansas, South Carolina and Tennessee (1903); Maryland and Mississippi (1904); Florida (1905); Alabama (1906); and Oklahoma (1907). Other laws filled in the gaps, segregating everything from water fountains, theaters, and public parks to residential neighborhoods. Blacks lost the power to challenge such statutes as they were stripped of the vote, state by state across Dixie, between 1890 and 1908. Wherever they turned in the South, their path to the ballot box was blocked by literacy tests, poll taxes, biased "understanding" tests that demanded strict interpretation of obscure state laws (invariably judged by whites), and "grandfather" clauses restricting suffrage to those whose (white) grandfathers had been legally enfranchised.[24]

The need for such restrictions on "race mixing" was explained in the early twentieth century by a new wave of racist propaganda. Titles told the story for such "scientific" works as Charles Carroll's *The Negro a Beast; or In the Image of God* (1900); William Calhoun's *The Caucasian and the Negro in the United States* (1902); William Smith's *The Color Line: A Brief in Behalf of the Unborn* (1905); and Robert Shufeldt's *The Negro, a Menace to American Civilization* (1907). The verdict of those tomes was buttressed by a revisionist "moonlight-and-magnolia" school of Southern history, exemplified by the writings of professors William Dunning, John Ford Rhodes, John Reynolds, and future president Woodrow Wilson. These and others painted "radical" Reconstruction as a heinous assault on white civilization in Dixie, while praising the Ku Klux Klan for its efforts to "restore law and order." Finally, skewed history and pseudoscience merged in the popular novels of Thomas Dixon, a North Carolina native born in 1864. A classmate of Woodrow Wilson at Johns Hopkins University, Dixon was elected to the North Carolina State Legislature before he reached voting age, later preaching a hell-fire Baptist gospel in New York City for nearly a decade, spicing his sermons with praise for white supremacy and warnings against "creeping negroidism." His popular novels, aptly described by one critic as "racist sermons in the guise of fiction," included *The Leopard's Spots: A Romance of the White Man's Burden—1865–1900* (1902), *The Clansman: An Historical Romance of the Ku Klux Klan* (1905), and *The Traitor: A Story of the Fall of the Invisible Empire* (1907).[25]

Fueled by such venom and encouraged by legislation demeaning to blacks, a new wave of racist violence swept the South. At least 2,883 blacks were lynched by white mobs between 1883 and 1907, without a single indictment returned against killers who often posed for photographs beside the mutilated bodies of their victims. Rioting by whites, sometimes with the participation of police, was also common in this period. Four blacks died in an outbreak at Danville, Virginia, in November 1883. Twenty were killed in the Carrollton, Mississippi, riot of March 1886. Six blacks lost their lives in a New Orleans riot during March 1895. Wilmington, North Carolina, saw eight blacks slain by white rioters in November 1898. Rowdy New Orleans suffered another three-day outbreak in July 1900, leaving two white policemen and an unspecified number of black victims dead. White terrorists in Atlanta killed 12 blacks and provoked a declaration of martial law in September 1906.[26]

Throughout that long reign of terror, black Americans still hypothetically enjoyed some measure of protection under federal law, albeit narrowly restricted by decisions of the U.S. Supreme Court. In fact, though, federal statutes languished in the absence of an agency mandated to enforce them. Finally, as 1907 drew to a close with 59 lynchings in Dixie, that void was about to be filled.

THE BUREAU OF INVESTIGATION (1908–1915)

The U.S. attorney general occupies one of four original cabinet posts in Washington, created in 1789, but the Justice Department he leads did not exist until June 1870, organized in the midst of Reconstruction. Since March 1871 it has been authorized to spend money in detecting and prosecuting crimes against the United States, but Justice had no detectives of its own at the outset of the twentieth century. President Theodore Roosevelt sometimes borrowed Secret Service agents from the Treasury Department, but Congress rebelled at the practice after two of its members from Oregon were investigated and convicted of land fraud. Attorney General Charles Bonaparte proposed creation of a new detective force in 1907, but congressional critics objected, voicing fears that such a unit might inaugurate "a system of spying upon and espionage of the people, such as has prevailed in Russia." The argument became more personal with references to Joseph Fouché, the sinister chief of internal security under Bonaparte's granduncle, French Emperor Napoleon I. On 27 May 1908, Congress specifically forbade Roosevelt and Bonaparte to use Secret Service agents at Justice, threatening suspension of any agent who accepted an assignment outside the Treasury Department.[27]

Undismayed by criticism or the law, Bonaparte waited for Congress to adjourn, then proceeded to create the Bureau of Investigation (BI) on 1 July 1908, with 34 employees under Chief Stanley Finch. Congressional opponents were furious when the House reconvened, grilling Bonaparte on the character and moral fiber of his agents, some complaining that the bureau had begun to shadow them and read their private mail. President Roosevelt denied all such charges, while Attorney General Bonaparte chose a different tack, insisting that the innocent had nothing to fear from surveillance. "Anybody can shadow me as much as they please," he declared. "They can watch my coming in and my going out. I do not care if there is somebody standing at the corner and watching where I go or do not go." Thus placed on the defensive, stung by White House claims that countless felons had escaped detection since the use of Secret Service agents was suspended, Congress grudgingly permitted the new bureau to survive.[28]

For all the sound and fury that attended its creation, the BI had few clear-cut duties in its first year of life. Agents were generally restricted to investigating crimes on Indian reservations or other government property, plus a few antitrust cases and incidents of fraud in Washington, D.C. The bureau got its first big boost in 1910 with passage of the Mann Act to suppress "white slavery." Chief Finch led the drive to crush commercial prostitution rings, which he portrayed as vicious syndicates of kidnappers invading homes and plucking victims off the streets. "Unless a girl was actually confined in a room and guarded," Finch warned, "there was no girl, regardless of her station in life, who was altogether safe.... There was need that every person be on his guard, because no one could tell when his daughter or his wife or his mother would be selected as a victim."[29]

Commercial vice was traditionally a local concern, but Congress found its window of opportunity in the U.S. Constitution's commerce clause, crafting legislation that forbade transportation of females across state lines for "immoral purposes." On 30 April 1912 Stanley Finch was detached from the BI with a platoon of agents named Special Commissioner for the Suppression of White Slave Traffic. In his place, A. Bruce Bielaski assumed control of the bureau and did his best to assist in the crusade for virtue. Before the "white slave" panic ran its course in 1914 and the agents loaned to Finch resumed their normal duties, hundreds of arrests were logged under the Mann Act. Many of those jailed had no involvement in the flesh trade, but were simply men who crossed state lines with women other than their wives. In such fashion the bureau learned a lesson vital to its future: The intent of federal laws is sometimes very different from their impact, and the Mann Act (still in force today) provided agents with new avenues of blackmail and intimidation, where their vocal critics were concerned.[30]

One of the decade's celebrated Mann Act cases also turned a spotlight on the BI's staunch support of racial orthodoxy in America's "Progressive" era. The target was Arthur "Jack" Johnson, a black prize fighter from Texas who infuriated racists by defeating white contenders to become boxing's first black heavyweight world champion in 1910. Whites rioted after Johnson's defeat of opponent Jim Jeffries in June 1910, and they were even more outraged by Johnson's penchant for marrying white women. His second wife committed suicide in September 1911, and bigots saw their chance to cage Johnson the following year, when he became engaged to 19-year-old Lucille Cameron. Cameron's mother was induced to charge Johnson with abduction in October 1912, when he traveled with Lucille from Minneapolis to Chicago. BI agents investigated the "crime," ignoring Lucille's denial of any coercion, and a federal grand jury indicted Johnson for Mann Act violations on 7 November 1912. In lieu of Cameron, the bureau obtained testimony from a white prostitute who said that Johnson had once paid her fare from Chicago to Philadelphia, where they allegedly had sex. Convicted by an all-white jury in May 1913, Johnson was fined $1,000 and sentenced to a prison term of one month to one year. Free on bond pending appeal, he fled to Paris with Lucille — now Mrs. Johnson — but returned to serve his time at Leavenworth in 1920. The conviction effectively ended Johnson's career, although he was posthumously drafted for the Boxing Hall of Fame in 1946.[31]

For all their concern over public morals, bureau agents showed no interest whatsoever in protecting civil rights. A minimum of 353 blacks were lynched in America between 1908 and 1915 without a single federal investigation or indictment. Three days of rioting by whites in August 1908 at Springfield, Illinois, left three blacks dead and 75 injured before troops intervened. BI agents ignored an outbreak in Tampa, Florida, where terrorists fired on a black church and killed three worshippers in July

1910; later the same month, they were likewise absent from Palestine, Texas, where terrorists murdered 18 blacks "without any real cause at all." No investigation was launched in March 1913 when nightriders raided a black home at Henderson, North Carolina, killing four persons and burning the house. On the rare occasions when white terrorists were convicted — in Kentucky (April 1909), Tennessee (May 1909), and Texas (December 1910)—federal investigators played no part in the proceedings.[32]

Texas, indeed, had returned to a state of near anarchy resembling Reconstruction as revolution in Mexico spilled across the border, sparking raids and pitched battles between Anglos and Hispanics. At least 500 persons were killed in border fighting between 1908 and 1925, with some estimates placing the final body count at 5,000. Whites were occasionally killed or wounded, usually by bandits crossing the border, but most of the victims were Hispanics singled out for vigilante mayhem on racial grounds. Between 20 August and 10 October 1915, white mobs lynched 26 Mexican Americans in five separate incidents. Federal agents remained invisible throughout the reign of terror, while Texas Rangers illegally invaded Mexico and white terrorists raided at will, ignored (when they were not actively assisted) by local police.[33]

With so much bigotry and racial violence in the land, the time was ripe for a revival of the Ku Klux Klan. Unknown to Southern partisans who cherished fantasies of Ku Klux "heroism" in the 1860s, its revival was about to get a boost from unexpected allies in the nation's capital — and in Hollywood.

The Invisible Empire Revived (1915–1916)

In April 1914, director D.W. Griffith purchased screen rights to *The Clansman,* Thomas Dixon's best-selling novel, and began production of America's first epic motion picture. The result, titled *The Birth of a Nation,* filled 12 reels and cost a record $110,000 to finish, premiering in Los Angeles on 8 January 1915. Blacks and liberal whites condemned the film's portrayal of brutish freedmen (played by white actors in blackface) and its glorification of the violent Ku Klux Klan. Dixon appealed to his friend Woodrow Wilson, now president of the United States, and Wilson viewed the film at a special White House screening on 18 February. Moved almost to tears, Wilson declared, "It is like writing history with lightning, and my only regret is that it is all so terribly true." Further endorsement came from Edward White, chief justice of the United States and a veteran of the Louisiana Klan (although White later grew embarrassed and recanted his support). The movie opened in New York in March to stern condemnation from critics including Jane Addams ("a pernicious caricature of the Negro race") and Upton Sinclair ("the most poisonous play"). Blacks were barred from the Boston premiere in April, but they sneaked into the theater and lobbed eggs at the screen. More protests erupted at screenings in Atlantic City, Pittsburgh, Milwaukee, Spokane and Portland, Oregon. White southern audiences were more appreciative, cheering the celluloid Klansmen and firing pistols at the first appearance of the film's black rapist. Admirers of the film urged Dixon to revive the

KKK, suggesting that he call it "Sons of the Clansmen," or perhaps the "Aryan League of America."[34]

While *The Birth of a Nation* made its way around the country, bigots found a new cause for excitement in Georgia. Fourteen-year-old Mary Phagan was murdered on 27 April 1913, at the Marietta pencil factory where she worked for Leo Frank, a Jew originally from New York. A black employee at the plant was first suspected, but he saved himself from jail (or lynching) by incriminating Frank. Convicted and condemned in a trial marked by anti–Semitic hysteria, Frank was spared from the gallows after Georgia's governor examined the flimsy evidence and commuted his sentence to life imprisonment. The governor's "traitorous" action galvanized racial propagandist Thomas Watson, a Populist campaigner from the 1890s so embittered by the failure of his liberal campaigns that he embraced racism and thus won election to Congress. In his spare time, Watson spewed venom at blacks, Jews and Catholics via two periodicals, *Watson's Magazine* and the *Weekly Jeffersonian*. His obsession with race-mixing sex and "libidinous priests" was so extreme that several issues of his magazines were banned from the U.S. mail as obscene, but bigots from coast to coast devoured each issue. Taking up the Frank case as a personal crusade, Watson cheered Frank's August 1915 lynching by a mob whose members called themselves the Knights of Mary Phagan. On 2 September, Watson called for the creation of "another Ku Klux Klan" in Georgia "to restore HOME RULE." Six weeks later, on 16 October, the Knights of Mary Phagan climbed Stone Mountain, near Atlanta, and lit America's first fiery cross in a scene lifted straight from the pages of *The Clansman*.[35]

For all their racist zeal, the self-styled knights weren't Klansmen — yet. The "honor" of a KKK revival fell to William Joseph Simmons, a defrocked Alabama minister who made his living as a recruiter and insurance salesman for fraternal lodges. In 1914 Simmons moved to Atlanta as district manager for the Woodmen of the World, which graced him with an honorary colonel's rank. While recuperating from an auto accident in early 1915, Simmons claimed to have had a vision of robed Klansmen galloping around his room on horseback. Thus inspired, he set about revising the Klan's original prescript, expanding it into a volume he called *The Kloran*. He dreamed up new ranks, titles, passwords and codes, most starting with the mystic letters "Kl." His Invisible Empire embraced the whole world — but membership was nonetheless restricted to white, native-born Protestant men. The Simmons Klan would stand for "an uncompromising standard of pure Americanism untrammeled by alien influences and free from the entanglements of foreign alliances." Simmons defined clannishness as "real fraternity practically applied," supporting "the soul of chivalry and virtue's impenetrable shield." His knights, if any were recruited, would "shield the sanctity of the home and the chastity of womanhood," while vowing "to forever maintain white supremacy." Above all, Klansmen were pledged "to protect the weak, the innocent, and the defenseless from the indignities, wrongs and outrages of the lawless, the violent, and the brutal; to relieve the injured and the oppressed; to succor the suffering and unfortunate, especially widows and orphans."[36]

Elaborate blueprints aside, Simmons let his dream lie dormant until October 1915. Ten days after the Stone Mountain cross-burning, on 26 October, Simmons

and 34 others— including two original Klansmen and several Knights of Mary Phagan —filed Georgia charter applications for the Knights of the Ku Klux Klan, described
as a "purely benevolent and eleemosynary order." On Thanksgiving night, Simmons
led a party to Stone Mountain, where they lit another cross. On 4 December 1915,
two days before *The Birth of a Nation* opened in Atlanta, local newspapers published
advertisements for the KKK, billed as "A Classy Order of the Highest Class." Black
models donned robes for publicity photos, and 92 members enlisted over the next
two weeks.[37]

The Klan was on its way, but no one seemed to know where it was going yet.
Racial violence continued in Dixie meanwhile: Fifty-six blacks were lynched in
1916 —15 of them in Georgia — but none of the mayhem was directly traceable to
Simmons or his knights. Another cause would spur the KKK to action soon, but it
was sparked by bloodshed overseas.[38]

Vigilantism in World War I (1917–1918)

War raged in Europe for nearly three years before the United States became
officially involved, on 6 April 1917. America's official declaration of hostilities was preceded, however, by long and furious debates over "preparedness," including widespread
agitation against German immigrants and other supposed "enemy aliens." The Bureau
of Investigation hired 100 new agents in the early weeks of 1917, but Chief Bielaski still
considered his manpower deficient for the coming struggle. On 20 March 1917 he forged
a working alliance with the American Protective League (APL), a private vigilante
group created by Chicago advertising executive Albert Briggs, active nationwide with
100,000 members in 1917 and claiming 250,000 a year later. Armed with badges that
identified them as "secret service" agents— later revised, after protests from Treasury,
to indicate an "auxiliary" function with Justice — APL members fanned out to comb
the land for spies and traitors. William Simmons collaborated with the APL's Georgia
commander, unleashing his Klansmen to harass "radical" labor unions and chase prostitutes away from military bases. The knights also coordinated their operations with
another, less prestigious vigilante group, the Citizens' Bureau of Investigation.[39]

Events moved swiftly after America's entry into World War I. On the day war
was declared, President Wilson ordered the Justice Department to arrest and detain
any identifiable "enemy aliens." In May, Congress passed the Selective Service Act,
requiring all men between the ages of 21 and 30 to register for military conscription.
A new Espionage Act (commonly called the Sedition Act) was passed on 15 June 1917,
penalizing any public opposition to the war, the draft, or sale of Liberty Bonds. BI
Chief Bielaski ordered his men to start hunting draft dodgers in July 1917, and vigilantes were encouraged by a $50 bounty offered for each "slacker" brought to jus-
tice. On 5 September 1917 the bureau and its private allies staged a series of nationwide
raids against a radical union, the Industrial Workers of the World (IWW). Hundreds
were arrested under the Espionage Act, and five tons of "seditious" literature was
seized by raiders in Chicago alone. Fears of lurking spies and saboteurs increased in
November 1917, when revolutionists deposed the Tsar in Russia.[40]

While war fever spread, the Justice Department acquired a new employee in the person of John Edgar Hoover, a 22-year-old native of Washington, D.C. A graduate of George Washington University Law School who had never practiced law, Hoover was employed at the Library of Congress when America entered the war. Three months later, on 26 July 1917, he transferred to Justice as a filing clerk. His new position paid only $1,200 per year, but it was deemed "essential" by the U.S. government and thus exempted him from military service in the conflict that would soon claim thousands of American lives.[41]

On 3 September 1918 the Bureau of Investigation teamed with APL vigilantes and local police officers to launch a massive roundup of suspected "slackers" across the United States. Statistics for the operation are confused and often contradictory. Officially, 125,317 men were arrested in New York and New Jersey, and 27,000 were jailed in Chicago; no reliable figures are available for the rest of the country, but similar raids occurred in most major cities. Arrests were indiscriminate, netting virtually any male of adolescent age or older found without a draft card on his person. (One of those detained in New York was a 75-year-old invalid hobbling on crutches.) Held for as long as three days in cramped quarters without food or water, the vast majority of those arrested were later released without charges. On 8 September, BI spokesmen admitted that only 1,525 of those arrested in New York and New Jersey were bona fide slackers. Nationwide, a Washington source declared, 199 of every 200 detained were found to be innocent. Public outcry following the sweeps included Senator Hiram Johnson's description of the raids as "terrorism." Gravely embarrassed, Attorney General Thomas Gregory called the raids "contrary to law" and insisted that they were executed "contrary to my express instructions"—but he qualified his condemnation with claims that the raiders merely suffered from an "excess of zeal for the public good."[42]

The bureau displayed no such zeal when it came to curbing acts of racist terrorism in the South. At least 111 black victims died at the hands of lynch mobs in 1917 and 1918, some of them returning combat veterans murdered in their military uniforms. Riots were also commonplace and not restricted to the South. White rioters killed one black victim in East St. Louis, Illinois, in May 1917; two months later, in the same city, another outbreak left at least 47 dead and hundreds injured and 312 buildings and 44 loaded railroad cars burned before troops intervened. White racists clashed with black soldiers at Houston, Texas, in August 1917, with two blacks and 11 whites killed; four months later, 13 black servicemen were hanged for murder in what critics called a "legal lynching." Pennsylvania witnessed two race riots in July 1918, claiming five lives in Chester and four in Philadelphia. President Wilson offered a mild denunciation of lynching in mid-1918, but no federal action was undertaken to curb the ongoing reign of terror against blacks.[43]

The First World War ended on 11 November 1918, although American rejection of the Versailles Treaty stalled the formalities and left the U.S. technically at war with Germany until 1922. The delay gave American troops an opportunity to invade Soviet Russia in September 1918, but their attempt to overthrow the fledgling communist regime was a failure, costing 500 casualties before they withdrew in June 1919. On the home front, meanwhile, there were enemies aplenty to consume the waking hours of federal agents and their vigilante allies in the private sector. The "War to End All Wars" was over, but another had begun — and it would span the next three-quarters of a century.[44]

RED SCARE (1919–1920)

White Protestant America's historic fear of swarthy "radicals" was greatly aggravated by the Russian revolution and its ominous echoes in the United States. Wartime inflation decimated salaries and prompted workers to demand more pay, which management indignantly refused. From coast to coast a stunning wave of strikes ensued — 3,600 in 1919 alone, when four million laborers left their jobs to walk picket lines. Some of the unions calling strikes were frankly socialistic, and a handful called for violence. It was a simple thing to brand all union organizers "Reds" and "Bolsheviks." The U.S. Senate convened hearings on American bolshevism in February 1919, but others preferred a more direct response. Increasingly, "radical" unions were met with brute force — from police, strike breakers, or super-patriots like the American Legion, whose members tortured and lynched an IWW organizer in Centralia, Washington, in November 1919.[45]

The left-wing threat was not a total fantasy. Chicago's federal building was bombed in September 1918 after the mass trial of IWW members for violations of the wartime Espionage Act. Several dozen bombs were mailed to prominent Americans, including financiers J.P. Morgan and John D. Rockefeller, in the closing days of April 1919. Most were held up by the post office for insufficient postage, but one maimed the housemaid of a retired Georgia senator. Near midnight on 2 June 1919 a blast rocked the Washington home of Attorney General A. Mitchell Palmer, damaging the house and killing two unidentified bombers. The bombers left behind a note signed by "THE ANARCHIST FIGHTERS" vowing murder to promote "the worldwide spread of revolution." Within hours, bombs were found in eight more American cities. Again, most were duds, but one killed a security guard at the home of a Boston judge.[46]

Bureau of Investigation agents chased the bombers to and fro without result. They blamed IWW "Wobblies" for the Chicago bombing in 1918, but no arrests were made. A series of conflicting BI press releases during June 1919 variously placed headquarters for the latest bombing plot in Philadelphia, New York and Paterson, New Jersey — but again, no bombers were identified. One statement from the bureau blamed the clumsy bombings on a team of Russian agents. Hopeful claims of "progress" and "good headway" on the several cases came to nothing. One immigrant suspect allegedly committed suicide by leaping from a window of the bureau's high-rise office in Manhattan, leaving BI agents to infer his guilt, but no indictments were returned in any of the bombings. They remain unsolved today.[47]

Attorney General Palmer was a prime target for radicals. A right-wing zealot who espoused a bare-knuckled brand of Americanism, he had passed the war years as alien property custodian before his appointment to head Justice in 1919. Now, seething from the apparent anarchist attempt on his life, Palmer appointed ex–Secret

Service Agent William Flynn to lead the Bureau of Investigation on a purge of foreign radicals. Their tool was the Immigration Act of October 1918, mandating deportation of foreigners who espoused "seditious" political or economic views. Convinced that the June 1919 bombers were "connected with Russian Bolshevism, aided by Hun money," Director Flynn joined Palmer for a special meeting on 17 June to plan mass arrests and deportation of "enemy" aliens. J. Edgar Hoover attended the meeting and clearly impressed his superiors. Two weeks later they promoted him to serve as Palmer's "special assistant" in charge of the roundup. Hoover's vehicle would be a new General Intelligence Division (GID), organized on 1 August 1919. Within three months of joining the bureau, Hoover had compiled a list of 150,000 radical targets, gleaned from left-wing mailing lists, informers, and agents of the American Protective League.[48]

The first raids, on 7 November 1919, targeted the Union of Russian Workers, organized in 1907 with headquarters in New York. Hundreds of members were jailed across the country, with 249 of the group's more outspoken members—including anarchists Emma Goldman and Alexander Berkman—transported to Ellis Island pending deportation. The collected "enemies" shipped out for Russia aboard the *SS Buford* (dubbed the "Soviet Ark") on 21 December 1919. Hoover was on hand to watch it sail.[49]

Six days after the *Buford* put to sea, Hoover ordered his men to prepare for another dragnet, this one targeting the Communist Party and the Communist Labor Party. Bureau spies within each group were told to arrange meetings on the night of 2 January 1920, thus facilitating mass arrests. Three thousand warrants were issued, but federal agents and their local allies did not stand on ceremony. BI spokesmen later conceded "some 4,000" arrests nationwide, while independent sources published estimates ranging from 6,000 to 10,000. One thousand were held in Detroit alone, and 800 in Boston, where one detainee killed himself and two others died of pneumonia in dank holding cells. Most were held incommunicado, sometimes for days, in cramped, unsanitary quarters—and, as in the "slacker" raids of 1918, the vast majority were later exonerated. Many of those were beaten in custody by their jailers. *The New York Times* described 150 men released without charges: "Most of them also had blackened eyes and lacerated scalps as souvenirs of the new attitude of aggressiveness which has been assumed by the Federal agents against Reds and suspected Reds." It remains unclear how many suspects were finally deported. Bureau-friendly author Don Whitehead, writing 35 years after the fact, said that 446 of "approximately 2,500" detainees were deported by 30 June 1921, but Assistant Secretary of Labor Louis Post told Congress that he had personally ordered "more than 500" deportations.[50]

As with the draft raids, protests followed close behind the mass arrests of 1920. A committee of lawyers from the prestigious National Popular Government League examined the public record and issued a report on 25 May 1920, denouncing Justice and the Bureau of Investigation for "continued violation of [the] Constitution and breaking of [federal] Laws." Attorney General Palmer, campaigning for the Democratic presidential nomination, was called before Congress six days later to justify the dragnets. "I apologize for nothing the Department of Justice has done on this matter," he told the House Rules Committee. "I glory in it." As for the beatings of inno-cent suspects, Palmer was willing to "forgive" his agents. "I do not defend it," he testified, "but I am not going to raise any row about it." That testimony failed to boost his presidential hopes. Rejected by the Democratic convention, Palmer watched Republican Warren Harding win in November, elected on his promise of "a return to normalcy" in America.[51]

J. Edgar Hoover demonstrated more political savvy than his boss at Justice, tak-ing steps to downplay his involvement in what history would call the "Palmer raids." Friendly journalists like Whitehead and Ralph de Toledano later minimized Hoover's role in the roundups, describing him as a fringe player who did no more than con-tribute a handful of memoranda and legal briefs; other reports make no mention of Hoover's involvement at all. As late as 1940, FBI spokesmen proclaimed that Hoover "was not in charge of, and had nothing to do with" the dragnets of 1919-1920. Hoover himself told the *New York Herald Tribune* in 1947, "I deplored the manner in which the raids were executed then, and my position has remained unchanged."[52]

Unfortunately for the legend, Hoover's interview with *The New York Times*, defending the raids on 26 January 1920, was a matter of permanent record. So was Palmer's congressional testimony, including the revelation that "Mr. Hoover was in charge of this in the Bureau of Investigation." In fact, Hoover seemed to believe that the raids had not gone far enough. He predicted a nationwide uprising of "Reds" on May Day 1920, then backpedaled a month later, saying that the raids and deporta-tions had produced "a marked cessation of revolutionary activity in the United States." He was presumably surprised when a massive bomb rocked Wall Street on 16 September 1920, killing 33 persons and wounding 200 more. Recent proclama-tions of victory notwithstanding, Hoover called the latest bombing part of "a gigan-tic plot to overthrow capitalism." He took personal charge of the case — and like the other bombings of the 12 months previous, it remains unsolved. Undaunted by that failure, Hoover pressed on with his work for the GID, expanding his list of suspected radicals.[53]

As in its execution of the Mann Act, the Bureau of Investigation took advan-tage of the Red Scare to investigate "suspicious" black Americans. The BI conducted a "nationwide investigation" of blacks before the postwar Red scare, and Hoover's GID would launch several more. Hoover himself issued at least two reports on rad-ical "agitation" among blacks, submitted to Congress by Attorney General Palmer in November 1919 and June 1920. One bureau statement warned: "The reds have done a vast amount of evil damage by carrying the doctrines of race revolt and the poi-son of Bolshevism to the Negroes. This business has been perhaps the most con-temptible and wicked performance of our American revolutionary fanatics." Hoover generally defined black "Bolshevism" as any criticism of white supremacy in action, as when the Chicago *Whip* editorialized, "The colored people...must...arouse them-selves to the fullness of their powers and inherent rights." That constituted "propa-ganda of a radical nature" in Hoover's eyes, and he was equally worried about the NAACP, with 350 chapters and 100,000 members nationwide. BI agents were dis-patched to monitor NAACP executive secretary James Weldon Johnson, noting with arch disapproval his criticism of Ku Klux Klan violence in the South. When *The Mes-*

senger, edited by A. Philip Randolph, advocated armed self-defense against lynch mobs and white rioters, BI critics condemned the periodical for spreading "race hatred" and striving "to create unrest among the negro element." In Boston, bureau agents accused a black newspaper of advocating "Bolshevik" and "Wobbly" methods to halt lynching.[54]

The specter of armed blacks defending themselves was worrisome for white terrorists. Southern lynch mobs killed at least 129 blacks without meeting resistance in 1919 and 1920, but white rioters were not always so fortunate. Twenty-six race riots rocked America during the "Red Summer" of 1919, scattered from Longview, Texas, to Omaha, Chicago and the nation's capital (six dead, more than 100 injured). Some of the outbreaks were grimly traditional, as with the massacre of 25 black sharecroppers in Phillips County, Arkansas, but even there five whites were killed as blacks fought back. The death toll in Chicago's riot was more nearly equal: 15 whites and 23 blacks killed in fighting that raged for three days. Although the violence was invariably started by white racists, blacks and "Reds" still got the blame. Arkansas governor Charles Brough condemned a black newspaper, the *Chicago Defender,* for encouraging a "conspiracy" in his state, and the Bureau of Investigation curiously cited Bolshevik propaganda as a primary cause of the white riots in Chicago and Washington. If such illogic troubled Hoover or his agents, they concealed it well.[55]

Hoover's willful blindness was a trait common to much of white America in 1920. After generations of unchallenged white supremacy, where even liberal opponents of lynch law stopped short of urging blacks to kill their tormentors, the threat of black "rebellion" conjured fear on both sides of the Mason-Dixon Line. That paranoia was to be a factor in the coming swift expansion of the Ku Klux Klan.

Nightriders Nationwide (1920–1922)

Despite its ardent war work and pursuit of radicals, despite a flood tide of violent racism in the "Red Summer" of 1919, the KKK was still pitifully small as a new decade dawned. Five years of sporadic recruiting, cross-burning and torchlight parades had lured no more than 3,000 members by spring 1920, with active klaverns (local units) confined to Georgia and Alabama. Wizard Simmons lived hand-to-mouth, barely making ends meet. A new approach was desperately needed if his empire was to thrive.[56]

In June 1920 Simmons struck a bargain with Edward Young Clarke and Elizabeth Tyler, proprietors of the Atlanta-based Southern Publicity Association. Tyler's son-in-law had lately joined the Klan, suggesting that the hooded knights might benefit from hiring a professional press agent. Clarke and Tyler, for their part, had organized fund-raisers for the Anti-Saloon League, the Red Cross, the YMCA and the Theodore Roosevelt Memorial League (which sued Clarke for embezzling $5,000). Furthermore, Clarke's brother was managing editor of the prestigious *Atlanta Constitution.* The partners were impressed with Simmons—described by Tyler as "a minister and a clean living man"—but also by the Klan's cash-cow potential. Simmons agreed to place Clarke and Tyler in charge of a new KKK propagation department, dispatching a sales force of "kleagles" (recruiters) to boost membership nationwide. The propagation department would keep eight dollars of each ten-dollar "kleckto-ken" (initiation fee), and the rest went to Simmons. By year's end, Clarke and Tyler had 1,100 kleagles in the field, ordered to cast their nets among fraternal lodges and fundamentalist Protestant churches, stressing issues and concerns of local interest in order to maximize sales.[57]

There was no shortage of such issues in 1920 and 1921. Racism was a staple of white society, exacerbated by the migration of 750,000 blacks from southern farms to northern cities during World War I, supported by propaganda broadsides such as Madison Grant's *The Passing of the Great Race* (1916) and Klansman Lothrop Stoddard's *The Rising Tide of Color Against White Supremacy* (1921). The arrival in America of 14.5 million immigrants, most of them from southern and eastern Europe, swelled urban ghettos between 1900 and 1920, while sparking a new wave of nativism unequaled since the "Know-Nothing" campaigns of the mid-nineteenth century. Resurgent anti–Semitism took its cue from European proto-fascists and from Henry Ford's newspaper diatribes against "The International Jew." War fever and the recent Red Scare left many Americans trembling in the grip of "100-percent Americanism" that verged on paranoia. Prohibition's advent and the crime wave it produced gave hard-line moralists no end of opportunities to scrutinize and criticize their neighbors. Finally, as in the Reconstruction era, many young men who had come of age in trenches and on battlefields found peacetime tedious. From coast to coast, wherever discontent stalked white America, the Klan's brigade of kleagles offered simple answers for a price.[58]

By late summer 1921 the KKK was flourishing. An estimated 850,000 "aliens" had been "naturalized" as new members of the Invisible Empire at ten dollars per head, plus expenses for costumes, monthly dues, Klan literature and memorabilia, life insurance and sundry incidentals. William Simmons, with 20 percent of the take, banked $170,000 plus $25,000 in back pay for the lean years, and acquired a $33,000 home in suburban Atlanta, dubbed Klan Krest. A new Imperial Headquarters, valued at $65,000, was established on Atlanta's Peachtree Street. Tax auditors would later estimate that the initial gold rush brought $1.5 million pouring into Klan coffers, with no end in sight.[59]

Wherever Klansmen marched and rallied in those glory days, violence inevitably followed. Texas blacks who fraternized with white women were flogged in Bolton, castrated in Houston, and branded with acid in Dallas. A white butcher in Birmingham, Alabama, was whipped for maintaining "friendly relations" with black customers. In Miami, a black Episcopal archdeacon was tarred and feathered by Klansmen for "preaching racial equality." Blacks in Ocoee, Florida, fought back when Klansmen attacked their homes on election day, in November 1920, but they still got the worst of the battle. Other communities scarred by race riots included Chicago and Waukegan, Illinois, (June 1920); Springfield, Ohio, (March 1921); and Augusta, Georgia, (August 1921). Oklahoma, soon to rank among the Klan's most violent realms, witnessed a grim outbreak at Tulsa in June 1921, and 60 blacks and 21 whites were left dead in the ruins. Across Dixie, at least 59 blacks were murdered by lynch mobs in 1921. Klansmen were not responsible for all the violence by any means, but they played on each new incident to recruit angry or frightened whites.[60]

Northern newspapers used the expanding Klan as a tool to increase circulation. The New York *Journal-American* focused primarily on reports of financial and political chicanery in Atlanta, while the competing New York *World* ran a two-week series on Klan activities in the 48 states, climaxed on 19 September 1921 with a list of 152 outrages that included four murders, 41 floggings, and 27 tar-and-feather parties. Inspired by those reports, the House Rules Committee convened hearings on the KKK in October 1921, with Wizard Simmons appearing as the Klan's star witness. Waxing eloquent, Simmons described his brainchild as a vehicle of "race pride" rather than bigotry; the Klan's white hood and robe, he vowed, were "as innocent as the breath of an angel." Proving once again that even bad publicity beats none at all, Klan membership increased 20 percent by December 1921, with more than 200 new klaverns organized. The following summer, with membership above one million and still rising, Clarke and Tyler received an average of 1,000 applications per day in Atlanta. Ten realms were chartered by 1922, spanning the South from Texas to the Carolinas, and active units were found in at least 23 other states. As Simmons told the press, "Congress gave us the best publicity we ever got. Congress made us."[61]

At the same time, albeit more modestly, the Bureau of Investigation was growing in Washington, D.C. It had increased from 34 agents in 1908 to 401 in 1922, with a support staff of 194. The bureau's budget had ballooned from $329,984 in 1911 (the first year with figures available) to $1,892,077 in 1922. Agents spent their time pursuing real and suspected communists, "radical" unionists, and critics of President Harding's corrupt "Ohio Gang." A new and lucrative crusade was launched in October 1919 with passage of the Dyer Act, making interstate transportation of stolen cars a federal crime. J. Edgar Hoover had tripled the size of his radical index since 1920, collecting an impressive 450,000 names. Promoted to serve as the bureau's assistant director on 22 August 1921, he pursued blacks and "Reds" with a zeal surpassing that of most Klansmen.[62]

Hoover didn't know it on the day he celebrated his promotion, but events were already in motion that would place his bureau and the KKK on a collision course within a year. From that point on, for good or ill, their histories would be forever intertwined.

1

Invisible Empires (1921–1944)

When did the Bureau of Investigation first turn its attention to the Ku Klux Klan? Official records shed no light upon that question, since the earliest records thus far released for public scrutiny date from September 1964. On 25 September 1921—16 days before Imperial Wizard Simmons addressed the House Rules Committee in Washington—*The New York Times* reported that Attorney General Harry Daugherty had ordered BI chief William Burns "to continue his inquiry" into Klan activities, but no legal basis for investigation was cited and no prosecutions resulted. Elsewhere, bureau-friendly authors date the BI's first clash with the KKK from autumn 1922.[1]

Federal agents clearly recognized the Klan before September 1921, but their attitude toward the order was hardly hostile. In December 1919, officers of the U.S. Army's Military Intelligence Division condemned *The Messenger,* a black newspaper, for its "vicious" attacks on the KKK. After all, they reported, the Klan was merely trying to prevent "the encroachment of the negroes [*sic*] in those neighborhoods populated by white people." Bureau agents likewise mounted surveillance on the Klan's opponents, rather than on Klansmen themselves. New York G-men reported NAACP criticism of Klan violence in August 1920, and July 1921 saw the Pittsburgh field office warn J. Edgar Hoover of a Communist Party leaflet urging blacks to use "organized force" against KKK terrorists. On 5 September 1922, *Messenger* editor A. Philip Randolph received a package containing a severed hand and a threatening note from the Klan. Bureau agents examined the gruesome relic and encouraged Randolph's suspicion that it was sent by rival black activist Marcus Garvey. Thus goaded, Randolph and other black leaders called for a federal investigation of Garvey, which sent him to prison for fraud.[2] It would require more serious complaints to launch surveillance of the Klan itself—and those, ironically, would come from a white governor below the Mason-Dixon Line.

ROUND ONE

Sometime in late September 1922, J. Edgar Hoover allegedly received a visit from Paul Wooton, Washington correspondent for the *New Orleans Times-Picayune*. Don Whitehead and others report that Wooton carried a letter from Louisiana Governor

John Parker, addressed to Attorney General Daugherty, describing the Klan's virtual seizure of power in Louisiana. No one has yet explained why Wooton bypassed Daugherty and bureau chief William Burns to contact Hoover, a relative unknown barely a year in office as the BI's assistant director. Although no documents have surfaced to support the story, it lives on in FBI legend. According to Whitehead and others, Hoover read Parker's letter and exclaimed, "Do you mean to say the Governor of Louisiana can't even use the telephone, telegraph, or the United States mails because of the Klan?"

"That's exactly what the Governor told me personally," Wooton replied, "when he sent for me to come to Louisiana. I brought you this letter because Governor Parker can't trust the mails. His mail is watched by the Klan and his telephone is tapped by Klansmen. He needs help."[3]

Instead of sending Wooton on to Burns or Daugherty, as protocol and logic might dictate, Hoover "decided to take personal charge of the matter" and telephoned Louisiana attorney general Adolph Coco to confirm Wooton's story. Bypassing his superiors, Hoover suggested that Governor Parker should write directly to President Harding.[4] This Parker did on 2 October 1922, with a letter that read in part:

> Due to the activities of an organized body reputed to be the Ku Klux Klan ... not only have the laws been violated, but men taken out, beaten and whipped. Two men have been brutally murdered without trial or charges.... [M]y information tonight is that six more citizens have been ordered to leave their homes (in Morehouse Parish) under penalty of death. These conditions are beyond the control of the Governor of this State.... [A] number of law officers and others charged with the enforcement of law in this State are publicly recognized as members of this Ku Klux Klan.[5]

While various Reconstruction-era anti–Klan statutes remained on the books, they had been undercut by rulings from the nineteenth-century Supreme Court, and white southern politicians had no interest in renewed federal scrutiny of crimes against blacks. Therefore, Parker sought limited intervention under Article IV, Section 4, of the U.S. Constitution, which provides that Washington "shall guarantee to every State in this union a republican form of government and shall protect each of them against invasion; and on application of the Legislature, or of the Executive (when the Legislature cannot be convened), against domestic violence."[6]

The sequence of events from that point forward remains hazy, shrouded by conflicting accounts. We know that Parker and Coco visited Washington in November 1922 for discussions with Harding and Daugherty, but bureau agents may have reached Louisiana sooner. Once again, the absence of official documents defeats all efforts to compose a timeline. Two teams of BI agents were apparently dispatched, one working publicly and enduring Klan threats while the other quietly collected details of Ku Klux mayhem, building a case for trial. Months later, on 29 January 1923, *The New York Times* announced that "[n]ew agents of the Department of Justice are taking up where their predecessors left off" in Louisiana, but no details of the prior investigation were provided.[7]

In any case, the facts were easily discerned. Klan members in Morehouse Parish included Sheriff Fred Carpenter, all of his deputies, District Attorney David Garrett, the local postmaster, and various municipal policemen. Dr. B.M. McKoin, "exalted cyclops" of the Mer Rouge Klan, had launched a flogging campaign to upgrade local morals, then staged an attempt on his own life and fingered two opponents of the KKK, Watt Daniel and Tom Richards, as the would-be assassins. On 24 August 1922, black-robed Klansmen kidnapped Daniel, Richards and three other victims from a baseball game at Bastrop. All five were whipped, and only three survived. Daniel and Richards were still missing in September when a Klan-ridden grand jury convened, briefly reviewed the case, and then reported "a marked decrease in crime in Morehouse Parish since the last grand jury was in session."[8]

On 19 December 1922, Governor Parker declared martial law in Morehouse Parish and sent National Guardsmen to find the missing men. Three days later, a mysterious dynamite blast rocked Lake Lafourche and brought two mangled, rotting corpses to the surface. Daniels and Richards were identified from articles of clothing, their gruesome deaths blamed on a "torture machine" later identified in conflicting reports as a piece of road-grading equipment or "old wagon wheels." Dr. McKoin and Klansman Jeff Burnett were charged as suspects in the case, and Parker and Coco convened an open hearing to solicit further evidence. Some 50 witnesses testified during January 1923, establishing Klan guilt in the murders and floggings, but when a new grand jury met in March, its members still found "insufficient evidence" for trial. In April 1923, Coco slapped McKoin and 17 komrades with various misdemeanor charges related to illegal liquor raids. Four defendants were convicted and fined ten dollars each in November 1923, and appellate courts dismissed the other cases three months later. By that time, Governor Parker had retired and Coco had lost his reelection bid.[9]

Most law enforcement agencies might consider the Morehouse Parish case a defeat, but FBI historians persist in calling it a victory. "Hoover was not discouraged," according to biographer Ralph de Toledano. "The publicity had hurt the Klan, turning some of its more prominent supporters and members against it." Harry and Bonaro Overstreet deem the case "a small success in the area of citizen education," and Whitehead opines that "[d]espite the lack of convictions, this fight helped turn public sentiment against the Klan."[10] When Hollywood filmed *The FBI Story* in 1959, it included a dramatic segment on the KKK: After raiding a newspaper office and trashing the presses, hooded Klansmen board a waiting truck to flee the crime scene. They are stunned when undercover G-man James Stewart doffs his mask and slams the tailgate, placing them under arrest — and well they should be, since no such event ever happened.

THE DEPARTMENT OF EASY VIRTUE

Whatever his opinion of the Morehouse Parish verdicts, Hoover had more pressing matters on his mind in 1922–24. As assistant director of the bureau, he served a Justice Department described by historians as "a national disgrace" and a "Department of Easy Virtue," mired in a "stygian darkness … of outright political corruption." Hoover's own bureau was "a dumping ground for political hacks," where agents hired for one dollar a year banked thousands in bribes every month.[11] As Ralph de Toledano described the situation:

> Appointment as a special agent was political, with senators and congressmen paying off favors by placing their friends and supporters on the BI's rolls. The Bureau's work was sloppy and the cases it presented to the Justice Department for prosecution were lacking in solid evidence and sketchily prepared. Repeatedly, the U.S. attorneys entrusted with cases submitted by the Bureau would never even take them to court. Rumors of bribery and corruption were rife, and there was talk in the press of abolishing the Federal government's major law enforcement agency.[12]

That situation derived from the advent of President Warren Harding's venal "Ohio Gang" in March 1921. Attorney General Harry Daugherty was Harding's longtime friend and campaign manager; the Justice Department was his reward for securing Harding's election. Bureau chief William Flynn fought to save his job, supported by various congressmen and federal judges, but all in vain. Daugherty fired him in August 1921 and replaced him with another childhood friend, notorious strikebreaker and "famous international sleuth" William Burns. On the same day, Daugherty promoted Hoover to serve Burns as the BI's assistant director.[13]

De Toledano claims that Hoover "was not particularly happy with the appointment, though he made no objections." Biographer Curt Gentry disagrees, stating that Hoover did not "wait shyly to be asked: he lobbied for the job he wanted."[14] The Overstreets describe the net result:

> Attorney General Daugherty, supported by Bureau Chief William J. Burns, specialized in three enterprises; and in no one of them did he let himself be inhibited by the law. He made war on the "Reds"—and on those whom it pleased him and his friends to have thus catalogued — with slight regard for rules of evidence or constitutional rights. He made "deals"—conducting, for example, an illegal but highly lucrative traffic in pardons and liquor permits. And he saw to it that those who might threaten his hold on the Attorney Generalship had reason to fear him.[15]

While bureau-friendly authors absolve Hoover of any role in that chicanery, Gentry reveals the future FBI director's role in guiding Daugherty: "Hoover … boosted his candidacy [for assistant BI director] with what was, in effect, a little Red scare of his own. When Daugherty first became attorney general, in March 1921, he'd shown no interest in 'the menace'; by August he had all the fanaticism of the newly converted. In the interim, Hoover had inundated the AG with memos, as well as a weekly intelligence digest, on radical activities both in the United States and abroad." Thus enlightened, "Daugherty soon discovered that [Hoover's] files contained information not only on radicals but also on Harding's political opponents, and that young Hoover was not averse to sharing it."[16]

The Justice Department had no monopoly on corruption in those years. Harding's Interior Department, under Secretary Albert Fall, was even worse. Fall accepted a six-figure "loan" from oilmen Edward Doheny and Harry Sinclair, after granting them rights to pump oil from U.S. Navy reserves at Elk Hills, California, and Teapot Dome, Wyoming. Various reports place the payoff somewhere between $100,000 and $135,000, described by Doheny as "an accommodation to an old friend." Montana senators Thomas Walsh and Burton Wheeler uncovered the scandal in early 1923, prompting presidential aide Jess Smith to kill himself in May. Smith left behind a $500,000 estate and a glut of rumors that he had been murdered to insure his silence. Similar tales circulated in August 1923, after President Harding died in San Francisco while returning from a trip to Alaska. Walsh and Wheeler held Senate hearings on the Teapot Dome scandal in October 1923, followed by investigation of Daugherty's conduct as attorney general.[17]

Though cornered, Daugherty was not prepared to go without a fight. Aided by Burns and Hoover, the attorney general launched a full-press counterattack on Walsh and Wheeler, tapping their phones, reading their mail, sending bureau agents to burglarize their homes and offices. G-men tried to snare Wheeler with prostitutes, but he spurned the bait. Foiled on that front, Burns and Hoover pressured witnesses to hide or defy Senate subpoenas; one bureau employee who testified under protest to avoid a criminal contempt citation was fired by Hoover the next day. The BI branded Wheeler a Red, citing a recent trip to Russia, but the mud would not stick. President Calvin Coolidge demanded Daugherty's resignation in March 1924, replacing him with Harlan Stone. Yet Burns and Hoover still pursued their critics. Six days after Stone's appointment, on 8 April, a federal grand jury in Montana charged Wheeler with bribery. Stone refused to drop the case, and Wheeler faced trial in April 1925, with Tom Walsh serving as his legal counsel. While 30 agents scoured the state, seeking any available means to smear Walsh and Wheeler, their case collapsed in court and Wheeler was acquitted. An embarrassed Harlan Stone later blamed the fiasco on Burns and Hoover, telling Senator John Kendrick, "They lied to me."[18]

Those lies did not prevent Stone from promoting Hoover to lead the Bureau of Investigation on 10 May 1924, nor did they end the bureau's covert war against Tom Walsh. In Montana, that fight was joined by Klansmen and ex-members of the defunct American Protective Association, an anti–Catholic group once led by Flathead Lake hotelkeeper Frank Linderman. Montana Republicans nominated Linderman as their senatorial candidate in 1924, opposing Walsh, and the Klan made Walsh's Catholicism a political issue. The divisive effort backfired in November, as Walsh defeated Linderman by some 8,000 votes.[19]

Hoover's promotion to serve as the BI's director, a post he held for nearly half a century, has been portrayed in identical terms by various authors since Don Whitehead first sketched the scene in 1956. In that scenario, Stone offers Hoover the job and Hoover accepts on condition that the bureau be "divorced from politics," with appointments and promotions based on merit. Stone "scowls" in response and tells Hoover, "I wouldn't give it to you under any other conditions."[20] It seems a curious exchange, after Hoover had deceived Stone while pursuing Walsh and Wheeler, but Whitehead details the provisions hammered out by Stone and Hoover three days later:

1. The Bureau would be a fact-gathering organization, its activities strictly limited to investigation of federal crimes.
2. Investigations would be personally ordered and directed by the attorney general.

3. Bureau personnel would be reduced insofar "as is consistent with the proper performance of its duties."

4. Any incompetents or suspect agents would be fired "as soon as possible."

5. The bureau's "dollar-a-year" men, "honorary" agents and other auxiliary employees would likewise be dismissed.

6. Future appointments would require the attorney general's approval, with preference given to men of "good character and ability" who possessed legal training.[21]

Stone trusted Hoover to live by those self-imposed rules, but as biographer Athan Theoharis observes, "Stone's trust was misplaced."[22] Hoover reformed some aspects of the bureau, but in time he violated every one of Stone's guidelines. Bureau surveillance of "radicals" never ceased; in fact, Hoover expanded it each year for the remainder of his tenure, far surpassing Burns in his defiance of the Constitution. And pursuit of lurking Reds left G-men little time for keeping tabs on members of the KKK.

"A CONCERTED DRIVE AGAINST THE KU KLUX KLAN"

The Overstreets maintain that after Morehouse Parish, Hoover's men pursued "a concerted drive against the Ku Klux Klan in the 1920s."[23] In fact, with the exception of a single case discussed below, there were no further federal arrests of Klansmen and no evidence of any ongoing investigations prior to World War II.

That paucity of bureau action did not mean the KKK had changed its ways. Wherever Klansmen rallied in the nation there were incidents of violence suggesting organized conspiracy to rob Klan victims of their civil rights. On 19 September 1921, six days before Attorney General Daugherty ordered the first known BI scrutiny of Klan affairs, the New York *World* published a list of 152 Ku Klux atrocities nationwide, including four murders, 41 whippings, and 27 tar-and-feather parties. Klan rallies sparked deadly riots in Delaware, Indiana, Maryland, Massachusetts, New Jersey, Ohio, Pennsylvania and Texas. An epidemic of nocturnal floggings scarred more than a thousand victims each in Oklahoma and Texas; more than 100 each in Alabama, Florida and Georgia; dozens in California and the Carolinas. Some victims were branded with hot irons or acid, and others were castrated. Two hundred Klansmen swept through Smackover, Arkansas, in November 1922, burning suspected vice dens, killing one man in the process, wounding and whipping dozens more. Pennsylvania knights shot up a black Boy Scout camp and wounded two policemen at a college campus rally. Klansmen in Niles, Ohio, bombed the mayor's home in October 1924, after he refused them a parade permit. In Talladega County, Alabama, Klansmen bombed two homes and burned a third, together with a school, a church, two dance halls and several barns.[24]

The 1920s Klan claimed fewer lives than its Reconstruction predecessor, yet it was lethal enough. At least five persons died in riots sparked by Klan activities in

Pennsylvania and Texas. Those deaths were likely unintended, but the same cannot be said for other homicides around the country. Kenneth Jackson counts six murders committed by southern Klansmen between 1920 and 1925, but his tally remains incomplete. In addition to the Mer Rouge victims and the fatal Smackover skirmish, other documented slayings from the period include an arson suspect lynched by Arkansas Klansmen in 1921; Father James Coyle, a Catholic priest, shot by a Birmingham Klansman in April 1921; Manolo Cabeza, lynched by Key West knights at Christmas 1921; Walter Gibbs, shot for dating black women in Nashville, Arkansas, in March 1922; Parks Banks, hanged near Yazoo, Mississippi, after quarreling with Klan leaders in August 1922; two unnamed blacks tortured and burned alive by Klansmen at Beaver Falls, Pennsylvania, in 1923; William Coburn, a Klan publicist, shot by one of his Atlanta komrades in 1923; a bootlegger shot in Ardmore, Oklahoma, in 1923; Joseph Zimmerman, vanished forever after Birmingham Klansmen kidnapped him in March 1925; and three victims killed when a Muskegon, Michigan, Klan leader bombed the home of a political rival in 1925. No final body count is available from Rosewood, Florida, where Klansmen and their allies razed a black community in January 1923, but published estimates range from eight victims to nearly 100.[25]

Klan homicides continued through the latter 1920s. In Herrin County, Illinois, battles between bootleggers and the KKK claimed at least 20 lives during 1924–26. Herman Bigby and neighbor Walton Adams were killed when Klansmen raided Bigby's home in Royston, Georgia, in March 1926. Toombs County, Georgia, saw at least two victims whipped to death in the same period. A Colorado knight was beaten to death when he tried to leave the order, and a three-year-old Pennsylvania girl never returned after Klansmen snatched her from her grandparents. An undercover policeman was ambushed and killed by Klan gunmen in Buffalo, New York. Outside Terrell, Texas, eight men condemned by a kangaroo court were burned alive while some 800 Klansmen watched.[26]

FBI apologists argue that the bureau was helpless in such cases, despite good intentions, since court rulings restricted federal prosecution of civil rights violations by private citizens. Such limitations never stopped Hoover's G-men from pursuing blacks or Reds, however, and the argument fails completely in cases where terrorists operated behind a shield of official authority. Under 18 USC Sec. 242, the bureau had free reign to investigate conspiracies hatched "under color of law," yet Hoover turned a blind eye while Klansmen infiltrated law enforcement agencies from coast to coast.

No comprehensive list of Klan cops from the 1920s is available, but a sampling proves the case. In Dallas, Police Commissioner Louis Turley was a Klansman. After three of his patrolmen were identified as Klan floggers, Turley ordered his detectives to "forget all about the charges brought against any member of the force." Other Dallas knights included Police Chief Henry Tanner, the county sheriff and his chief deputies and the district attorney. Portland, Oregon's police department commissioned 100 Klansmen as auxiliary officers, handpicked by Grand Dragon Fred Gifford. Denver's Klan roster included the mayor, city attorney, manager of public safety, police chief, scores of policemen, four judges, two federal narcotics officers, and at least two deputy sheriffs. In Waco, Texas, the mayor and board of police commissioners signed on en masse. White knights in Baton Rouge, Louisiana, included Sheriff Horace Lyons and a district judge and his court clerk. In Morehouse Parish, scene of at least two unpunished murders, Sheriff Fred Carpenter, his deputies, and D.A. David Garrett were Klansmen. When California's Klan rolls were revealed, members included ten percent of the public officials in every major city. Sacramento's kleagle was a deputy sheriff who recruited many other policemen and firefighters; at least 25 policemen and 81 federal employees joined the Klan in San Francisco; seven Fresno patrolmen paid dues to the Invisible Empire; Bakersfield's police chief and police judge were members; in Los Angeles, the list included Sheriff William Traeger, Police Chief Louis Oaks, and U.S. Attorney Joseph Burke. The Klan controlled law enforcement in Birmingham, Alabama, where knights paraded with police motorcycle escorts. Known members on the public payroll included Sheriff T.J. Shirley and Chief Deputy Henry Hill. Historian William Snell reports that most Birmingham policemen, "if not all of them," were Klansmen.[27]

Nor can it be argued that law enforcement officers joined the Klan as a mere fraternal exercise. Seven members of the Alabama National Guard were jailed for lynching a black man in January 1921, but the charges were dismissed. Nationwide, between 1920 and 1929, at least 42 other blacks were lynched in circumstances suggesting police collusion. After the Smackover, Arkansas, raids of November 1922, Ouachita County's sheriff praised the KKK for driving away "undesirables." Birmingham Public Safety Commissioner W.B. Cloe likewise expressed gratitude for illegal Klan vice raids, and off-duty policemen led hooded knights against local Chinese cafés in 1926. Key West's Ku Klux sheriff, Roland Curry, surrendered Manolo Cabeza to Klan lynchers in December 1923. Police Chief B.M. Lawson was one of three Klansmen arrested for flogging two women in Lumberton, North Carolina, in April 1923. A policeman who joined the Klan's raid on a Pennsylvania Boy Scout camp was fired in July 1924, but he faced no criminal charges. The police chief of Taft, California, joined Klansmen to cheer the flogging of a dentist who filed divorce papers. In Inglewood, California, Klan raiders traded shots with a patrolmen who caught them kidnapping a suspected bootlegger; Klansmen killed or wounded in the battle included a town constable and a deputy sheriff.[28] In no case did the bureau lift a hand against the lawless officers.

A KLEAGLE'S FALL

Atlanta publicist Edward Clarke deserves as much credit (or condemnation) for the Klan's growth in 1920–22 as any other single individual. With partner Elizabeth Tyler, he profited greatly from Ku Klux recruiting and helped set the tone for modern Klan attacks on Catholics and Jews. By summer 1921, however, Clarke was nervous and uncertain of his future with the KKK.

The trouble stemmed from October 1919, when Atlanta police caught Clarke in Tyler's bed. Both were jailed for disorderly conduct and paid five-dollar fines, with Clarke blaming his wife for the raid. The official report on that incident later vanished from police files, doubtless lifted by some Klansman on the force, but the New York *World* had a photocopy of the document and cheerfully resurrected the story in 1921. On 25 September, the same day William Burns received his order to investigate the KKK, Clarke publicly announced his resignation from the order. Citing Tyler's tender feelings, Clarke declared a wish to spare her further criticism, adding that without her aid he was "neither physically nor financial able" to remain as imperial kleagle. Tyler fired back with a statement branding Clarke's decision "a mistake," urging him to remain with the Klan and fight their malicious detractors. Clarke reconsidered and withdrew his resignation, but it was a choice he soon had reason to regret.[29]

By Thanksgiving 1922, Imperial Wizard Simmons was under siege in Atlanta, surrounded by ambitious underlings who coveted his title and the Klan's ballooning income. Kleagle Z.R. Upchurch resigned in disgust, accusing Clarke of feeding liquor to Simmons and looting the Klan's treasury. Other kleagles followed suit, calling the Klan a cash cow for its leaders in Atlanta. At the Klan's November Klonvokation, Simmons was persuaded to resign and yield his throne to Dallas Klansman Hiram Evans. Clarke still remained an obstacle to Evans and his team, however, banking an estimated $40,000 per month from his kleagles at large.[30] Before Evans could hatch a plot to ease Clarke out of office, though, the Bureau of Investigation came to the new wizard's rescue.

Once again, it was Clarke's eye for the ladies that landed him in trouble. In February 1921 he traveled from Houston to New Orleans with a companion, one Laurel Martin, for what the BI deemed "immoral purposes." Accounts differ as to whether Clarke was arrested in New Orleans, but a federal grand jury indicted him there on 1 March 1923, charging a violation of the Mann Act. A few days later, Hiram Evans announced cancellation of Clarke's contract "for the good of the order." Clarke was prepared to fight the move, but September 1923 saw him placed on bond for traveling with liquor in his luggage. A meeting of grand dragons voted to expel Clarke from the Klan on 11 January 1924, and he pleaded guilty in New Orleans on 10 March, paying a $5,000 fine. David Chalmers reports that Clarke was later indicted for mail fraud, but no further information is available on that case, and it appears that he was never prosecuted.[31]

Recalling those events four decades later, in April 1965, Hoover told a group of journalists that "several other" Klan leaders were indicted with Clarke and that "the red faces which occurred at that time as a result of those convictions [*sic*] soon ended the Klan in the South." The first part of his statement was entirely false — Clarke stood alone in court — and historian Kenneth O'Reilly confirms that Hoover's assessment of the case was "wildly exaggerated." The FBI's website reports, more modestly, that "[t]he Bureau of Investigation used the Mann Act to bring Louisiana's [*sic*] philandering KKK 'Imperial Kleagle' to justice."[32] As for Hoover's role, if any, Clarke's offense occurred six months before Hoover's promotion to assistant bureau director, and Clarke pleaded guilty exactly two months before Hoover assumed command of the BI. Any record of his personal involvement in the case remains hidden from public view in the FBI's files.

KLAN POWER AND DECLINE

The Overstreets contend that, thanks to bureau intervention, the Klan's "huge membership dissolved as swiftly as it had formed." Don Whitehead, estimating total membership at "almost one million in forty-six states," is wrong on both counts. In fact, the order was found in all 48 states and the District of Columbia, with active outposts in Canada and Germany. Peak membership was not attained until 1925, a full year after Clarke's guilty plea and three years after the fruitless Mer Rouge arrests. Published estimates of total membership range from 2,028,000 to an improbably precise 8,904,887, with most tallies falling somewhere in the three-to-five-million range.[33]

Whatever the final hood count, those numbers spelled power as the Klan plunged headlong into politics. No denizen of Washington, D.C., was ever more attuned to realpolitik than J. Edgar Hoover, forging alliances with any politician who could help (or harm) him, strongly favoring conservatives of every stripe. Hoover cannot have missed the fact that United States Chief Justice Edward White was a confessed former Klansman, or that Georgia Senator Tom Watson dropped in to support Wizard Simmons during his 1921 appearance before Congress. On that same occasion, Georgia congressman William Upshaw praised Simmons for "his sterling character," hailing "his every utterance as the truth of an honest, patriotic man." Rumors of President Harding's White House initiation circulated widely during 1921, and Imperial Klokard Alton Young confirmed them on his deathbed in the 1940s. According to Young, a five-man induction team led by William Simmons ushered Harding into the Invisible Empire and were rewarded for their service with War Department license plates that exempted them from speeding tickets. Attorney General Daugherty denied that either he or Harding were Klansmen, yet the stories persisted. The Klan mourned Harding's death with public demonstrations in August 1923, and Ohio Klansmen stood guard at his tomb.[34]

Nationwide, Klan votes elected 75 congressmen, 16 U.S. senators, 11 governors and countless other officials. Georgia Governor Thomas Hardwick praised the KKK, and successor Clifford Walker was himself a Klansman, and Richard Russell — chief justice of Georgia's Supreme Court, later U.S. senator — sought Klan political advice. Colorado's knights included Secretary of State Carl Milliken, Denver Mayor Ben Stapleton and City Attorney Clarence Morley. Ohio Klansmen elected 12 mayors in 1923, including those of Akron, Columbus and Toledo. In Oregon, where Klansman K.K. Kubli served as speaker of the house and a fellow knight ruled the state senate, legislators banned parochial schools. Indiana knights or friends beholden to Grand Dragon D.C. Stephenson included Governor Ed Jackson, state Prohibition Director Charles Orbison, Congressman Harry Rowbottom, and the mayors of various cities including Indianapolis, Kokomo and Evansville. Arkansas governor Thomas McRae practiced "friendly neutrality" toward the Klan, while appointing a knight as his personal secretary. In California, Governor Friend Richardson chose Sacramento's kludd (chaplain) as chaplain of the state Senate. Alabama surpassed even Georgia in Klan infestation: known members in the Cotton State included Governor Bibb Graves, U.S. senators Hugo Black and Thomas Heflin, Attorney General Charles McCall, Supreme

Court Justice John Anderson, and Birmingham Mayor Cooper Green. Governor Graves sponsored a bill imposing $25,000 fines on anyone who uttered "libelous" criticism of Klansmen in office, and Birmingham attorney Irving Engle offered this assessment of the state at large: "When I say powerful, they took over the state. You couldn't be an officer, couldn't win an election unless you were a member of the Klan, that was true of [the] counties and the cities."[35]

J. Edgar Hoover had few (if any) philosophical quarrels with the KKK, and his bureau's success in crime-fighting relied in large part on local police who were often Klansmen. Those officers recovered most of the stolen cars for which Hoover claimed credit each year in his bids for increased appropriations, and they tipped Hoover's agents to "subversive" stirrings among blacks and leftists. In short, Hoover had no incentive to tackle the Klan, and no evidence exists that he did so after 1923.

Still, Klan strength *did* plummet in the last half of the decade. More than 40,000 Klansmen and women marched through Washington, D.C., on 8 August 1925, but less than half as many returned for a second parade one year later. Published estimates of the declining Ku Klux membership include 321,000 in 1927; "no more than several hundred thousand" in 1928; 82,600 in 1929; and 35,000 to 45,000 in 1930. The latter counts are too conservative, since 30,000 knights remained in Florida alone, but there is no doubt that the Klan's great wave had crested and retired.[36]

The Klan's precipitous decline in 1926–30 owed nothing to the Bureau of Investigation. Primary causes of the slump included disillusionment with Ku Klux violence, extremism and rampant financial corruption. Local arrests revealed some Klansmen as sadistic thugs. Time after time, Klan officers absconded with cash or indulged in luxuries the rank and file could not afford. Embarrassment and plunging membership drove many politicians to desert the KKK, while some urged Klan endorsement of opponents on election day.[37] A murder case in Indiana and a civil trial in Pennsylvania ultimately dominated reasons for the Klan's downfall.

No Klansman in the 1920s enjoyed more personal power than Indiana Grand Dragon D.C. Stephenson. Alone, he handpicked Hoosier officeholders from small towns to Congress and the governor's mansion, obtaining from each written pledges of loyalty. Stephenson liked to call himself "the law in Indiana," and he had his sights fixed on a U.S. Senate vacancy in 1928, when passion intervened and ruined everything. On 15 March 1925, Stephenson invited a Hagerstown schoolteacher, Madge Oberholtzer, to join him on a journey to Chicago. In their train compartment, shared with a Klan bodyguard, Stephenson swilled alcohol and assaulted his date, inflicting deep bite marks all over her body. When the train stopped at Hammond, Indiana, Stephenson checked into a hotel and made the grievous error of allowing Madge to go out shopping with his gunman. She bought poison at a local pharmacy and drank it, leading to her death on 14 April. Stephenson was charged with second-degree murder and later convicted at trial. When Governor Ed Jackson failed to pardon him, Stephenson shared his files with journalists and prosecutors, resulting in scandal, impeachments and criminal trials throughout the state. Within a year, Klan membership in Indiana dropped by 96 percent, from 350,000 to an estimated 15,000. Historian Wyn Wade suggests that Stephenson's downfall did "more than any [other] single factor" to defeat the KKK.[38]

In western Pennsylvania, meanwhile, Klansmen complained to imperial head-quarters about the high-handed style of Grand Dragon Sam Rich. Hiram Evans fired Rich, but his replacement — the Rev. Herbert Shaw — proved no more popular with the unhappy knights. When their complaints resumed, Evans banished spokesman John Strayer (a minister and state legislator), then revoked the charters of eight dissident klaverns. The ousted Klansmen continued to meet on their own, prompting Evans to file suit in 1927 for their regalia and $100,000 in damages. Strayer and five codefendants countered with a $15 million claim against the wizard for misuse of dues collected prior to their expulsion. The trial, in April 1928, was disastrous for Evans, facing a parade of witnesses who detailed in open court Klan corruption and atrocities. Klansman J.R. Ramsey described nocturnal raids, ordered by Evans and Rich, that included "burning barns, tar-and-feather parties and other ruthlessness." Two black men had been tortured and burned to death, Ramsey said, at a July 1923 "castration party" outside Beaver Falls. Other witnesses fingered Sam Rich himself in the still-unsolved kidnapping of a three-year-old Pittsburgh girl and described the ritual burning of seven or eight men in Texas. On the witness stand, Evans grudgingly admitted that he could have stopped a riotous parade through Carnegie that left one Klansman dead in 1923. In his summation, defense attorney Van Barrickman denounced the Klan as "supreme in its rottenness," and Judge W.H.S. Thompson agreed.[39] On 13 April 1928, Thompson dismissed both claims with a judgment that read:

> I find as a fact that the Ku Klux Klan has established and is maintaining a form of despotic rule, which is being operated in secret under the direct sanction and authority of the plaintiff's chief officers; that, in violation of the rights and liberties of the people, it has set up tribunals not known to law, before which citizens of the Commonwealth, not members of the Klan are brought, subjected to some form of trial, and, upon conviction, severe corporal punishments are imposed, painful, humiliating and often brutal in their character, and in some instances destructive of life itself.
>
> I also find as a fact that in the secret operation of the corporation's activities and in hostility to the civil authorities, military organizations are established and maintained with arms, regalia and equipment, with officers of varying rank and military titles, these officers being bound to obey without question the commands of the superior officer in authority of the plaintiff corporation. In addition to this, bands known as "night-riders," or the "black-robed gang," armed, equipped and masked, are formed and operated here and there throughout the country, both organizations being used as instruments of terror, oppression and violence, and being thus a continued menace to the public peace and destructive of the public order.
>
> I also find as a fact that Hiram Wesley Evans was present and spoke to the assembled multitude in Carnegie immediately before the riot; that he and Rich were well aware that the civil authorities of Carnegie had forbidden the parade, and that in defiance of this position and in utter disregard of the consequences which might naturally follow, he gave the order to march, which resulted in the serious riot in which men were beaten and severely injured. At least one man was wounded by gunfire and another man was shot to death. Under these circumstances, he [Evans] was directly responsible for the riot and bloodshed which ensued.
>
> The evidence also disclosed that in the State of Texas men were brought before

the Klan, tried and convicted. And in some instances were subjected to brutal beatings and in others were condemned to death and burned at the stake.

In view of all the facts disclosed by the evidence, the plaintiff corporation, stigmatized as it is by its unlawful acts and conduct, could hardly hope for judicial assistance in a court of the United States which is commissioned to extend to all litigants before it, without distinction of race, creed, color or condition, those high guarantees of liberty and equality vouchsafed by the Constitution of the United States.

This unlawful organization, so destructive of the rights and liberties of the people, has come in vain asking this court of equity for injunction or other relief. They come with filthy hands and can get no assistance here.[40]

That ringing condemnation from a federal court had no impact on Hoover or his agents, who remained aloof from anything resembling an investigation of the Klan. Eighteen months after Judge Thompson threw the Klan out of court, Wall Street's stock market crash rocked the nation, inaugurating the Great Depression and leaving countless Klansmen either unemployed or desperately short of cash with which to pay their dues. Klan membership continued its long downhill slide, while Hoover — if he noticed the order at all — was soon distracted by new adventures.

A New Deal for the Bureau

The early 1930s brought a rash of headline-grabbing crimes, including celebrity ransom kidnappings and daring bank holdups, which Hoover portrayed as a national menace requiring more money, more agents and broader authority for the Bureau of Investigation. The abduction of Charles Lindbergh, Jr., in March 1932 prompted Congress to make interstate kidnapping a federal crime. A year to the day from that vote, on 17 June 1933, four lawmen and their prisoner were shot and killed at Kansas City's Union Station while en route to the federal prison at Leavenworth. The casualties included one BI agent dead and two others wounded — accidentally shot, it turned out, by a fourth agent armed with an illegal weapon. Hoover suppressed that evidence and blamed the massacre on an Oklahoma bandit, Charles "Pretty Boy" Floyd, who was run to earth and killed in October 1934. Meanwhile, Hoover and Attorney General Homer Cummings prevailed on Congress to pass legislation expanding bureau authority on the criminal front. The new laws made bank robbery a federal crime, restricted private ownership of certain weapons, and added a death penalty clause to the Lindbergh Law. They also empowered BI agents (allegedly for the first time) to carry weapons and to make arrests.[41]

The new laws launched Hoover's bureau into what Don Whitehead calls "a strange kind of guerrilla warfare against the armed forces of the underworld." Organized crime was exempt — indeed, Hoover publicly denied its very existence until 1964 — but agents made headlines in pursuit of transient outlaws such as John Dillinger, "Baby Face" Nelson and "Machine Gun" Kelly. In the process, Hoover's bureau gained its present title, while press agents tagged his agents with their famous "G-man" nickname. Almost before the gunsmoke cleared from that crusade, in summer 1936, President Franklin Roosevelt ordered a sweeping FBI investigation of right-

and left-wing extremists across the country, thus legitimizing the very domestic surveillance that Hoover had practiced illegally since 1918. On 5 September 1936, Hoover
ordered FBI field offices "to obtain from all possible sources information concerning subversive activities conducted in the United States by Communists, Fascisti, and
representatives or advocates of other organizations or groups advocating the overthrow or replacement of the Government of the United States."[42]

Despite his new authority, Hoover recognized that some of the FBI's activities
were still blatantly illegal. He resolved the problem with semantics, outlining dis-
tinctions between "investigations" and collection of "intelligence." In Hoover's mind,
an *investigation* was "conducted when there is a specific violation of a Criminal Statute
involved, always presuppose [*sic*] an overt act and is proceeded upon with the very
definite intention of developing facts and information that will enable prosecution
under such legislation." *Intelligence* activities proceeded under "an entirely different
premise," since "[m]uch of the activity indulged in by Communists and subversive
elements does not, in the original stage, involve an overt act or violation of a specific
statute. These subversive groups direct their attention to the dissemination of propaganda and to the boring from within processes, much of which is not a violation of
a Federal statute at the time it is indulged in, but which may become a very definite
violation of the law in the event of a declaration of war or of the declaration of a
national emergency."[43]

Neither theory, it seems, applied to members of the Klan or other racist groups
who continued a veritable reign of terror during the Depression. G-men did nothing in July 1930 when masked nightriders kidnapped and killed S.S. Mincey, a
black Republican leader in Montgomery County, Georgia. By 1939, at least 63
blacks were lynched by racists acting with police cooperation, yet Hoover saw no
cause to act under 18 USC Sec. 242. The FBI was deaf in January 1935 when
Franklinton, Kentucky's sheriff said of a murder in his jail: "There wasn't any
lynching. There wasn't any mob. There were just about six or eight men who were
going about their business." Hoover's hearing was no better in November 1938
when another sheriff in Wiggins, Mississippi, praised 200 participants in "an orderly
lynching," conducted with "no shooting and no disorder in the mob." Hoover was
blind in 1935 when Klansmen joined ranks with police to slaughter members of
the Southern Tenant Farmers Union, and again in 1936 when Tampa police delivered three white "radicals" to a Klan flogging party. One of the victims, Joseph
Shoemaker, was tortured to death by his captors, none of whom were punished
for their crime.[44]

One of the decade's worst cases—and one in which the FBI had clear-cut jurisdiction—was the October 1934 lynching of Claude Neal. A black resident of Jackson
County, Florida, Neal was accused of killing a teenage white girl on 18 October.
Threats of lynching prompted Florida authorities to jail Neal in Brewton, in neighboring Alabama, for safekeeping. It was wasted effort, as the lynchers declared their
intent to kidnap Neal and bring him back to Florida for execution. This they did on
26 October, accompanied by radio and newspaper announcement of their plans and
movements. A caravan of 300 to 400 persons removed Neal from jail and drove him
back to Florida, thus violating the Lindbergh Law with an obvious interstate kid-

napping. Back in Jackson, the mob held Neal alive for two days of "interrogation"—i.e., mutilation and torture—while newspapers reported his impending fate. Headlines in the Dothan (Alabama) *Eagle* boldly declared: "Florida to Burn Negro at Stake: Sex Criminal Seized from Brewton Jail, Will be Mutilated, Set Afire in Extra-Legal Vengeance for Deed." Florida's governor declined to move against the mob, which finally put Neal out of his misery. Despite the public nature of the crime, a November grand jury declined to indict the killers.[45]

No other kidnapping in U.S. history has been the subject of advance publicity and blow-by-blow media reports of the crime's progress. Under the Lindbergh Law, each member of the mob was subject to federal trial and execution for Neal's murder—and yet, the FBI did not investigate, much less arrest the guilty parties. Author James McGovern blames Attorney General Cummings for the lapse, reporting that his "strict construction" of the Lindbergh Law applied its terms only to cases where a ransom was demanded. On 29 October 1935, Hoover received an order from Assistant Attorney General Angus MacLean, dictating that the FBI should not investigate Neal's case. That order theoretically absolves Hoover, but it does not explain why he remained inactive during the preceding week.[46]

In most cases, Hoover required no order to abstain from civil rights investigations, and he ignored directions that obstructed his pursuit of blacks or Reds. Another case that failed to interest him was that of the Black Legion, a Klan splinter group active in the Midwest during 1934–36. Media reports identified the Legion's leaders as ex–Klansmen William Shepard (city health officer of Bellaire, Ohio) and V.F. Effinger. Shepard denied involvement with the group but admitted forming a team of black-robed nightriders in Ohio. Michigan was the Legion's greatest stronghold, with recruits including nearly a hundred public officials in Oakland County alone. Identified members included Pontiac's city treasurer, high-ranking police and firefighters, various judges, municipal officers and a member of the state Legislature. Frank Donner reports that the Legion also included "numerous supporters and sympathizers among the Detroit police, as well as among the officials of suburban communities." The Legion also worked with Harry Bennett, chief of the Ford Motor Company's brutish "service department," who kept Mafia goons and Nazis from the German-American Bund on his payroll as strikebreakers.[47]

The Black Legion's reign of terror was exposed in May 1936 with the murder of Michigan victim Charles Poole. Sensational reports blamed the group for 50 slayings, though prosecutor Duncan McRae called that tally "a fantastic rumor." Michigan state police dubbed the Legion a "strong-arm agency of the Ku Klux Klan," and Detroit police commissioner Heinrich Pickert clung to his job by a thread when his department's close ties to the terrorist group were revealed. His officers had used the Legion to identify and punish labor organizers in the Motor City's auto plants. Eleven Black Legion defendants were convicted of Poole's murder in autumn 1936, and 40 others faced charges of arson, kidnapping, flogging and conspiracy. Once again, despite clear violations of 18 USC Sec. 242, the FBI made no investigation or arrests.[48]

WINDS OF WAR

Federal concern with Fascist groups increased as Adolf Hitler's Germany expanded to consume Europe and Nazi agitators circulated throughout the United States, attacking various minorities and Roosevelt's "Jew Deal" relief programs. The FBI investigated six pro–Nazi groups before the U.S. entered World War II, but still found little time to scrutinize the Klan. Don Whitehead contends that two Klan leaders lobbied for Hoover's dismissal in 1939, but he provides no evidence, and it is difficult to understand why any Klansman of that era would regard the FBI director as a threat. James Colescott, replacing Hiram Evans as imperial wizard in June 1939, admired the FBI and lavished praise on Hoover's allies from the Red-hunting Dies Committee.[49]

Hoover *was* attacked in the pro–Nazi press, and Robert Edmondson's *American Vigilante Review* ironically branded Hoover a dangerous leftist. Chief among Hoover's far-right targets was the German-American Bund, which rallied with New Jersey Klansmen at Camp Nordland in 1940. There, flanked by swastikas and fiery crosses, Grand Dragon Arthur Bell shared the dais with Bund leader August Klapprott, who proclaimed, "The principles of the Bund and the principles of the Klan are the same." Wizard Colescott disagreed, exiling Bell with the announcement that "[t]here can be no sympathy on the part of the Bund and the Klan." Bell fired back with a claim that Colescott had approved the rally and produced a letter from the wizard, which was read to the assembled knights and Nazis. Still, Colescott weathered the storm, telling the Dies Committee that his shrunken Klan was still "100 percent American." Committee member Joe Starnes, from Alabama, emerged from the hearing with word that "the Klan was just as American as the Baptist or Methodist Church, as the Lions Club or the Rotary Club."[50]

Even when investigating Nazis, Hoover's agents managed to find black offenders in the fold. In 1942, the Philadelphia field office reported to Hoover that "many Negroes have expressed pleasure over Japanese victories in the Pacific and in the Far East." A handful of Fascist defendants were charged with sedition in federal court, but all were finally acquitted, while Black Muslim leader Elijah Muhammad was imprisoned for counseling blacks to resist military conscription.[51]

Had Hoover wished to track the Klan and allied terrorists, there was no shortage of activity. At least five lynchings were committed with police complicity in 1939–44. Elbert Williams, a black resident of Tennessee, was kidnapped and murdered after he registered to vote in June 1940. Robed Klansmen joined a riotous mob that barred blacks from Detroit's federally-funded Sojourner Truth housing project in February 1942, and while three mob leaders were later indicted, no knights were among them. Members of the Atlanta Klan's nightriding Klavalier Klub killed at least three victims in 1939–40 and whipped 50 more. On 5 February 1939, when they snatched six persons from the streets on charges of "inciting niggers against the whites," bystanders complained to Patrolman Roy Edelman. "This is none of your business!" Edelman replied. "If you don't watch out, they'll get you, too!" Eight floggers were finally captured and sent to state prison — including deputy sheriffs Edwin Burdette, Herb Eidson and W.W. Scarborough (exalted cyclops of the East

Point klavern)—but all were pardoned in December 1941 by Governor Eugene Talmadge.[52]

"Old Gene" personified the flagrant violations of 18 USC Sec. 242 that occurred daily in Dixie. Himself a lifelong ally of the Klan who bragged of flogging blacks, as governor in 1941–43 Talmadge named Samuel Roper, an Atlanta policeman and high-ranking Klansman, to lead the Georgia Bureau of Investigation. When Roper and a group of fellow knights asked Talmadge's opinion on the best means of deterring black voters, the governor scrawled "pistols" on a slip of paper. Upon leaving the governor's mansion in 1943, Talmadge founded his own "secret, patriotic white man's organization" called Vigilantes Inc., led by Major John Goodwin of the Georgia Highway Patrol. Klansmen and Vigilantes—if, indeed, there was any real difference between the two groups—held joint meetings with Talmadge, Goodwin and various Klan leaders as featured speakers. At one such meeting, in December 1943, Talmadge and Goodwin shared the stage with James Colescott, Grand Dragon Samuel Green, and State Treasurer George Hamilton.[53] Hoover's agents ignored the ongoing collusion between state authorities and terrorists as if it did not exist.

On those rare occasions when the FBI bestirred itself to safeguard civil rights, the results were mixed at best. Agents arrested two Houston policemen for beating a black soldier in August 1942, but they were absent in May 1940, when three officers and a civilian gunman murdered inmate O'Dee Henderson in his Alabama jail cell. In 1943, Attorney General Francis Biddle ordered Hoover to investigate a case from Baker County, Georgia. Sheriff Claude Screws and two deputies faced federal charges for the beating death of a black prisoner. They were convicted, but the Supreme Court overturned the verdict by a vote of five to four. According to that judgment, officers could be convicted on a federal charge only if they tortured and killed victims "with the specific intent and purpose of denying their prisoner a Constitutional right" such as suffrage.[54] Hoover's reaction to that ruling is unknown, but he never blamed police for using brutal force, and the Screws case guaranteed that he would not be criticized for shunning future civil rights investigations.

The bureau played no role whatever in the final dissolution of the KKK. In spring 1944, Internal Revenue agent Marion Allen surprised James Colescott with a bill for $685,355 in unpaid taxes from the 1920s. Klan assets were sold to pay part of the debt, then Colescott convened a special klonvokation on 23 April, revoking all Klan charters nationwide and disbanding provisional klaverns. Far from blaming the FBI, Colescott told reporters, "It was that nigger-lover Roosevelt and that Jew [Henry] Morgenthau who was his Secretary of the Treasury who did it!" On a more plaintive note, the wizard added, "Maybe the government can make something out of the Klan. I never could."[55]

2

Terrorism Resurgent (1945–1953)

Disbandment of the national Klan in April 1944 did not spell death for the order, as Colescott proclaimed. Active klaverns clung to life in several states, notably Georgia, Alabama, Florida and Tennessee. Dr. Samuel Green organized the Association of Georgia Klans (AGK) in May 1944, mimicked by the Ku Klux Klan of Florida four months later. Alabama's Klan formally revived on 27 March 1946, with eight crosses fired in Birmingham the next night. The same month saw a cross-burning in Knoxville, Tennessee, followed by similar demonstrations in New Jersey (August), Miami (October) and at Stone Mountain, Georgia (October). A Jewish merchant closed her shop in Red Bank, Tennessee, after repeated cross-burnings. Within a single week of June 1946, two crosses were burned in Los Angeles and a Hollywood synagogue was vandalized with racist graffiti. Three months later, a new Federated Ku Klux Klans filed its incorporation papers in Alabama.[1]

The spate of post-war Klan activity provoked federal attention. In May 1946, Attorney General Tom Clark announced his intent to use every available statute against racist organizations. Two months later, Clark reported that the FBI was investigating Klan activities in California, Florida, Michigan, Mississippi, New York and Tennessee. No prosecutions resulted, but Clark listed the Klan as a subversive organization in December 1947, theoretically barring its members from federal employment in Cold War America. On a more practical level, between May and December 1946, Klan charters were revoked by state authorities in California, Georgia, Kentucky, New Jersey, New York and Wisconsin. Several states and cities passed anti-mask laws, and New York went further still, imposing six-month jail terms and $10,000 fines on would-be Klan recruiters.[2]

"Blood Will Flow in the Streets"

Six decades after the fact, no documents concerning the FBI's 1946 Klan investigations are available for public scrutiny. No federal charges were filed against Klansmen in the years 1945–48, despite a wave of racist violence spanning the Deep South that claimed scores of lives and left countless other victims traumatized. Whatever marginal impact the bureau had on Klansmen in that period, it must be gleaned from secondary sources.

Georgia, as ever since the KKK's rebirth in 1915, was the heart of postwar Klan activity. Members of Atlanta's Klavalier Klub resumed nightly floggings and bragged of killing a black cab driver in August 1945. Eugene Talmadge, pursuing his third term as governor in July 1946, warned black voters to stay away from the polls during Georgia's Democratic primary, and FBI agents reported a "well-organized plot" to murder incumbent governor Ellis Arnall. On primary day, 17 July, Sam Green boasted that the Klan had delivered 100,000 votes for "Old Gene." Nine days later, an unmasked vigilante firing squad executed four "uppity" blacks—George Dorsey, Roger Malcolm and their wives—outside Monroe. Those crimes remained officially unsolved, at least in part, because of police complicity. Sam Roper, back on the Atlanta force after his stint with the Georgia Bureau of Investigation, doubled as a detective and the exalted cyclops of Klan Post 297. Elsewhere in Atlanta, 11 uniformed policemen attended a Klan meeting on 3 June 1946, and 38 turned out for another rally ten days later. One of those compromised lawmen assured his fellow Klansmen that they would be granted leave to handle any local race riots "in their own way."[3]

Talmadge won election in November 1946, but Klansmen were stunned by his sudden death on 21 December. They backed a hasty plan to replace Old Gene with son Herman Talmadge, but the coup lasted barely two months, until Lieutenant Governor Melvin Thompson replaced the younger Talmadge. Terrorism resumed that summer, escalating into the 1948 primary season, as Herman Talmadge planned his first full-fledged gubernatorial bid. In Wrightsville, on primary eve, Grand Dragon Green proclaimed that "blood will flow in the streets" if Georgia blacks sought equality with whites. Klansmen circulated through the neighborhood after that rally, and none of Wrightsville's 400 black voters cast ballots the next day. In Swainsboro, cardboard coffins marked with the initials "KKK" were left at black homes overnight, persuading two-thirds of all registered blacks to refrain from voting. One black who voted, Isaiah Newton, was murdered in Alton, and his killer was acquitted on a plea of self-defense. Another black man, Robert Mallard, was ambushed and shot by robed Klansmen soon after November's election. Sam Green announced his own investigation of the case, and Sheriff R.E. Gray proclaimed Mallard "a bad Negro" who "was hated by all who knew him." GBI agents arrested Mallard's widow for murder at her husband's funeral. Although those charges were dropped, Lieutenant W.E. McDuffle insisted that "the Ku Klux Klan has been wrongfully accused in this case."[4]

Once again, the Klan was free to kill and maim where politicians and police supported it. Herman Talmadge celebrated his inauguration by naming Green as a lieutenant colonel and aide-de-camp on his staff. Talmadge later denied any knowledge of the appointment, but Green had a framed certificate to prove it. Talmadge was less bashful at Green's 1948 birthday party, where he delivered the keynote speech. Georgia and the nation were lucky, he said, to have Klansmen who "will save America for Americans," standing "ready to fight for the preservation of our American traditions against the Communists, foreign agitators, Negroes, Catholics and Jews." Others shared the governor's view. In Atlanta, "Brother Judge" Caleb Callaway received a Ku Klux letter of commendation for his rulings "conforming with the principles of Klannishness." At a November 1948 Klan meeting, three Atlanta police-men gave speeches. One of them, Patrolman "Trigger" Nash, was honored for killing his 13th black victim "in the line of duty." To loud applause, Nash "said he hoped he wouldn't have the honor of killing all the niggers in the South and he hoped the people would do something about it themselves." Columnist Drew Pearson gave the speech national publicity, yet Hoover's G-men found no reason to investigate a con-fession of racist serial murder committed "under color of law."[5]

Georgia was not the only state plagued by Klan mayhem and official inaction during 1946–48. Senator Theodore Bilbo, campaigning for reelection in Mississippi, confessed Klan membership in August 1946. In fact, he said, Bilbo Klan No. 40 was named in his honor. Bilbo "was not in sympathy" with certain Klan activities, but he solemnly declared, "No man can ever leave the Klan. He takes an oath not to do that. Once a Ku Klux, always a Ku Klux." His message to Mississippi whites was straightforward: "If you never voted for me before, vote for me now. Let me go back to Washington. I'll represent you in the Senate so that you'll be proud and never regret it. I'll fight and fight, and I'll kill and kill." As for black voters, he suggested, "The best way to keep the nigger from the polls is to visit him the night before the election." Taking those words to heart, whites flogged a black man to death in Lex-ington on 22 July 1946. A month later, racists mobbed blacks in Magee. The floggers were acquitted by an all-white jury, and the rioters escaped indictment. FBI agents were nowhere to be found in the Magnolia State.[6]

Alabama hosted several competing Klan factions in 1946–48, all of them vio-lent. A union organizer was kidnapped from Elba and whipped in December 1946. In 1947, "Parson" Jack Johnston's Original Southern Klan stormed a Phenix City courthouse and staged a demonstration in the jury box. Other knights raided a black Girl Scout camp outside Bessemer. Birmingham Klansmen bombed the first of many black homes in August 1947. The city's public safety commissioner, Eugene "Bull" Connor, warned another black resident that his presence in a once-white neighbor-hood "might lead to violence and if [Connor] were in his place he would move imme-diately." In April 1948, soon after another black home was bombed in the district nicknamed "Dynamite Hill," Connor warned the pastor of Birmingham's Sixteenth Street Baptist Church that God — acting through the KKK — would "strike the church down" if it hosted a meeting of the Southern Negro Youth Congress. In 1948, Alabama's attorney general wrote to Senator Lister Hill: "The Ala. Klan *is* unques-tionably and undoubtedly directed from tall buildings and, its [sic] most likely that its [sic] directed from one certain tall building" — a reference to U.S. Steel's corpo-rate office, which employed Exalted Cyclops E.E. Campbell.[7]

Sporadic violence also flared in other southern states. In Columbia, Tennessee, rioting whites swept through a black neighborhood on 26 February 1946, injuring ten persons, vandalizing homes and shops with KKK graffiti. Police responded by jailing 70 blacks and fatally shooting two of them during a jailhouse interrogation on 28 February. Two months later, Klan threats and nocturnal shootings kept all but one of Perry, Florida's 150 black voters from casting ballots in the Democratic pri-mary. A black union activist was threatened by Miami Klansmen in August 1946. On 1 November 1948, Mayor Thomas Cummings reported that black neighborhoods in

Nashville, Tennessee, were "flooded" with threats against potential voters in the next day's election.[8] As in Georgia and Alabama, the FBI remained invisible.

"EDGAR SAYS NO"

J. Edgar Hoover despised President Harry Truman (1945–53). Truman's lack of deference toward the FBI director was a daily irritant, compounded by his refusal to fire certain federal employees branded by Hoover as Reds. Another strike against the president was his desegregation of the U.S. military and creation of a Fair Employment Practices Commission. As described by assistant FBI director William Sullivan in his memoirs, "Hoover's hatred of Truman knew no bounds."[9] Still, Truman *was* the president and Hoover had to work with him after a fashion, through Attorney General Clark. As for the quality of service Hoover's agents rendered, though, there was no guarantee.

Southern lynchings proved the point. Barely five weeks after VJ-Day, on 11 October 1945, black inmate Jesse Payne was taken from jail with the sheriff's apparent complicity and lynched in Madison, Florida. Tom Clark ordered G-men to investigate, under pressure from the NAACP, but no suspects were identified. In January 1946, Leroy Bradwell was arrested for the "crime" of writing love notes to a white woman in Midway, Florida. Last seen with Gadsden County's sheriff, Bradwell inexplicably vanished en route to jail and was never seen again. FBI agents proved that Bradwell had not written the notes in question, but they said "no facts have been uncovered to evidence foul play" and the case remains unsolved. Georgia's governor requested federal aid in the July 1946 Dorsey-Malcolm lynching. FBI agents questioned some 2,800 persons, but no charges were filed. (In 1992 an aging witness identified several of the lynchers, all deceased.)[10]

Some cases *did* lead to arrests. In August 1946, black cousins Albert Harris and John Jones were beaten and dragged from jail in Minden, Louisiana, by a gang including both deputy sheriffs and civilians. Driven to an isolated bayou, both captives were beaten, then Jones was murdered with a blowtorch and meat cleaver. Harris survived his wounds and described the attack to G-men, resulting in the October indictment of five lynchers under 18 USC 242. All were acquitted at trial when their lawyers accused the FBI of "Gestapo tactics" and said the NAACP had coached prosecution witnesses. In February 1947, another lynch mob tortured murder suspect Willie Earle to death in Pickens County, South Carolina. Clark ordered Hoover to investigate and 31 lynchers were identified, 26 of whom confessed in custody. Notwithstanding their admissions of guilt, a judge directed acquittal of three defendants, and jurors freed the other 28. One day after that verdict, on 23 May 1947, Godwin Bush escaped from would-be lynchers in North Carolina and sought protection from FBI agents. Seven whites were arrested on 27 May, but a grand jury declined to indict them. The only racist killer convicted as a result of FBI investigation in that era was Constable Tom Crews of Jacksonville, Florida. Crews whipped and murdered a black farmhand in September 1945, was convicted in October 1946, and received the maximum one-year prison term.[11]

Civil rights activists were unimpressed with the bureau's performance in Dixie. In 1946, NAACP attorney (and future Supreme Court justice) Thurgood Marshall addressed a complaint to Tom Clark. "The FBI," Marshall wrote, "has established for itself an uncomparable [*sic*] record for ferreting out persons violating our federal laws. This great record extends from the prosecution of vicious spies and saboteurs, who are trained in the methods of evading identification and arrest, to nondescript hoodlums who steal cheap automobiles and drive them across state lines." Citing Clark's expressed hope of broadening federal civil rights laws, Marshall noted that "there would be very little use to strengthen these Civil Rights Statutes if the FBI continues its policy of being unable to produce the names of persons guilty of [lynchings]." In a memo to NAACP Director Walter White, Marshall spoke more bluntly: "I have no faith in either Mr. Hoover or his investigators and there is no use in my saying I do."[12]

When confronted with Marshall's complaint, Hoover fired off a letter to White, insisting that the NAACP should not address concerns to the attorney general without first consulting Hoover. Recounting the FBI's frustration with white Southern juries, Hoover added: "As you realize, [the FBI] has nothing whatsoever to do with the nature or context of Federal statutes which are initiated, approved and placed on the statute books by the Congress of the United States. If these statutes are defective or inadequate, the responsibility is that of Congress." President Truman, meanwhile, declared in the wake of the Dorsey-Mallard investigation, "When the mob gangs can take four people out and shoot them in the back, and everybody in the county is acquainted with who did the shooting and nothing is done about it, this country is in a pretty bad fix from the law enforcement standpoint."[13]

Disgusted, Hoover wrote to Clark on 12 September 1946, requesting that the bureau be relieved of any further civil rights responsibilities. Hoover complained that his men were "expending a considerable amount of manpower" on "murders, lynchings and assaults, particularly in the Southern states, in which there cannot conceivably be any violation of a Federal statute." While Hoover did not "condone the type of activities" seen in hate crimes, he believed they should be left to state authorities. The director ignored white racism and blamed "nebulous" federal laws for the low conviction rate in civil rights cases. More to the point, he bemoaned the fact that "[a]n increasingly large number of people are taking a critical attitude toward the [Justice] Department because of its failure to 'get results' in these cases." Hoover regretted that "the public judges the efficiency of law enforcement ... upon the basis of prosecutions," leaving his bureau saddled "in the public mind and in the press with the responsibility" for solving difficult cases. His team suffered from a widespread "feeling and belief that the Bureau has failed to 'solve' many cases into which it has entered." Hoover lamented that "completely ineffective" civil rights efforts let state authorities "slide out of these cases as soon as the Department and the Bureau enter them," urging Clark to stop his prosecutors from "rushing pell-mell into cases where there is no apparent violation of a Federal statute."[14]

Clark responded cautiously on 24 September, admitting that "a large percentage of the investigations initiated in this field prove in the end to be fruitless." Still, he felt that Justice had no choice, since "in each case the complaint made is indicative of a violation. If we do not investigate we are placed in the position of having received a complaint of a violation and of having failed to satisfy ourselves that it is or is not such a violation. I know of no way to avoid at least a preliminary inquiry into the facts of a complaint which alleges a civil rights offense. I am sure you agree that we should not be in the position of avoiding such actions." Furthermore, Clark noted, the department's Civil Rights Section had "requested only limited investigations in almost every case."[15]

Hoover did not agree with Clark, and he devised a covert plan to rid himself of "liberal" assignments by unseating Truman in the 1948 presidential election. Secretly, he met with Republican contender Thomas Dewey and hatched a campaign strategy: In exchange for dirt from bureau files and any other aid G-men could furnish, Dewey promised Hoover a seat on the U.S. Supreme Court, with the ultimate goal of becoming chief justice. Hoover's coaching helped Dewey wrestle the GOP nomination from rival Harold Stassen in May 1948, then shifted to an avalanche of derogatory data on the Truman administration. Nothing was omitted, from Truman's links with the Pendergast political machine and Tom Clark's underworld connections to the lurking threat of "Communists in government." Dewey's command of facts and polls was so impressive that the *Chicago Tribune* headlined its election-day early edition with a banner reading "Dewey Defeats Truman." When Truman carried the election, Hoover was so angry that sulked at home for two weeks, feigning illness.[16]

To punish Truman and expand his own influence, Hoover undertook promotion of a new Red scare, pursuing Russian spies and "parlor pinks" with equal zeal, reserving primary attention for those targets likely to embarrass the White House. Illegal leaks to congressional allies such as Richard Nixon, Pat McCarran and Joseph McCarthy fueled marathon witch hunts by the House Un-American Activities Committee, the Senate Internal Security Subcommittee, and the Subversive Activities Control Board. Author Curt Gentry is correct in noting that "'McCarthyism' was, from start to finish, the creation of one man, FBI Director J. Edgar Hoover." The benefits of that campaign to Hoover were both emotional and material. In addition to the pleasure of tormenting his enemies, Hoover watched his own salary double between 1945 and 1950. In the latter year, when Congress slashed $979 million from the federal budget, Hoover's FBI received every penny the director requested, plus an additional 700 employees to help fight "subversive activities."[17]

Hoover's arrogance grew with the strength of his bureau, revealed by an incident in 1949. That year saw the latest in a series of underworld attempts to kill Victor and Walter Reuther, Michigan leaders of the United Automobile Workers. Two days after Victor was shot at his home, the U.S. Senate adopted a unanimous resolution calling for an FBI investigation. Tom Clark passed the order to Hoover, but soon reported back to UAW attorney Joseph Rauh that "Edgar says no. He says he's not going to get involved every time some nigger woman gets raped." The strange non sequitur revealed Hoover's pathological racism and suggested an unbalanced mind. It should also have seen him dismissed on the spot for rank insubordination, but Clark could not afford to stir a hornet's nest at FBI headquarters. Mere weeks from an appointment to the U.S. Supreme Court, Clark had accepted bribes to arrange the early parole of convicted gangsters, a fact well known to Hoover and his aides.[18]

As Hoover went undisciplined, so did most of the Klan's invisible empire during 1949–53. In Georgia, shortly before an August 1949 heart attack claimed his life, Sam Green boasted that FBI agents used Klansmen to collect intelligence on Southern race problems. Days after Green's death, IRS agent Marion Allen slapped the AGK with a bill for $9,332, representing unpaid taxes from 1946–48, and earned more death threats in the process. Assaults and whippings were rife throughout the state, including an attack on Soperton's mayor and two raids against one-armed Mayor C.L. Drake in Iron City. Lynchings with probable police complicity were recorded — and ignored–in Irwinton (September 1949) and Bainbridge (May 1950). Klan bombing targets included a black family in Atlanta and a newsman who exposed corruption within the Talmadge regime. One case with clear federal jurisdiction involved the February 1949 abduction of three black high-school students from Columbus, Georgia. Klansmen drove them across the state line to Phenix City, Alabama, where they were whipped, grilled about their rumored ties to the NAACP, then released on foot with a flurry of shots to speed them on their way. As in the Claude Neal case, G-men were not concerned with racist violations of the Lindbergh Law.[19]

Alabama's knights kept pace with their Georgia brethren where violence was concerned. The Federated Klans, led by William Morris and Dr. E.P. Pruitt, flogged so many victims around Birmingham in early 1949 that Governor James Folsom reminded his constituents, "Your home is your castle. Defend it in any way necessary." Seventeen Klansmen were finally indicted by state authorities, but only two faced trial and both were acquitted. William Morris was the only knight incarcerated, spending 67 days in jail on a contempt citation for refusing to identify his Klansmen. The same month he emerged from custody, Birmingham Klansmen pulled down the tower of a black radio station. In Mobile, nightriders bombed three homes and burned a fourth, together with an elementary school. Other racist bombings jarred Cottonwood, Crossville and Phenix City. In "Bombingham," Bull Conner's police left seven more bombings unsolved in 1949–50. Assistant police chief Jack Warren admitted that racist bombings "would not be truly adequately investigated," yet Washington saw no cause to intervene. Blacks finally ambushed a group of Birmingham nightriders, killing one man and wounding another. Police and white-owned newspapers ignored the shooting, but it brought six years of relative quiet to Dynamite Hill.[20]

Elsewhere across the South, Klansmen struck when and where they could. Virginia's knights whipped a Columbus County woman in January 1951 and bombed three Norfolk County homes in summer 1953. Authorities in Dallas, Texas, recorded 17 racist bombings between March 1949 and January 1952, and another series of blasts rocked Houston in August 1953. One of the nation's most violent klaverns was found in Chattanooga, Tennessee, where Klansman Jesse Stoner called for deportation of blacks and mass execution of Jews. Sam Green expelled the klavern from his Klan in August 1949 after reports of 16 floggings and a bombing, but the mayhem continued with another home bombed in May 1950. In Nashville, occupancy of a new housing project was switched from blacks to whites in January 1950, after cross-burnings and a dynamite blast. Emboldened by their victory, Klansmen bombed another black family's home in March 1951. Between January 1951 and June 1952, more than 40 racist bombings scarred the Southern states.[21] The FBI remained invisible in nearly all those cases, but the tide was bound to shift. In Georgia and the Carolinas, cases were about to break that would allow the bureau to save face.

"Beyond the Line of Duty"

Mamie Clay was a problem for white supremacists in Dade County, Georgia. A resourceful black landowner who rejected lowball offers on her property, Clay soon became a target of harassment by police and Klansmen alike. First, sheriff's deputies raided her home and accused her of running a brothel. When that charge failed to stick, a series of cross-burnings caused Clay to fear for her life. She invited friends to share her home, but Georgia blacks found no safety in numbers. On the night of 2 April 1949, another cross blazed on a nearby hilltop. Moments later, Sheriff John Lynch and three of his deputies arrived at Clay's house with a mob of masked Klansmen. Lynch arrested seven of the blacks on false drunk-and-disorderly charges, then delivered them to the Klan. Driven to a nearby schoolyard, the seven were whipped, then ordered to "Get on over that hill and get out of here."[22]

Clay complained to the Justice Department, and Tom Clark ordered an FBI investigation of the case. A federal grand jury convened in Rome, Georgia, on 3 August 1949, prompting Samuel Green to banish the Trenton klavern from his AGK five days later. Twelve defendants were indicted on civil rights charges, including Sheriff Lynch, three deputies and eight civilian knights. When their trial opened on 22 November, five past or present Klansmen were excluded from the jury pool, but one acknowledged knight was seated as an alternate juror. FBI agents testified that Sheriff Lynch admitted working with the KKK "to get this thing cleaned up," and that the morning after the assaults he said, "I don't think we'll be bothered about anything that happened last night." Lynch said his presence at Clay's home on the night of the whippings was "a coincidence," and that he tried to save her guests but had been "too slow on the draw." Deputy William Hartline confessed to helping build and deliver the cross that was burned near Clay's home, but he denied any knowledge of the floggings. Klan witnesses for the defense included Sam Roper (who denied the existence of a Dade County klavern), Walter Arp (acknowledging the presence of a provisional unit), and Katherine Rogers (Dr. Green's former secretary, detailing robe sales in the county).[23]

Judge Frank Hooper directed acquittal of two defendants, L.C. Spears and Trenton City Recorder John Wilkins, on 1 December 1949, then declared a mistrial on 17 December, when jurors deadlocked on the other ten defendants. Victory celebrations were premature, however, as the Justice Department scheduled a new trial for March 1950. A second jury convicted Lynch and Hartline on 9 March, while acquitting their eight codefendants. Both lawmen received the maximum sentence of 12 months in prison and a $1,000 fine, with the verdicts upheld on appeal. In the meantime, on 12 December 1949, Rome's federal grand jury passed a resolution praising G-men for "their great fidelity and singleness of purpose," having "gone far beyond the line of duty to aid, assist, and protect the citizens of the United States and to further the cause of equity and justice in America."[24] The service was real enough, albeit rendered grudgingly by Hoover, and Sheriff Lynch was barely settled in his prison cell before the bureau had another opportunity to sting the Klan.

CAROLINA CRACKDOWN

Atlanta wholesale grocer Thomas Hamilton moved to Leesville, South Carolina, in 1948, representing Samuel Green and the Association of Georgia Klans. His knights liked action and committed their first known flogging at Sandy Bottoms on 24 July 1949, when four blacks were whipped with the warning that "This is your civil rights." Four months later, Hamilton defected from the AGK to found his own Association of Carolina Klans, with strength concentrated in Horry County, South Carolina, and neighboring Columbus County, North Carolina. Nocturnal kidnappings and beatings proliferated over the next two years, scarring an uncertain number of victims. Whites and blacks alike were flogged, typically for some alleged infraction of Klan "morals." Known victims included war veterans, farmers, a pregnant woman and two disabled brothers. Hamilton's knights also set off a bomb in Wake Forest, North Carolina, and stoned the home of federal Judge J. Waites Waring, who had invalidated South Carolina's white primary. On 26 August 1950, Klansmen raided Charlie Fitzgerald's nightclub at Myrtle Beach, South Carolina, firing some 300 shots and leaving one of their own dead at the scene. When the corpse was unmasked, authorities recognized an off-duty Conway policeman, recently elected magistrate. Another of Hamilton's men was killed three months later while whipping victim Clayton Moore in Greenwood, South Carolina.[25]

Five days after the Myrtle Beach skirmish, Sheriff C.E. Sasser charged Hamilton with conspiracy to incite mob violence, but a Horry County grand jury refused to indict him. The same result occurred, on an identical charge, after Hamilton was briefly jailed for the beating of Leslie Boney, a YWCA swim instructor who stumbled upon a Klan meeting near Bishopville, South Carolina. Emboldened, the grand dragon launched a new series of raids on both sides of the border. Most of the whippings were carried out by members of Fair Bluff, North Carolina's "Southlands Sport Club"—led by Exalted Cyclops (and former police chief) Early Brooks—but some were more public affairs. On 25 August 1951, two black men were pummeled at a Klan rally while police stood and watched. Six months later, candidate C.L.C. Glymph blamed Klan threats for his decision to quit the race for town council in Gaffney, South Carolina. Tom Hamilton's first conviction, for criminal libel, was recorded on 30 October 1951, but he escaped with a $1,000 fine.[26]

By that time, FBI agents were on the dragon's case. Their focus was the Fair Bluff abduction of white victims Ben Grainger and Dorothy Martin on 6 October 1951. Klansmen had driven their captives across the state line into South Carolina, thus violating the Lindbergh Law, and injuries inflicted on the couple made their kidnappers eligible for capital punishment. G-men spent four months collecting evidence, then joined Sheriff Hugh Nance for synchronized raids that bagged ten Columbus

County Klansmen at midnight on 18 February 1952. Those held included Early Brooks and his son Bobby; ex-policeman Horace Strickland and son Pittman from Tabor City; brothers George and Sherwood Miller; Steve Edmonds; Bobby Hayes; and L.C. Worley. The morning after those arrests, J. Edgar Hoover told reporters that he had ordered his men to "find the criminals and bring them to court regardless of how tedious the job is and how long it takes."[27]

The federal arrests encouraged state authorities to tackle Klansmen on their own. Nine days after the midnight raids, agents from North Carolina's State Bureau of Investigation (SBI) charged Early Brooks and seven other knights with the November 1951 flogging of pregnant victim Esther Floyd. On 5 March 1952, SBI officers arrested four knights—including Fair Bluff Police Chief Frank Lewis—for the December 1951 kidnapping and whipping of Woodrow Johnson. At the same time, SBI spokesmen announced that the Klansmen already charged with beating Esther Floyd would also be indicted for whipping Chadbourn resident Dorsey Robinson the same night. Robeson County, North Carolina, had suffered no violence, but authorities there dusted off an 1868 statute banning membership in "secret political or military organizations" and fined 16 of Hamilton's knights on general principles. Hamilton himself joined the list on 23 May 1952, charged with conspiracy to kidnap and assault victim Evergreen Flowers, beaten in Chadbourn in January 1951. A month later, Hamilton and 24 disciples were indicted for conspiracy against four other victims. In South Carolina, Constable T.M. Floyd was fired for joining the Fitzgerald raid, and 27 Klansmen (including Fair Bluff policeman Jack Ashley) were indicted in a series of Horry County floggings.[28]

The flurry of indictments spelled doom for Hamilton's Klan. State charges in the Grainger-Martin case were tried in May 1952. Seven defendants pleaded "no contest" on reduced charges, while seven more took their chances with a jury; two of those were acquitted on all counts, and the rest were convicted of assault but acquitted of kidnapping. Early Brooks received a two-year prison sentence, but the rest had their jail time suspended on payment of various fines. Federal trial in the same case convened three days after those verdicts were rendered and lasted two days. Ten defendants were convicted, and one teenager was discharged on a plea that older Klansmen forced him to participate. Early Brooks received another five-year sentence, three others drew shorter terms, and four more escaped with probation. In the Flowers case, Tom Hamilton pleaded guilty and received a four-year sentence; Klansman Joe Hardee also received that penalty; Russell Hammacher drew a maximum sentence of 18 months; Tabor City Commissioner Troy Bennett died before sentencing; and eight others paid fines in lieu of prison time. Throughout the Carolinas, 51 other Klansmen faced various charges, all but eight of them finally convicted. Ten entered prison on 1 September 1952, and 24 others paid fines totaling $15,850. Seven appealed their sentences on grounds that "church whippings" were not criminal, but that specious plea was rejected on 6 October 1952.[29]

The FBI struck again on 21 January 1953, charging 19 Klansmen with kidnapping and conspiracy in an assault on victim George Smith, flogged at Nichols, South Carolina, in October 1951. The list of defendants included five already jailed for other crimes, but they would not escape another federal trial. In court on 18 May 1953, 18 pled guilty as charged; seven received additional prison terms, and the rest were given probation. In October 1953, Tom Hamilton wrote an open letter from prison urging "my Klan friends everywhere to disband wherever you are." Hamilton served one-third of his sentence and was released on 22 February 1954.[30] Strangely, the bureau's greatest victory against the KKK to date was omitted when Don Whitehead published *The FBI Story* two years later.

FAILURE IN FLORIDA

Florida had been the Klan's strongest realm in 1930–44, and its knights remained violently active in the postwar era. By 1949, at least three rival Klans competed for members and money in the Sunshine State, but their core "values" of white supremacy and anti–Semitism were unchanged. Immediate postwar concerns included "radical" labor unions invading the state's citrus industry and the threat of black suffrage pursued by Harry Moore's Progressive Voters League. To hold those threats at bay, Klansmen pursued their normal tactics—terrorism and alliances with racist lawmen.[31]

There was no shortage of Klan-friendly sheriffs in Florida, but the most notorious was Willis McCall, who ruled Lake County like a fiefdom from 1945 to 1973. McCall denied Klan membership, but various informants from the 1950s named him as a high-ranking knight who called the shots for local nightriders. McCall earned his reputation beating union organizers and threatening journalists in 1947–48, but it took the Groveland rape case to give him a national audience. In July 1949, white teenager Norma Padgett quarreled with her abusive husband, briefly disappeared, and then returned to say she had been raped by four black strangers. McCall's deputies singled out suspects Charles Greenlee, Walter Irvin, Sam Shepherd and Ernest Thomas. Thomas was killed by a vigilante posse, and the others were jailed and savagely beaten. Klansmen ran amok through Lake County for three days, burning black homes and stores, but McCall frustrated lynchers by moving his battered captives to another county. On 5 August 1949, Assistant U.S. Attorney General Alexander Campbell ordered the FBI to make a "full and exhaustive investigation into the entire matter of the arrest mistreatment" in Groveland. Agents interviewed and photographed the suspects, noting many cuts and bruises, then moved on to investigate the rape and riots. That investigation was abruptly halted on 31 August by order of U.S. Attorney Herbert Phillips in Miami after black activists Harry Moore and Thurgood Marshall called for release of the suspects. Phillips ordered G-men to stand down "pending outcome" of the rape trial in Lake County.[32]

That trial was a farce, employing perjured testimony and fabricated evidence to convict all three defendants. Irvin and Shepherd were sentenced to die, and 16-year-old Greenlee received a life prison term. Five days later, Campbell ordered Herbert Phillips to proceed with indictments against police who had beaten the Groveland defendants. Phillips resisted, warning that prosecution "might result in another effort to commit serious violence on the defendants or victims," but he finally agreed to convene a grand jury. At the same time, however, Phillips ordered G-men to make no more inquiries about police brutality in Lake County. Author

Ben Green calls Phillips's handling of the April 1950 grand jury proceedings "questionable at best." His worst lapse was failure to present medical testimony corroborating the torture suffered by Greenlee, Irvin and Shepherd, thus leading the panel to offer Sheriff McCall "the highest praise" for his handling of the case. Justice spokesmen pronounced themselves "disturbed and disappointed in the inaction of the grand jury," but Phillips declined to reopen the case. It remained for the U.S. Supreme Court to overturn the Groveland convictions in April 1951 on grounds that the 1949 proceedings failed to "meet any civilized conception of due process of law."[33]

A new trial was ordered for Irvin and Shepherd. On 6 November 1951, McCall retrieved them from state prison for a pretrial hearing in Lake County. He allegedly stopped to change a flat tire near Umatilla at 9:30 P.M., whereupon the handcuffed prisoners attacked him, forcing McCall to shoot both "in self-defense." Shepherd died at the scene, but Irvin survived to tell a very different story. In his version, the shooting was a summary execution, assisted by deputy sheriff James Yates. FBI agents launched an immediate investigation, and Governor Fuller Warren (a confessed former Klansman) named Jefferson Elliott to head the state's probe. A Georgian who once served as Eugene Talmadge's personal bodyguard, Elliott admitted joining the KKK in Atlanta, but said he left the order after Talmadge fired him for arresting his son Herman on a drunken-driving charge. Florida Klan-fighter Stetson Kennedy challenged that claim, saying Elliott responded to Klan passwords and recognition signs, greeting Kennedy as a fellow knight. A local grand jury cleared McCall of any wrongdoing on 10 November 1951, whereupon Kennedy said that Elliott told him "Florida FBI agents had been partners in the conspiracy." Kennedy rushed to Washington and met with Leonard Kaufman, assistant chief of the Justice Department's Civil Rights Section, but Hoover dismissed Kennedy as a "phony" and ordered G-men not to "waste any more time" on him. In Miami, Herbert Phillips refused to convene another federal grand jury.[34]

While Sheriff McCall basked in the limelight of local adulation, Florida Klansmen were busy defending their state against blacks and Reds. They beat and murdered black victim Melvin Womack in Winter Garden, in March 1951, then went on to detonate a series of bombs in Miami and Orlando. Black homes were favored targets—Miami's Carver Village housing project was bombed three times in as many months—but synagogues and a Catholic church were also included. A second murder victim, Willie Vincent, was pitched from a speeding car in Tampa. In Orlando, nightriders beat Arthur Holland and grazed his scalp with a bullet "as a lesson to other Negroes." State investigators failed to move against the terrorists, prompting the Anti-Defamation League to create a private Coordinating Committee Against Bombing. FBI leaders shared the state's apathy until spokesmen for Florida's tourist industry complained to Washington. Justice then ordered the FBI to "investigate to see whether it could investigate." Miami's agent-in-charge told reporters, "There was a mailbox damaged in one of the explosions. Maybe that gives us an entrée into the case."[35]

Still, no Klansmen had been charged by 25 December 1951, when a powerful bomb exploded beneath Harry Moore's home in Mims. Moore was killed outright;

his wife lingered nine days before succumbing to her wounds. Jefferson Elliott led the state's investigation once again, and U.S. Attorney General Howard McGrath told reporters that "every facility of the FBI ... is being used to the fullest extent" in pursuit of the bombers. A "special team" of 14 G-men scoured Mims for clues, armed with "unprecedented authority" to identify the bombers without regard for federal jurisdiction. NAACP director Walter White described Hoover as "deeply aroused" by the bombing, hot on the trail of "three suspects." Agents collected soil and other evidence from Moore's home for scientific analysis, interviewed his dying wife three times, and monitored his funeral for signs of radical fervor. In June 1952, with no arrests in sight, Assistant FBI Director Louis Nichols told Walter White, "There is nothing additional we can say at this time." One week later, the NAACP issued a statement condemning the "failure of the county, state, and Federal officials who, after more than six months, have proceeded no further than an investigation of the crime." That resolution echoed Thurgood Marshall's 1946 complaint to Tom Clark, noting that while G-men had a reputation for catching the "cleverest criminals in history," they seemed "almost invariably unable to cope with violent criminal action by bigoted, prejudiced Americans against Negro Americans."[36]

Hoover's agents were making *some* progress, however. They learned that Orange County law enforcement was riddled with Klansmen, from Sheriff Dave Starr to Apopka Police Chief William Dunnaway and most of his officers, County Commissioner John Talton, the clerk of Orange County's criminal court and a justice of the peace in Winter Garden. One informant estimated that three-fourths of Apopka's white male population was linked to the Klan "in one way or another." Some of those interviewed confessed participation in floggings, but most remained stubbornly silent. Joseph Cox, kligrapp (secretary) of the Orlando klavern, committed suicide after his second FBI interview in March 1952. G-men tapped the telephones of two early suspects, "renegade" Klansmen Tillman Belvin and Earl Brooklyn, but neither was charged and both died within a year of Moore's murder. On 28 April 1952, Hoover told his superiors at Justice, "Our hope is that some Klan members will begin to talk if subpoenaed before a Federal Grand Jury."[37]

Attorney General McGrath acquiesced to that plan on 4 October 1952, announcing that a grand jury would meet in Miami to examine Florida's long reign of terror. "We believe," he told reporters, "there have been violations of the civil rights statutes and other laws." The first phase of the hearings focused on violence in Miami; 47 witnesses appeared, including Jefferson Elliott and a dozen Klansmen summoned with subpoenas. On 9 December the panel indicted three Miami knights and a woman who had organized protests at Carver Village — not for terrorism, but for lying to FBI agents or the grand jury, or falsely denying Klan membership on federal job applications. Prosecutors vowed, "This is only the beginning of the investigation. There will be much more." The panel reconvened in February 1953 to study Moore's case and grilled 100 witnesses over the next six weeks. Its final report called the Florida Klan a "cancerous growth ... founded on the worst instincts of mankind" and listed 19 incidents in "a catalogue of terror that seems incredible," as reported from Miami and Orlando during 1943–51. That list barely scratched the surface, and Harry Moore's murder remained unsolved, but the grand jury charged seven more Klansmen with perjury on 3 June 1953. One day later, the NAACP wired Attorney General Herbert Brownell congratulations for "the splendid work of the FBI" in "securing indictments of six Klansmen allegedly involved in acts of terror in Florida between 1949 and 1952."[38]

That praise was both inaccurate and premature. No Klansmen had been charged with any violent crimes, and none of those indicted for lying under oath were ever punished. On 30 December 1953, federal Judge George Whitehurst dismissed Klansman Harvey Reisner's indictment on grounds that the FBI had no jurisdiction in local crimes such as floggings. The remaining indictments were dismissed on 11 January 1954. Federal prosecutors announced plans to appeal that ruling on 25 June 1954, then changed their minds without fanfare on 2 September, and "the case just slowly faded away"—leaving a false impression that the FBI had scored another victory against the KKK. Despite renewed flurries of interest in 1978, 1982 and 1991, the Moore assassination remains unsolved. No one was punished for the Klan's long reign of terror in the Sunshine State.[39]

"THE SQUAD"

One final incident deserves inclusion here. In 1989, pseudonymous author "Michael Milan" published a memoir entitled *The Squad,* describing his alleged adventures as a member of "J. Edgar Hoover's private Squad … a top-secret operations unit that did jobs so dirty even the other intelligence services were afraid of it." Milan detailed supposed activities occurring between 1947 and 1971, with one chapter devoted to his disruption of the KKK in Georgia. According to Milan, he was summoned by Hoover "late in the summer of 1953" and given a perilous assignment.[40] Milan describes that meeting and his mission:

> Hoover explained to me that he was sending me to Atlanta, Georgia, where the Ku Klux Klan was beginning a new round of activity. They had been attacking black civil rights groups for the past four years, but had now turned their attention to Jewish organizations and the Catholic Church as well. Mr. Hoover was concerned, he said, that the Klan would set off a chain reaction that would provoke violent retaliations from both Jews and blacks. He said that intelligence reports had revealed that men like Jacob Druckman were planning demonstrations all over the South, and a highly respected and formidable black minister from Atlanta, Martin Luther King, Jr., was organizing black congregations in Mobile [Alabama]. The Klan had targeted King as a major threat, and Hoover was worried that the whole situation would flare up into violence unless he could get his people inside the Klan to gather intelligence and disrupt their activities. He was starting another counter-intelligence program.[41]

Milan describes his trip to Georgia under orders "to infiltrate a local group" and report "names and plans." After joining the Klan, he allegedly participated in several raids—burning a black church at Smyrna, looting an Atlanta synagogue and pummeling the rabbi, finally torching a police car to scatter rioting Klansmen outside another Jewish temple. Hoover ordered him back to New York, Milan says, after G-men arrested local knights and "turned" them as informants.[42]

While not inherently implausible, Milan's story is riddled with errors, inconsistencies and outright fabrications. Jacob Druckman (1928–96) was a Pulitzer Prize-winning symphony conductor in New York, with no connection to the black civil rights movement. Dr. King led his first protest against segregation in Montgomery, Alabama, (not Mobile) during 1955–56. Milan further describes New York gangster Benjamin "Bugsy" Siegel as living in Las Vegas when Milan returned to New York — but Siegel was murdered in June 1947.[43] And despite Milan's claims to the contrary, none of the violent events he describes were reported by *The Atlanta Constitution* or any other newspaper in 1953. Finally, as we shall see in Chapter 7, Hoover's counter-intelligence program ("COINTELPRO") against the KKK was not launched until September 1964.

In short, we must conclude that *The Squad* is a work of sensational fiction.

3

Beyond "Black Monday" (1954–1962)

On 17 May 1954 the U.S. Supreme Court issued its landmark ruling on school desegregation in the case of *Brown v. the Board of Education*. That unanimous judgment overturned the 1896 *Plessy* rule of "separate but equal" facilities for different races, proclaiming that segregated classrooms were "inherently unequal," and thus unconstitutional. Twelve months later, when no all-white school had admitted a single black pupil, the court demanded "a prompt and reasonable start" on integration, proceeding "with all deliberate speed."[1]

Below the Mason-Dixon Line, *Brown* was a call to arms unrivaled since the outbreak of the Civil War. In darkest Mississippi, Judge Tom Brady scorned the ruling as "Black Monday" and called for organized resistance, and Senator James Eastland told his white constituents, "You are not required to obey any court which passes out such a ruling. In fact, you are obligated to defy it." Shrunken Klan factions found a new lease on life while facing rampant competition. By May 1956, Dixie boasted 90 active segregationist groups claiming 250,000 to 300,000 members. Most pledged themselves to "lawful" means of resisting integration, but actions spoke louder than words. In 1959 the Southern Regional Council published a five-year roster of 530 incidents involving "racial violence, reprisal and intimidation." The tab included six murders, 44 nonfatal shootings, 57 bombings, 11 arson attacks on homes or public buildings, and 17 riots. Georgia Klansman James Venable spoke for many "segs," in and out of the Klan, when he said of public schools, "Let's close them up. Let's burn them up, if it comes to that."[2]

J. Edgar Hoover blamed the Supreme Court and militant blacks for any disturbance in Dixie, but he also recognized the danger of embarrassment if G-men bungled future civil rights investigations. Hoover would fight that battle in Washington, with President Dwight Eisenhower's administration, but he also ordered Clement McGowan — then supervising the civil rights desk at FBI headquarters — to "personally caution [agents] that the Supreme Court justices didn't ask anybody's opinion when they were passing on the [*Brown*] case and they didn't need any dissenting opinions or concurring opinions when you're out conducting investigations." As McGowan reminded author Kenneth O'Reilly, "Nothing can hurt you quicker than somebody opening his mouth. The biggest enemy most of the agents had was their own little mouths — or big mouths."[3]

"White-Collar Klans"

While the KKK enjoyed its most successful recruiting drive in 30 years, new organizations took the forefront in resisting integration. Chief among them were the loosely-knit Citizens' Councils, spawned by Mississippi businessmen and politicians in July 1954. The Councils expanded to Alabama, Arkansas, Florida, Louisiana, South Carolina and Texas in 1955, and Governor Herman Talmadge presided at the birth of Georgia's States' Rights Council in September of that year. Council leaders followed Tom Brady's lead in dissociating themselves from the "nefarious Ku Klux Klans." Brady himself condemned Klansmen "because they hid their faces, because they did things that you and I wouldn't approve of." Still, perhaps inevitably, the Councils were branded by blacks and northern liberals as "white-collar Klans," "button-down Klans," or "the uptown KKK."[4]

In fact, despite public denials, there were many contact points between Councils and Klans. Georgia councilor Roy Harris had served as campaign manager for several of the Peach State's Klan-allied governors, including Klansman E.D. Rivers (1936), Eugene Talmadge (1946), and Herman Talmadge (1948 and 1950). Asa Carter's North Alabama Citizens' Council was little more than a front for his Birmingham-based Original Ku Klux Klan of the Confederacy, and Klan terrorist "Dynamite Bob" Chambliss ranked among the group's first Birmingham members. John Kasper, organizer of the Seaboard White Citizens' Council, welcomed hooded Klansmen to his public rallies. Dr. Edward Fields worked for the Louisville, Kentucky, Council in 1957, then left to found a Klan-allied neo–Nazi group, the National States Rights Party (NSRP). (Five years earlier, the U.S. Army had classified Fields as "one step away from being totally insane.") Homer Barrs, secretary-treasurer of Florida's Council, was a close friend of Klan leader J.E. Fraser; Fraser praised Barrs as a "fine, right-thinking boy," and Barrs welcomed knights to his ranks. In 1959, Council leaders in South Carolina complained that Klansmen had infiltrated and subverted their organization. Louisiana Council spokesmen treated Ku Klux crowds to anti–Semitic rants in 1961. Klan literature was distributed at a Birmingham Council meeting in June 1963, and robed knights joined councilmen a month later to picket the city's new biracial commission. As late as September 1970, Council members and Klansmen marched together outside the Memphis school board, protesting ethnic diversity in education.[5]

Nor were Council members always peaceable and law-abiding, as they claimed. On 9 September 1954, while praising the newborn Citizens' Council, a Mississippi legislator opined that "a few killings" might "save a lot of bloodshed later on."[6] Two years later, a flier distributed at a Council rally in Montgomery, Alabama bore this message:

> When in the course of human events it becomes necessary to abolish the Negro race, proper methods should be used. Among these are guns, bows and arrows, sling shots and knives. We hold these truths to be self-evident, that all whites ate created equal with certain rights, among these are life, liberty and the pursuit of dead niggers.
>
> In every stage of the bus boycott, we have been oppressed and degraded because

of black, slimy, juicy unbearably stinking niggers. Their conduct should not be dwelt upon because behind them they have an ancestral background of Pygmies, Head Hunters and snot suckers. My friends, it is time we wised up to these black devils. I tell you they are a group of two-legged agitators who persist in walking up and down our streets protruding their black lips. If we don't stop helping these African flesh eaters, we will soon wake up and find Reverend [Martin Luther] King in the white house.

LET'S GET ON THE BALL WHITE CITIZENS.[7]

As with the KKK, wherever Council members gathered in the South, racist rhetoric gave way to violent deeds. Mississippi set the standard in May 1955, when black suffrage activist George Lee was shot and killed at Belzoni after ignoring repeated threats from local Council members. Sheriff Isaac Shelton first declared that shotgun pellets taken from Lee's face were "fillings from his teeth"; after an FBI report identified the buckshot, Shelton blamed "some jealous nigger" for the slaying. Attorney General Herbert Brownell Jr. ordered an FBI investigation of Lee's death, under pressure from the NAACP and American Civil Liberties Union, but the killers remained at large. Three months after Lee's assassination, black activist Lamar Smith was gunned down in broad daylight outside the Brookhaven courthouse. The FBI ignored that case, and while three whites were briefly detained, a grand jury refused to indict them. Another black resident of Belzoni, Gus Courts, was threatened by racists in 1955 for his voter registration efforts. That autumn, a known Council member warned Courts, "They're planning to get rid of you." Courts was wounded in a drive-by shooting on 25 November 1955, with Sheriff Shelton once again declaring that "some nigger had it in for him." Three days later, Attorney General Brownell announced that the FBI had "automatically" opened a "preliminary investigation" of the incident, but the effort was perfunctory at best. Courts complained that G-men never spoke with him beyond a brief hospital interview, and when his physician presented the shotgun pellets extracted from Courts, two Memphis agents told him to "keep them." Once again, the case remained unsolved.[8]

Another shocking case from Mississippi was the August 1955 "wolf-whistle murder" of Chicago teenager Emmett Till. While visiting relatives at Money, in LeFlore County, Till allegedly whistled at a white woman or asked her for a date (accounts differ). A short time later, Till was kidnapped and murdered by the woman's husband and brother-in-law. The killers were acquitted by an all-white jury, then sold their story of the murder to *Look* magazine. Historian William Manchester says that the FBI "painstakingly assembled irrefutable evidence" in Till's case, then "reluctantly closed its file" when grand jurors refused to vote kidnap indictments, but the truth is rather different. Governor James Coleman appointed ex–FBI agent Robert Smith III to investigate Till's murder for the state, and Hoover advised Justice to forgo federal prosecution. When Chicago Mayor Richard Daley called for federal intervention, Hoover informed the White House that while "Mayor Daley is not a Communist," certain "pressures engineered by the Communists were brought to bear on him." Don Whitehead blames Hoover's superiors for his inaction, while insisting that: "The clamor for federal intervention in civil rights cases such as the Till case was like an echo from the early 1930's, when the cry rang out for a federalized police force to stamp out gangsterism. But the real answer to the problem is stronger local law enforcement backed by intelligent public opinion."[9] Whitehead neglects to mention that Hoover led the call for expanded FBI powers in 1933–34, and that Congress gave him everything he wanted. There would be no such demands from FBI headquarters where civil rights were concerned.

Elsewhere in Dixie, the Citizens' Councils were linked to other acts of racist violence. Alabama councilors joined in the February 1956 riot that drove black coed Autherine Lucy from the state university at Tuscaloosa; when Bob Chambliss and three others were arrested, they filed a $4 million lawsuit against the NAACP. Two months later, members of "Ace" Carter's group attacked singer Nat "King" Cole at Birmingham's municipal auditorium. John Kasper led riots against school integration in Clinton, Tennessee, in September 1956. Council leaders in Little Rock, Arkansas, participated in two Ku Klux bomb plots during 1959–60. Attendees of a Council rally in New Orleans rioted on 15 November 1960 after keynote speaker Leander Perez warned them, "Don't wait for these Congolese to rape your daughters."[10]

Hoover's bureau generally ignored the Citizens' Councils. A rare exception occurred in October 1956 after Assistant Attorney General Warren Olney informed the U.S. Senate that Louisiana councilmen were engaged in "mass disfranchisement" of blacks. In Ouachita Parish alone, three-fourths of all registered blacks had been stricken from the voting rolls after challenges filed by the Council. Olney explained that "[o]ne of the principal objects and purposes of the Ouachita Citizens' Council was and is to prevent and discourage persons of the Negro race from participating in elections in the parish." FBI investigation revealed that some 8,500 Louisiana blacks had been stripped of the franchise by October, a figure that rose to 11,000 the following month. Council president William Rainach, meanwhile, denounced a "vast conspiracy" to "nullify" southern political power; he further accused President Eisenhower of using the FBI to "build a black Republican Party in the South." A federal grand jury convened in December 1956 but found no impropriety in the purge of black voters. Rainach crowed that he had foiled a "plot to clamp a reign of terror on the South." As Neil McMillen notes, the failed investigation "served only to embolden the purgers," and thousands more blacks were stricken from Louisiana's voting rolls thereafter.[11]

Hoover Chooses Sides

On 9 March 1956, Hoover accompanied Attorney General Brownell to a meeting of Eisenhower's Cabinet. Brownell used the occasion to promote his plan for new civil rights legislation, calling for an increased federal role in the South. When Brownell finished, Hoover took the floor and presented his view of the Southern situation, titled "Racial Tension and Civil Rights." Despite his own prior warnings to agents in the field, Hoover could not resist the opportunity to undercut Brownell and take his stand with those defending segregation.

The director opened with a warning that "[t]he South is in a state of explosive resentment over what they consider an unfair portrayal of their way of life, and what they consider intermeddling." For that condition, Hoover blamed the *Brown* decision and "a lack of objectivity and balance in the treatment of race relations by the press." Behind the conflict over "mixed education," he continued, "stalks the specter of racial intermarriages." And if that was not bad enough, white parents harbored yet another fear, since "colored parents are not as careful in looking after the health and cleanliness of their children."[12]

Who else shared blame for the impending crisis? "Delicate situations are aggravated," Hoover said, "by some overzealous but ill-advised leaders of the NAACP and by the Communist Party, which seeks to use incidents to further the so-called class struggle." The "crusade for integration," he claimed, was led by rabble-rousers who had "learned the techniques of mobilization, pressure, and propaganda to build momentum for their cause." He accused black leaders of preaching "racial hatred" and called special attention to a coming convention of the NAACP. According to Hoover, "The Communist Party plans to use this conference to embarrass the administration and Dixiecrats who have supported it, by forcing the administration to take a stand on civil rights legislation with the present Congress. The party hopes through a rift to affect the 1956 elections." He touched briefly on "the alleged lynching" of Emmett Till for "whistling at a distaff white," then veered off-course to misrepresent the black-separatist Nation of Islam as one of the "organizations presently advancing integration" that "figures in the rising tensions."[13]

"This mounting tension," Hoover said, "has manifested itself in overt acts on the part of individuals, organized resistance in legislative bodies, and the creation of organizations on a widespread basis in the South to resist integration.... The area of danger lies in friction between extremists on both sides ... both those who stand for and against segregation ready with violence." The KKK, in Hoover's view, was "pretty much defunct." As for the Citizens' Council, Hoover called its members "the leading citizens of the South ... bankers, lawyers, doctors, state legislators and industrialists." Its violence troubled Hoover less than "Negro publications" which ran "inflammatory articles concerning these councils."[14] Hoover went on:

> If the bloodshed which both the proponents and opponents of integration now discuss is to be avoided, there needs to be real understanding and public education with regard to the factors contributing to the present situation which can boil over at any moment into acts of extreme violence....
> The law-abiding people of the South neither approve nor condone acts of brutality and the lawless taking of human lives. On the other hand, historic traditions and customs are a part of a heritage with which they will not part without a struggle. The mounting tension can be met only with understanding and a realization of the motivating forces.[15]

Thus, at one stroke, Hoover pled the case for "understanding" of Dixie's white-supremacist "heritage" while presenting the lie that "opponents of integration" were somewhere "discussing" plans for "bloodshed." Hoover must have known that claim was false, since his agents had shadowed every black civil rights group in America from its inception. None preached violence — and, in fact, the movement would not launch its "direct action" phase of nonviolent civil disobedience until early 1960. Hoover had raised another phantom "menace" to support his private bigotry — and once again, he would succeed.

As the director finished speaking, Eisenhower told his cabinet, "These people in the South were not breaking the law for the past sixty years, but ever since the 'separate but equal decision,' they have been *obeying* the Constitution of the United States. Now, we cannot erase the emotions of three generations overnight." Historian J.W. Anderson writes that Hoover's presentation "reinforced the president's inclination to passivity" on civil rights; Sanford Ungar agrees, calling the speech "a major factor" in Ike's decision to reject Brownell's civil rights program. In Birmingham, perennial Klan target Fred Shuttlesworth called Eisenhower "a president who sees nothing, hears nothing, thinks nothing, feels nothing, and winds up doing nothing." When William Rogers replaced Brownell as attorney general in November 1957, he "virtually dropped" enforcement of federal civil rights statutes. Despite passage of new civil rights legislation in 1957, banning intimidation of voters in any election involving candidates for federal office, the U.S. Civil Rights Commission found "hardly any" FBI investigations in the field during 1957–60. Rogers also barred any Justice Department attorney from keeping written records of complaints against the FBI, and a handpicked Hoover aide joined the department's Civil Rights Division to "help" with requests for FBI assistance.[16]

Even in victory, however, the director still faced difficulties on the racial front. In 1957, South Carolina congressman Mendel Rivers warned headquarters that "the Bureau is getting itself in a bad situation when it is forced to do the work of the NAACP." When Senator Eastland aired a similar complaint, Assistant Director Lou Nichols replied, "A lot of the Southern folks never know what a position [Hoover] has been put in." In 1958, an aide to South Carolina Senator Olin Johnson, one H.L. Edwards, warned FBI leaders that "many of the Southern senators" had taken "definite steps" to get Hoover dismissed. Although "the matter had gradually calmed down," Edwards recommended "pressure" on Eisenhower "to set up an investigative staff for the Civil Rights Division of the Department," which would let the FBI "keep away from such matters entirely." Edwards opined that "this could be accomplished if sufficient interest was aroused in Congress," suggesting that Hoover "speak to his close friends" on Capitol Hill. Hoover, ever reluctant to share power, panned the notion as "completely untenable."[17]

"PRETTY MUCH DEFUNCT"

The Klans Hoover dismissed so casually were anything but "pretty much defunct" in early 1956. The Invisible Empire was growing rapidly, both in membership and in the number of competing Klans. Atlanta auto worker Eldon Edwards led the country's largest faction, chartered in October 1955. His U.S. Klans had chapters in eight Southern states by 1956. A year later, Edwards faced competition from at least 23 rival Klans, including six each in Alabama and South Carolina, four in Florida, two each in Georgia and Texas, plus one each in Louisiana, Mississippi and North Carolina. Membership estimates for the late 1950s vary widely. The Anti-Defamation League granted Edwards 12,000 to 15,000 knights in 1956, increasing by January 1961 to a probable 20,000. According to the ADL, independent Klans claimed

7,000 to 10,500 members in 1956, versus 20,000 to 37,000 in early 1961. Historian Arnold Rice pegs the figure much higher, counting "well over 100,000" knights in "more than 500 new chapters" by mid-1958.[18]

Don Whitehead took his cue from Hoover, contending that the KKK had "been run to cover as an effective hate group" by 1956, but the evidence fails to support that contention. Alabama set the standard for Klan terrorism with violence surrounding the Montgomery bus boycott of 1955–57. Montgomery Klansmen also murdered Willie Edwards, a black truck driver, in January 1957, and his death was dismissed as an "accident" until 1976. Elsewhere in Alabama, more than a dozen blacks were whipped by nightriders in August 1957 alone. The following month, on 2 September, members of Ace Carter's Klan kidnapped victim Edward Aaron in Birmingham and castrated him in a Ku Klux initiation ceremony. A week after that heinous crime, other knights mobbed and chain-whipped the Rev. Fred Shuttlesworth as he escorted four black children into a newly integrated school. Bull Connor's all-white Birmingham police force recruited known Klansmen, including "Dynamite Bob" Chambliss, as auxiliary officers to patrol black neighborhoods. Saraland's police chief and six other whites were jailed for illegal cross-burnings in September 1958. Reporters speculated that the seven might be linked to the mayor's recent murder, but no indictments were filed. Alabama G-men, led by future FBI director Clarence Kelley in Birmingham, did nothing to quell the reign of terror.[19]

South Carolina, another traditional stronghold of klancraft, witnessed violence on a par with Alabama's in the late 1950s. Klansmen burned the Summerton home of one black activist, the Rev. Joseph Delaine, then vandalized his new home in Lake City and burned down his church. When another masked party came for him in October 1955, Delaine scattered them with gunfire. In September 1956, Clarendon County knights fired on the home of a local NAACP leader, then torched his uncle's church. Four Klansmen were jailed for the July 1957 whipping of Claude Cruell in Greenville, and six more were arrested for the beating of a white high-school band teacher at Camden. Elsewhere in Dixie, arsonists burned two rural schools slated for integration near Deep Creek, North Carolina, in August 1958. Another arson fire struck the home of C.G. Hall, Arkansas' secretary of state, after he criticized the Klan in June 1959. Four masked kidnappers snatched a black man, Felton Turner, from Houston in March 1960; they hung him upside down, whipped him, and carved "KKK" on his chest. Five months later, Klansmen from Florida and Georgia staged three days of rioting against sit-in demonstrators in Jacksonville. In no case is there any record of an FBI investigation.[20]

Mississippi contributed two more of the decade's worst cases. In May 1958, Yalobusha County Sheriff Buck Treolar faced manslaughter charges after he beat a black prisoner to death. Acquitted by a local all-white jury, Treolar retrieved his blackjack from the prosecution table and said with a smirk, "Now I can get back to rounding up moonshiners and niggers." G-men ignored that case, but they were forced to act at Poplarville after lynchers dragged rape suspect Mack Parker from jail on 25 April 1959. Governor Coleman requested federal aid under the Lindbergh Act, which permits FBI investigation of any kidnapping still unsolved after 24 hours. Sixty agents worked the case, assuming federal jurisdiction after Parker's corpse was pulled from the Pearl River in Louisiana. The G-men identified 23 suspects, including mob leader J.P. Walker, a one-time deputy sheriff; they also concluded that jailer Jewel Alford furnished the killers with keys. One suspect died during the FBI's investigation, another suffered a stroke, and a third was hospitalized for a "nervous breakdown." Attorney General Rogers called the bureau's 378-page report "one of the most complete investigations I've ever seen," yet a federal grand jury refused to indict the surviving suspects in January 1960. The district attorney of Pearl River County convened his own panel but withheld the FBI report and declined to call any agents as witnesses. Once again, murder went unpunished in Mississippi.[21]

DEFIANCE AND DYNAMITE

A trademark of Klan terrorism in the 1950s was an increasing reliance on explosives. Statistics on the plague of racist bombings vary. One media report from December 1954 counted 195 bombings for that year alone, and a May 1963 article in *New South* listed 142 explosions since January 1956. Whatever the actual tally, Klansmen and their allies on the neo–Nazi fringe clearly had launched an all-out war against blacks, Jews and anyone who counseled moderation on the race issue. One early case was "solved" at Louisville, Kentucky, where liberals Carl and Anne Braden purchased a home for a black friend, Andrew Wade IV, in an all-white neighborhood. Soon after Wade moved in, a cross was burned in his yard, and bombers struck the house in June 1954. Instead of searching for the nightriders, local police raided the Braden home and seized "Communist" literature. A grand jury found it "very significant that the case seems to follow the pattern used by the Communist party in this country to create trouble between the respective races." The Bradens and three friends were indicted for "advocating sedition," and another of Wade's acquaintances was charged with the bombing. Only Carl Braden faced trial, receiving a 15-year prison term in December 1954. Ten years later, right-wing groups such as the John Birch Society still cited the Braden case as "proof" of Red guilt in American race bombings.[22]

While no part of the country was immune to terrorism, most bombings occurred in the South, at or near flashpoints in the struggle for integration. A black boycott of segregated buses lit the fuse in Montgomery, Alabama, where ten bombings shook the city during 1956–57. Five Klansmen were charged with those crimes, and two were acquitted at trial despite signed confessions; charges against the other three were dropped as part of a general amnesty that also freed black boycott leaders.[23] (Twenty years later, one bombing defendant implicated two others in the 1957 Willie Edwards murder, but neither went to trial.) Terrorism continued apace in "Bombingham," where Bull Connor's police repeatedly seized weapons from blacks guarding churches and homes during 1957–58; the late 1950s saw at least 17 bombings in Birmingham, Bessemer and Mobile. Atlanta recorded 18 racist bombings between 1957 and 1960, and a black activist's wife was killed in the bombing of her home in Ringgold, Georgia, in November 1957. Tennessee Klansmen were equally bomb-happy, touching off eight blasts in Clinton and 13 in Chattanooga (where they also burned two homes).[24]

White terrorists were not always anonymous, however. FBI informants named

Bob Chambliss as the bomber of a Birmingham church in December 1956, but no charges were filed. Seven Tennessee Klansmen were jailed for destroying Nashville's Hattie Cotton School in September 1957, and John Kasper and 19 accomplices faced charges of defying federal injunctions against protests at the school. Five more knights were arrested in December 1957 for bombing the Gaffney, South Carolina, home of a "moderate" physician. In March 1958, three Klansmen received state prison terms for plotting to bomb a black school in Charlotte, North Carolina. Four months later, blacks captured a slow-footed knight near the scene of a Birmingham explosion; jurors convicted defendant Hubert Wilcutt in December and gave him a ten-year sentence, then recommended probation.[25]

On 3 May 1958, officials from 28 cities met in Jacksonville, Florida, to create the Southern Conference on Bombing (SCB). Spurred by 46 reported blasts since January 1957, the delegates offered rewards totaling $55,700 for information leading to the capture and conviction of racial terrorists. Milton Ellerin, a former G-man working for the Anti-Defamation League, provided a roster of notorious anti–Semites and racists—including the name of Birmingham delegate Bull Connor. The ADL's national director wired Connor an apology for the "clerical error," but any anti-terrorist group including such members was destined to fail. J. Edgar Hoover withheld FBI cooperation from the SCB, and while conference agents infiltrated several racist groups, including Klan factions and the National States Rights Party, its reward went unclaimed.[26]

Back in Birmingham on 8 May 1958, Bull Connor met with William Morris from the Federated Klans—himself an FBI informant—to discuss rival terrorist Jesse Stoner. A longtime Klansman soon to be a founder of the brown-shirted NSRP, Stoner bossed a team of transient bombers-for-hire that operated throughout Dixie, executing contracts to order. He was well known in Birmingham, and Morris hoped to trap him for whatever reason. Connor agreed and sent two of his men, Capt. G.L. Pattie and Sgt. Tom Cook, to "pose" as racists in a meeting with Stoner on 14 June. Connor staked out the meeting with agent-in-charge Clarence Kelley and two other G-men, but their microphones malfunctioned, failing to capture the conversation in which Stoner agreed to bomb Fred Shuttlesworth's church for $2,000. Stoner's men, led by Richard Bowling, carried out the bombing on 29 June and fled back to Georgia, leaving Connor empty-handed. Suddenly worried, since his own men had commissioned the bombing, Connor rushed to Washington for an emergency meeting at FBI headquarters.[27] There, he spun a fable for G-men, reporting that:

> [We] called our informer long distance ... and told him of the bombing and asked him if he thought Stoner had anything to do with it and he said no he didn't believe so. About twenty minutes later, our informer called back and said Stoner had just called him long distance and told him that they had bombed the church and he wanted him to get some money out of us for the job. Our man told our informer that we had never told him that we would give him any money to bomb any place or any church. We said we might could get some people to give us some money. He said he told Stoner that those people had not told him that we would give him any money to bomb this church.
>
> There is no question in my mind after reading their statements and talking with my informer for eight hours Sunday that we have got to have help from the

FBI to catch [Stoner] because he or his crowd do not live in the state of Alabama and we do not have men that we can put on to tail him 24 hours a day. I think this is one man who must be tailed every hour until he is caught or he and his crowd are going to do a lot of damage in the Southeast.[28]

Unknown to Connor, the FBI already had a spy inside the NSRP, but bureau leaders declined to help Bull with his predicament. Accordingly, Connor and Morris tried another sting on Stoner, this time furnishing a hit list of civil rights leaders. Dr. King topped the list, with a $1,500 bounty on his head, but Stoner smelled a rat and passed on the contract. Meanwhile, Connor promoted Tom Cook to serve as his "subversives" specialist and personal liaison with the local KKK. On 24 July 1958, Hoover warned G-men to "hold contacts with Connor to a minimum because of his unsavory background."[29]

Stoner's gang struck again on 12 October 1958 with the bombing of an Atlanta synagogue. Moments after the blast, police received a call from "General Gordon of the Confederate Underground," claiming credit for the attack. FBI spokesmen reported that the crime and phone call "almost exactly paralleled" earlier synagogue bombings in Miami, Jacksonville and Birmingham. Local police arrested NSRP member Chester Griffin on 12 October and obtained a confession implicating others in the party. Four more (Richard Bowling among them) were soon jailed without bond and indicted on 18 October, and suspect George Bright was chosen for trial in December. Defense attorney James Venable, a Klansman since the 1920s and onetime mayor of Stone Mountain (1946–49), used the courtroom as a forum for attacking Jews. While prosecutors relied on FBI informant Leslie Rogers, Venable called Eldon Edwards and other high-ranking Klansmen to attack the spy's credibility. An inmate of the state asylum, enjoying a moment of "temporary lucidity," furnished Bright with an alibi, and Bright and NSRP chairman Arthur Cole named Rogers as the temple bomber. Rogers was damaged by admitting that the FBI had paid him for reports, a total of $1,150 by October 1958. On 10 December 1958, jurors deadlocked eight-to-four for conviction, and a mistrial was declared. Bright won acquittal at his second trial in January 1959, though new attorney Reuben Garland received a six-week jail term for contempt of court.[30] After the verdict, juror Manley Morrison told reporters:

A lot of people on the witness stand didn't seem too bright to me. The FBI did not impress me. I guess they were trained not to give out information, but you'd think they would know more than what they are telling or admitting to. I personally got the impression they were holding back some things. Now what they were, I couldn't tell you. But you know, you expect them to be more knowledgeable. In my own mind, they did not bring out sufficient evidence to place [Bright] anywhere near the scene of the crime.[31]

The next crop of racist bombers arrested were bagged in Little Rock, Arkansas. There, in August and September 1959, explosions hit the local school board's headquarters, the mayor's office and the fire chief's car, and a fourth bomb failed to explode at the city manager's office. City police, acting with no apparent federal aid, determined that the bombings were planned at a KKK meeting — but the mastermind and ultimate defendant was E.A. Lauderdale, Jr., a director of the "respectable" Capital Citizens' Council. Convicted at trial and sentenced to three years confinement,

Lauderdale entered prison in February 1961. Six months later, he was pardoned by racist Governor Orval Faubus.[32]

Congress reacted to the wave of Southern bombings with the Civil Rights Act of 1960. The new law penalized common racist behavior, including (a) willful interference with or obstruction of any federal court order, judgment or decree; (b) interstate flight to avoid prosecution or imprisonment for bombing or burning any vehicle or building, or to avoid giving testimony in such cases; (c) interstate transportation of explosives with knowledge or intent that they will be used in bombing; and (d) use of the mails, telephone or any other instrument to convey threats of arson or bombing.[33] Every racist who telephoned a bomb threat was now a federal offender under FBI jurisdiction — but would the bureau act?

The answer to that question came from troubled Little Rock, where bombings continued despite E.A. Lauderdale's arrest. On 9 February 1960, bombers did "considerable damage" to the home of a black student newly enrolled at Central High School. Police arrested two black suspects, later releasing one; the other was convicted by an all-white jury and received a five-year prison term. Next, in the predawn hours of 12 July 1960, G-men caught two terrorists red-handed, planting a bomb at all-black Philander Smith College. Bombers Emmett Miller and Robert Parks were barely in jail when a blast wrecked the local school board warehouse. That crime was never solved, but FBI agents bagged a third conspirator, Hugh Adams, on the afternoon of 12 July. Little Rock's agent-in-charge told reporters the arrests derived from "coverage of activities of Klansmen and other racist hate mongers" in Arkansas. In fact, Miller was both a Klan recruiter and the founding president of Crittenden County's Citizens' Council. A tip put agents on his trail, and they had watched him drive with Adams to West Memphis, there retrieving 40 sticks of dynamite. G-men were present when Miller met Parks after dark, and they were ready to pounce as he lit the bomb's fuse.[34] So far, it seemed like a case to make Washington proud.

Miller, Adams and Parks were charged with violating the 1960 Civil Rights Act, but federal prosecutors dropped those charges in October 1960, ruefully admitting that they had no evidence of any interstate activity. In January 1961, a local grand jury indicted Miller on the misdemeanor charge of attempting to commit a felony. If convicted, he faced a maximum penalty of 90 days in jail and a $100 fine. Four months later, however, a Justice spokesman sought dismissal of even that trivial charge in order to protect the FBI's "effective investigative techniques and operational procedures." Washington said that "Miller and those working in concert with him now seek a trial in the hope that they may discover how an FBI corps managed to be at the scene to thwart the principal crime." Judge William Kirby agreed and empanelled a jury long enough to thank them for their service and direct a verdict of acquittal. Emmett Miller, free to carry on his war, soon founded two Arkansas chapters of the rabid National States Rights Party.[35]

Typically, when FBI spokesmen seek dismissal of a case to protect "techniques and procedures," it means one of two things: either the bureau has informants planted in a suspect group, or evidence was gathered by illegal means and would be inadmissible at trial. Whichever was the case in Little Rock, questions remain: How "effective" are the FBI's investigative methods if they don't put terrorists in jail? How valuable are informants if their testimony can't be used at trial? Were federal agents breaking laws in Little Rock, as they have done in countless other cases nationwide throughout the bureau's history? And if they were, what punishment was meted out to those who scuttled Miller's case? The answers to those questions, like so much about the FBI, remain a closely guarded secret.

A Failed Crusade

By spring 1962, eight years after the *Brown* decision, only 2,725 of Dixie's 2.5 million black students were attending integrated classes. That tally included 12 of Louisiana's 295,000 black children, eight of 303,000 in Georgia, and none in Alabama, Mississippi and South Carolina. At that rate, "all deliberate speed" would see Southern schools fully integrated by the year 9256. Klansmen deserved a share of credit for the slowdown, as in Athens, Georgia, during January 1961. The state university admitted its first black student on 10 January, and 600 whites staged a riot on campus the following day; of 16 arrested, eight were Klan members. A new United Klans of America (UKA) was created in July 1961, soon shifting its headquarters from traditional Atlanta to the Tuscaloosa, Alabama, home of Imperial Wizard Robert Shelton. By September 1962, its rallies drew thousands in Alabama, Florida and Georgia.[36]

Dr. Martin Luther King, meanwhile, could claim no triumph for his Southern Christian Leadership Conference (SCLC) since the Montgomery bus boycott of 1955–56. Accordingly, he charted a campaign of civil disobedience to end segregation in Albany, Georgia, 182 miles south of Atlanta. Southwestern Georgia was hardcore Klan country in 1962, notorious for a legacy of lynchings and modern-day police brutality against black citizens. In April 1958, James Brazier was fatally beaten in Dawson's jail, his killer later promoted to serve as chief of police. In July 1962, police in Albany clubbed the pregnant wife of a civil rights worker, inducing a miscarriage. In that atmosphere, King hoped for strident opposition that would bring much-needed publicity and support to himself and the SCLC. He was stymied, however, by Police Chief Laurie Pritchett, who restrained his officers and knelt beside black protesters to pray in the street, effectively stealing the wind from King's sails.[37]

The Georgia Klan was pledged to no such wily moderation, though. Its knights craved action, and they found it in the small communities surrounding Albany, where young volunteers from the Student Nonviolent Coordinating Committee (SNCC) risked life and limb to register black voters. Nightriders raided the homes where SNCC activists slept, shooting up four houses at Leesburg on 31 August 1962, wounding two volunteers at Dawson on 5 September, and losing one of their own the same night when a Dallas homeowner replied with deadly gunfire. Churches suspected of hosting voter-registration meetings were burned in Sasser, Leesburg, Dawson and Chickasawhatchee. A Labor Day rally of the United Klans in Albany brought some 6,000 racists out to cheer the lighting of a 40-foot cross.[38]

The violent acts in Georgia targeting black voters clearly qualified as violations of the 1957 Civil Rights Act. G-men investigated the church-burnings and reportedly reached one site while the flames were still leaping. At another fire scene on 9

September 1962 a white man was arrested for assaulting Agent Paul Mohr, but grand jurors refused to indict him. Eight days after that incident, newspapers reported that FBI agents had delivered four confessed arsonists to local authorities, but no more was heard of those suspects. Historian Howard Zinn, observing events at first hand, reported: "There is a considerable amount of distrust among Albany Negroes for local members of the Federal Bureau of Investigation.... FBI men appear to Albany Negroes as vaguely-interested observers of injustice, who diffidently write down complaints and do no more. With all of the clear violations by local police of constitutional rights, ... the FBI has not made a single arrest on behalf of Negro citizens." Dr. King echoed that sentiment, telling reporters, "One of the great problems we face with the FBI in the South is that the agents are white Southerners who have been influenced by the mores of the community. To maintain their status, they have to be friendly with local police and people who are promoting segregation. Every time I saw FBI men in Albany, they were with the local police force."[39]

Hoover responded to that criticism in time-honored fashion by launching a full-scale investigation of Dr. King. Citing alleged "Communist influence" inside the SCLC, Hoover persuaded Attorney General Robert Kennedy to approve limited wiretaps on King's telephones—and then proceeded to shadow King's every move for the rest of his life, long after official sanctions for surveillance were revoked. Over the next two years, Hoover's vendetta ranged from public denunciation of King as America's "most notorious liar" to unsigned letters urging King toward suicide. In Albany, meanwhile, no terrorists faced any charges, but the bureau did arrest nine local blacks. Their "crime" was picketing a store in a black neighborhood, owned by a member of the all-white jury that acquitted Sheriff Warren "Gator" Johnson (successor to Claude Screws) of shooting a handcuffed black prisoner. Washington indicted the nine on federal charges of "interfering with the jury process" and held them over for trial. Perjury charges against a tenth defendant failed because the bureau used illegal wiretaps to eavesdrop on attorney-client conversations.[40]

4

"Segregation Forever"

Next to Georgia, Alabama is the state where Klansmen have enjoyed their greatest strength and closest ties to public officeholders. Montgomery witnessed the foundation of the Confederacy in February 1861 and served for three years as the rebel nation's capital. William Simmons was a son of Alabama, and his resurrected Klan drew its first non-Georgian members from Mobile and Birmingham in 1915. A century after secession, many white supremacists still viewed Alabama as the heart of resistance to desegregation. Birmingham proudly billed itself as America's "most segregated" city, where even interracial checker games were banned by law, and Bull Connor's police worked hand-in-hand with Klansmen to crush black aspirations.[1]

On 19 March 1958, state Attorney General John Patterson launched his gubernatorial race with a mass-mailing of letters to Alabama Klansmen. The missives solicited votes in the name of "a mutual friend, Mr. R.M. (Bob) Shelton," who had recently defected from the U.S. Klans to lead the independent Alabama Knights. When the *Montgomery Advertiser* reported his ploy, Patterson feigned ignorance. "That's amazing," he blustered. "I am not a member of the Ku Klux Klan. I have never been a member. I don't know anyone named Shelton." One day later, the newspaper printed a copy of his campaign letter (typed on Patterson's official letterhead) and detailed Shelton's role in the campaign. Rival candidate George Wallace denounced Klansmen as "pistol-toters and toughs," chastising Patterson for "rolling with the new wave of the Klan and its terrible tradition of lawlessness." On election day, Patterson trounced Wallace by a margin of 35,000 votes, and Shelton — then a salesman for the B.F. Goodrich Company — celebrated his candidate's victory with a million-dollar contract for new tires on state vehicles.[2] Whatever blows it may have suffered in the South at large, the KKK was not about to fade away in Alabama.

HOLDING THE COLOR LINE (1958–1961)

For Alabama segregationists, the Montgomery bus boycott of 1955–56 was a setback but not a defeat. Resistance was a way of life not easily surrendered. The state recorded seven racist bombings during 1958–60, four of them in Birmingham, where terrorists faced prosecution only if blacks caught them at the scene and physically detained them. In May 1958, Birmingham Klansmen vandalized the same black-owned radio station whose tower they had cut down nine years earlier. The following year, on 10 April 1959, they kidnapped three black men, whipped them with chains and branded one—Medal of Honor-winner Charles Billups—with the initials "KKK." The FBI's local field office, commanded by agent-in-charge Clarence Kelley, kept loose tabs on the Klan but made no effort to restrain or prosecute known criminals within its ranks.[3]

The bureau's leading Klan informant was Gary Thomas Rowe, Jr., a hard-drinking police groupie whose lack of self-restraint and education barred him from the law-enforcement career he craved. In September 1956, Rowe was fined $30 for impersonating a Birmingham policeman. Three years later, he had graduated to the status of a phony G-man, finally drawing attention from the real-life FBI. A rookie agent, Barrett Kemp, was sent to chastise Rowe but somehow wound up asking him about the Klan. Rowe had an open invitation to the Alabama Knights, which valued barroom brawlers for its "missionary work," but he had balked at signing on until Kemp offered him an opportunity to serve the bureau "in the best interests of my country." Rowe later said that he took the assignment "toward the end of 1959," assuming the code-name "Karl Cross," yet his FBI file was not opened until 18 April 1960, listing Rowe as BH 248-PCI(RAC)—that is, "Birmingham, Code Number 248, potential confidential informant (racial)." Rowe was initiated into Eastview Klavern 13 of the Alabama Knights on 23 June 1960 and promoted two months later to the rank of nighthawk, with responsibility for investigating prospective members.[4]

Eastview 13 already ranked among the Alabama Klan's most violent chapters, with a membership including "Dynamite Bob" Chambliss and other notorious racists, but its mayhem increased as Rowe rose through the ranks. Clarence Kelley turned a blind eye to Rowe's part in the mayhem, informing Hoover in November 1960 that the new informant furnished data of "unusual value." Specifically, Rowe reported on Klan ties to the police in Birmingham and Irondale, where Chief Olin Bragg asked helpful knights for "assistance or advice" on racial matters. In spring 1961, Thomas Jenkins replaced Kelley as agent-in-charge, but Rowe remained a loose cannon, vaguely cautioned to "be careful" in the course of midnight "missionary work." The message he received was simple and explicit: Don't get caught.[5]

Rowe had his first near miss on 20 April 1961, when Robert Shelton and Eastview Exalted Cyclops Robert Thomas sent him to confer with Sgt. Tom Cook at police headquarters. Cook provided Rowe with a dossier on the Alabama Council on Human Relations, including details of the group's supposed "Communist and Jewish connections." Cook also warned the Klan to drop its plans for raiding a meeting in honor of liberal poet John Ciardi, since the gathering "would definitely be covered" by FBI agents. When Rowe returned the file on 24 April, Cook warned him of a leak in Eastview 13. The local FBI—fully aware of Cook's liaison with the KKK from Rowe's own lips—had tipped him to an impending church raid, reported by Rowe. The spy would soon be located, Cook said, and once he was identified, Connor's police intended to arrest him on false charges. "The jury could be fixed," Cook said, "to have the individual sent to the penitentiary." Rowe dodged that bullet and the church raid was aborted, but FBI communication with Cook continued, reaching a bloody climax three weeks later.[6]

In the meantime, Rowe furnished his handlers with another report that struck closer to home. In January 1961, Bull Connor nominated Arthur Hanes as his candidate for mayor of Birmingham. Hanes was a former FBI agent, lately employed as chief of security at Hayes Aircraft, where he recruited pilots for the CIA's disastrous Bay of Pigs invasion. On the side, he was a frequent "patriotic" orator, taking the stage at gatherings of the John Birch Society and Ace Carter's violent Citizens' Council. Birmingham's knights collected donations for Hanes and turned out en masse to support him in the May primary, where Hanes ran second to opponent Tom King. A runoff election was scheduled, with Hanes supported by a "Committee to Keep Birmingham White," but his Klan supporters were soon distracted by more immediate concerns in the form of the integrated Freedom Rides.[7]

"FREEBUS"

The "freedom ride" concept did not originate in 1961. Fifteen years earlier, on 3 June 1946, the Supreme Court's ruling in *Morgan v. Virginia* had banned segregated seating on interstate buses and trains. The Congress of Racial Equality (CORE) dispatched 16 volunteers on an integrated "Journey of Reconciliation" in April 1947, but the effort drew little attention. In June 1950, the court's judgment in *Henderson v. the United States* ordered desegregation of railway dining cars, but Presidents Truman and Eisenhower balked at supporting federal legislation to enforce the rulings, and segregation remained firmly in place below the Mason-Dixon Line. Protests were belatedly triggered on 5 December 1960, when ex–Klansman Hugo Black announced the court's ruling in *Boynton v. Virginia*. That decision expanded the *Morgan* rule to bus and train terminals, barring segregation in waiting rooms, restaurants and restrooms.[8] By New Year's Day, CORE leaders were planning a fresh wave of demonstrations to test the court's latest decision.

Bull Connor and his allies in the Klan stood ready to defend the Alabama color line. On 4 May 1961, as 13 Freedom Riders boarded their buses in Washington, D.C., Gary Rowe was summoned to a meeting with Tom Cook and Birmingham detective W.W. "Red" Self. The officers warned Rowe of "a group of niggers and whites coming into the state of Alabama on what was to be a so-called Freedom Ride." Cook wanted Klansmen to waylay the riders on arrival. Rowe quoted Cook as saying, "I don't give a damn if you beat them, bomb them, murder or kill them. I don't give a shit. We don't ever want to see another nigger ride on the bus into Birmingham again." That evening, the knights of Eastview 13 were told to stay alert and "remain in close touch with their telephones." Rowe later testified that he arranged other meetings between Connor, Cook, Robert Shelton and Hubert Page, an Eastview Klansman who served as Grand Titan for northern Alabama. Cook and Connor visited Atlanta on 11 May to gather more intelligence on the Freedom Ride itinerary, and Eastview's knights held another meeting that night to plan details of their "intervention." At that meeting, Page ordered his Klansmen to stay away from the Greyhound bus depot when demonstrators arrived on 14 May. A team of 60 knights hand-picked by Shelton would attack the riders, Page explained, during a 15-minute grace period granted by Connor. A message was conveyed from the police commissioner himself: "By God, if you are going to do this thing, do it right." Specifically, Connor instructed that the demonstrators should be beaten until they "looked like a bulldog got hold of them," then stripped of their clothes and chased from the depot — where police would charge them with indecent exposure. Klansmen were warned to leave their membership cards and unlicensed pistols at home. Any knights who overstayed their welcome and wound up in jail were guaranteed light sentences.[9]

Gary Rowe was chosen as a squad leader to coordinate the assaults. When informed of the Connor-Klan conspiracy, Rowe's bureau contact allegedly replied, "Jesus Christ, I can't believe this. This could never be allowed to happen. The American people would never stand for this." The G-man vowed to "get five thousand marshals or ten thousand troops in here, if necessary. We've got the 82nd Airborne, the 101st Airborne. We can pull more damn people in here than the Klan ever heard of. The Old Man [Hoover] will not allow this to go down." In fact, Hoover had known of Cook's ties to the Klan since 5 May, at the latest. On 12 May, he received a telex from the Birmingham field office detailing the Klan's riot plan. One day later, Clement McGowan — chief of the FBI's civil rights section — ordered Birmingham to warn police chief Jamie Moore "that apparently several groups are interested in the arrival of the CORE party ... and there could be some violence." The warning should be couched in "general terms," McGowan said, with no specific mention of the KKK or any particular bus depot. No information should be shared with Connor personally, since "we have to be careful to protect our informant and be alert to any possible 'trap.'" (Police in Anniston, 66 miles east of Birmingham, received a similar warning, devoid of details.) G-men apparently trusted Moore, a graduate of the FBI National Academy, to do his duty in spite of Connor, but their faith was misplaced. At 9:30 P.M. on 13 May, Moore called Agent Jenkins to say that he was leaving town to visit family for Mother's Day. Moore left Tom Cook in charge, thereby effectively ceding control to the Klan.[10]

CORE's team met only intermittent opposition in the first week of its odyssey. One rider was arrested in Charlotte, North Carolina, on 8 May; another was assaulted at Rock Hill, South Carolina, on 10 May; and two more were briefly jailed in Winnsboro, South Carolina, the same afternoon. By 14 May, when they left Atlanta bound for Birmingham, their numbers had swelled and the riders occupied two buses, one Greyhound and one Trailways. Atlanta's FBI office cabled Birmingham at 11:59 A.M. on 14 May, reporting that the first busload of riders should arrive by 3:30 P.M., with the second (Trailways) scheduled to reach Birmingham at 4:05. A mob led by Klansman Kenneth Adams met the Greyhound in Anniston, bashed the bus with clubs and slashed at its tires with knives. The driver fled, pursued by a caravan of 40 or 50 cars, but two of his tires went flat a few miles west of town. Surrounded, the riders huddled in the bus until one Klansman pitched a firebomb through a window and set it ablaze. State Trooper Eli Cowling held the would-be lynchers at bay, firing shots over their heads until the mob dispersed. The riders were hospitalized for smoke inhalation, while their bus burned down to a blackened skeleton at roadside.[11]

The Trailways bus reached Anniston an hour later, and found the Klan waiting. FBI agents and at least three local policemen watched the knights rush aboard, assaulting the riders and beating one — Walter Bergman — so severely that he suffered permanent brain damage. One smiling officer boarded the bus and told Klansmen, "Don't worry about no lawsuits. I ain't seen a thing." The bus pulled out with eight knights still aboard, escorted by four police cars. Word flashed ahead to Birmingham, where Agent Jenkins telephoned Tom Cook and told him that the bus was on its way — this despite standing orders from Washington that G-men should furnish "information relating to racial matters … only to reliable law enforcement officials and agencies." Cook wasted no time in alerting the Klan and the National States Rights Party (whose contingent, led by Jesse Stoner and Ed Fields, had turned up uninvited for the party).[12]

The Anniston ambush derailed Connor's initial plan in Birmingham. Despite the selection of a 60-man strike team, eyewitnesses on 14 May describe 150 to 1,000 Klansmen milling around the Greyhound depot by 3:00 P.M., across the street from City Hall. Tom Cook kept a phone line open for Gary Rowe at headquarters and made "a number of trips back and forth" to the Greyhound terminal, according to *Birmingham News* editor John Bloomer. After the Greyhound bus was burned at Anniston, Cook briefed Rowe on the incident and ordered Klansmen to wait for the next load of riders. He signed off with "Give 'em hell," apparently still unaware that the remaining target was a Trailways bus. At 4:00 P.M., an unknown man — identified by Rowe as a policeman — turned up at the Greyhound station, barking orders for the knights assembled there to rally at the Trailways depot. When the hijacked bus arrived at 4:15, Klansmen were waiting for the demonstrators, wielding blackjacks, pipes, and leaded baseball bats. Gary Rowe waded in with the rest, beating riders and bystanders alike. His known victims included George Webb, a black man unconnected to the freedom riders, and a photographer from the *Birmingham Post-Herald*, whose camera Rowe smashed. Rowe was clubbing an unidentified black woman when Red Self arrived to warn him that the Klan's 15 minutes were up. Retreating from the depot, Rowe and fellow knights attacked Clancy Lake, news director for a local radio station, and pummeled several blacks who were writing down the license numbers of Klan vehicles. In parting, Detective Self thanked Rowe and company for doing "a good job."[13]

Craving more action, Rowe and Klansman Billy Holt went prowling for fresh victims on Sunday evening. They misjudged their quarry that time, and one of the blacks they assaulted drew a knife and slashed Rowe's throat. A Klan physician stitched the wound, but it was after midnight when Rowe called his FBI contact to report the day's activities. Rowe said he had been injured at the Trailways depot, whereupon his handler called the incident "a goddamn shame" and promised to cover the medical bill. A quarter-century later, in his published memoirs, Rowe preserved the fiction of a stabbing at the Trailways depot and described a second, nonexistent riot at the Greyhound terminal on 14 May.[14]

On Monday morning, Tom Cook telephoned Rowe and thanked him for doing "a goddamn good job down there. People [will] always love you for it." Unfortunately for Rowe, when he broke the *Post-Herald* photographer's camera he had not exposed its film. The paper ran a front-page picture of the riot, with a chunky Klansman who resembled Gary Rowe in the thick of the action. Rowe's handler was furious, allegedly raging, "The Old Man's going to shit. He's going to climb the wall." When Rowe admitted that he was the subject in the photo, his contact replied, "Just think very carefully. Who else does that look like besides you?" Thus prodded, Rowe fingered a brother knight, Charles "Arnie" Cagle. "That's it," his handler said. "Cagle. To the day you die, if you're 99 damn years old, I don't care who asks you — if the director comes down and looks you in the eyes and says, 'Goddamnit, Gary Thomas Rowe, Jr., I know that's you' — you're going to look him in the eye and say, 'No, sir. That's not me. That's Arnie Cagle.'" In a wire to FBI headquarters, Agent Jenkins told Hoover that Rowe "advised he was not personally involved in the fighting at the Trailways bus depot," and that Rowe had merely "obtained film from photographers' cameras peacefully and without incident." The bureau later gave Rowe $50 for the doctor's tab and provided another $150 "for services rendered."[15]

Bull Connor, meanwhile, faced a storm of criticism for his failure to prevent the riot, or at least to intervene in timely fashion once it started. Journalist Howard Smith was technically incorrect in stating that the Trailways melee "took place just under Police Commissioner Connor's window," but he captured the spirit of events. Connor said he was short-handed, with most of his men celebrating Mother's Day at home. The trouble, he declared, was sparked by "out-of-town meddlers" who had no business in Birmingham. A new mob rallied at the Greyhound depot on 17 May, when a busload of freedom riders rolled in from Nashville, but this time police were out in force with snarling dogs to hold Klansmen at bay. Connor placed the demonstrators in protective custody and had them driven safely back to Nashville the next day.[16]

The action shifted northward to Montgomery on 20 May 1961. Once again, G-men warned authorities that freedom riders were on their way — and once again, police did nothing to prevent mayhem. At least 200 thugs were waiting when the bus arrived, reenacting the Birmingham riot while police commissioner L.B. Sullivan watched from his car, telling reporters, "We have no intention of standing guard for a bunch of troublemakers coming into our city." Ten minutes into the riot, police straggled onto the scene and watched from the sidelines. The mob, grown to at least a thousand by that time, turned from the freedom riders to assault black bystanders and journalists. Floyd Mann, the state's public safety director, flashed his pistol to protect two victims, but most were not so fortunate. When Mann asked a patrolman why Commissioner Sullivan had not summoned more police, the officer replied, "The men he would send out probably would join the mob." John Siegenthaler, a Justice Department attorney dispatched by Robert Kennedy, was clubbed unconscious in full view of FBI agents — who did nothing. He lay on the pavement while Sullivan told newsmen that "every white ambulance in town reported their vehicles had broken down." Finally, after an hour and 15 minutes, police reinforcements and sheriff's deputies arrived to disperse the rioters with tear gas. The only persons arrested were a white couple, Fred and Anna Gach, jailed for "disorderly conduct" after shielding riot victims from their attackers.[17]

Upon regaining consciousness, Siegenthaler was furious at the G-men who had watched his beating, blandly taking notes. "They had agents all over the place," he recalled. "When I got out of the hospital and got back to my office, there was a letterhead memo on my desk, from Hoover to the attorney general, indicating who the assailants were. It galls me to think that the FBI stood there and watched me get clubbed." Bureau headquarters replied by quoting policy: "If the agent should become personally involved in the action, he would be deserting his assigned task and would be unable to fulfill his primary responsibility of making objective observations." On a more personal level, Hoover responded to Siegenthaler's criticism by investigating the victim, opening a file on Siegenthaler that included baseless allegations of "relations with young girls."[18]

Dr. Martin Luther King flew into Montgomery on 20 May, to address a freedom rally at a local church. White rioters surrounded the building, whereupon Attorney General Kennedy rushed 400 U.S. marshals to the scene. In the predawn hours of 21 May, Governor Patterson declared martial law in Montgomery and called out the National Guard. At the same time, Patterson ordered Floyd Mann to sever his department's "working relationship with the FBI." Any state trooper caught helping G-men investigate acts of racial violence, Patterson warned, would be fired on the spot.[19]

After the Birmingham riot, FBI agents questioned various members of Eastview 13. Without exception, the Klansmen said their presence at the bus depot on Mother's Day was mere coincidence. Photos disproved that, but no federal charges were filed. Local police made a face-saving move on 16 May, bypassing Shelton's Alabama Knights to arrest three members of the U.S. Klans. A fourth knight — the proverbial "outside agitator" from Rome, Georgia — was charged on 26 May with beating a reporter. The defendants paid fines and received short jail terms for disorderly conduct, and more serious charges of assault with intent to murder were dismissed.[20] Meanwhile, on 21 May, Assistant Attorney General William Orrick complained to Robert Kennedy about the FBI's negligence in Montgomery. Within an hour of that call, Montgomery's agent-in-charge promised Orrick "eager cooperation"— if he would stop criticizing the bureau. Early next morning, agents began arresting Klansmen for the Anniston bus-burning under a federal statute banning destruction of vehicles used in interstate commerce. A federal grand jury indicted nine knights on 1 September 1961. Two cases were soon dismissed, leaving seven defendants to face trial in October. On 3 November 1961, alleged ringleader Kenneth Adams was acquitted, and the judge declared a mistrial for his codefendants. Juror Lewis Parker was jailed for perjury on 28 November for falsely denying Klan membership when he was picked for the panel. At their second trial, in January 1962, six defendants were convicted. Judge Hobart Grooms placed five on probation, subject to severance of all Klan ties, and defendant Robert Couch received a one-year prison term, concurrent with an outstanding burglary sentence. The convictions encouraged Governor Patterson to distance himself from the KKK. An FBI informant told headquarters that the governor advised one knight, "You need not think that because you all supported me you can take the law into your own hands. I'm going to start arresting you every time you get out of line and start causing trouble."[21]

While the Anniston case wound its way through the courts, Justice attorney John Doar sought a federal injunction barring Alabama Klansmen and police from conspiring against freedom riders. Doar's suit was filed before Judge Frank Johnson, a longtime Klan opponent who lived under guard from U.S. marshals. Tom Cook advised Robert Shelton to duck subpoenas for the hearing, scheduled to begin on 26 May 1961, but process servers traced the dragon to his lair. In court, Shelton drew a warning for evasive answers, then admitted knowing various Mother's Day conspirators, including Ken Adams, Hubert Page and Robert Thomas. Johnson ultimately banned three Ku Klux factions—the Alabama Knights, the Federated Knights and U.S. Klans—from interfering with the Freedom Rides. Also named in the injunction were Shelton, Grand Dragon Alvin Horn (of the U.S. Klans), and Commissioner L.B. Sullivan and his police chief. Doar said the lawmen had "deliberately failed to take measures to insure the safety of the students and to prevent unlawful acts and violence upon their persons."[22]

Doar sought a similar injunction against Bull Connor and Chief Moore in Birmingham, but Judge Johnson dismissed them from the lawsuit on 30 May 1961. That decision was prompted in part by Agent Jenkins, who defended Connor on the witness stand, swearing that Klansmen and police had not conspired to mob the Trailways bus on 14 May; he was not asked and did not volunteer anything about Rowe's information that a plot was hatched against the Greyhound riders. Connor's case was strengthened by affidavits from two patrolmen, allegedly detailed to the Greyhound depot area at 3:00 P.M. on Mother's Day. The officers described a 4:15 radio alert reporting "a fight in progress" at the Trailways terminal, followed by announcements that two cars assigned to that district "were tied up." A time-stamped dispatch record indicated that other cars were sent to the Trailways depot "two minutes after the call was received." Outside the hearing room, Chief Moore told reporters, "There was no prearrangement [with the Klan] that I know of. Bull was certainly not in sympathy with those people, but he wouldn't shirk his duty." Neither Johnson nor the press were privy to comments from another Birmingham patrolman, who recalled his lieutenant's orders to remain at least six blocks distant from the Greyhound depot on Mother's Day. "If a call goes out to go to the bus station," he was told, "you don't hear it."[23]

A sideshow of the Freedom Rides occurred in August 1961, when NAACP leader Robert Williams invited a group of demonstrators to strife-torn Monroe, North Carolina. The freedom riders arrived on 21 August, and Klansmen raided Monroe's black neighborhood three nights later. During the exchange of gunfire, a hapless white couple blundered into the war zone, and blacks armed with rifles escorted them to a nearby home for safety's sake. When the smoke cleared, an FBI task force moved in to arrest Williams and various members of his NAACP chapter for "kidnapping," despite the obvious fact that no interstate crime was involved. Williams escaped to Cuba, and several of his comrades were jailed and held for trial. One female suspect was traced to Ohio, surrounded at her arrest by 25 G-men with guns drawn. The case eventually fell apart, with Williams later acquitted on all charges.[24]

The FREEBUS fiasco initially proved beneficial to the FBI. While Hoover treated Southern congressmen and right-wing columnists to "inside" information on CORE's supposed Communist ties, his superiors gushed with praise for the bureau. Robert Kennedy described the FBI's work in Anniston as "magnificent," and Justice attorney Burke Marshall told Hoover he "appreciated the promptness with which we went into this matter." The director, typically ungracious, replied that Kennedy should "tell off 'bellyachers' like Doar" who demanded further action. Specifically, Hoover resented Doar's request for a rundown "of all assaults and violent activities engaged in by the Klan or Klan members in this general area within the last five years." (Instead, Hoover spent his time checking for criminal records among the freedom riders.) While Jesse Stoner and the NSRP hung Hoover and Kennedy in effigy, Hoover dismissed all criticism of his dealings with the Klan-infested Birmingham police force. In reporting crimes, he said, "[i]t is immaterial whether the law enforcement agency is trustworthy and also whether it will properly fulfill its responsibility." Agent Jenkins won promotion to serve as assistant director of the FBI, and John Siegenthaler remarked, "I think Gary Thomas Rowe made him."[25]

Fifteen years after the Mother's Day riot, Rowe appeared as a witness before the U.S. Senate's Church Committee, describing his work for the bureau. Those revelations prompted freedom riders Walter Bergman and James Peck to sue the FBI in 1983, charging that Hoover's agents knew about the ambush in advance and were responsible for failing to prevent it. The plaintiffs won their case in February 1984, with federal judge Richard Enslen finding that the freedom riders had faced a "statewide conspiracy and official involvement" in 1961. The court awarded Bergman $45,000 in damages, and Peck received $25,000.[26]

THE POLITICS OF HATRED (1961–1963)

Alabama's knights were not entirely preoccupied by the Freedom Rides in 1961. One day before the Trailways depot riot in Birmingham, Talladega Klansmen whipped three whites who had allowed a black baby sitter to discipline their children. Nine days later, on 22 May, bomb threats were received at two Montgomery schools scheduled for integration. Identical threats to the Montgomery bus depot preceded the arrival of more freedom riders on 20 June 1961, but the FBI declined to investigate those clear violations of the 1960 Civil Rights Act. Threats gave way to violence on 16 January 1962, when bombs damaged three black churches in Birmingham. Gary Rowe informed FBI agent Byron McFall that the bombers were part of an Eastview team led by Earl Thompson, including Bobby Cherry (suspected in various blasts since 1958). The bureau ignored that report, while pursuing its investigation of Dr. King with all available resources.[27]

Meanwhile, on 30 May 1961, former G-man Arthur Hanes faced his runoff election with rival Tom King in Birmingham. King had an early lead, but his campaign hit a snag when photos of his handshake with a black man — engineered by Bull Connor — appeared on fliers with a caption urging whites to "Defeat the NAACP Bloc Vote." Hanes, meanwhile, told voters, "You may be assured, if my opponent is elected tomorrow that this will be hailed as the fall of the South's greatest segregation stronghold." On election day, King trailed Hanes by some 4,000 votes, giving the local KKK another cause for celebration.[28]

Hanes's election changed nothing for the better in Birmingham. On 19 July 1962, Sgt. Tom Cook paid another visit to the Eastview klavern, informing Klansmen that Hanes and Bull Connor were "tired of the way things are going in the racial situation in Birmingham but that their hands are tied." Cook told the knights that Fred Shuttlesworth would be leading other blacks to integrate a local restaurant on 22 July. Rowe quoted Cook as saying that "city hall was relying on the Klan" to kill Shuttlesworth, with police complicity. Two officers were stationed at the restaurant, one prepared to fake a heart attack while the other would be "overpowered" by Klansmen. In the confusion, alcoholic truck driver John Wesley Hall (dubbed "Nigger" for his dark complexion) would stab Shuttlesworth. Rowe tipped G-men to the plot, whereupon agent-in-charge Henry Fitzgibbon alerted Hanes and Chief Moore. Agents also warned Shuttlesworth, and he decided to stay home. The demonstration passed without incident, except at Eastview 13, where Hubert Page vowed to uncover the informant. When he was identified, Page said, the spy's life "would not be worth a plugged nickel."[29]

The Klan's great hope in 1962 was former opponent George Wallace. After his defeat in the 1958 governor's race, Wallace had vowed that "no son of a bitch will ever out-nigger me again." For the 1962 campaign, he chose ex-wizard Asa Carter as his primary speech writer and dispatched him to address Klan rallies in the hinterlands. "He'd get the crowds all churned up," Robert Shelton recalled. "He was really good at doing that." Other knights, including "Dynamite Bob" Chambliss, distributed Wallace campaign signs, and Shelton himself received $7,500 to "cover expenses." The National States Rights Party threw its meager weight behind Wallace, and their candidate told state legislators, "I'm gonna make race the basis of politics in this state, and I'm gonna make it the basis of politics in this country." Wallace's inaugural speech, written by Carter, included a promise to "stand in the schoolhouse door" against desegregation, closing with a vow cribbed from the Klan's own motto: "Segregation today! Segregation tomorrow! Segregation forever!" As governor, Wallace renamed the state's highway patrolmen "state troopers" and placed them under the command of "Colonel" Albert Lingo, a "dangerously unstable" man known for being "hell on niggers," who gobbled tranquilizers "by the handful." Soon after his appointment, Lingo appeared on the dais at a Klan rally, where he was introduced to the assembled knights as "a good friend of ours." Another Klansman on Wallace's staff was Ralph Roton, a high-school dropout who qualified as an "investigator" for the state's Peace Committee by virtue of his membership in Shelton's Klan Bureau of Investigation. Ace Carter maintained covert contact with the Klan and NSRP throughout Wallace's tenure as governor. Birmingham's knights celebrated Wallace's election with another bombing of Shuttlesworth's church, on 14 December 1962.[30]

Dr. King launched his epic civil rights campaign in Birmingham on 2 April 1963, with no fear that Bull Connor would benefit from Laurie Pritchett's example in Georgia six months earlier. In place of prayers, Connor unleashed fire hoses and attack dogs, jailing thousands by the time George Wallace sent Al Lingo and 250 troopers to reinforce local police on 7 May. In turn, Connor sent Lt. Maurice House to order Klansmen off the streets of Birmingham. "We want to keep our friendship with the Klan," House said, "but if you try to help us you'll be arrested." Harassing demonstrators by daylight might be forbidden, but Klansmen still owned the night in "Bombingham." On 11 May 1963, after a huge Klan rally in Bessemer, two blasts rocked the home of Dr. King's brother, the Rev. A.D. King. A black witness, Roosevelt Tatum, told G-men that a uniformed patrolman had planted one bomb on King's porch, then pitched another from the window of Car 22 as he drove away. The first small blast drew a crowd to the site, and the second blast wrecked the façade of King's house. Gary Rowe missed a scheduled ten o'clock call to his FBI handler that night, preoccupied with a Klan "wrecking crew" that included Charles Cagle, John Hall and Eugene Thomas. They were still on the street when another bomb struck the Gaston Motel, where Dr. King was registered. By the time Rowe touched base with Byron McFall at 3:00 A.M., a riot was in progress.[31]

After years of terror and weeks of police assaults on passive demonstrators, Birmingham blacks raged against Connor's patrolmen, pelting them with stones. Al Lingo turned up at the scene, appearing "half drunk" to Chief Moore, and ordered a counterattack by his troopers. "We don't need any guns down here," Moore told Lingo. "You all might get somebody killed." Sneering, Lingo replied, "You're damned right it'll kill somebody. Get your cowardly ass back to your office or your house, because I'm in charge now and my orders are to put these black bastards to bed." His men swept the streets, then finished by attacking black residents on their own porches. "And so the battle ended," a New York reporter wrote, "with the state policemen, who had played only a very minor role in the actual quelling of the riot, rapping old Negro men in rocking chairs."[32]

Bob Chambliss, no stranger to terrorism, later said that Gary Rowe bombed the Gaston Motel. His companions on the raid, said Chambliss, were Klansmen Billy Holt, Don Luna and Hubert Page. The team allegedly received a police escort to and from the crime scene in the person of Patrolman Floyd Garrett — a nephew of Chambliss and one of two officers who supplied affidavits for Bull Connor at the May 1961 hearings before Judge Frank Johnson. Chambliss also told his konfidants that he would trust Rowe "to kill a nigger and never talk." Three days after the latest blasts, Mayor Hanes addressed a Klan front group, the United Americans for Conservative Government (UACG) in Birmingham. To applause from a crowd that included Chambliss, Bobby Cherry, John Hall and Hubert Page, Hanes described Dr. King as a "witch doctor," his marchers as a "Congolese mob." While blasting "weak-kneed quisling traitors" who would compromise on segregation, ex–Agent Hanes promised that he would "never negotiate or meet with the Communists or the rabble rousers of the King type because they haven't got anything to negotiate with. They haven't got a thing that we want. We have what they want."[33]

The University of Alabama faced court-ordered integration in spring 1963. Located at Tuscaloosa, in Wizard Shelton's backyard, the school enjoyed tremendous symbolic significance — and it offered a test of George Wallace's vow to "stand in the schoolhouse door" against blacks and federal invaders. That May, Shelton had promised "the bloodiest rioting ever seen in the U.S." if 'Bama was forced to integrate, but Wallace recognized his moment in the sun and issued orders for the Klan to mind its manners. On 5 June 1963, FBI informants related a warning from Al Lingo to the KKK: Any knights who ruined Wallace's big day would be arrested. Bull Connor addressed a Tuscaloosa Citizens' Council rally two days later, then lingered to repeat Lingo's message in a private meeting with Klansmen. Asa Carter took time off from scripting Wallace's performance to warn Ed Fields and the NSRP. Robert

Shelton promptly changed his tune, announcing that his knights had "no intention of bringing any form of violence on the campus."[34]

As always, though, a portion of the Ku Klux rank and file was uncontrollable. Gary Rowe told his FBI handlers that a UKA "action squad" would be driving a small arsenal of weapons from Birmingham to Tuscaloosa on 8 June 1963. As later detailed in Rowe's memoirs, the stash reportedly included a bazooka and six rockets, five carbines, four shotguns, a submachine gun, six tear-gas grenades, a dozen fragmentation grenades, 12 sticks of dynamite with blasting caps, and four bayonets. G-men told Rowe to haul the weapons in his car, but his companions insisted on using another vehicle. State troopers stopped the car outside Tuscaloosa, detaining Rowe, Charles Cagle and four other knights. Officially, the list of weapons confiscated from their car included six pistols, two sabers, two bayonets, two nightsticks and a baling hook. At the arrest, one trooper told the Klansmen, "Some bastard called the FBI and told them you had all these weapons." The prisoners were soon released, and their weapons were returned by a judge who hosted Klan meetings in his courtroom after hours. As they left, the judge remarked, "If Tuscaloosa had a thousand more men like Bobby Shelton, it would be a better place to live." Rowe later showed the weapons to his FBI contact but refused to surrender them. No charges were filed for violation of the 1934 National Firearms Act.[35]

George Wallace briefly lingered in the schoolhouse door at Tuscaloosa, mouthing words prepared by Asa Carter, but the university was integrated without bloodshed. Still, politicians and police in Alabama were committed to resistance. A few days after Wallace's charade, Sgt. Tom Cook attended an NSRP meeting in Birmingham, where Jesse Stoner offered instruction on how to make time bombs. In July 1963, a plainclothes officer escorted Ed Fields to an Anniston motel, where Al Lingo waited with instructions for the brownshirts. Specifically, Lingo— speaking for Governor Wallace — asked Fields and his neo–Nazis to disrupt integration of Birmingham schools by "any means necessary." Fields made the pledge and kept it to the best of his ability, sending 125 fascists to scuffle with police outside a newly integrated school on 8 September 1963. Bob Chambliss, meanwhile, helped the NSRP collect signatures on a petition requested by Wallace, condemning "mixed education." Gary Rowe informed his bureau handlers of the Klan-NSRP power struggle, complaining that innocent knights had been blamed for violent acts committed by Fields and company. If G-men cared, they gave no sign.[36]

While the FBI vacillated between investigating the Alabama Klan and concealing its crimes, the U.S. Army chose outright collaboration. Intelligence agents from the Army's 20th Special Forces Group in Birmingham solicited Robert Shelton's help in collecting data on "subversive" civil rights groups. As revealed three decades later by the Memphis *Commercial Appeal*, "In return for paramilitary training at a farm in Cullman, Alabama, Klansmen soon became the 20th's intelligence network, whose information was passed on to the Pentagon." We may only speculate on whether military weapons (like the Klan's bazooka) were also provided as part of the payoff. Thus far, the Army has no comment on its secret dealings with the KKK. Another Birmingham Klansman from the 1960s, Martin McWhorter, later said the order's "primary objective" during 1961-69 "was information supply, to the CIA and the FBI."[37]

Whatever the arrangement, Klansmen put their training to good use. On 10 August 1963, Gary Rowe and 30-odd confederates staged a diversion at a carnival in Warrior, Alabama, while Charles Cagle and another knight burned down a local church. (The minister was black, but he had played no part in recent demonstrations.) Ten days later, a bomb damaged the home of black attorney Arthur Shores in Birmingham. Neighbors turned out once more to stone police, whereupon U.S. Attorney Macon Weaver blamed the riot on "false charges" filed against lawmen by bombing witness Roosevelt Tatum in April. Weaver had convened a federal grand jury on 28 June 1963, seeking to indict Tatum for "lying" to FBI agents—an offense committed daily by Klansmen, yet never punished—but Justice refused to press charges. The mood in Washington changed two months later, and Tatum was indicted on 26 August, the first federal defendant charged in "Bombingham's" 16 years of terror. Jurors convicted him on 18 November 1963, and he received a sentence of 366 days in prison. The FBI's message to future witnesses was crystal-clear.[38]

In August 1963, George Wallace sent Ralph Roton to observe and analyze Dr. King's epic march on Washington, D.C. The Klansman's conclusion was preordained: the Reds did it. Terrorists bombed the Shores home a second time and sparked another riot on 4 September. Birmingham police killed an unarmed black man in the melee, and Gary Rowe later claimed a drive-by shooting of a black pedestrian the same night. In Rowe's account of that incident, he shot the victim with a pistol and was then stopped by an officer who told him, "Get the hell out of here, OK? Good shooting!" Two days later, Governor Wallace addressed a UACG rally in Birmingham, with Robert Shelton, Bob Chambliss and other knights in the audience. His speech inspired another raid, this time against the rural home of black businessman A.G. Gaston, owner of the Gaston Motel and an alleged conduit of weapons to Black Muslims. Rowe later gave two versions of the incident. In one, he joined a squad including Herman Cash, Eugene Thomas and future grand dragon Robert Creel, lobbing firebombs at Gaston's house before searchlights and bursting flares drove them away. The other story, published 20 years later, describes a bungled raid on a Muslim "training camp," aborted when the knights found themselves storming a state prison's fence.[39]

"BAPBOMB"

The Klan's most notorious atrocity of the 1960s occurred at 10:22 A.M. on 15 September 1963, when a powerful bomb exploded during Sunday services at Birmingham's Sixteenth Street Baptist Church, killing four black girls aged 11 to 14 and leaving 14 other persons injured. Bull Connor had delivered the church's first bomb threat in 1948, but Birmingham's knights had taken 15 years to plan the attack.[40]

The church bombing was Birmingham's twenty-first since 1955, and the first to claim lives. Two more blacks died in the riot that followed: Police killed 16-year-old Johnnie Robinson after he lobbed a stone at cars decorated with racist slogans, and two teenage motorcycle thugs shot 13-year-old Virgil Ware. The culprits in that case had earlier visited the NSRP's headquarters and attended a rally of the Klan-front

UACG. The shooter received six months' juvenile detention for the murder, and his driver escaped with probation. Al Lingo's state troopers also shot an elderly black bystander near the Sixteenth Street church, but their victim survived his head wound. Dr. King spoke to President John Kennedy soon after the blast and reported that JFK had shown "the kind of federal concern needed" and "made it clear that the federal government would not stand idly by and allow the lives and property and rights of Negro citizens to be trampled." From Washington, J. Edgar Hoover announced the greatest FBI manhunt since the 1930s pursuit of John Dillinger, but warned his agents not to provide the Justice Department with "a 'blow-by-blow' account" of the investigation, fearing that their statements "will appear in the [Washington] *Star* or the *Saturday Evening Post.*"[41]

A total of 231 G-men were assigned to the case Hoover dubbed "BAPBOMB," but some of them were quickly led astray by racist rumors linking Black Muslims to the Birmingham bombings. Hoover wanted "all angles" of that dead-end inquiry explored. Assistant Director Cartha Deloach entertained suggestions from Georgia senator Richard Russell—a Klan ally since the 1920s—that civil rights activists bombed the church to get sympathetic attention. Governor Wallace aired the same allegation, attributing the deadly blast to "communists or other Negroes who had a lot to gain by the ensuing publicity." Hoover, meanwhile, blamed "Negro elements" for obstructing the manhunt with baseless criticism that created "a gulf" between FBI agents and local police.[42]

In fact, as G-men must have known, the bombing was a Klan "project," carried out by members of the Cahaba River Group, a dissident faction organized by members of Eastview 13 in August 1963. Bob Chambliss was among its members, all of them well known to Gary Rowe. Informant Rowe allegedly learned of the blast moments after it happened, from a girlfriend on the Birmingham Police Department, and then favored his FBI handlers with their first report of the crime. Still, Rowe unaccountably waited seven months to tell agents that two Klan terrorists, John Hall and Ross Keith, had missed an appointment with Rowe the same morning. After speaking to the bureau, Rowe called several other knights—including Herman Cash, Billy Holt, Robert Thomas and Earl Thompson—but all were "out working" that Sunday. Rowe's personal role in the bombing remains uncertain today. Bob Chambliss later said that Rowe confessed to the crime, complaining that "we" had used an insufficient charge, when he should have "put out enough to level the damn thing." Birmingham detective Red Self testified that Rowe said, "I'll tell you one thing: they will never solve the Sixteenth Street bombing because me and another guy handled it." On yet another occasion, Rowe floated the ludicrous story that black singer Harry Belafonte had financed the bombing. Various sources report that Rowe failed two polygraph tests in which he denied bombing the church.[43]

Klansmen were busy in the days surrounding the fatal church bombing. On 14 September, Bob Chambliss told niece Elizabeth Hood that he had "enough stuff put away to flatten half of Birmingham." He added, "You just wait till after Sunday morning. They will beg us to let them segregate." Jesse Stoner was in Birmingham the same day, seen by police at the home of Ed Fields. In the predawn hours of 15 September, multiple bomb threats diverted police from the neighborhood of Sixteenth

Street. Black witnesses reported two white men lurking around the church that night in a car resembling one owned by Klansman Thomas Blanton, Jr.; one of them limped when he walked, and Blanton had recently broken a toe. At 10 A.M. on Sunday, Patrolman Floyd Garrett visited his aunt (sister of Bob Chambliss), Viola Hillhouse. A young cousin heard Garrett tell Hillhouse that a bomb was planted at the church. "Keep your damn mouth shut," he warned. "If anybody asks, you don't know anything, understand?" Moments after the explosion, Garrett called on Uncle Bob and told him, "They will get your ass on this one. You have gone too far." At 2 P.M. on Sunday, Cahaba River knights gathered at a Midfield rally held by West End Parents for Private Schools. Robert Shelton was also present but later denied speaking to the dissident Klansmen. Deputy Sheriff James Hancock told a different story, saying he possessed a tape recording of their conversation, wherein Shelton said the bomb should have exploded at midnight. (No copy of that tape has surfaced yet.)[44]

Floyd Garrett made the first BAPBOMB arrest and jailed a black dishwasher from a local cafeteria after a white co-worker accused him of planting the bomb. Other officers locked up the church's janitor. At the same time, Garrett told Lt. Maurice House that Bob Chambliss was probably responsible. An FBI agent scuttled that lead on 16 September, visiting House to report (falsely) that bureau surveillance placed Chambliss at home throughout Saturday night. In a weak response to the bombing, a federal grand jury convened and indicted several NSRP members for obstructing school integration (while ignoring Al Lingo's role in the conspiracy). On 19 September, after another bomb exploded near a public school, G-men collected soil samples but ultimately learned nothing. Local police took a different approach: they arrested a neighbor who reported the bombing, drove him to an isolated spot and beat him, then jailed him on a charge of public drunkenness. Three days later, Cahaba River Klansmen held a "kiss-of-death" meeting, clasping hands and vowing to kill the first man who revealed their link to the Sixteenth Street blast.[45]

Fear of capture did not stop the bombers, however. At 1:34 A.M. on 25 September, Gary Rowe called his FBI contact to report an explosion. He was driving around one of Birmingham's black neighborhoods, Rowe said, when he heard the blast. Fifteen minutes later, a second bomb exploded, this one packed with nails. The blast damaged eight homes but wounded no one, since the crowd drawn by the first explosion had dispersed. Klansman John Hall, cruising the same streets with a girlfriend, heard the second bomb and told his companion, "That son of a bitch was a good one." Inspector J.W. Haley described the second charge as "a booby trap meant to kill." An informant inside the Cahaba River group told state investigator William Posey that Hubert Page had planned and supervised the latest bombing. On 28 September, Capt. R.W. Godwin drove Page to Huntsville for a polygraph test. Analyst Lee Greene reported that Page "definitely has knowledge" of the second Shores bombing, the Sixteenth Street blast, and the recent shrapnel charge. "He is lying about his participation in these bombings," Greene said, "and definitely attended the Cahaba [kiss-of-death] meeting. The man is a fanatic." Nonetheless, state authorities concealed those test results until 1965, while G-men assured Page that he was not a suspect in the quadruple murder. Author Diane McWhorter suggests that the bureau may have mollified Page in an effort to conceal Gary Rowe's part — with Page — in the April 1963 Gaston Motel bombing.[46]

On 26 September, Charles Cagle led FBI agents to a field where stolen dynamite had once been hidden, but the stash was gone. Two days later, nearly two weeks after the fatal bombing, G-men questioned Bob Chambliss for the first time but learned nothing from the tight-lipped Klansman. On the same day in Detroit, two agents questioned Kirthus Glenn, a woman who had seen three suspects near the church at 2:10 A.M. on 15 September and recorded their car's license number. Birmingham knights took advantage of the leisurely federal investigation to coordinate alibis, while Governor Wallace and Al Lingo schemed to "solve" the case without FBI help. On 29 September, Lingo met twice with a group of Klansmen including Shelton, Page, John Hall, Robert Thomas, Bobby Cherry and UACG president Bill Morgan; the second gathering also included Arthur Hanes and attorney Wade Wallace (a UACG member and cousin of the governor). That night, state troopers accompanied by two Klansmen arrested Bob Chambliss at home. John Hall and Charles Cagle soon joined him in jail, charged with misdemeanor counts of illegally possessing dynamite. Gary Rowe, warned in advance by Red Self, neglected to inform his bureau handlers of the impending arrests.[47]

While George Wallace gloated over "beating the Kennedy crowd to the punch," Justice officials scrambled to make sense of the arrests. Lingo's predecessor, Floyd Mann, told Washington that the charges were filed to scuttle the FBI's BAPBOMB investigation and take the leading suspects "out of circulation." Bob Chambliss, seemingly unconcerned, fell asleep during his polygraph test and left jail with his cohorts on 1 October after posting $300 bond. Another Klan suspect, Troy Ingram, had failed an FBI polygraph the previous day. Tom Blanton, Jr., failed an identical test on 1 October, but G-men waited another full day before quizzing his girlfriend about Blanton's movements on 15 September, thus granting him time to prepare her answers. Six agents raided Blanton's home on 4 October, finding six guns but no trace of explosives; they planted bugs at the same time, but the poor quality of their equipment rendered Blanton's conversations unintelligible.[48]

By that time, paranoia was at work within the local Klan. At a Cahaba River meeting, held on 6 October, Chambliss accused Robert Shelton of selling him out to police. He was correct, but there were others on the quisling list as well. Months later, Rowe informed G-men, "The Klan met and discussed [Hubert] Page getting $15,000 from Gov. Wallace and there was a large shortage with some believing that Page embezzled some of it." Troy Ingram failed a second polygraph test on 6 October, but it hardly mattered. Defendants Cagle, Chambliss and Hall were convicted of misdemeanor charges three days later, their 90-day jail terms and $100 fines suspended when they threatened to appeal the verdict. Disillusioned with Gary Rowe's erratic and contradictory reports, Birmingham agents hired a new informant in October — mass-murder suspect "Nigger" Hall. Delighted with his new assignment, Hall prepared a list of suspects in the fatal bombing that included Blanton, Cagle, Chambliss and Ingram. He further named Gary Rowe as one member of a three-man team that held veto power over all Klan "missionary work" in Birmingham.[49]

G-men working the BAPBOMB case were not restricted to the testimony of Ku

Klux informants. Elizabeth Hood sat with agents on 11 October 1963, detailing her uncle's remarks on the eve of the explosion and his Sunday comment that "It wasn't meant to hurt anybody. It didn't go off when it was supposed to." Eleven days later, Kirthus Glenn identified Bob Chambliss from FBI mug shots as one of the Klansmen she saw near the church on 15 September. (In that and every other photo lineup they prepared for witnesses, G-men omitted pictures of Gary Rowe and his car.) The Birmingham field office asked Hoover for permission to arrest Chambliss, but the director refused, complaining that the "chance of a successful conviction is remote." Five months later, when agents reported an "airtight" case against Chambliss, Hoover once more declined to inform his superiors at Justice. The same was true of suspect Tom Blanton, Jr. in 1965, after informant Mitchell Burns recorded Blanton saying, "They ain't gonna catch me when I bomb my next church. The boys done a good job on this one. There are a few Negroes now who won't grow up to bother us." Yet again, Hoover refused to share the information with federal prosecutors.[50]

While suppressing evidence against the Birmingham bombers, Hoover also managed to ignore an interstate terrorist conspiracy hatched by members of another Ku Klux faction called Nacirema, Inc. Chartered in Georgia on 25 July 1961, Nacirema—"American" spelled backwards—was incorporated by Klansmen Clyde Newborn and R.H. Wynn of Mableton. William Anderson and William Crowe, both members of the UKA, led the group "composed almost entirely of present and former Klansmen who joined Nacirema to get more violent action." In August and October 1961, Anderson and Crowe conducted "explosive schools" for Nacirema members outside Macon, Georgia, at the farm of O.C. Mixon (known as "Klansman's Hill"). Congressional investigators later said those classes were conducted "with the knowledge and consent" of Robert Shelton and Georgia Grand Dragon Calvin Craig, both of whom reportedly attended the August session. Georgia authorities "discovered" Nacirema in 1963 when an Atlanta prostitute informed police of her boyfriend's involvement in the black-robed gang. An October 1963 article in *Life* magazine exposed Nacirema to public scrutiny, reporting that its 60 members—including both Klansmen and brownshirts from the NSRP—were suspected in 138 bombings spanning 11 southern states. Two unnamed members of the group were seen in Birmingham on 14 September 1963, suggesting Nacirema involvement in the Sixteenth Street church bombing. Atlanta police captain Everett Little told *Life*, "These fellas were the real hoods of the whole racist movement, guys who would take a contract to blow up a place, just like an underworld hood would take a contract to kill a man."[51] Although Jesse Stoner was never publicly linked to Nacirema, the bombing-for-hire operation was strikingly similar to his own activities in the late 1950s.

Robert Shelton was unfazed by Nacirema's exposure, and he seemed to have no fear of FBI investigators. G-men who questioned him on 20 November 1963 began with an apology for the inconvenience and blandly accepted the wizard's denial of any involvement in violence. Before leaving his office, they "assured Shelton that as long as Mr. Hoover was head of the FBI the organization would be in fact an investigative organization without malice or opinion and dedicated to serving the public without preference or discrimination. Shelton stated he has always been an admirer of the Bureau and Mr. Hoover and hoped that his leadership in the FBI would continue."[52]

The BAPBOMB case remained officially unsolved until 1977, when Alabama Attorney General William Baxley reopened the state's investigation. Elected in 1970 with support from Governor Wallace, Baxley sought to prosecute the church bombers in 1971, but Hoover refused to cooperate. Undaunted, Baxley established a reputation for pursuing corrupt politicians and sheriffs. After Hoover's death in May 1972, Baxley tackled the Birmingham bombers again, but obstacles remained. Suspects John Hall, Troy Ingram and Ross Keith died before Baxley could quiz them, and Gary Rowe and Herman Cash reportedly passed state polygraph tests. New requests for FBI assistance were blocked by "stonewalling" until Baxley threatened a Washington press conference with parents of the four murdered girls. At last, the bureau budged, providing Baxley with sufficient evidence to indict Bob Chambliss in September 1977. Two months later, on 17 November, an integrated jury convicted Chambliss of murdering victim Denise McNair, and he received a life sentence. A spokesman for Justice observed that the jury "heard less direct evidence than was available to Mr. Hoover in 1964, when the director ruled against prosecution." On the same day Chambliss was convicted, Baxley served subpoenas on suspects Bobby Cherry and Tom Blanton, Jr., but both knights stood silent behind their lawyers and no further charges were filed. Chambliss died in prison on 19 October 1985, and a sex scandal ended Baxley's political career in 1986.[53]

There matters rested for another decade, until Tuscaloosa native Robert Langford took charge of the Birmingham field office. Journalist Robert Kessler says that Langford reopened the BAPBOMB case in 1993 "without telling headquarters," and that he subsequently "found" recordings made of suspect Blanton during 1963–65. A contradictory report maintains that the FBI revived its investigation in 1997, a year after Langford retired, upon discovery of "new and credible evidence." In either case, a county grand jury convened to review the case in November 1998, culminating in the May 2000 murder indictments of Blanton and Cherry. Even then, controversy endured: Cherry said G-men had offered to reduce his charges if he would "lie" under oath about Blanton; Blanton's daughter told reporters, "The FBI told Dad, 'We're going to pin it on somebody. We don't care who.'" Agent Craig Dahle officially denied both accusations, assuring journalists, "It wouldn't happen that way."[54]

Blanton was convicted of murder on 1 May 2001 and received one life prison term for each of his four victims. On the day he was convicted, FBI Director Louis Freeh told the U.S. Senate that the BAPBOMB case was "a disgrace to the FBI. That case should have been prosecuted in 1964. It could have been prosecuted in 1964. The evidence was there." A judge initially excused Bobby Cherry from trial on grounds of dementia, then reversed his ruling and found Cherry competent in January 2002. Four months later, jurors convicted Cherry of murder, and he drew four terms of life imprisonment. In the wake of that verdict, Bill Baxley asked, "What excuse can the FBI have for allowing Mr. Blanton to go free for twenty-four years with that smoking-gun evidence hidden in its files? If we had had those tapes, we would have unequivocally been able to convict Blanton [in 1977]. The FBI, for all intents and purposes, gave a 'get out of jail free card' to Tommy Blanton." John Yung, Baxley's former assistant, recalled of the Chambliss case, "[The FBI] denied having any more evidence than what they gave us, and it was hard enough getting what we got."[55]

In Birmingham, Agent Dahle told reporters there was "no easy answer" to Baxley's questions, but he insisted, "I think it is wrong to assert that there was any effort to block anything." Kessler, meanwhile, blames the bureau's failure on simple ignorance. "Instead of withholding evidence from … Baxley in 1977, as Baxley claimed," Kessler writes, "the FBI did not realize it had the material." If that explanation strained credulity to the breaking point, it paled beside Kessler's description of the BAP-BOMB case as "an FBI success story." Ignoring the fact that Blanton and Cherry were convicted in a state court nearly four decades after their crime, Kessler contends that "the FBI brought to justice a man who had blown up four girls because of the color of their skin."[56]

5

Murder in Mississippi (1961–1963)

In 1963, Mississippi native James Silver described his home state as a "closed society," impervious to the currents of change sweeping over America at large. "Mississippi's spiritual secession from modern America has never ended," Silver wrote. "For more than a century Mississippians have refused to be bound by the will of the national society." That defiance revealed itself in official rhetoric, through the militant Citizens' Councils, and in the daily toll of racist violence suffered by black citizens of the state. The FBI closed its Mississippi field office in Jackson after World War II, subsisting thereafter with scattered one-man "resident agencies" and loose supervision from Birmingham. J. Edgar Hoover had no interest in the plight of Mississippi blacks, nor in the machinations of police and vigilantes who oppressed them. Since 1956 he had not wavered from his view of Council members as "the leading citizens of the South."[1]

Ironically, for all its racist fervor, Mississippi was the one Deep South state where Hoover's description of the "defunct" KKK seemed accurate. Despite reported Ku Klux stirrings in 1946, 1950 and 1956–57, the Klan had failed to prosper in postwar Mississippi. Its full-scale return is usually dated from autumn 1963, when kleagles from Louisiana's Original Knights recruited 300 Mississippi converts, but no records exist to pinpoint the date.[2] With or without hoods and robes, however, Mississippi terrorists were clearly organized and armed by April 1960 — and the FBI saw no reason to interfere.

"LAWLESS AND RECKLESS PEOPLE"

Addressing founders of the first Mississippi Citizens' Council in 1954, Tom Brady warned his followers, "This thing will die a-borning if lawless and reckless people are brought into it." Six years later, Brady deemed the Council's membership "impeccable," but mounting bloodshed proved the fallacy of that evaluation. Mob violence rocked Biloxi in April 1960 when whites mobbed blacks at a segregated beach. Four months later, another mob including identified Council members stormed an unfinished ministerial college for blacks in Union, beat a white pastor and chased away other workers. In May 1961, white thugs in Jackson lassoed a nine-year-old black girl and dragged her through the streets behind their car. In no case did police arrest the guilty parties.[3]

Civil rights activists realized that the key to racial equality in Mississippi was political power. Few Mississippi blacks were registered to vote in 1961, and fewer still cast ballots. The worst resistance to black suffrage lay in southwestern Mississippi, adjacent to Louisiana. There, in Pike County, only 250 of 6,939 voting-age blacks were registered; Amite County had one registered voter among 3,560 adult blacks; Walthall County, with 2,490 blacks of voting age, had none. Robert Moses, a member of SNCC from New York, arrived to remedy that situation in July 1961. Operating from McComb, he toured surrounding districts with local activist Herbert Lee and E.W. Steptoe, president of Amite County's small NAACP chapter. On 15 August, Moses was arrested after leading three blacks to register in Liberty. Two weeks later, SNCC worker Marion Barry (later mayor of Washington, D.C.) was beaten while escorting two would-be voters to the Liberty courthouse. Travis Britt, another SNCC member, got the same treatment on 5 September, when he accompanied Moses and four other blacks to the Liberty registrar's office. Two days later, SNCC worker John Hardy was pistol-whipped by the Walthall County registrar in Tylertown, then arrested by Sheriff Ed Craft for "disturbing the peace." Justice Department attorneys filed suit to block Hardy's prosecution under the 1957 Civil Rights Act, but FBI agents made no move against the racists who had violated criminal provisions of the same federal statute.[4]

Incessant violence soon discouraged local blacks from cooperating with Moses and Steptoe, but Herbert Lee remained loyal. "A lot dropped out," Lee's wife recalled, "but he kept going." On 25 September 1961, Lee drove a truckload of cotton to the gin outside Liberty. There, he was approached by state legislator E.H. Hurst, who began shouting at Lee, then drew a pistol and shot him in the head. Lee's corpse lay on the ground for two hours before a black mortician arrived from McComb. In the interim, a white bystander approached black witness Louis Allen, saying, "They found a tire iron in that nigger's hand." When Allen said he had seen no such weapon, the stranger repeated, "They found a piece of iron, you hear?" In fear for his life, Allen repeated the lie at a coroner's inquest convened the same afternoon. Hurst told the panel Lee had threatened him with a tire tool as they argued over an unpaid $500 debt. Hurst said that he struck Lee with his pistol in self-defense and "must have pulled the trigger unconsciously." Lee's voter-registration work, Hurst said, "had nothing to do with it." The jury ruled Lee's death a case of "justifiable homicide," and Hurst was released. Louis Allen subsequently told his story to FBI agents, but he refused to testify before a state grand jury after Justice spokesmen told him "there was no way possible to provide protection for a witness at such a hearing." Hoover's agents—who would jail nine Georgia blacks in 1962 for "interfering with the jury process" in a racial case—filed no such charges against white conspirators in Mississippi. John Doar at Justice ordered an FBI examination of Lee's body, but Hoover stalled transmission of the message and Lee was buried without an autopsy.[5]

Violence escalated after the unpunished murder of Herbert Lee. On 11 October 1961, when 115 black students marched through McComb to protest the shooting, white hoodlums assaulted two reporters on the sidelines. Seven weeks later, riotous mobs attacked freedom riders at McComb's bus depot, unrestrained by police during three days of mayhem. Indeed, lawless lawmen were a constant threat to Mississippi blacks. Roman Duckworth Jr., a black soldier home on leave, was shot and killed by a Taylorsville patrolman on 9 April 1962 when he refused to take a segregated bus seat. The following month, Neshoba County Sheriff Ethel "Hop" Barnett and Deputy Lawrence Rainey (both later members of the KKK) killed Willie Nash, a black epileptic handcuffed in their custody. On 6 June 1962, police in Clarksdale stripped Bessie Turner, a black theft suspect, and forced her to lie on her back while they whipped her with belts. Two weeks later, Jackson police beat a black newspaper editor en route to investigate a rumored racial murder. In July 1962, 14-year-old Welton McSwine was jailed at Greenwood for "peeping" into a white woman's house. Patrolmen forced him to strip, then flogged him with a bullwhip in his cell. Attorneys sent McSwine's affidavit and photos of his wounds to FBI headquarters and to the Justice Department, but they received no answer from Washington. In no case did the bureau see fit to investigate.[6]

"ANOTHER WAR BETWEEN THE STATES"

On 25 June 1962, a federal court ordered the University of Mississippi — "Ole Miss" at Oxford — to admit its first black student, Kosciusko resident James Meredith. Supreme Court justice Hugo Black dismissed various legal stays on 6 August, and a federal injunction of 25 September barred state interference with Meredith's enrollment. Governor Ross Barnett earned a contempt citation that same afternoon, followed by Lieutenant Governor Paul Johnson on 26 September, before the way was cleared for Meredith's admission on 30 September 1962.[7]

Outside agitators quickly seized upon the Oxford crisis, but they weren't the blacks and Reds depicted in segregationist propaganda. In Alabama, Robert Shelton huddled with officers of the United Klans, declaring that Meredith's admission to Ole Miss might launch "another War Between the States." The UKA's leaders decided "that if they went to Mississippi to help defend Ole Miss, they would be armed and ready to fight." A "standby alert" flashed across the South via telephone and CB radio, warning all UKA members to arm themselves and be ready to move on command from Tuscaloosa. Two crosses blazed on campus the night of 26 September, and Shelton's first "observers" reached Oxford the following day, joined by a team of 19 Klansmen from northeastern Louisiana.[8] In the meantime, another call to arms had gone out nationwide, this one broadcast by a self-styled patriot in Texas.

Major General Edwin Walker had commanded U.S. troops assigned to protect the first black students at Little Rock's Central High School, in 1957. He performed that duty in a professional manner, but the experience seems to have unhinged his mind. Four years later, he resigned from the Army after his superiors reprimanded him for indoctrinating his troops with far-right literature denouncing President Truman and Eleanor Roosevelt (among others) as Reds. In civilian life, Walker served as a paid orator for the John Birch Society, espousing doctrines so bizarre that even

William Simmons of the Citizens' Councils branded him an extremist. Now, on 26 September 1962, Walker told a national radio audience, "It is time to make a move.... We have listened and we have been pushed around by the anti–Christ Supreme Court. It's time to rise. To make a stand beside Governor Ross Barnett at Jackson, Mississippi. He is showing the way. Now is the time to be heard. Ten thousand strong from every state in the nation. Rally to the cause of freedom. The battle cry of the Republic: Barnett, yes! Castro, no! Bring your flag, your tent and your skillet. It's now or never! I have been on the other side in such situations in a place called Little Rock, and I was on the wrong side. This time I will be in Jackson, Mississippi, on the right side."[9]

Faulty geography aside, Walker's summons struck a responsive chord. Overnight, Barnett's office was flooded with telegrams and phone calls from militant racists offering to "bring our guns and fight." FBI offices around the country logged tips on armed groups gathering as far away as Southern California. L.P. Davis, head of the Gentilly, Louisiana, Citizen's Council, cabled Walker: "You called for 10,000 volunteers nationwide for Ole Miss to fight against federal tyranny. Will pledge 10,000 from Louisiana alone, under your command." Louisiana Council boss William Rainach pledged another 10,000 to Governor Barnett. Fred Hockett, executive secretary of the Florida Citizens' Council, offered 1,500 men. Sheriff Jim Clark of Selma, Alabama, announced that he and Sheriff Hugh Champion were ready with "posses" of 500 deputies each. Georgia Grand Dragon Calvin Craig declared that when his orders came, "a volunteer force of several thousand men would be on its way to Mississippi straight off." FBI informants reported 600 knights already in Jackson, and a ham radio broadcast from Kansas City alerted "all Minuteman organizations, all ranger units, Illinois civilian control units, Washington militia" and allied groups to stand ready. The National States Rights Party wired Barnett from Alabama with a claim of "thousands" en route to Oxford. Milwaukee's field office warned Hoover that a wealthy racist was flying four P-51 fighter planes to Ole Miss, but they never arrived. Mississippi Sheriff James Grimsley chartered buses for members of his Jackson County Citizens' Emergency Unit (JCCEU), embarking for Oxford on 27 September. Melvin Bruce, a sometime chauffeur for American Nazi Party leader George Rockwell, wired Barnett from Georgia on 30 September: "I volunteer my services, arms and munitions to you as a combat infantryman, and will serve under any officer you might designate. I would consider it an honor to serve under the patriot, General Walker." The same day, a caravan of "Citizens for the Preservation of Democracy" left Prichard, Alabama, trailed by journalists and an FBI surveillance team.[10]

Edwin Walker landed in Jackson on 29 September with a small band of Texas cronies. Before driving to Oxford, he held a press conference on the airport tarmac, telling reporters, "I am in Mississippi beside Governor Ross Barnett. I call for a national protest against the conspiracy from within. Rally to the cause of freedom.... There are thousands, possibly tens of thousands of people on their way to Mississippi from across the nation." James Meredith arrived at Ole Miss on 30 September, guarded by 300 U.S. marshals. At five o'clock that afternoon, Oxford's airport denied Robert Shelton permission to land, whereupon his UKA contingent circled briefly, then returned to Alabama. FBI resident agent Robin Cotton persuaded his superiors to send another dozen G-men, who fanned out to infiltrate the growing mob on campus. Rioting erupted after nightfall, with some 2,500 racists of all ages besieging Meredith's federal guards in the Lyceum, where they defended themselves with tear gas. Walker led one charge, followed by an estimated thousand rioters, while others rushed the Lyceum with a hijacked fire engine. Mississippi lawmen watched and did nothing as gunfire erupted between snipers and the outnumbered marshals. Also on hand were two observers from Alabama, Al Lingo and Hunter Phillips, dispatched by gubernatorial candidate George Wallace to chart the progress of Mississippi's uprising for future reference.[11]

At 10 P.M., Agent Cotton saw dozens of men armed with rifles and shotguns leaping from pickup trucks on the campus outskirts. Soon they were blazing away at the Lyceum in what author William Doyle calls "the beginnings of a Ku Klux Klan rebellion." Out-of-state knights by the dozens infested Ole Miss, mingling with students and apathetic police to burn cars, pummel bystanders and bombard the Lyceum with everything from bricks to high-powered rifle fire. An old school bus bearing Louisiana license plates was parked outside the campus football stadium, loudspeakers blaring a fight song titled "Cajun Ku Klux Klan." Its lyrics ran: "You niggers listen now. I'm gonna tell you how to keep from being tortured when the Klan is on the prowl. Stay at home at night, lock your doors up tight. Don't go outside, or you will find them crosses burning bright." The racist guerrillas met no opposition from Mississippi officers, and Attorney General Kennedy later complained that "approximately 150 of the police were observed sitting in their automobiles within half a mile of the rioting and shooting."[12]

The Ole Miss riot claimed two lives. One victim, Abbeville jukebox repairman Ray Gunter, had gone to Ole Miss with a friend "to see what's going on." A stray bullet struck him in the head as he stood watching rioters attack the Lyceum. Victim Paul "Flash" Guihard was a reporter for Agence France-Presse, assigned to cover the disorder. He arrived on campus at 8:40 P.M. and was found dying moments later, 165 yards northeast of the Lyceum. Unlike Gunter, Guihard was no accidental shooting victim. Forensic evidence revealed that he was shot in the back with a .38-caliber pistol from a distance of less than 12 inches. Investigators believe that Guihard's camera and goatee marked him for rioters or some "rogue" lawman as a "liberal" reporter, deserving of death. FBI technicians ultimately tested 450 weapons carried by federal officers during the riot without identifying the guns that killed Guihard and Gunter. No tests were performed on the .38-caliber weapons carried by Mississippi officers at the scene.[13]

The campus riot was quelled around 5:30 A.M. on 1 October 1962, then burst to life again at 9 A.M. in downtown Oxford. Some 13,500 troops—more than double the number of Oxford's year-round residents—crushed the second outbreak by noon. On campus, 30 U.S. marshals suffered gunshot wounds, and 136 more were otherwise injured; 48 soldiers also suffered various injuries. Within hours of the riot's end, Oxford was overrun by 50 FBI agents, 200 other Justice personnel, 20 Army intelligence agents and 31,000 regular troops. Ironically, black troops dispatched to Oxford were stripped of their rank, weapons and helmets to avoid offending local whites. *The New York Times* estimated that 375 civilians were injured, and 300 others were arrested by federal officers. (Mississippi lawmen made no arrests.) Those detained ranged in age from 14 to 57. They listed home addresses from California to Georgia, but the majority came from Mississippi, Alabama, Louisiana and Tennessee. Hundreds of weapons were seized in the riot, including a submachine gun and a souvenir Japanese pistol from World War II. On 1 October, troops raided the Sigma Nu fraternity house, confiscating 25 guns from frat brothers led by future U.S. Senator Trent Lott. Of those arrested, only 40 were registered college students; eight of those received mild disciplinary action from the student judicial council, but none were expelled. Most prisoners were freed by 3 October, after FBI interrogation.[14]

Only four Ole Miss rioters, all from out of state, faced criminal charges. Edwin Walker stood accused of assaulting or opposing federal officers, preventing a federal officer from discharging his duty, inciting or engaging in an insurrection against the United States, and conspiracy to forcibly overthrow or oppose execution of U.S. laws. Briefly detained at the U.S. Medical Center in Springfield, Missouri, Walker posted $50,000 bond on 6 October 1962 and was released with a court order for psychiatric testing. A federal grand jury convened in January 1963 refused to indict Walker, and all charges were dropped. Melvin Bruce and three of Prichard's "Alabama volunteers" *were* indicted on federal charges, but one case was dropped, and the three other defendants were acquitted after lawyer Jesse Stoner convinced jurors that the accused had been beaten by U.S. marshals. State authorities filed no charges.[15]

Echoes from the battle of Ole Miss were heard for months to come. Leaders of the United Klans gathered in Bessemer, Alabama, on 2 October 1962, voting to "lay low for awhile and then try to get Meredith and hang him from a gate on the campus when the situation permitted." That same night, an FBI informant from Columbus, Georgia, warned G-men of a Klan plot to bomb troops in Oxford with explosives charges dropped from small airplanes. Another group with designs on Meredith was Sheriff Grimsley's Jackson County Citizens' Emergency Unit, 600 members strong, described in FBI memos as "being organized ... to secretly go to the University of Mississippi ... 'to get' or kidnap" Meredith. A separate Justice file confirmed that the JCCEU's "main purpose, apparently, is to kill Meredith," though members also threatened and harassed moderate newspaper editor Ira Harkey in Pascagoula. Informants reported that Grimsley—a notorious drunkard known for corruption and sexual assaults on female prisoners—had conspired to murder Harkey, while his cronies bragged "that none had outdone them in brick throwing and vehicle burning" in Oxford. Nonetheless, the FBI's investigation of Grimsley was "suddenly dropped" in early 1963, "as if the government lost interest." On 23 December 1963, unidentified nightriders fired shotgun blasts into James Meredith's home in Kosciusko, Mississippi.[16]

Emboldened by dismissal of his federal charges, Edwin Walker sued the Associated Press for libel, seeking $35 million in damages from reports of the Oxford riot. Sympathetic Texas jurors awarded Walker $800,000 in June 1964, but the U.S. Supreme Court voided that judgment in 1967. Walker remained a fixture on the far-right lecture circuit and was cheered by Atlanta members of the John Birch Society in September 1965, when he told them, "There will be a KKK in the USA longer than there will be an LBJ." Walker's next two arrests, in 1976 and 1977, included charges of sexually fondling undercover policemen in Dallas. Despite his long history of outré and criminal behavior, President Ronald Reagan's Pentagon restored Walker's $45,000 yearly pension in 1982, proclaiming him "a truly dedicated American soldier." Walker collected $495,000 more from American taxpayers before his death in 1993.[17]

"RABID ON THE SUBJECT OF SEGREGATION"

White-on-black racial violence remained a way of life in Mississippi after Oxford, practiced by police and private citizens alike. An unarmed black man, Eli Brumfield, was killed by police in McComb in October 1962. Nightriders fired into Ira Harkey's Pascagoula newspaper office on 1 November 1962. Two months later, terrorists forced a carload of SNCC workers off the road and fired shots into their vehicle near Natchez. On 24 February 1963, four black activists in Greenville were wounded by machine-gun fire from a passing car. Four days later, a similar shooting wounded another civil rights worker in Leflore County. March brought terror to Greenwood, where racists fired at black motorists, shot up the home of a black family whose son applied to Ole Miss, and burned a voter registration office. Clarksdale witnessed the firebombing of a black activist's home on 12 April 1963; two days later, police whipped a black theft suspect until he confessed; and the local sheriff blamed lightning for the fire that destroyed an NAACP leader's store on 4 May. Vera Pigee, secretary of the Clarksdale NAACP, was beaten by a white man on 23 April 1963, then jailed for "disturbing the peace"; on 8 June, gunmen fired shots into her home. The same day saw federal charges filed against Winona's sheriff and police chief for brutalizing black prisoners, but that was the FBI's only achievement in Mississippi, and it solved nothing. One day later, six more Winona blacks were beaten and jailed for trying to integrate a local bus depot.[18]

The main target of white rage in Mississippi during 1954–63 was Medgar Evers, state chairman of the NAACP. The State Sovereignty Commission — a spy network established by Mississippi officials in 1956 to investigate and harass civil rights activists — opened one of its first files on "Medgar Evers — Race Agitator," and Governor James Coleman ordered a series of "spot checks" on Evers "to determine whether he is violating any law." (During 1956–58, the commission also funneled $250,000 in taxpayers' money to the Citizens' Councils.) The commission's chief investigator, ex–FBI agent Zack Van Landingham, placed Evers under constant surveillance, yet he was unable to identify the terrorists who firebombed Evers's carport in Jackson on 27 May 1963. Two weeks later, on 11 June, Evers informed the FBI that police cars followed wherever he went. One had tried to hit him on 8 June, the driver laughing. A G-man took the message and told Evers he would pass it along to the Justice Department.[19]

On 12 June 1963, a sniper killed Evers in his driveway with one shot through the back. Governor Barnett called the murder "a dastardly act," and Mayor Allen Thompson described Jackson's citizens as "dreadfully shocked, humiliated and sick at heart." Worldwide, the question was not whether Mississippi grieved, but whether the latest murder would be added to the growing list of "unsolved" racial crimes.

James Wechsler, writing for the *New York Post* on 13 June, captured the spirit of the moment with his observation that Evers "went to a lonely death, as he had feared he would, while the G-men slept."[20]

Jackson police found a rifle at the murder scene, and while the FBI offered assistance with the evidence or any out-of-state leads, Assistant Director Alex Rosen said that Justice attorney Burke Marshall "indicated he desired no further action taken by the FBI." Hoover normally would have welcomed that order, yet Rosen says the director defied it with a memo to all bureau field offices, commanding agents "to immediately alert racial informants and other sources to our interest in this matter, and if these offices obtain any information which might have a bearing on the Evers killing, we want to be immediately advised." Still, Hoover's pursuit of the case may have been a nose-thumbing gesture toward Marshall and Robert Kennedy, rather than a bid to solve the crime. When Rosen suggested that any information received on the case should be passed to Kennedy, Hoover wrote "No" across the memo. And when Jackson police removed the murder rifle's scope to process it for fingerprints on 12 June, Hoover penned a note reading: "Well at least they are not using our facilities."[21]

That quickly changed with a police request for FBI examination of the crime scene evidence. The bureau's lab in Washington received the rifle, ammunition from its magazine, the telescopic sight, a partial fingerprint from the scope, and a bullet that had passed through Evers's body before striking his house. Technicians could not match the mutilated slug to any certain weapon, but its composition was consistent with the unfired ammo in the rifle. A photo of the rifle, published nationwide on 13 June, brought a call to Jackson police from Innes McIntyre in Itta Bena, Mississippi. McIntyre thought the weapon was one he had recently sold to a Greenwood "segregation fanatic" named Byron De La Beckwith Jr. Detectives filed the name but kept it from the FBI, while G-men tried in vain to match the partial fingerprint to subjects in the bureau's files. Agents also checked prints of some 300 suspects in Mississippi, but Beckwith's name did not make the list. On 20 June, Hoover informed Attorney General Kennedy that "no logical suspect has been developed as of the present time." A parallel line of investigation tracked the imported telescopic sight from its entry port (Chicago) to a gun shop in Grenada, Mississippi. There, on 21 June, agents reportedly obtained the name of buyer Byron De La Beckwith, pinpointing his address from the Greenwood telephone directory. Comparison of Beckwith's military records to the Jackson fingerprint then identified him as the sniper.[22] It was another triumph for the FBI.

But was it true?

Hoover biographer Curt Gentry notes that identity cannot be proved from a partial fingerprint, even one described as a "fresh" specimen with "moisture along the ridges." Instead, Gentry and others contend, the bureau found Beckwith via less orthodox methods. First, bribes and informants allegedly identified several Mississippians involved in a plot to kill Evers, but the triggerman remained anonymous. Then, according to retired G-man Anthony Villano, agents forged a devil's pact to solve the case. After singling out a Jackson Citizens' Council member involved in the murder conspiracy, FBI agents contacted Gregory Scarpa, a New York mobster facing federal charges of interstate flight to avoid prosecution. They offered Scarpa a free pass in that case if he would help them crack the Evers murder. Scarpa agreed and flew to Miami with a girlfriend, to establish an alibi, then drove from Florida to Jackson and kidnapped the Council suspect. Followed by G-men, Scarpa allegedly took his captive to a remote cabin in Louisiana's bayou country, there torturing the suspect until he confessed his role in the plot and named Beckwith as the sniper. Agents crouched outside an open window, taking notes, then flashed Beckwith's name to Washington, where the fingerprint "match" was contrived. Villano paid Scarpa $1,500 for his services, preserving a receipt, and Scarpa avoided prosecution on the pending charge. When the story broke years later, Scarpa refused to comment on the case. New state and federal indictments sent him to prison in the 1990s.[23]

Whatever the source of their information, FBI agents approached Byron De La Beckwith on 21 June 1963, but he refused to speak with them. At 4:45 P.M. the next day, Justice charged Beckwith with conspiracy under the 1957 Civil Rights Act. Beckwith conferred with lawyer Hardy Lott—Greenwood's city attorney and past president of the local Citizens' Council—before surrendering to G-men at 10:35 P.M. Federal prosecutors dropped their charge after a local grand jury indicted Beckwith for murder on 2 July 1963—his victim's thirty-eighth birthday.[24]

(FBI involvement in the Evers case was not confined to solving the murder. Several agents monitored the victim's funeral for seditious speeches, noting comments by NAACP president Roy Wilkins that condemned "the Southern political system." After police clubbed Tougaloo College professor John Salter during a Jackson protest demonstration, G-men professed themselves unable to identify the officers from films of the event. One headquarters memo described Salter as "a chronic complainant" and "a determined, belligerent, and confused young man ... [who] obviously does not like the FBI." Helpful agents also fed police the anonymous tip that widow Myrlie Evers "had gotten jealous of [actress-singer] Lena Horne and might have gotten her brother-in-law to kill Evers." Detectives pursued the lead, seeking "any loose talk that is going around," and pronounced the victim's next-door neighbor "a sound, sane Negro not addicted to the demonstrations [who] has no part of this movement."[25])

Beckwith was a distant relative of Senator James Eastland and a charter member of the Greenwood Citizens' Council, outspoken in matters of race. On 16 May 1956 he had written a letter to Governor Coleman seeking a job with the State Sovereignty Commission "uncovering plots by the NAACP to intergrate [sic] our beloved State." In that letter, Beckwith described himself as being "expert with a pistol, good with a rifle and fair with a shotgun—and—RABID ON THE SUBJECT OF SEGREGATION!" In 1957, he wrote to the Jackson *Daily News*: "I believe in segregation as I believe in God. I shall combat the evils of integration and shall bend every effort to rid the USA of the integrationist, whoever and wherever he may be." Another letter, to the Memphis *Press-Scimitar*, advised fellow bigots, "Don't waste a lot of time going around asking a lot of fool questions and wondering: 'How are we going to get rid of integration?' You must strike first." Now his rifle had been found at the scene of a racial homicide, and Beckwith's forehead bore a fresh wound from the recoil of its telescopic sight.[26]

The case should have been open-and-shut, but this was 1960s Mississippi. Beck-with enjoyed full support from the Citizens' Council, which established a White Cit-izens' Legal Fund to pay his expenses. His defense team included Hardy Lott and Hugh Cunningham, a partner in the Jackson legal firm to which ex–Governor Bar-nett returned in January 1964. When jury selection began on 27 January, District Attorney William Waller asked each potential venireman, "Do you think it's a crime to kill a nigger in Mississippi?" (Those who had to think about their answer were excused.) Barnett himself visited the courtroom, shaking hands with Beckwith while the jury watched, and Ole Miss agitator Edwin Walker also dropped in to encour-age the defendant. FBI agents testified for the state, building the circumstantial case against Beckwith, but two policemen surprised prosecutors with claims that they had seen Beckwith in Greenwood, 60-odd miles from Jackson, at the time of the shooting. (Neither could explain why the sightings went unreported until Beckwith's trial.) Judge Leon Hendricks declared a mistrial on 7 February 1964, with jurors deadlocked seven to five for acquittal. A second trial ended the same way on 17 April 1964, with the panel deadlocked eight to four in Beckwith's favor. Six months later, Hoover assessed the bureau's performance in the Evers case as follows: "There was certainly good *investigative* work done in this case by our Agts., but at the same time our Laboratory runs true to form in being *inconclusive* on matters checked by it."[27] Still, he could not resist chastising the victim's brother, Charles Evers, when they met briefly in July 1964. As Hoover recalled that conversation:

> I told Mr. Evers that along with his position of aggressive leadership went a responsibility for the truth and observance of all laws. I specifically made the point that the FBI had solved the murder of his brother at great cost and sacrifice, yet we had never hesitated in our quest for solution. I added that despite this hard-earned success, a number of Mr. Evers's followers, both before and after the solution of the murder, had unjustly criticized the FBI. I told him that such tactics are divisive and do nothing to resolve the troublesome issues confronting the American people today. Mr. Evers denied that he or Mrs. Medgar Evers had ever criticized the FBI.[28]

What role, if any, did the Klan or Citizens' Council play in killing Medgar Evers? Soon after the shooting, Klan fliers circulated throughout Mississippi bearing pho-tos of Evers, James Meredith, John Salter, Bob Moses, Emmett Till and other blacks. The pictures of Evers and Till were crossed out. Author Reed Massengill, a relative of Beckwith but no racist himself, contends that Evers "was on a Ku Klux Klan hit list, even though the Klan was not formally organized in Mississippi." Massengill con-cluded that the Evers slaying "may have marked the Klan's unofficial launch in Mis-sissippi." In October 1963, an informant told G-men of a conversation overheard between Beckwith and fellow members of the Greenwood Citizens' Council two or three days before the murder. "They were talking about shooting someone," he recalled. Beckwith had ranted about "goddamned niggers" and said, "I'll do what-ever has to be done. I don't mind shooting the S.O.B." An unidentified companion said, "If someone can do the shooting, I'll do the driving." Agents noted that their informant would not sign a statement, for fear of being murdered. After Beckwith's second mistrial, fiery crosses blazed in several Jackson neighborhoods. Eight months later, on 6 December 1964, informant Delmar Dennis reported the comments of Neshoba County's exalted cyclops, Edgar Killen, to his FBI contacts. According to Dennis, Killen "boasted that the Klan could infiltrate every jury selected in Mississippi. As an example, he cited the slaying of Medgar Evers. He said that this murder was a Klan project and that the Klan protected Beckwith by arranging to have Klansmen on the jury." In December 1990, a member of Beckwith's original jury confirmed rumors that another panel member "was in the pocket of the Klan." FBI files declassified around the same time claimed that "the murder was a Klan hit, with the Citizens' Council implicated as well."[29]

Beckwith himself was certainly a Klansman, though dates and details of his enlistment remain obscure. On 26 June 1963, during a police interrogation, Beckwith told detectives "that we definitely needed a Ku Klux Klan at this time, that it could do a lot of good." (The officers noted that Beckwith was "also way overboard when Masonry is mentioned.") A letter Beckwith wrote from jail in early 1964 declared: "When the KKK needs me enough, then I will be happy to serve them — they've asked me and I haven't said no." Most accounts agree that Beckwith was recruited by Kleagle Gordon Lackey of the Mississippi White Knights, but some versions place his initiation as late as August 1965. Beckwith and Lackey both appeared before the House Committee on Un-American Activities in Washington on 12 January 1966. Both were represented by attorney Travis Buckley, an active member of the White Knights, and both refused to answer all substantive questions. Curiously, Beckwith's subpoena demanded documents from both the White Knights and from Robert Shelton's rival United Klans of America. Congressional sources also linked Beckwith to acts of Klan violence committed in March and May 1965, well before his supposed August initiation.[30]

By the time he went to Washington, Beckwith had been promoted to serve the White Knights as a kleagle. Delmar Dennis recalled that "Beckwith was a recruiting man. He was out getting members all over the state." He also helped publish a pro–Klan newspaper, *The Southern Review,* while serving the KKK as a motivational speaker. At one gathering, convened on 8 August 1965 at a fishing camp run by Klansman L.C. Matthews near Byram, Beckwith told his fellow knights, "Killing that nigger gave me no more inner discomfort than our wives endure when they give birth to our children. We ask them to do that for us. We should do just as much. So, let's get in there and kill those enemies, including the President, from the top down!" After his speech, Beckwith signed autographs for the faithful — including one obtained by Dennis and delivered to his FBI handlers with a report of Beckwith's self-incriminating comments. Agent Tom Van Riper remembered that report years later, and Beckwith's FBI file listed "several different sources" who described the speech. At another meeting, in Laurel, Beckwith told Klansmen that he had sworn "a Shriner's oath" to kill Charles Evers, as well.[31]

It was doubly curious, then, that G-men kept silent on 19 June 1966, when D.A. William Waller informed the bureau that he could not try Beckwith for murder again unless he received substantial new evidence. A public confession should have done the trick, but Hoover and company suppressed the 1965 reports. On 13 July 1966, a memo from Jackson to FBI headquarters revealed more startling evidence from a "reliable" informant in the Mississippi Klan. That source described a conversation with Gordon Lackey in which Lackey boasted of helping Beckwith murder Evers. According to the memo, Lackey said "that he and Beckwith made two or three trips to the [Evers] residence in order to determine his actions and activities and to make necessary plans. In each instance they used a white or light colored Valiant, which was also used on the night of the shooting." Lackey further "stated that he and Beckwith were hiding in some bushes near Evers's home and shot him when he returned to his residence late one night." Finally, the informant said, "Lackey stated, 'They got the wrong man. Beckwith did not do the shooting.'" The same memo noted that G-men had questioned Lackey as a suspect in June 1963, then dismissed him after two National Guardsmen said they were drinking with Lackey in Hattiesburg on the night of the murder.[32]

J. Edgar Hoover was impressed with the 13 July report. Eight days later, he sent Jackson agent-in-charge Roy Moore a cable that read: "In view of the importance of this case and the importance of the information furnished by this informant, it is felt that every effort should be made to induce him to become a willing witness at this time." Moore offered cash, but no amount of money could persuade the still-unnamed informant to testify. He rejected each new bid with the remark that he "loved life" and would not risk it on a public move against the Klan or Beckwith. G-men kept the secret from state prosecutors, and the Evers case was not reopened for another quarter-century.[33]

Meanwhile, Beckwith had turned his hand to politics, seeking election as Mississippi's lieutenant governor in 1967. Adopting the slogan "He's a Straight-Shooter," Beckwith campaigned for office on a platform of "absolute white supremacy under white Christian rule." He seemed to take the race seriously, but the Klan leaders who bankrolled it viewed the crusade as a flamboyant recruiting device. "He was conned into it," one knight told author Adam Nossiter. "I was given a large sum of money to finance the campaign. They were using him. I guess it was just a big joke." In the end, Beckwith polled only five percent of the statewide vote tally.[34]

If the loss discouraged him, Beckwith concealed the fact with rare self-discipline, continuing his labors on behalf of various hate groups. In 1973 he addressed the NSRP's annual convention, and September of that year found Beckwith at a Citizens' Council rally in Jackson, where Alabama's George Wallace delivered the keynote address. Three weeks later, an informant warned Al Binder — a Jewish attorney in Jackson — of a Klan plot against A.I. Botnick, the Anti-Defamation League's chief spokesman in New Orleans. Binder and an FBI agent were present when Beckwith met Klansman L.E. Matthews at a Jackson café, then followed Matthews to his home. A third Klansman, bureau informant Gordon Clark, stood by while Matthews constructed a bomb and showed Beckwith how to arm it. Clark furnished Agent Thompson Webb with Beckwith's itinerary, and Louisiana police stopped Beckwith's car outside New Orleans. In addition to the bomb, they seized three rifles, a pistol, and a map of New Orleans with the route to Botnick's home traced in red ink.[35]

Beckwith denied any knowledge of the bomb in his car, suggesting that the explosives were planted by persons unknown, either to frame or kill him. A wealthy Greenwood businessman posted Beckwith's $36,000 bail, and another flew him home to Mississippi on a private plane. At Beckwith's federal trial for conspiracy and illegal interstate transportation of explosives, Botnick's secretary described Beckwith's visit to the ADL office on 13 September 1973, asking questions about her employer. A jury of 11 whites and one black acquitted Beckwith of all charges on 20 January 1974, leaving the stunned judge to tell Beckwith, "You have literally walked through the valley of the shadow of death. You are a very lucky man." That luck ran out in May 1975, when Beckwith faced an all-black jury on state charges of transporting dynamite without a permit. The second panel convicted Beckwith, and he received the maximum five-year sentence. An appellate court rejected his appeal in May 1977, but Beckwith missed his surrender date, causing officers to arrest him as a fugitive. In March 1978, Beckwith wrote a letter from prison to *The Tribal Chronicle,* a newspaper published by Aryan Nations leader Richard Butler. In that correspondence, Beckwith discussed his "accused" membership in "the top super secret White Knights of the KKK of Mississippi.... Now a White Knight looks at all other KKK groups as Boy Scouts or Cub Scouts or John Birchers at the most — I think — I really don't know. Ha! But I mix and mingle with all KKK groups."[36]

State authorities reopened the Evers case in autumn 1989, by which time Beckwith had moved to southeastern Tennessee. On 9 January 1990, Agent Al Waites of the Jackson field office told prosecutor Bobby DeLaughter, "The FBI wants to cooperate in every way, but it has certain policies and procedures." Four months later, DeLaughter requested "all reports and information" on informant Delmar Dennis, supporting the plea with a signed release from Dennis himself. In September 1990, Waites produced "mountains of reports," cleared for release to DeLaughter as soon as Waites excised "any information regarding any federal grand jury or information concerning informants." When reminded that such data was the one thing DeLaughter needed, Waites cited "bureau procedure" to demand a second release from Dennis.[37] A decade later, DeLaughter recounted his Kafkaesque conversation with Waites:

Waites: I can safely tell you that what you wanted concerning Delmar Dennis is not in there, but there is something else regarding another informant that would be of great interest and benefit to you. But I can't let you have that.

DeLaughter: Al, please tell me what I need to do to get clearance for the information that will help me.

Waites: You write a letter asking for it.

DeLaughter: I did that almost a year ago.

Waites: You didn't ask specifically for this.

DeLaughter: I asked for *everything* concerning Beckwith and Medgar Evers.

Waites: You can't ask for it generally like that. It has to be a specific request.

DeLaughter: Okay, tell me what it is. You don't have to show me anything now or let me copy anything.

Waites: I can't. You don't have clearance for me to tell you.

DeLaughter: How can I possibly be expected to ask for something with specificity if you don't tell me what I need to specifically ask for?

Waites: I see the bind you're in, but it's bureau policy.[38]

Waites finally let DeLaughter read various reports, in which all names but Beck-with's were blacked out, yet a request for copies was denied. Waites also "read aloud a few things from an outline his analyst had prepared from a review of those reports," which DeLaughter was not privileged to see. The gradual release of heavily censored FBI documents continued through April 1992, including a surprise revelation that Klan bomb-maker L.E. Matthews was also an FBI informant. A May 1966 report from Delmar Dennis declared that "Beckwith wants people to know he is a member of the Klan and furthermore he wants people to know that he got away with mur-der." Mary Adams, an IRS employee, met Beckwith in 1967 and recalled that "he openly bragged that he had killed Medgar Evers." Louisiana prison inmate Lester Hockman served time with Beckwith and shared "critical information" on the Evers slaying while collaborating with G-men on an unrelated case. Specifically, Beckwith named another Klansman who ordered the murder, "as well as several bombings that resulted in the deaths of innocent persons." Beckwith allegedly told Hockman that "he had watched Evers's house for some time before the shooting" and "that he alone had shot Medgar Evers." Informant Matthews reported that while planning the Bot-nick bombing in 1973, "Beckwith told Matthews it had taken him about five weeks to get lined up on Medgar Evers, to which Matthews responded that Beckwith had botched the job — that after all the planning, he had to go off and leave his gun at the scene.... Beckwith claimed that he hid the gun ... and that he probably would have been all right if the previous owner of the gun had not gone to the prosecuting attorney's office and reported that he had sold it to Beckwith."[39]

Beckwith's third murder trial began on 27 January 1994, 30 years to the day from the beginning of his first. Bailiffs ejected a lone Klansman who came to honor Beck-with, and the case proceeded without further incident. New evidence included the testimony from six witnesses describing Beckwith's murder boasts. Delmar Dennis appeared for the state, followed by his former FBI handler. Ex-agent Tom Van Riper explained why the bureau had concealed Beckwith's 1965 confession, saving Dennis for a triple-murder case in Neshoba County. "That was the most important thing going at the time," Van Riper said. "The FBI would never have blown an informer as important" as Dennis on the Evers case. Another informant, Dick Davis, recalled a conversation with Beckwith in October 1969. After discussing a mutual friend in the United Klans, Beckwith identified himself as a member of the "White Knights of the Camellia in Mississippi" and spoke "brightly" about killing Jews. Mark Reiley, a Louisiana correctional officer, recounted Beckwith's confrontation with a black prison nurse. "If I could get rid of an uppity nigger like Medgar Evers," Beckwith told her, "I can get rid of a no-account nigger like you." Beckwith had often boasted to the prison staff about his powerful connections, once telling Reiley that "if he was lying and didn't have the power and connections he said he had, he would be serving time in prison for getting rid of that nigger Medgar Evers."[40]

After 90 minutes of deliberation, a jury of eight black and four whites convicted Beckwith on 5 February 1994. Judge Breland Hilburn sentenced Beckwith to a life term in state prison, where he died on 19 January 2001, at age 80.[41] Beckwith's con-viction paved the way for other long-delayed prosecutions, even as it raised new crit-icism of the FBI's role in obstructing justice.

6

Dixie Burning

The year 1964 was pivotal for America's civil rights movement and for the crusade's white opponents. Dramatic campaigns were launched in the South, aided by new federal legislation, while Klansmen waged guerrilla warfare from the Carolinas to Louisiana. Hoover's FBI was finally, reluctantly compelled to move against the KKK, but only after more lives had been sacrificed.

Reviewing that tumultuous year from a comfortable retirement three decades after the fact, Deputy FBI Director Cartha Deloach said that "[t]he Klan in the 1960s was not a large organization.... For a while, the revived Klan numbered no more than a few hundred men in Mississippi." In fact, Deloach's statement addressed only one of 15 Klans active in 1964, Mississippi's White Knights of the KKK, which started small but claimed a peak membership of 10,000 by early 1965. Overall estimates of Klan membership in 1964 typically fall between 40,000 and 50,000 knights. Deloach also ignored the evidence of history and FBI investigation with his claim that "[c]ontrary to popular myth, the Klan had little success recruiting members among state and local lawmen."[1] Throughout the South, from Reconstruction to the 1980s, Klan infiltration of police departments posed a major threat to public safety—and events in 1964 would emphasize that well-known fact.

"A Segregated Super-Bomb"

Racial tensions had simmered in northern Florida since mid-1963, when Dr. R.N. Hayling's NAACP chapter launched a campaign to integrate St. Augustine. White residents of the nation's oldest city cherished their racist history, preserving St. Augustine's antebellum slave market as a tourist attraction while maintaining segregation in every walk of life, from cradle to grave. Klansmen held their first modern rally outside town on 18 September 1963, gathering in white-robed finery to hear the Rev. Charles "Connie" Lynch attack Hayling and praise Alabama's church bombers. Hayling and three other blacks were caught while spying on the rally, viciously beaten and doused with gasoline in preparation for burning, while an observer–the Rev. Irvin Cheney, of Florida's Council on Human Relations—fled to telephone the FBI and the sheriff's office. G-men ignored the call, but Sheriff L.O. Davis arrived in time to arrest four Jacksonville Klansmen and to charge the victims with assault. At trial, white jurors acquitted the knights and convicted Hayling of attacking his would-be killers. The NAACP's call for a federal investigation went unanswered, though the U.S. Civil Rights Commission pronounced St. Augustine's racial situation "considerably worse than in most if not all other cities in the state."[2]

A primary source of violence in St. Augustine was Holstead "Hoss" Manucy's Ancient City Hunting Club (ACHC), organized sometime in 1961 or '62. Manucy denied any formal links to the Klan, but other sources note that the KKK and ACHC "worked intimately together." Federal reports went further yet: FBI memos named Manucy as the Klan's exalted cyclops for St. Augustine, and a congressional report identified the ACHC as a front for Klavern 519 of the United Florida Ku Klux Klan. Federal judge Bryan Simpson declared in June 1964 that the Klan and ACHC were "one and the same thing." Manucy often claimed that his Catholicism barred him from the KKK, but some Florida factions dropped their ban on Catholics in the 1950s, and Jesse Stoner later admitted that "there was some overlap" in membership between the two organizations. On 25 October 1963, when armed ACHC members circled the home of NAACP leader Goldie Eubanks, a shot from the darkness killed nightrider William Kinard and put his friends to flight. Three nights later, another caravan returned, firing into black homes and business establishments, lobbing a hand grenade (which failed to explode) at the Harlem Gardens nightclub. Klan minister Connie Lynch presided at Kinard's funeral, and the pallbearers included Manucy, three Klan officials, and a spokesman for the National States Rights Party. Eubanks, his son and a neighbor were charged with Kinard's murder, but a "key witness" vanished in November and the case was dropped.[3]

Sheriff Davis was also a friend of the Klan. While he denied joining the hooded order, saying that "the initiation is so horrible that I don't believe I could stand it," he hosted Klan meetings in his office and loaned official vehicles to visiting out-of-town knights. Davis was friendly with Stoner and Lynch, prompting *Life* magazine to report that many (if not all) of his part-time "special deputies" were Klansmen. The sheriff denied that charge as well but admitted deputizing members of the Ancient City Hunting Club, and Manucy (a convicted bootlegger) served Davis as a "liaison officer" to local vigilantes. "If whites got too rowdy," Davis explained, "Hoss would get 'em in line." Restraint was not an issue with the sheriff, though; in fact, he was notorious for brutal treatment of black prisoners in general and civil rights protesters in particular. Judge Simpson condemned Davis's techniques in June 1964, proclaiming from the bench: "More than cruel and unusual punishment is shown. Here is exposed, in its raw ugliness, studied and cynical brutality, deliberately contrived to break men physically and mentally." The FBI, whose files included evidence of Sheriff Davis helping Klansmen hide a federal fugitive, failed to pursue a case against the rogue lawman.[4]

Violence increased in St. Augustine during the latter weeks of 1963 and early 1964. Gunfire and arson became commonplace as Klansmen battled efforts to desegregate the city's schools, motels and restaurants. A local grand jury blamed the incidents on "two outside militant elements"— the KKK and NAACP — though only one used violence, and both drew members from the local populace. Mayhem accelerated in March 1964, when the SCLC launched its "Florida Spring Project" in St.

Augustine, and peaked in June with a series of free-wheeling riots led by Klansmen, spurred by the inflammatory rhetoric of agitators Lynch and Stoner. The Civil Rights Commission called St. Augustine a "segregated super-bomb ... [with a] short fuse," and Dr. Martin Luther King dubbed it "the most lawless city I have ever seen." Judge Simpson finally stepped in, barring official interference with nonviolent protests, and Hoss Manucy spent an hour in jail before complying with Simpson's order to name his "club" members. Even then, he proved evasive, picking names at random from the telephone directory, but he escaped official sanction. Stoner, Lynch and three other knights were briefly detained for illegally burning a cross on private property, but otherwise the violent Klansmen of St. Augustine went unpunished.[5]

Jacksonville was the modern Klan's traditional Florida stronghold. With six active klaverns in 1964, the city harbored knights who had forged a close relationship with Mayor Haydon Burns, backing his race that year for the governor's mansion. Connie Lynch claimed membership in Jacksonville Klavern 502 of the United Florida KKK, and his hell-fire rhetoric fairly represented the militancy of Duval County's knights. In September 1963, after six-year-old Donald Godfrey breached the all-white bastion of Lackawana Elementary School, Klansmen stole 13 cases of dynamite from local construction sites and used some of the 2,145 sticks to make crude fragmentation grenades that they hurled at the Jacksonville NAACP office and a black-owned liquor store. Chief among the militants was Indiana transplant William Rosecrans, recruited by Exalted Cyclops Bart Griffin "to fight niggers." Rosecrans was driving on 6 February 1964 when fellow Klansman Robert Gentry fired shotgun blasts at a black truck driver (afterward saying that he missed deliberately). Ten days later, it was also Rosecrans who planted a bomb at the Godfrey home, demolishing most of the house. In the wake of that blast Rosecrans fled to St. Augustine, where he found work in a boatyard under an assumed name. FBI reports said that Sheriff Davis "was also instrumental in helping the Klan hide" Rosecrans, but he was never charged.[6]

Ironically, despite the tacit official sanction of racial violence in St. Augustine, the city proved too hot for Rosecrans. FBI agents were under pressure to solve a 27 February bombing of the strikebound Florida East Coast Railway. The bombing occurred during a visit by President Lyndon Johnson, and the reward the FBI offered bore some unexpected fruit. Sheriff Davis offered Hoss Manucy a share of the reward, and Manucy mistakenly fingered Rosecrans as the railroad bomber. A polygraph test absolved Rosecrans in that crime but pointed to his guilt in other cases. Charged with the Godfrey bombing on 3 March 1964, he confessed and named accomplices, prompting a series of arrests in Jacksonville. Those charged with conspiracy included Klansmen Bart Griffin, Robert Gentry, Jacky Harden, Donald Spegal and Willie Wilson. Rosecrans pled guilty on 13 March and received a seven-year sentence on 17 April. His komrades faced trial in federal court on 30 June, two days before President Johnson signed a new civil rights act into law. Attorney Jesse Stoner contended that G-men had framed his clients, thus persuading jurors to acquit Gentry and Harden on 5 July, and the jury deadlocked on their codefendants. A second panel acquitted the remaining knights on 25 November 1964, leaving Rosecrans to serve his time alone.[7]

"A Ticket to the Eternal"

If Florida presented stiff resistance to desegregation, Mississippi was a veritable fortress, pledged to maintenance of white supremacy at any cost. Paul Johnson, fresh from the Ole Miss debacle and a federal contempt citation, was elected governor in 1963 after he stumped the state with speeches branding the NAACP a collection of "Niggers, Apes, Alligators, Coons and Possums." Proponents of a new civil rights offensive joined forces in January 1964 to create the Council of Federated Organizations (COFO), made up of representatives from CORE, SNCC, SCLC and the NAACP. At the same time, a new Mississippi Freedom Democratic Party (MFDP) organized to challenge the state's all-white delegation to the Democratic National Convention. Together, COFO and MFDP laid plans for a "Freedom Summer" that would radically change life in the Magnolia State.[8]

Opposing that "invasion" were Governor Johnson, the State Sovereignty Commission, thousands of white lawmen, the Citizens' Council — and a reborn Ku Klux Klan. As previously noted, kleagles from Louisiana's Original Knights of the KKK enlisted their first Mississippi converts sometime in 1963. Grand Dragon E.L. McDaniel of Natchez led a dissident faction that reorganized as White Knights of the KKK in February 1964. He was replaced two months later by Samuel Bowers from Laurel. McDaniel emerged in April 1964 as Grand Dragon of the UKA's Mississippi realm, competing with Bowers for members and headlines. On 24 April 1964, cross-burnings were reported in 64 of the state's 82 counties, with membership in the White Knights climbing toward 10,000 at year's end. A front group established by Bowers, called Americans for Preservation of the White Race, claimed 30,000 members— including numerous lawmen — by late 1964. Edgar Killen, the exalted cyclops of Neshoba County, visited Senator James Eastland's home in Doddsville "very, very frequently," but the modern Mississippi KKK had little interest in politics. A bulletin issued by Bowers on 3 May 1964 described his Klan as "the physical Spear upon which the enemy will either impale himself and perish, or sweep aside, then to proceed almost unhindered in his evil work of destroying civilization." All knights were advised to "roll with the mass punch which they will deliver in the streets during the day, and ... counterattack the individual leaders at night.... [A]ttacks against these selected, individual targets should, of course, be as severe as circumstances and conditions will permit." A later leaflet warned: "We are not going to sit back and permit our rights to be negotiated away by a group of Jewish priests, bluegum black savages and mongrelized money worshippers. We will buy you a ticket to the Eternal if you insist."[9]

Before that bloody summer ended, Klansmen made good on their threats. Between May and September 1964, at least seven blacks and two white civil rights workers were murdered in Mississippi; three other activists were wounded by gunfire; 35 other shootings were reported; at least 80 victims were beaten; 68 buildings were bombed or burned (including 37 churches); and ten cars were damaged or destroyed. No part of Mississippi was secure for "race-mixers," but the epicenters of white terror were McComb (with 25 attacks) and Greenwood (home of Byron De La Beckwith).[10] No such concentrated plague of mayhem had been seen in Dixie since the days of Reconstruction after the Civil War.

The first to die in Mississippi's new race war was Louis Allen, witness to the death of Herbert Lee in Liberty in 1961. G-men had shunned Allen while leaking details of his confidential statement to the Amite County sheriff's office — and thus, in effect, to local terrorists. Allen endured two years of harassment, including a May 1962 incident in which a deputy sheriff threatened his life, fractured his jaw, then arrested Allen and fined him $17.50 for "interfering with the law." Allen reported that attack to the FBI, but agents did nothing. In autumn 1963, E.W. Steptoe's wife warned Allen of a plot against his life, and Allen finally decided to leave Mississippi. White employers refused him references on grounds that they "might be helping a communist," but Allen forged ahead with his departure plans. On 31 January 1964 — the day before he was scheduled to leave for Wisconsin and the first day of Byron De La Beckwith's murder trial — gunmen killed Allen in his driveway. FBI agents made no appearance on the scene, and a coroner's jury blamed the slaying on "an unknown assailant." Days later, the McComb *Enterprise-Journal* published a rumor that Allen "may have become a 'tip-off man' for the integration-minded Justice Department."[11]

Whippings of Mississippi blacks by hooded nightriders began in mid-February 1964 in Adams and Lincoln Counties. Several sources also refer to the Klan murder of a black Centreville resident on 29 February 1964, but none provide the victim's name, and no further details are now available. On 30 May 1964 in Neshoba County, Sheriff Lawrence Rainey and Deputy Cecil Price (both Klansmen) arrested black teen-ager Wilmer Jones on suspicion of telephoning a white girl. After Jones had spent several hours in jail, the officers released him to a gang of White Knights who drove him to a rural shack and questioned him at length about his nonexistent "civil rights activities."[12]

By the time that incident occurred, Klansmen had already killed two more victims. On 2 May 1964, they kidnapped two black Meadville students, Henry Dee and Charles Moore, to question them about rumors of Black Muslims stockpiling guns around Natchez. There were no Muslims and no guns, thus nothing to confess. Unsatisfied, the knights beat their two victims unconscious, then drove them across the border to Louisiana and dropped their weighted bodies in the Mississippi River near Tallulah. Moore's mother reported her son missing on 4 May, whereupon the Franklin County sheriff informed her that both young men were staying with a relative of Dee's in Louisiana. That lie collapsed on 12 July 1964, when a fisherman found part of a decomposed corpse in the river. More remains were discovered that day and the next in the midst of a search for three Klan victims murdered in Neshoba County. G-men arrested two White Knights from Meadville, Charles Edwards and James Seale, on 6 November 1964. Edwards signed a confession, implicating Seale and other suspects, but state murder charges were quickly dismissed. FBI agents did not pursue the case, although they had clear jurisdiction. If Dee and Moore were killed in Louisiana, their slayers should have been tried under the Lindbergh Law; if the victims died in Mississippi, it was *still* a federal case, since they were beaten on U.S. government land in the Homochitto National Forest. More than 35 years later, in January 2000, FBI spokesmen announced a reopening of the case, but no charges had been filed when this volume went to press in 2005.[13]

FBI headquarters paid little attention to the Mississippi Klan in early 1964. As late as 12 June, Hoover ordered all field offices to identify college students who joined COFO and check their names against bureau files for "subversive" associations. Hoover's agents were assisted in that effort by the Mississippi Highway Patrol, which claimed to have dossiers on "all known agitators in the state." Zack Van Landingham, a G-man for 27 years before he joined Mississippi's racist State Sovereignty Commission, also "turned over information on subversives to the FBI." Agents would follow student volunteers back to their homes when they left Mississippi, grilling those who criticized the FBI in public. Bureau files reveal descriptions of the volunteers as "immature, unreliable and obnoxious."[14]

Two summer volunteers who rated bureau files were James Chaney and Michael Schwerner in Meridian. Chaney was black, a Meridian native already active in CORE when the Freedom Summer began. Schwerner was every Klansman's *bête noire*, a liberal Jewish New Yorker whose beard earned him the nickname "Goatee." Already marked for death as the full-scale "invasion" began, Schwerner drove Chaney north to Oxford, Ohio, for a COFO training seminar on 14 June 1964. There, they met volunteer Andrew Goodman, an anthropology student from Queens College in New York City. The trio reached Meridian on 20 June, and there learned of the latest Klan atrocity. Four days earlier, a hooded raiding party had attacked the all-black congregation of Mt. Zion Church in Longdale, beating several worshipers before they burned the church. G-men interviewed the victims on 19 June and filed a report with the New Orleans field office, then resumed their investigation of civil rights workers. Schwerner, Chaney and Goodman drove to Longdale on 21 June, but they never made it back. Arrested by Deputy Price in Neshoba County, they were held in jail in Philadelphia while a Klan lynching party gathered. Price released the prisoners after nightfall, then stopped them again outside town and delivered them to his fellow knights. The three were shot, then buried in an earthen dam on a farm owned by Klansman Olen Burrage.[15]

The triple disappearance sounded national alarms. Before midnight on 21 June, COFO workers in Meridian telephoned FBI resident agent Hunter Helgeson in Jackson to report the trio missing. Helgeson curtly informed the caller "that the FBI is not a police force." When another volunteer called back, Helgeson "took in the information curtly and did not allow a chance for further conversation." NAACP leader Aaron Henry received similar treatment. On 22 June, Justice attorney John Doar promised SNCC spokesmen that the FBI would "look into the matter." Meridian resident agent John Proctor visited Cecil Price that afternoon, but his "investigation" was brief, ending with a drink of confiscated bootleg liquor in the Klansman's patrol car. Attorney General Kennedy, meanwhile, had lost all faith in Hoover, whom he termed "senile" and "rather a psycho," the "frightening" chief of "a very dangerous organization." Since the JFK assassination in November 1963, Kennedy understood that Hoover "no longer had to pay attention to me; and it was in the interest, evidently of … President Johnson to have that kind of arrangement and relationship." Johnson, for his part, despised Kennedy and feared Hoover. In regard to Mississippi's Freedom Summer, Johnson observed, "There are three sovereignties involved. There's the United States and there's the state of Mississippi and there's J. Edgar Hoover."[16]

Still, Washington could not ignore the disappearances. President Johnson dispatched former CIA boss Allen Dulles to Jackson on 23 June, and the bureau's New Orleans field office sent an inspector and five more agents to join in the search, code-named "MIBURN" (for "Mississippi Burning"). That same afternoon, Klan crony Al Lingo announced that witnesses had seen the missing volunteers cheerfully munching cheeseburgers in Marion, Alabama, but the fable collapsed by day's end, when Schwerner's burned-out car was found in Neshoba County's Bogue Chitto Swamp. On 24 June, Assistant Director Al Rosen arrived from FBI headquarters with a team of lab technicians, ready for a "full-court press" to find the missing men. Three busloads of U.S. Navy seamen joined the search on 25 June, dragging murky rivers while state highway patrolmen watched from the shore and shouted out helpful advice: "If you want to find that damn nigger, just float a relief check out there. That black bastard will reach up and grab it." In Jackson, Schwerner's widow confronted Governor Johnson and a visitor, Alabama's George Wallace. She arrived just as Johnson told reporters, "Governor Wallace and I are the only two people who know where they are, and we're not telling." When Rita Schwerner informed Allen Dulles of Johnson's remark, Dulles insisted she must be mistaken. She repeated the governor's comment, whereupon an FBI bystander chastised her for being "impertinent." Klan wizard Robert Shelton, meanwhile, dropped in for a personal "inspection tour," assuring journalists that "my people will continue the investigation."[17]

At Justice, Burke Marshall hatched a plan for FBI infiltration of the KKK and passed it to Attorney General Kennedy. Kennedy, in turn, relayed the plan to President Johnson. Noting that "the information gathering techniques used by the Bureau on Communist or Communist related organizations have of course been spectacularly efficient," Kennedy went on:

> The unique difficulty that seems to me to be presented by the situation in Mississippi ... is in gathering information on fundamentally lawless activities which have the sanction of local law enforcement agencies, political officials, and a substantial segment of the white population. The techniques followed in the use of specially trained, special assignment agents in the infiltration of Communist groups should be of value. If you approve, I recommend taking up with the Bureau the possibility of developing a similar effort to meet this new problem. It might be desirable to ask for a report to you by the end of the month giving in detail what information the Bureau had been able to develop in the various counties of Mississippi on the members of the Klan group and of the Americans for the Preservation of the White Race, or any similar organizations, as well as their present activities and plans for the immediate future.[18]

Confronted with an ultimatum from the White House, Hoover could only obey. By 30 June he had 100 G-men prowling the Magnolia State, identifying Klansmen and their allies, but his clean-cut agents could not do the job alone. Neshoba County, for example, was a region whose official history boasted that "she enjoyed the largest annual per capita consumption of snuff and chewing tobacco of any county in the country." Klansmen controlled the sheriff's office and the Philadelphia police force, thereby ruling out federal collaboration with local authorities. Under those circumstances, Hoover launched a two-pronged attack. On 2 July 1964, he sent 50 more agents into Mississippi, including a muscular squad dubbed the "Big Ten," so-called "because of the agents' size and their readiness to overlook such niceties as 'due process' in getting answers from Klan leaders." Simultaneously, Hoover authorized recruitment of paid informants to create "the best intelligence system possible" and identify every Klansman in the state. That same day, President Johnson signed the 1964 Civil Rights Act, saddling Hoover with responsibility for investigating racial discrimination in public accommodations, facilities and education.[19]

Even as he implemented Burke Marshall's plan to infiltrate the Klan, Hoover wrote letters to Governor Johnson and to Mississippi's U.S. senators, informing them that the bureau would open a full-time field office in Jackson on 10 July 1964, "so that we can keep in even closer contact and cooperate more fully with the Mississippi law enforcement agencies." G-man Roy Moore was drafted to serve as agent-in-charge, so pressed for time that he was forced to fabricate a mock-up office for Hoover's arrival on 10 July. False walls and borrowed furniture created the illusion on the second floor of an uncompleted bank in Jackson, with two New Orleans bureau secretaries posing as receptionists. Hoover played to the cameras, and one reporter leaned against a flimsy wall and almost brought the stage set crashing down on the director's head. Once Hoover left, the dummy office was demolished and construction on the real one proceeded at a more leisurely pace. In keeping with the grand illusion, Hoover lavished praise on Governor Johnson, calling him "a man I have long admired from a distance" and saying that Johnson "was most outspoken in deploring the violence which had occurred in his state. He emphasized that as long as he sat in the governor's chair, ignorance, hatred, and prejudice would not take over in his state." At their private meeting, Hoover handed Johnson a list of Mississippi lawmen in the Klan, including several members of the state Highway Patrol. Johnson promised to fire those offenders at once, though sheriffs and city policemen were beyond his reach as governor. Hoover's public claim that Mississippi harbored only 480 Klansmen — and that every one had been interrogated by his agents—combined gross understatement with wishful thinking.[20]

The Klan was not intimidated by Hoover's fleeting photo opportunity. Within a week of the director's visit, nightriders burned seven more churches across Mississippi, for a total of 16 since June. Threats against G-men were so common that Hoover made Jackson a "voluntary office," while allegedly instructing agents in the field to meet any challenge from Klansmen head-on. Don Whitehead and other bureau-approved authors describe numerous high-noon confrontations with gun-toting knights who always backed down in the face of steely-eyed FBI courage, but the stories are invariably stripped of names and other details necessary for substantiation. Otherwise, it was business as usual in the Magnolia State. Klan victims complained that bureau agents "questioned them in an accusatory and skeptical manner," while treating white police "with deference and respect." Author Sanford Ungar observes that "the agents did not like, or approve of, the civil rights workers, and they were disinclined to risk a deterioration of their good working relationship with local police." Coahoma County's sheriff was a case in point, telling reporters, "The FBI comes in here everyday and we have coffee everyday. We're good friends." Meanwhile, Neil Welch — Jackson's assistant agent-in-charge — declared that "a few Civil Rights Division attorneys actually manufactured" brutality complaints against Mississippi policemen.[21]

The FBI's main focus in Mississippi during summer 1964 was to find the missing trio from Meridian. The discovery of other corpses—including those of Ku Klux victims Dee and Moore — was strictly incidental. Alex Rosen made the bureau's priority clear in a memo to headquarters, dated 31 July 1964:

> The FBI is interested in but one thing at this time and that [is] to find the victims. If such information came directly to the FBI or through an intermediary or through any other imaginable means, we would be interested only in having pinpointed for us the location of the bodies of the victims if they were dead, and we would then have to establish that the victims were the individuals being sought. Once we established that the victims were actually recovered we would then pay a substantial amount of money, indicated to be from $5,000 to $30,000. In addition to this we pointed out that money was no object, as our primary objective at this time was to locate the victims.[22]

The bid paid off on 4 August 1964, after 44 days of fruitless interviews and searching. That morning, G-men equipped with heavy machinery invaded the Burrage farm and unearthed the hidden corpses as if they had a map of their location — which they did. Directions were provided by a still-unnamed White Knights informant who received either $25,000 or $30,000 for the information (reports vary). Either way, the FBI considered it a bargain. "We'd have paid a lot more if we'd had to," one agent admitted. "We'd have paid anything." FBI technicians soon discovered that Goodman and Schwerner both died from one pistol shot to the chest, and Chaney had been shot three times with a different weapon. Chaney had also suffered other injuries, consistent either with a savage beating or with damage from the bulldozer that uncovered his corpse. Despite that scientific evidence, a local coroner's jury that convened on 25 August refused to list a cause of death for any of the three victims.[23]

By that time, agents were distracted from their manhunt by another White House order. President Johnson wanted round-the-clock surveillance of the Mississippi Freedom Democratic Party's delegation to the Democratic National Convention, meeting from 24 to 26 August 1964 in Atlantic City, New Jersey. Hoover cheerfully obliged, sending Cartha Deloach with a team of specialists to bug the delegates' hotel rooms and tap their telephones. Other G-men "counseled" presidential aides on means of barring MFDP members from the convention floor. Upon completion of that illegal errand, Hoover told Deloach that LBJ "thought the job the Bureau had done in Atlantic City was one of the finest [he] had ever seen." Furthermore, "There were a lot of bad elements up there and because of the work some of the Bureau people did [Johnson's aides] knew exactly where they were and what they were doing." Thirty years after the fact, Deloach admitted that "the line between national security and political activism had been blurred" in Atlantic City. That should not have surprised Deloach, an agent with 22 years in the bureau who had worked at Hoover's side since 1953, yet he declared, "We felt we had been compromised. At that point I resolved never to be used again in that fashion. But I found it was a resolution I could not keep." In fact, Deloach accepted a "meritorious award" from Hoover for his work in Atlantic City and remained as Hoover's third-in-command until July 1970, when he retired to become a vice president of Pepsi-Cola Corporation.[24]

Violence continued unabated in Mississippi while G-men slowly gathered evidence against the Neshoba County killers. Shootings and beatings were routine, and August saw sixteen more arson and bombing attacks. Hooded knights invaded the home of an MFDP member in Oak Ridge, beating three residents and riddling the walls with gunfire. Fifteen Klansmen disrupted a black picnic outside Laurel, pummeling several victims and firing shots overhead as they fled. In McComb, they kidnapped a white man who befriended blacks and abused him for three hours. Police also participated in the terror with no apparent fear of federal intervention. Neimiah Montgomery, an elderly, unarmed black man, was killed by patrolmen in Marigold for arguing with a white gas station attendant who short-changed him. In Aberdeen, after a COFO Freedom House was tear-gassed by nightriders, police disposed of the canisters before G-men could check fingerprints. A black resident of Cleveland, Mississippi, said that Police Chief W.H. Griffin had offered him $300 to "get rid of" voter registration workers. Officers in Columbus jailed a civil rights attorney for "reckless driving" after white thugs forced his car off the road. In Canton on 26 August, shots were fired from a city patrol car at COFO volunteers on three occasions. Through it all, G-men remained impassive, and Hoover openly sided with Mississippi's whites. In an interview with the *Jackson Daily News*, the director termed himself a "states' righter," praised the Mississippi Highway Patrol, and denounced "the harsh approach toward Mississippi taken by the Justice Department during the past three years." For the record, he added, "We don't guard anybody. We are fact-finders. The FBI can't wet-nurse everybody who goes down and tries to reform or educate Negroes in the South." In Jackson, SNCC workers hung a new sign in their office. It read: "There is a place in Mississippi called Liberty; There is a department in Washington called Justice."[25]

Neshoba County judge O.H. Barnett convened a local grand jury to investigate the triple murder in September 1964. He cabled bureau headquarters in Washington, requesting that all agents having knowledge of the crime present themselves for questioning on 28 September. Cartha Deloach drafted an answer, signed by Hoover, which explained that agents working on the case "have been instructed by the acting attorney general not to disclose before that grand jury any information relating to material or information contained in the files of the Department of Justice, or any information obtained in connection with any official Department of Justice investigation." In fact, Hoover was fearful of unmasking his informants, as he had been in the Emmett Miller bombing case in Little Rock. Contributing to his decision was the fact that Judge Barnett was an outspoken white supremacist, a cousin of ex–Governor Ross Barnett, and a blood relative of several suspects in the case. He may, in fact, have been a Klansman. As noted in a memo from Roy Moore to Hoover, written on 3 December 1964, "A Klansman judge is unlikely to disqualify himself or to eliminate Klan members as an impediment to service on a grand jury or petit jury."[26]

While that drama evolved in Neshoba County, a federal grand jury convened in Biloxi to review the case. It named no killers, but on 2 October 1964 the panel indicted five lawmen—Rainey, Price, ex-sheriff Ethel "Hop" Barnett, and two Philadelphia policemen, Otha Burkes and Richard Willis—for illegally detaining and beating seven blacks between October 1962 and January 1964. All five were Klansmen and prime suspects in the recent murders. (None were ever tried.) By October, bureau agents had recruited two key informants in the White Knights hierarchy. The Rev. Delmar Dennis was a kludd and confidant of Samuel Bowers, who joined the FBI team to avoid conspiracy charges while "serving God and country" for $100 a week. Kleagle Wallace Miller was a sergeant with Meridian's police force. Both informants would report on Klan activities over the next three years. Meanwhile, G-men obtained confessions from two members of the murder party itself. James Jordan cracked in October 1964, saying he heard but did not see the shootings. Horace Barnette told a different story, naming Jordan as James Chaney's killer. The other triggerman, he said, was Klansman Alton Roberts. Ballistics evidence confirmed the accusation against Jordan.[27]

After meeting with Governor Johnson on 2 December 1964, Justice officials realized that Mississippi authorities had no intention of charging the killers. Accordingly, two days later, G-men arrested 21 Klansmen on federal conspiracy charges. Ten of those jailed, including Deputy Price, were named as members of the lynching party; the rest were accused of peripheral roles in planning or concealing the crime. Esther Carter, appointed to serve as a U.S. commissioner without any vestige of legal training, set bonds for the defendants ranging from $1,000 to $5,000, then dismissed all charges against them on 12 December after branding Horace Barnette's confession inadmissible "hearsay." A new grand jury in Jackson indicted 18 defendants on 15 January 1965, but Judge Harold Cox—a Kennedy appointee to the federal bench who once compared black voters in his state to chimpanzees—dismissed the latest felony indictments on 24 February. In a second ruling, issued the following day, Cox held that the defendants should be tried only on misdemeanor charges of inflicting "summary punishment" on the three murder victims "without due process of law." There the matter rested until March 1966, when the U.S. Supreme Court reversed Cox's ruling. A third grand jury reissued conspiracy indictments against 19 White Knights on 27 February 1967, this time including Sam Bowers among the defendants.[28]

So it was that the Neshoba County killers finally faced trial in October 1967, more than three years after the slayings. In the interim, defendant Cecil Price had lost his bid to replace Lawrence Rainey as sheriff, edged out by codefendant Hop Barnett. Judge Cox presided at the trial, bad news for prosecutors as he ruled that signed confessions from defendants Jordan and Barnette must have all other names removed before they could be read aloud in court. A rude surprise for Klansmen came when FBI informants Delmar Dennis and Wallace Miller testified for the government, describing the Klan's plot to kill Michael Schwerner. Turncoat James Jordan also gave his version of the murders while admitting that the FBI had paid $8,000 for his testimony. On 20 October, an all-white jury convicted seven knights (including Bowers, Price and Alton Roberts), acquitted eight (Sheriff Rainey among them), and deadlocked on three (including Hop Barnett and Edgar Killen). At sentencing, Bowers and Roberts received ten-year prison terms; Price and plotter Billy Posey, six years each; and three others, three-year terms. Jordan pled guilty in separate proceedings and was sentenced to four years. The three deadlocked cases were never retried. All convicted defendants remained free on bond until the Supreme Court rejected their final appeals on 27 February 1970. They entered federal prison three weeks later.[29]

Even with the convictions on record, Mississippi whites still made excuses for the Klan. Ex-governor Johnson, interviewed in 1970, said that Klansmen "did not actually intend to kill those people." He explained:

> What happened was that they had been taken from jail and brought to this partic-ular spot. There were a good many people in the group besides the sheriff and the deputy sheriff and that group. What they were going to do, they were going to hang those three persons up in a big cotton sack and leave them hanging in a tree for about a day and a half, then come out there at night and turn them loose. They thought that they'd more or less scare them off. While they were talking this Negro, the Negro boy from over at Meridian — he seemed to be the ringleader of the three — he was acting kind of smart-aleck, and talking pretty big, and one of the Klansmen walked up behind him and hit him over the head with a trace chain.... The chain came across his head and hit him on the bridge of the nose and killed him as dead as a nit. After this boy had been killed, then is when they determined, "Well, we've got to dispose of the other two."[30]

Johnson's statement, while appearing to claim inside knowledge of the crime, flies in the face of sworn testimony that Bowers and other White Knights began plot-ting Schwerner's murder in April or May 1964. He also contradicts attorneys and wit-nesses for both sides by placing Sheriff Rainey at the murder scene. Judge Cox avoided such troubling discrepancies when asked about his verdict in July 1983. "They killed one nigger, one Jew, and a white man," he told the *Clarion-Ledger*. "I gave them all what I thought they deserved."[31]

GEORGIA JUSTICE

J. Edgar Hoover was airborne, returning from his launch of Jackson's faux field office on 11 July 1964, when he learned of yet another Klan atrocity. At 4:45 that morning, unknown gunmen had fired shotgun blasts into a car occupied by three black men near Colbert, Georgia. The driver was killed instantly, but his passengers escaped injury. The three were officers in the U.S. Army Reserve, returning home to Washington, D.C., from summer training at Fort Benning, Georgia. The murdered victim, Lt. Col. Lemuel Penn, served in civilian life as the director of adult and voca-tional education for Washington's public schools.[32]

The Penn murder climaxed six months of violence by Georgia Klansmen, begin-ning when knights brawled repeatedly with sit-in demonstrators in Atlanta during January 1964. In the predawn hours of 21 June, after a United Klans rally near Cov-ington, two carloads of Klansmen invaded a black housing project in Athens, firing shotguns into various apartments. Two persons were wounded in that spree, one los-ing an eye. Three members of Clarke County Klavern No. 244 — Herbert Guest, Den-ver Phillips and Paul Strickland — were arrested for the shootings; Guest and Strickland were fined $100 each for firing guns inside the city limits, but more seri-ous charges of assault with intent to murder were dropped without trial. On 3 July 1964, Klansmen mobbed an integrated party leaving a theater in Americus, Georgia. The following day in Atlanta, Grand Dragon Calvin Craig took the stage at a segre-gationist rally with future Georgia Governor Lester Maddox and Alabama Governor

George Wallace, while racists in the crowd beat three black spectators with folding chairs. The day before Penn's murder, 10 July, nightriders had fired on another black motorist outside Colbert, but they missed their target.[33]

Hoover might have ducked the Penn case, but as in Mississippi, circumstances beyond his control forced the FBI's hand. Early on 11 July, President Johnson telephoned Governor Carl Sanders to request federal-state cooperation in the manhunt, and Sanders—who had vowed that he would "not rest easy" while Penn's slayers were at large—agreed. Later that day, Attorney General Kennedy ordered a full-scale FBI investigation of the crime. Compelled to act, Hoover dispatched Assistant Director J.J. Casper and 20 agents to Athens with orders to "leave no stone unturned" in their search for the killers. On 6 August 1964, G-men arrested four members of Clarke County's klavern—including Herbert Guest, James Lackey, Cecil Myers and Joseph Sims—on charges of conspiring to deprive Penn of his civil rights.[34]

Lackey and Guest confessed in custody, describing events of the fatal morning. Lackey admitted driving the murder car, with Myers and Sims as passengers. They had seen Penn's car at a stoplight in Athens at 4:10 A.M. and assumed from its Washington license plates that the black occupants must be "some of President Johnson's boys." As Lackey explained, "The original reason for our following the colored men was because we heard Martin Luther King might make Georgia a testing ground for the civil rights bill. We thought some out-of-town niggers might stir up some trouble in Athens." As they overtook Penn's vehicle on Highway 172, Sims declared, "I'm going to kill me a nigger," then he and Myers opened fire with sawed-off shotguns. One of their weapons belonged to Herbert Guest and regularly hung on the wall of his garage, described by Lackey as "a frequent gathering place" for Klansmen. Another UKA member, Thomas "Horsefly" Follendore, admitted seeing Myers and Sims return the guns to Guest's garage at 5:00 A.M. on 11 July. Guest, meanwhile, allegedly heard Myers and Sims boast of Penn's murder for the first time on 13 July, granting that Myers had taken guns from his garage on several occasions without Guest's permission.[35]

Adverse publicity prompted confused reactions from the United Klans' leadership. Clarke County Klavern No. 244 was dissolved after the latest arrests, its members dispersed between Oglethorpe County Klavern No. 244 and Walton County's Vinegar Hill Klavern No. 53, where Myers and Sims appeared on the membership roll. A special meeting of the UKA's Georgia realm convened on 18 August 1964 to arrange defense funding. Imperial Wizard Robert Shelton sent a letter to all klaverns in seven Southern states asking each knight to donate at least one dollar toward support of the Georgia defendants. By such means, Exalted Cyclops Tom Whitehead in Athens collected some $3,000 for defense of Myers and Sims.[36]

Hoover later told Congress that his agents delivered "some 800 pages of interviews with witnesses and subjects" to authorities in Madison County. A local grand jury indicted Lackey, Myers and Sims for murder on 25 August 1964, while naming Guest as an unindicted accessory after the fact. By the time Myers and Sims faced trial in Danielsville on 2 September 1964, Lackey had recanted his confession, accusing G-men of unlawful arrest and coercion and extracting his statement "under fears and threats." Judge William Skelton admitted the confession. Defense attorney James

Hudson cited Lackey's low IQ (90) and Agent Jack Simpson's comment to Lackey that the bureau might pay $3,000 for testimony in "complicated cases such as this." Hudson asked jurors, "What do you think this meant to James Lackey, a mentally ill person working in a filling station?" Herbert Guest also withdrew his statement to the FBI, saying, "I don't know what they got in it. I blacked out or something happened to me.... I don't remember nothing about it.... I really don't know what went on the last three or four hours." The defense capped its case with a parade of witnesses (including one black woman) who said they saw Myers and Sims at a café in Athens at 5:00 A.M. on 11 July. Jurors acquitted both defendants on 4 September, prompting Klan attorney James Venable to remark, "You'll never be able to convict a white man that kills a nigger what encroaches on the white race of the South." Prosecutor Clete Johnson shook hands with Myers and Sims as they left the courtroom, and Madison County's sheriff attended a victory banquet for the Klan triggermen in Lawrenceville.[37]

James Lackey's murder case was dropped after his codefendants were acquitted. Myers and Sims remained active in the Vinegar Hill klavern after their trial, then left (or were expelled from) the UKA to join James Venable's National Knights of the KKK. They soon enlisted with a violent faction known as the Black Shirts or Black Knights, led by Klansmen Earl Holcombe (who participated as a member of the U.S. Klans in a 1961 riot in Athens, Georgia) and Colbert McGriff (expelled from the UKA after a shooting incident in Griffin). On 16 October 1964, a federal grand jury indicted six Klansmen — Guest, Lackey, Myers, Sims, Denver Phillips and George Turner — for conspiring to violate Penn's civil rights. Federal judge William Bootle dismissed those charges on 19 December 1964, claiming lack of federal jurisdiction in the case. Myers and Sims were still at liberty in October 1965, twice arrested with fellow Klansmen that month for assaulting blacks in Crawfordsville. The U.S. Supreme Court reversed Judge Bootle's ruling on 28 March 1966, thereby reinstating the federal indictments and clearing the way for a summer trial.[38]

Prosecutors split their case, trying defendants Myers, Sims and Turner together. Guest, Lackey and Phillips faced a separate jury. Both cases were tried between 28 June and 7 July 1966. Confessions from Lackey and Guest were produced and disputed once more. Black victims from Crawfordsville described their beatings by Myers and Sims in October 1965, and an arsenal of confiscated weapons was displayed in court, including sawed-off shotguns, knives, chain flails, and wooden clubs adorned with swastikas. Defense counsel conceded that his clients "may be guilty of a little violence, even a little bad violence," but said they were simply trying to "help out" by "letting the colored people of Athens know that somebody else other than the police was watching them." Verdicts from the first trial were sealed until the second jury finished its deliberations. On 8 July, Judge Bootle announced that Myers and Sims had been convicted and that their codefendants were acquitted. The next day, Bootle sentenced Myers and Sims to the maximum ten-year sentence permitted under federal law. Sims got another ten years on 13 August 1966 after pleading guilty to attempted murder of his wife.[39]

So it was that Hoover's FBI, despite resistance at the top and in the field, cracked two notorious Klan murder cases in Mississippi and Georgia during 1964–67. Before any defendants faced trial on those charges, however, FBI headquarters launched all-out guerrilla war against the KKK and its allies nationwide. In the process—perhaps predictably, considering the bureau's history—G-men strayed outside the law and brought their agency more disrepute.

7

COINTELPRO

Between September 1964 and April 1971, the FBI waged full-scale covert war against various Klan factions and their allies on the neo–Nazi fringe. Some aspects of the long crusade were leaked to friendly journalists, invariably edited and fictionalized to exalt the bureau's image, but most details of the struggle were concealed from public scrutiny until 1975–76, when congressional investigators finally bared the secrets of J. Edgar Hoover's campaign against political dissent in the United States. Those revelations posed a salutary lesson on the perils of excessive zeal in law enforcement's efforts to eradicate "subversive" elements.

While the FBI spared no effort in surveillance and harassment of left-wing political dissenters from its birth in 1908, bureau headquarters did not launch its first official counterintelligence program — COINTELPRO, for short — until August 1956. Hoover's target was the U.S. Communist Party, and his tactics ranged from traditional bugging and wiretaps to such bizarre schemes as "Operation Hoodwink," a plan to foment violence between Reds and the Mafia by means of forged letters and pamphlets. In August 1960, Hoover initiated a second COINTELPRO crusade against advocates of Puerto Rican independence. A third campaign, against the Socialist Workers Party, was inaugurated in October 1961. Other targets included radicals of the "New Left" and members of "Black Nationalist Hate Groups" — a class that ranged, in Hoover's eyes, from militant Black Panthers to the nonviolent SCLC and the conservative NAACP. Before Hoover officially pulled the plug on COINTELPRO in April 1971, he approved 2,340 "actions" against various groups or individuals, but that tally barely scratched the surface of FBI covert activity. According to U.S. Senate reports published in 1976, the FBI admitted conducting 4,102 illegal wiretaps during 1960–1971, planting 567 illicit "bugs" during the same period, and unlawfully opening 56,371 pieces of personal mail during 1958–1971.[1] Each of those 61,040 confessed transgressions was a federal crime, committed by Hoover's G-men in the name of "national security." No one will ever know how many other violations were "forgotten" or suppressed during the COINTELPRO era.

"COINTELPRO — WHITE HATE GROUPS"

The Overstreets, writing in 1969, asserted that FBI infiltration of the KKK had been "continuous for decades." Nonetheless, Hoover issued his first memo on the subject to all field offices in January 1963, coaching agents-in-charge on the proper identification of "Klan-type and hate-type organizations," requesting full information on "the formation and identities" of "'rightist or extremist' groups" from coast to coast. Even then, he ordered no disruptive action, simply broad collection of intelligence. Seventeen months later, on 27 August 1964, William Sullivan's Domestic Intelligence Division (DID) answered Hoover's request for a feasibility study on anti–Klan activity by proposing a campaign to "expose, disrupt and otherwise neutralize the KKK." Sullivan wished to continue the FBI's "policy of aggressively seeking out persons addicted to violence even though they have not violated a Federal law as yet." By that means, he suggested, G-men might achieve results rivaling "our accomplishments in similar-type programs directed against [left-wing] subversives."[2]

Hoover issued a memo to the field on 2 September 1964, cribbing from Sullivan in his announcement of a new COINTELPRO— White Hate Groups. It was designed "to expose, disrupt and otherwise neutralize the activities of the various Klans and hate organizations, their leadership and adherents." The memo continued:

> The activities of these groups must be followed on a continuous basis so we may take advantage of all opportunities for counterintelligence and also inspire action in instances where circumstances warrant. The devious maneuvers and duplicity of these groups must be exposed to public scrutiny through the cooperation of reliable news media sources, both locally and at the Seat of Government [Washington, D.C.]. We must frustrate any effort of the groups to consolidate their forces or to recruit new or youthful adherents. In every instance, consideration should be given to disrupting the organized activity of these groups and no opportunity should be missed to capitalize upon organizational and personal conflicts of their leadership.... All Special Agent personnel responsible for the investigation of Klan-type and hate organizations and their membership should be alerted to our counterintelligence plans relating to these groups. Counterintelligence action directed at these groups is intended to complement and stimulate our accelerated intelligence investigations.... In instances where a reliable and cooperative news media representative or other source outside the Bureau is to be contacted or utilized in connection with the proposed counterintelligence operation, it will be incumbent upon the recommending office to furnish assurances that the source will not reveal the Bureau's interest or betray our confidence.... You are cautioned that the nature of this new endeavor is such that under no circumstances should the existence of the program be made known outside the Bureau and appropriate within-office security should be afforded this sensitive operation.... To insure our success in this new endeavor, the Agent to whom the program is assigned in each office must have a detailed knowledge of the activities of racist groups in the territory and that knowledge must be coupled with interest, initiative and imagination. The Agent must be alert for information which has a disruptive potential. The information will not come to him — he must look for it.[3]

Hoover's plan, like the other COINTELPRO operations mounted before it, belied frequent claims that FBI activities were strictly limited to "fact-finding" missions. Indeed, his order stepped beyond the bounds of any legitimate police activity, a fact acknowledged by his order that "[m]ature experienced agents should be utilized and any investigation conducted should be done in a most discreet manner in order to avoid any possibility of embarrassment to the Bureau." Before its termination, COIN-TELPRO—White Hate would target 17 Klan factions and nine other organizations, including the National States Rights Party and the American Nazi Party, with Hoover claiming credit for the effective demise of all concerned. Between 1964 and 1971, Hoover authorized 287 specific operations against racist groups—an average of 40 per year, versus 100 per year against the Communist Party (which committed no violent acts).[4]

COINTELPRO—White Hate proceeded on three distinct fronts. The first (and only legitimate) effort involved field investigation of actual crimes. The second encompassed myriad "dirty tricks," many illegal and all outside the FBI's purview, and the third comprised a publicity campaign heralding the bureau's "secret war" in articles and books written by "reliable and cooperative" authors. Phase three served the FBI's "educational purpose" of bringing Klansmen "into disrepute before the American public," while simultaneously casting Hoover and his agents as champions of the civil rights movement. The overall campaign was justified by Hoover's finding that "the KKK and supporting groups" were "essentially subversive." Unable to resist the comparison, he declared, "They hold principles and recommend courses of action that are [as] inimical to the Constitution as are the viewpoints of the Communist Party." With that in mind, responsibility for the White Hate crusade was transferred from the FBI's Criminal Investigation Division to Sullivan's cloak-and-dagger DID.[5]

The FBI's first line of attack on hate groups was infiltration by hired informants. Contrary to public perception, no G-men themselves joined the Klan. Rather, they paid "civilians" to join, as in Gary Rowe's case — or more commonly, persuaded active knights to spy on their fellow Klansmen. Agent Roy Moore listed the common recruitment techniques for newsman Jack Nelson as follow: "One, we explained the facts of life. Two, money might be involved. Three might be a threat against them that they didn't know about within the Klan group itself." According to Nelson, "Translated, 'explaining the facts of life' meant threatening and frightening the prospective informant in every possible way." Subjects who resisted such methods were sometimes punished with a method dubbed "snitch-jacketing," in which G-men falsely branded them traitors, thus subjecting them to violent harassment (or murder) by fellow Klansmen. By such means, Hoover claimed in February 1965 that the bureau's efforts had "resulted in a complete infiltration of the Klan to the extent that the FBI now is aware of its plans and activities." A month later, Hoover told Congress that his spies within the KKK were "highly qualified sources consisting of not only rank-and-file members but also individuals who are in a position to have access to plans and policies."[6]

Recruitment of informants proceeded at a frenzied pace throughout the Invisible Empire, adding 774 new spies to the FBI's payroll, for an acknowledged total of 2,014. A memo to the White House, written by Hoover in 1965, said that informants were enlisted at "an average of more than two each day for every day in the past twelve months." Soon, FBI headquarters reported that one in five active-duty Klansmen were turncoats, and that "at least half" of all Klan units had bureau spies in top leadership posts. That raised the question of ongoing violence committed by those very klaverns, a fact explained in equal parts by the quality of informants retained and their shoddy supervision by FBI handlers. In theory, Klan informants were disowned for criminal activity, excessive drinking or "sex perversion," and the bureau allegedly tried to weed out the "screwballs," but such guidelines were honored more in the breach than in observance. Gary Rowe was a prime example, and he was no isolated case. Agent Harold Leinbaugh said of hired informants, "Most of them were unguided missiles. You can't tell a criminal informant too much. You hope and pray a lot. He's probably not too bright, he's certainly unreliable, but you've got to ... hook him somewhere." Assistant Director Fred Baumgardner agreed that informants "did not have to be lily white," and Agent Fred Woodcock noted that while violence was officially discouraged, if a spy did not "get selected for the inner group ... he may never know what is actually going on." In a pinch, Baumgardner noted, "The Bureau is willing to pay an informant to give you negative information, that nothing is going to happen or that nothing is going on."[7]

Aside from tips on criminal activity, informants were pressed to furnish "compromising-type data." In some states, G-men obtained tax information from the IRS Intelligence Division without informing the Disclosure Branch, as required by law. A memo dated 15 May 1965 observes that "[t]hrough analysis of their income tax returns, we may be able to determine whether or not sources of their income or depositories used by them for their respective klan organizations are legitimate." Agents assigned to Imperial Wizard Robert Shelton compiled "a summary of information concerning [his] close associations, likes and dislikes, drinking habits, and social habits ... his relationship with his wife, any other females or males." The file included such minutiae as Shelton's dislike for grits. When Klan wives complained to G-men about domestic violence, agents sometimes informed the abusive husbands, thus "generating pressure within the families that the FBI could exploit." In a similar vein, Gary Rowe enthusiastically complied with bureau orders to bed the wives of other Klansmen, thereby creating further turmoil.[8]

Where paid informants failed to disrupt the Klan, FBI agents created "notional" organizations to do the job. One such fictional group, the National Committee for Domestic Tranquility, was "a Bureau-approved vehicle for attacking Klan policies and disputes from a low-key, common sense, and patriotic position." It boasted paper chapters in 11 states and published monthly newsletters under the byline of editor "Harmon Blennerhasset," an obscure nineteenth-century ally of Aaron Burr. Typical articles included false reports of collapsing klaverns, pieces urging Klansmen to desert the KKK and support "our boys" in Vietnam, and others attacking Klan leaders for acting "in league with the Anti–Christ." On the side, agents running the NCDT mailed critical letters and fliers to knights involved in policy disputes within the KKK, or to those deemed ripe for "turning" as informants.[9]

As the NCDT's cover wore thin, FBI headquarters created a new "National Intelligence Committee," advertised by well-placed informants as a secret branch of the United Klans, created "by the people to protect them from the leadership." An FBI memo released in 1975 admitted that: "The so-called supersecret NIC ... is a fictitious organization originated and controlled by the Bureau in our continuing program to disrupt the Klan on a nationwide scale. The purpose behind this fictitious committee is to circulate misleading information which will continue to neutralize and disrupt the Klan and discredit Klan leaders." One such gambit was a 1967 letter falsely stating that Robert Shelton and North Carolina Grand Dragon J.R. Jones had been fired for embezzling Klan funds. Shelton filed a complaint of mail fraud with the U.S. Post Office, whereupon nervous G-men approached the chief postal inspector and asking about potential felony charges. The agents concealed their role in drafting and mailing the letter, gratefully accepting the postal inspector's judgment that Shelton's complaints "appear to involve an internal struggle" within the UKA. The postal investigation was dropped "since the evidence of mail fraud was somewhat tenuous in nature," and FBI agents promptly wrote another letter to continue the charade.[10]

Anonymous mailings and false accusations ranked high among FBI stratagems during the White Hate campaign. Klan mailing lists were copied for the bureau by informants or stolen outright during illicit break-ins known as "black bag jobs." Noting that "Klansmen are not intellectuals," the bureau peppered them with postcards bearing various cartoons and captions. One portrayed a hooded knight above the statement "I am an informant, color me fed!" Another with the heading "FBI Infiltrates Klan" showed two knights in a sinking rowboat, one of them declaring, "We seem to have sprung a leak!" In April 1966, G-men mailed 6,000 postcards with a message reading: "KLANSMAN, trying to hide your identity behind your sheet? You received this. Someone KNOWS who you are." When members of the UKA scheduled an Alabama klonvokation, agents from the Birmingham field office mailed letters canceling their hotel reservations. Also on tap was a joke book titled *United Klowns of America*, described by FBI headquarters as "light in presentation" but "a serious effort at counterintelligence." One of the mass-mailing proposals rejected by Hoover involved a "critical cartoon" portraying Charlotte, North Carolina, Klansmen dressed in women's clothing. The notion arose from reports that local knights were patrolling ghetto neighborhoods in drag, hoping to catch black rapists, but Hoover scrubbed the plan, fearing that it would "make 'heroes' of the Klan" for protecting white women.[11]

Anonymous postcards struck at Klansmen in four ways, as outlined by Assistant Director Baumgardner in a memo to William Sullivan, dated 24 February 1966. It read:

> Using postal cards of this nature would serve several purposes along the following lines:
> (1) Since these messages are not in sealed envelopes, a number of persons could read them before delivery, thus exposing klansmen and removing one of the Klan's most potent weapons—its veil of secrecy.
> (2) Widespread mailing would undoubtedly be reported to the leadership and since the source will not be identified, apprehension regarding the Klan's security could cause them a major problem.
> (3) The wives and families of klansmen will probably feel uneasy about these messages and may influence members to disassociate themselves.
> (4) Some of the messages could be sent to business addresses rather than residences further spreading the word as to Klan membership.[12]

The technique was so effective that in June 1966, Florida knights printed 14,000 copies of one FBI postcard for mailing to non-Klansmen, in hopes that the blizzard of false accusations would divert focus from actual members. That prospect worried Hoover, prompting him to warn field agents that "you should discreetly endeavor to develop information which could be used to identify one or more klansmen as being responsible for the mailing of these cards. It is possible that some situation will arise leading to an arrest by local authorities, at which time a supply of these cards would be found in the possession of a klansman. Each office should consider requesting a handwriting examination if cards of this type are received by prominent individuals and brought to your attention."[13]

As often as not, anonymous mailings included false charges of theft or immoral behavior. One FBI postcard widely circulated in 1965 portrayed two knights drinking in a tavern, with the caption reading: "Klansman — Which Klan leaders are spending your money tonight? Think!" Other letters were directed more specifically, accusing individual knights of embezzlement, adultery, and so forth. One message, typed by G-men "on plain paper in an amateurish style," was addressed to a particular Klansman's wife from "a God-fearing klanswoman."[14] It read:

> Yes, Mrs. [name deleted], he has been committing adultery. My menfolk say they don't believe this but I think they do. I feel like crying. I saw her with my own eyes. They call her Ruby.... I know this. I saw her strut around at a rally with her lustfilled eyes and smart aleck figure.... They never believed the stories that he stole money from the klans in [deleted] or that he is now making over $25,000 a year. They never believed the stories that your house in [deleted] has a new refrigerator, washer, dryer and yet one year ago, was threadbare. They refuse to believe that your husband now owns three cars and a truck, including the new white car. But I believe all these things and I can forgive them for a man wants to do for his family the best way he can.[15]

Klansman Uriel Miles, an Alabama truck driver, was the target of one such FBI "action," designed to disrupt his marriage. A memo to headquarters from the Birmingham field office, dated 25 August 1966, identified Miles as a heavy drinker and philanderer who neglected his family. The memo recommended mailing of a letter to Miles, which read in part:

> I know what sorry things you have been doing lately and how you have neglected and mistreated your family. You and I are sworn to put an end to such lowdown and sorry carrying on as you have been doing. I have put up with it as long as I am going to. I'm letting the imperial wizard know about you. If he don't do something, or you don't straighten up and act right, me and some of your buddies are going to learn you a lesson.[16]

Headquarters granted permission for the scheme on 9 September 1966: "Authority granted to prepare the letter proposed and to forward a copy to [Imperial Wizard Robert] Shelton. The letter should be prepared with a manual typewriter on commercially purchased stationery and should contain a representative number of grammatical and typing errors. Post the letters in the area of Miles' Klan activity and take all the usual precautions to insure they cannot be associated with the bureau. Advise the bureau of any positive results and be alerted to recommend appropriate follow-up counterintelligence action." Miles and his wife sued the FBI for $250,000 in April 1977, but their claim was dismissed.[17]

A more peculiar bureau effort branded one KKK leader as a personal friend of

Cuban dictator Fidel Castro. Despite the ludicrous nature of that accusation, it prompted an internal Klan investigation during which the accused knight resigned and his klavern was officially disbanded by imperial headquarters.[18]

Other tactics utilized in COINTELPRO—White Hate included illegal bugs and wiretaps; official harassment by local, state and federal agencies of all varieties; FBI pressure on employers to fire Klan employees; exertion of influence on school administrators to dismiss employees or expel students; and persistent leakage of information (false or otherwise) to "cooperative news media." One such contact was Ralph McGill, the publisher of the Atlanta *Constitution*, described in FBI memos as a "staunch and proven friend" who would "not betray our confidence." Data from confidential FBI files, often consisting of unfounded rumors or information fabricated by the bureau, thus became "public source material" employed to the Klan's detriment.[19]

On 2 September 1965, the first anniversary of COINTELPRO—White Hate's inception, Hoover sent a memo to Attorney General Nicholas Katzenbach, captioned "Penetration and disruption of Klan organizations—racial matters." Hoover wrote that high-level "penetration" of the Klan had solved "a number of cases involving racial violence in the South," contributed to recovery of stolen weapons and ammunition, and quietly "forestall[ed] violence in certain racially explosive areas," while informants gave the bureau "up-to-date intelligence data concerning racial matters."[20] Hoover's only reference to a specific covert action appeared in the following paragraph:

> We also are seizing every opportunity to disrupt the activities of Klan organizations. Typical is the manner in which we exposed and thwarted a "kick back" scheme a Klan group was using in one southern state to help finance its activities. One member of the group was selling insurance to other Klan members and would deposit a generous portion of the premiums in the Klan treasury. As a result of the action we took, the insurance company learned of the scheme and cancelled all the policies held by Klan members, thereby cutting off a sizeable source of revenue which had been used to finance Klan activities.[21]

The FBI also claimed (but never documented) its covert frustration of various Klan murder plots. In one case, a group of Georgia knights allegedly met on 8 February 1965 to plot the assassination of Martin Luther King Jr. G-men reportedly learned of the plan one day later, then "saw to it" that King was not molested on the target dates of 15 February (in Marion, Alabama) or 26 February (in Hollywood, California). Another Georgia hit squad, dubbed the "Secret Six," was allegedly foiled when "an FBI shortwave radio message" frustrated a plot to kill Atlanta vice-mayor Sam Massell and Morris Abrams, president of the American Jewish Committee.[22] While entirely feasible, those triumphs may as easily be products of the FBI's propaganda mill, unrelated to real-world events.

BEYOND "MIBURN"

The FBI's White Hate crusade grew from the MIBURN case in Mississippi, yet enjoyed its slowest progress there. Cartha Deloach later admitted that the campaign proceeded "only by inches" in cracking close-knit klaverns, despite William Sullivan's dramatic sketch of its beginnings.[23] Sullivan wrote:

> Toward the end of the summer of 1964, Roy Wall, The special agent in charge of [the Philadelphia, Mississippi] office, called me. I told Roy, "Let's destroy these fellows. Just utterly destroy them." I trusted Roy; he was an outstanding agent. He said that in Mississippi there were three different Klan organizations and that we were in a position either to keep them separated and have them compete and fight with each other for support, or to merge them into one organization. I asked Roy, "If we merge them into one, can you control it and if necessary destroy it?" Roy said, "Yes, we can do that." I told him to go ahead and merge them, through the use of informants. From that time on, the Klan never again raised its head in Mississippi.[24]

Whatever orders may have passed from Sullivan to Wall, the rival Klans in Mississippi were not merged — in fact, the UKA's realm split to form a fourth faction, the Knights of the Green Forest — and by no stretch of the imagination can it be shown that the KKK "never again raised its head in Mississippi" after 1964. In fact, Roy Moore later reported that "we averaged 250 acts of violence per annum" across the Magnolia State, during 1964–1970. "After 1970," he continued, "[it was] practically nil. It took us that long to put the fire out."[25] SNCC activist Abbie Hoffman described his experience with the Klan at McComb, in 1965:

> The Ku Klux Klan was so strong they once held a rally in the middle of Route 80. Cars had to pass the meeting on side roads. It was hard to believe, but there were two hundred white sheets, flaming crosses and all.... [T]he Klan was no outmoded joke. A faceless nightmare, they were furnished by police with a list of our license-plate numbers, and they patrolled the borders of each black community, gunning for organizers. "Coon huntin,'" the local whites called it.... Daily picket lines were scenes of vicious Klan beatings. Once I was thrown to the curb and kicked repeatedly. An FBI agent leaned over and asked sarcastically if my civil rights had been violated. No one ever got arrested except SNCC workers.[26]

Pike County, surrounding McComb, harbored eight UKA klaverns and at least one chapter of the White Knights front, Americans for Preservation of the White Race. It was also a center of nightriding violence supported by Sheriff R.R. Warren, who said on 24 September 1964 that local bombings were "staged" by blacks to provoke federal intervention. Governor Johnson sounded a similar note six days later, saying that a state investigation of McComb's bombing epidemic revealed that some blasts "were plants set by COFO people" and "some were bombings by white people." In fact, all the bombers were UKA knights, as revealed when G-men arrested 11 members of a self-styled "Pike County Wolf Pack" between 30 September and 5 October. Klansmen Paul Wilson and Ernest Zeeck confessed in custody and named accomplices. A local grand jury indicted nine suspects, all of whom pled guilty or "no contest" when they appeared before Judge W.H. Watkins on 23 October 1964. Wilson and Zeeck received 15-year sentences, and their codefendants drew terms ranging from six months to five years in prison. Then, in a stunning turnaround, Judge Watkins suspended all jail time on grounds that the defendants' acts of terrorism were "to some extent at least provoked and brought about by outside influences." All were freed the same day after six paid trifling fines of $500 each. The cash was raised by Grand Dragon E.L. McDaniel, who solicited funds for the Wolf Pack while denying they were Klansmen.[27]

On balance, the Mississippi Klan seemed barely inconvenienced by the FBI's White Hate crusade in 1964–65. At a Jackson rally on 18 July 1965, Sam Bowers boasted that his White Knights were responsible for 16 arson fires in his hometown of Laurel alone. Statewide, the butcher's bill for 1965 included at least three murders, four floggings, one nonfatal stabbing, 11 shootings, four bombings and 52 arson attacks. One fatality was Meadville resident Earl Hodges, beaten to death on 16 August 1965 by fellow Klansmen who mistook him for an FBI informant. His death was ruled "accidental" by local police and remains unpunished.[28]

At the same time, FBI handling of Mississippi knights ranged from slapstick comic efforts to blatant counter-terrorism. Roy Moore vetoed William Sullivan's scheme to embarrass the White Knights by ordering 12 cases of embalming fluid in the name of the APWR, but infiltrators spread dissent and fostered paranoia in the ranks. At one Klan gathering, false accusations of embezzlement produced an armed confrontation between Hattiesburg knights and bodyguards of Sam Bowers, but the conflict stopped short of bloodshed. In Natchez, after White Knights threatened bureau personnel, Agent Paul Cummings "organized a squad of G-men and headed for the Klansmen's favorite bar." When the knights refused to step outside, agents shot out the tavern's windows. "We were at war," Cummings explained, "and we used muscle."[29] Even then, it took three more years to produce results.

"Klantown USA"

Mississippi was not the only scene of Ku Klux terrorism during the White Hate crusade. Louisiana witnessed its own rash of violence during 1964–66, including three known murders, seven bombings, ten arson incidents (including five black churches burned), and 13 riots led by Klansmen. Much of the mayhem occurred around Bogalusa, in Washington Parish. Although 40 percent of its residents were black, Bogalusa also harbored some 800 Klansmen, earning the nickname "Klantown USA" because no other American city had a higher per capita number of knights. Aside from drive-by shootings, midnight whippings and the like, Bogalusa Klansmen fired by Jesse Stoner's oratory mobbed civil rights marchers on at least ten occasions in July 1965, while police stood by and watched from the sidelines.[30]

Despite inside knowledge of at least one Ku Klux murder (detailed in Chapter 8), FBI agents arrested only one Louisiana Klansman during their White Hate crusade. Howard Lee was a member of the Original Knights who also held a federal firearms license. He ignored mandatory record-keeping guidelines when he sold 521 weapons to members of his own Klan, the White Knights and UKA. G-men ultimately charged Lee with 216 violations of the National Firearms Act, and he was imprisoned in early 1965. Otherwise, the only federal action undertaken was a Justice Department lawsuit filed against the Original Knights and its front group, the Anti-Communist Christian Association, on 19 July 1965. As a result of FBI investigation, Justice lawyers established a pervasive pattern of intimidation designed to forestall integration in Washington Parish. On 1 December 1965, a three-judge federal court issued injunctions against both groups and 38 specific Bogalusa Klansmen, barring any further interference with civil rights demonstrations.[31]

Still, violence continued in Washington Parish and elsewhere, with no arrests. Angry black victims organized an armed group of their own, the Deacons for Defense and Justice, in Jonesboro in 1964. Other chapters quickly formed, fighting skirmishes with Klansmen on several occasions. The FBI responded, as it always had to signs of black assertiveness, with a full-scale investigation that branded the Deacons "subversive." A memo from early 1965 reveals that bureau headquarters had sent reports on the "gun-carrying black vigilante group" to all "appropriate ... authorities in the state of Louisiana."[32]

Viola Liuzzo

SNCC volunteers launched a voter-registration drive in Dallas County, Alabama, during 1964, augmented in early 1965 by Martin Luther King and his SCLC. King's goal was a historic march from Selma to Montgomery, where Governor George Wallace remained a staunch friend of the Klan. The Alabama campaign cost four lives, and King's first march was crushed on 7 March 1965 — "Bloody Sunday" — by the combined force of Al Lingo's state trooper's and Sheriff Jim Clark's civilian "posse" (said to include many Klansmen, though Selma itself had no klavern). A federal court order allowed the march to proceed under military guard two weeks later, and one of those participating in the protest was Viola Liuzzo, a middle-aged mother of five from Detroit who had answered King's call for volunteers.[33]

J. Edgar Hoover, typically, was more concerned with watching King and peaceful black protesters than the Klansmen who terrorized them. A team of 26 G-men shadowed voter-registration workers around Selma from January 1965 onward, increased to 70 agents by mid-March. The fresh troops were sent on 12 March, after Attorney General Katzenbach asked Hoover "whether an operation like [the FBI] ran in Neshoba County, with a special detail" might "keep the situation from getting too out of hand." Heedless of Klan threats to the marchers, Hoover privately complained that Selma was "a situation where almost everyone is having hallucinations." Unaware of Hoover's attitude, Katzenbach thanked the director on 23 March "for the help Bureau people have been on the march in Alabama, particularly the way they are getting information to the Army and to [Assistant Attorney General] Ramsey Clark."[34]

In fact, Hoover's agents had done their best to obstruct King's march. Before the protest, two white men posing as city fire inspectors toured the SCLC's office in Montgomery, planting several hidden recorders that the staff discovered and destroyed. The Rev. Meryl Ross had no doubt about the spies' identity. He blamed: "The FBI. They were very hostile. The Montgomery police and the sheriff's office were antagonistic, but those [FBI] guys were hostile. Early in the week we wanted to walk around the perimeter of the capitol building to plan our security, but the FBI wouldn't let us near it. They had ordered armed patrols to seal it off and wouldn't give us permission to get through."[35] The bureau, of course, had no jurisdiction for such interference.

Ironically, while Hoover had warned Congress on 4 March 1965 of "a marked increase in Klan membership" during the past twelve months, he had no inkling that violence was about to erupt once again. At the protest's end on 25 March, Viola Liuzzo used her car to ferry groups of demonstrators back to Selma from Montgomery. On her last trip from the capital, she reported that a carload of white men had given chase, nudging her bumper several times. Undaunted, she left for Montgomery again at 7:34 P.M., accompanied by a black teenager, Leroy Moton. At 8 P.M., while traveling along Highway 80 in Lowndes County, Liuzzo was fatally wounded by gunshots from another car, and her vehicle crashed into a barbed-wire fence. Moton, uninjured but spattered with Liuzzo's blood, staggered to the highway and flagged down a passing truck filled with marchers returning to Selma.[36]

The tale is simply told, yet confusion still surrounds the events of Liuzzo's murder four decades after the fact. Indeed, the riddles began hours before the shooting when the morning edition of Montgomery's *Alabama Journal* ran a short article refuting "persistent rumors that a white female civil rights demonstrator had died here or in Selma." Author Mary Stanton suggests that the article contained "some sort of encoded message" anticipating Liuzzo's murder, but the question remains unanswered. That same morning, Alabama state troopers patrolling Highway 80 received radio orders to watch for a gray Ford with out-of-state license plates, and sworn testimony in court also referred to alerts for a red Sprite — neither matching the description of the supposed murder car. Their significance, if any, is unknown today.[37]

As for the slaying itself, contradictions abound in official descriptions of the event. One FBI report said six shots were fired into Liuzzo's car from two different pistols, one .38 caliber and the other .22 caliber. John Doar, representing Justice in Selma, was told the fatal shots came from a rifle. Leroy Moton agreed that a high-powered rifle was used, but he heard no gunfire and believed the weapon must have been equipped with a silencer. Al Lingo, meanwhile, told reporters that only *two* shots had been fired, insisting that no one could determine whether Liuzzo was shot from a passing car or by a roadside sniper. A revolver found discarded on the highway's shoulder was never dusted for fingerprints by G-men or police, a fact that prompted a flurry of furious memos from FBI headquarters to the Birmingham field office. Leroy Moton's description of the chase and shooting further confused matters. Moton swore that two cars had pursued Liuzzo's green Oldsmobile. A black Ford tried to force Liuzzo off the road soon after leaving Selma, he said, but the fatal gunshots came from a different car. After the shooting, Moton said, a carload of men returned to the scene and shined flashlight's into Liuzzo's car while he lay covered in the dead woman's blood. FBI files noted statements from three other witnesses who described a dark-colored Ford cruising the highway near Big Swamp (where the shooting occurred) or 25 March. SCLC headquarters in Montgomery also received a telephone call at 8 P.M. on 25 March, reporting "something funny" on Highway 80; more specifically, the caller said a green Oldsmobile with Michigan plates was being followed by a two-tone 1959 or 1960 Chevrolet convertible, "red and some other light color." *Newsweek* magazine reported the pursuit with two chase cars in its issue of 5 April 1965.[38]

Soon after news outlets reported the shooting, President Johnson called J. Edgar

Hoover with orders to "find the perpetrators of this heinous crime" and "do everything possible around the clock" to solve the case. Johnson and Hoover spoke repeatedly throughout that night, continuing sporadic conversations until 6 A.M. on 26 March. Hoover immediately launched a smear campaign against Liuzzo and her family, telling Johnson in their first conversation that Liuzzo's husband "doesn't have too good a background and the woman had indications of needle marks in her arms." Furthermore, he said, Liuzzo "was sitting very, very close to the Negro in the car. It had the appearance of a necking party." When LBJ called back a short time later, Hoover amended his assessment of Anthony Liuzzo: "I don't say the man has a bad character but he is well known as a Teamster strongarm man." Hoover quickly added, "On the woman's body we found numerous needle marks indicating she had been taking dope, although we can't say definitely, because she's dead."[39]

Although Liuzzo's husband *was* a Teamster, every other statement made by Hoover in his conversations with the president was false. Published reports differ on the source of his malicious information, alternately crediting "agents in Mississippi" or Agent Spencer Robb in Birmingham, who allegedly wrote a memo falsely claiming that Viola Liuzzo "had puncture marks in her arms indicating recent use of a hypodermic needle." No such needle marks existed, and the memo was suppressed for two decades, but its false contents quickly leaked to right-wing journalists—and to the Klan. Biographer Curt Gentry says that Hoover, an undoubted racist, "wanted to believe this lie" that validated claims of civil rights activity as a prelude to "race-mixing." (The first test performed on Liuzzo's corpse by state investigators was an examination for signs of recent sexual intercourse. The results were negative.) The director also had another motive, for by sunrise on 26 March he knew that an FBI informant — none other than Gary Rowe — had been a member of the Ku Klux murder team.[40]

Accounts differ as to when Rowe informed his bureau handlers of his presence at the crime scene. Don Whitehead maintains that Rowe met an agent in the parking lot of a Birmingham hospital at 11:15 P.M. on 25 March, but Mary Stanton places his first call to the FBI some three hours later. In fact, as Rowe himself later admitted, his FBI contact had approved Rowe's participation in the latest "missionary work" sometime "early in the morning" of 25 March — a fact long suppressed by the bureau. As Rowe described the shooting, he was riding in the backseat of a red-and-white Chevrolet Impala driven by Klansman Eugene Thomas, accompanied by UKA members William Eaton and Collie Wilkins, Jr. They had followed Liuzzo's car through Lowndes County, debating the best method of attack. Thomas wanted to ram the Oldsmobile, but Wilkins warned him that the FBI could trace paint chips and thus identify them. Finally, Rowe said, during a high-speed chase, Eaton and Wilkins "emptied their guns" into Liuzzo's Oldsmobile. Rowe denied firing at Liuzzo but admitted aiming his gun out the window, pretending to shoot.[41]

The case was officially solved by 8 A.M. on 26 March, when President Johnson got word from Attorney General Katzenbach. At 12:40 P.M., Johnson appeared on television, flanked by Katzenbach and Hoover, to announce the arrest of four Klansmen for Liuzzo's murder. Rowe was named with the rest, but he was not identified as an FBI informant. Johnson lavished praise for the arrests upon that "honored public servant, Mr. Hoover. I cannot express myself too strongly in praising Mr. Hoover and the men of the FBI for their prompt and expeditious performance in handling this investigation." After branding the KKK "a hooded society of bigots," Johnson urged all knights within the sound of his voice "to get out of the Ku Klux Klan now and return to a decent society before it is too late." From Tuscaloosa, Robert Shelton called LBJ a "damn liar," describing Liuzzo's murder as a "trumped-up plot" by "Communists and sex perverts" to "frame the Ku Klux Klan." After their arraignment on murder charges, UKA headquarters posted a $150,000 bond for the accused.[42]

Sheriff Clark in Selma sparked new controversy with his own press conference on 27 March 1965. Specifically, Clark charged that the FBI could have saved Liuzzo's life. "They had a carload of Ku Klux Klansmen under surveillance," Clark said, yet failed to share that information with state or local police. At 6:20 P.M. on 25 March, Clark revealed, state troopers had given Eugene Thomas a warning ticket for excessive speed. His car was stopped within ten miles of the Liuzzo murder site, but no further action was taken because of the FBI blackout. "The FBI agents have always worked closely with us in the past," Clark declared, "but this time for some reason they didn't. If we had known about it, we would have tried to keep that car under surveillance. The shooting didn't happen in my county. I regret that it happened, but I've been getting telegrams from all over the country blaming me for it. We had a march today on the courthouse and the demonstrators indicated that I was to blame for what happened. If they want to blame anybody, they ought to march on the federal building."[43]

FBI headquarters responded furiously on 28 March, calling Clark a "malicious liar" whose public statements were "typical of his weakness in handling his responsibilities." Bureau spokesmen admitted seeing Thomas's car in a Klan motorcade in Montgomery on 21 March and said that the FBI had provided a list of license plate numbers to Alabama law enforcement agencies over the next four days. Headquarters also said that shortly after Thomas and his "wrecking crew" left Bessemer for Montgomery on 25 March, "[a]n all-points bulletin was put out immediately by police notifying the U.S. Army and the Alabama Department of Public Safety." A story in the *New York Journal American* hailed Rowe as a hero, falsely stating that he came within minutes of saving Liuzzo. On 30 March, the *Los Angeles Times* reported: "[Hoover] said his agency is doing everything possible to investigate violations of civil rights laws, but he stressed that its role is that of an investigator — not an accuser, prosecutor, jury or judge. 'I refuse to let the FBI be forced into practices which smack of police state actions, regardless of the circumstances,' he said. 'To my mind the freedom and rights of our nation can be implemented as well as preserved without resorting to totalitarian tactics.'"[44]

Two decades later, marking the anniversary of Liuzzo's murder in the *Washington Post*, columnist Jack Anderson captured Hoover's true role in the case. "Evidently aware of the embarrassment the FBI would suffer from the presence of its undercover informer in the murderer's car," Anderson wrote, "J. Edgar Hoover marshaled the Bureau's resources to blacken the dead woman's reputation." A collaborator in that effort, welcome or otherwise, was Robert Shelton of the UKA. On 28 March, Shelton told reporters that Liuzzo was "set up to become a martyr and another rallying point for the civil rights movement. If this woman was at home with the children where she belonged, she wouldn't have been in jeopardy." Shelton also said he had inside information on Liuzzo's "police record"—she was fined $50 in 1964 for home schooling her children—and on her "liberated relationship" with husband Anthony. Klansmen contended that Liuzzo had engaged in sex with Selma blacks, but the promised witnesses never appeared.[45]

Hoover's malice extended to Liuzzo's funeral and beyond. On learning that Dr. King planned to address the Detroit gathering, G-men turned out in force to watch and photograph the crowd. King also congratulated agents for their quick solution of the crime, but headquarters was stoically silent, "because a reply would only help build up this character." Teamster president James Hoffa flew Liuzzo's body home from Selma on a union plane, prompting Hoover to renew his false charges that Anthony Liuzzo was a "strong-arm extortionist" with Mafia ties. When Liuzzo sought to recover his late wife's personal effects, the FBI ignored him. A letter to the White House seeking return of her wedding ring was routed to bureau headquarters, where it sat unanswered for a decade. (Liuzzo finally got the ring back in 1976, two years before his death.) Meanwhile, Hoover preserved in his files every letter written to the FBI about Liuzzo's murder. One letter, preserved for no rational reason, came from a woman in Corpus Christi, Texas, who mourned "what an insult Mrs. Liuzzo made to the people of Alabama by cavorting around with a Negro Buck after dark in their state." Investigative files were opened on other correspondents, including several junior high school students who sent letters of praise to the bureau for catching Liuzzo's killers.[46]

On 31 March 1965, agents of the FBI's Crime Records Division briefed Douglas Smith, an aide to Alabama Congressman George Anderson, on the "subversive" leadership of CORE, the SCLC and SNCC. Smith admitted that "an urgent request from Governor George Wallace" had "precipitated" his visit to Washington, seeking "information indicating communist connections on the part of civil rights leaders." Despite Hoover's best efforts, Smith left the meeting convinced that the FBI's data "would not satisfy the Governor." Still, it was not for lack of trying, as Hoover's campaign of character assassination against Viola Liuzzo proceeded apace. As noted by historian Wyn Wade, "In less than a month, the national topic changed from the willful murder of Liuzzo to her moral character." In April, Hoover thoughtfully reminded Northern journalists, "White citizens [in Alabama] are primarily decent, but frightened for their lives. The colored people are quite ignorant, mostly uneducated."[47]

A federal grand jury indicted all four Klansmen on 6 April 1965 for conspiracy to violate Liuzzo's rights, then corrected its error on 15 April by dismissing charges against Gary Rowe. A Lowndes County grand jury indicted Eaton, Thomas and Wilkins for first-degree murder on 22 April. All were represented by the UKA's imperial klonsel (attorney), Matt Murphy, who had earlier defended Robert Chambliss and other knights on bombing charges in Birmingham. Now, as the FBI removed Rowe from his client list, Murphy filed suit to recover $6,000 in fees from the turncoat Klansman. G-men in Mobile, Alabama, countered that move with a memo to Hoover on 4 May 1965 proposing a leak to the House Un-American Activities Committee (HUAC) concerning "the role of a subversive lawyer in promulgating the aims of the KKK."[48]

Collie Wilson was first to face trial in Hayneville that May, named as the trig-german in Liuzzo's death. In addition to their plans for Murphy, G-men checked Lowndes County prosecutors and impaneled jurors for links to the Klan or the Cit-izens' Council (which held regular meetings in the county courthouse). Expert tes-timony linked the fatal slug and several cartridges discarded along Highway 80 to a .38-caliber revolver seized at the home of Eugene Thomas. Gary Rowe appeared for the state, describing the murder and Thomas's loan of his pistol to Wilkins. Mur-phy attacked Rowe for breaking his "sacred" Klan secrecy oath, then capped his per-formance with a hysterical rant against "niggers," Communists and the United Nations. Ten white jurors voted to convict Wilkins on a reduced charge of manslaughter, but two held out for acquittal, and the judge declared a mistrial on 7 May 1965. A second trial was scheduled for October, and Wilkins rushed off to sign autographs at Klan rallies.[49]

The next controversy in Liuzzo's case erupted four days later in Detroit. On 11 May 1965, Tony Liuzzo learned from local journalists that Marvin Lane —former chief of detectives with the Detroit Police Department, then police commissioner in suburban Warren, Michigan — had furnished Sheriff Clark in Selma with a confiden-tial report on Liuzzo in April. Robert Shelton distributed copies to reporters cover-ing the Wilkins trial, continuing the campaign of posthumous slander initiated by Hoover at FBI headquarters. Lane's cover letter to Clark revealed without explana-tion that Detroit's "Criminal Intelligence Bureau began an investigation regarding the background of Viola Liuzzo" on 26 March 1965. Lane further told Clark, "We would like if it is at all possible to determine the method of transportation to Selma by Mrs. Liuzzo, and who may have accompanied her." The purpose of that query was unclear, since the Liuzzos never lived in Warren and Liuzzo was not killed within Clark's jurisdiction (much less Lane's). Clark admitted knowing Lane through a "national police organization," contending that he had received death threats from callers who identified themselves as Teamsters. On 17 May, Inspector Earl Miller — director of Detroit P.D.'s Criminal Intelligence Division — admitted leaking confiden-tial files to Lane (his former boss). Earl Miller, ex-sheriff of St. Clair County, Michigan, and executive director of the National Sheriff's Association in Washing-ton, D.C., admitted putting Clark in touch with Lane. Detroit police chief Vincent Piersante followed those admissions with a claim that he ordered the background check, in order to prepare "security" for Liuzzo's funeral.[50]

Detroit's interest in Liuzzo may be no surprise, as the police department had recruited heavily from displaced Southern whites since the 1920s and was soon infested by members of the KKK and the spin-off Black Legion. That racist tradition endured through the 1960s and went far toward explaining Lane's interest in Liuzzo's movements 500 miles outside his jurisdiction. The report itself was a six-page col-lection of fact, fabrication and innuendo, documenting Liuzzo's marriages and civil rights activity, her education and work history, a nervous breakdown and her $50 fine from 1964. A former co-worker described Liuzzo as "disruptive" and "of ques-tionable character," cited nonexistent psychiatric treatment and falsely said that Liuzzo was fired from her job. As the lies and distortions piled up, Mississippi's *Jack-son Daily News* reported that Liuzzo had a "four-page police record" in Detroit. The

Detroit Free Press countered by calling Lane's report "inaccurate, derogatory and totally uncalled for. It makes insinuations which are not supported by facts, and dwells on irrelevant and unfavorable minutiae not only about Mrs. Liuzzo, but about her whole family. What Lane ignored was that Mrs. Liuzzo was not accused of any crime, and her murder was not the result of any provocation on her part. She was involved in no bar room brawl. She had broken no laws."[51]

The FBI publicly ignored Tony Liuzzo's complaint against Lane, but Hoover quietly retaliated by banning Warren police officers from the bureau's National Academy. The director bristled on 17 May 1965 when columnist Inez Robb told readers of 132 newspapers nationwide, "What troubles me is the moral aspect of Rowe's presence in the car when an innocent woman was gunned down. Under what kind of secret orders did Rowe work? Was the infiltration of the Ku Klux Klan more important than the saving of an innocent woman? ... [T]he FBI owes the nation an explanation of its actions in the Liuzzo case." In lieu of explanation, Hoover wrote snide memos about Tony Liuzzo. Liuzzo had stopped payments on his wife's car when it was seized as evidence in Alabama. Later, it was repossessed and auctioned to a private bidder who advertised the vehicle for sale in Birmingham "with bullet holes and everything still intact, ideal to bring in a crowd." When Liuzzo complained, Hoover filed a memo saying he "seems more interested in cash ... than in grief."[52]

In the wake of Liuzzo's murder, Hoover sent more "detailed information" on the White Hate crusade to Attorney General Katzenbach. When Katzenbach urged even stronger action, Hoover wrote that his agents were "getting on the Klan—that this was well begun in Alabama but has not been developed as far in Mississippi."[53] One such Alabama action was embodied in a memo to Hoover from the Birmingham field office, dated 4 August 1965, which read:

> Racial informants have advised in April, 1965, that a meeting of the United Klans of America, Inc., Knights of the Ku Klux Klan (UKA), was held in Bessemer, Alabama, and this was a state meeting. [Name deleted] advised that [deleted], one of the three defendants to be tried on the murder charge in Hayneville, Alabama, was present at this meeting. It was announced that [deleted] had received a letter addressed to him at Bessemer, Alabama, from Chicago, Illinois, and this letter was signed "Mafia." There was a black glove cut out of construction paper, with the words "Mafia," and "Vendetta," on it. Reportedly, this letter stated that all the Klan was marked for death, and if anything happened to the Negro boy who was riding with Mrs. Liuzzo when she was shot, then the Mafia would cut up [deleted's] family, piece by piece, before killing them. Reportedly, the letter had been postmarked at Chicago, Illinois. It was also reported by Birmingham informants that the receipt of the above described letter by [deleted] not only placed him in a state of fear and great concern, concerning the situation, but caused quite a number of the other Klansmen to be similarly concerned and in somewhat of a fearful state of mind. The Bureau is herewith requested to prepare an anonymous communication to [deleted] and other known Klansmen and/or officials of the UKA, in an attempt to exploit the situation. The Bureau is herewith requested to give consideration to preparing an original cartoon or drawing setting out a black glove with the wording "Mafia" and "Vendetta," appropriately arranged in or on the drawing of the black glove.

A suggested letter is as follows:

> Klansman:
>   You know what happened to Mrs. Viola Liuzzo. The Mafia knows what you
> have been doing and what you are doing now. Your so-called "non-violence" will
> receive proper action soon.[54]

Matt Murphy missed the second Wilkins trial. He was killed on 20 August 1965 when a tanker truck hit his car on the highway between Birmingham and Tuscaloosa. His replacement as defense counsel, ex-mayor and former G-man Arthur Hanes, was yet another grave embarrassment for FBI headquarters. Hanes told reporters, "I was hired by these boys, but as far as I know the Klan has nothing to do with paying me." Bureau headquarters thought otherwise, noting that Hanes had served as one of Murphy's pallbearers. A personal memo from Hoover branded Hanes "no good," "a very strong supporter" of Bull Connor and "a fellow who has certainly a strong smell of the Klan about him." Hanes, for his part, found the "Bureau boys" in Alabama "very friendly."[55]

The Liuzzo prosecution team changed in late summer as well, with state attorney general Richmond Flowers replacing county solicitor Arthur Gamble, Jr. Despite his personal belief in segregation, Flowers was an enemy of both the KKK and Governor George Wallace. He complained in 1965, when Wallace allies in the state Senate killed a dynamite control bill passed by the Alabama House of Representatives to curb Klan terrorism. Wallace subsequently called for voters to impeach Flowers on grounds of his "collaborating with the federal government," yet Flowers got no help from FBI headquarters. On a visit to Justice in Washington, he was "greeted warmly and left with a confident guarantee of assistance," then six weeks elapsed before he received a meager packet including some newspaper clippings, a Florida grand jury report on the KKK from 1952, a copy of the Klan's 1915 constitution, and three old copies of the *Fiery Cross* (then available on most newsstands in Alabama).[56]

Tension ran high in the weeks before Wilkins's second trial in Hayneville. Two hundred Klansmen gathered for a local rally on 10 July 1965, and the Citizens' Council continued its weekly courthouse meetings. Eight past or present council members were selected for the Wilkins jury over angry objections from Flowers, yet Flowers remained confident, declaring it "the strongest case I've ever had, complete with the eyewitness testimony of an FBI agent [sic]." It mattered not to Art Hanes and a stacked racist jury, however. The all-white panel acquitted Wilkins on 22 October 1965, and he left court to a hero's reception. Another jury, including eight blacks and four whites, acquitted Eugene Thomas of murder on 27 September 1966. William Eaton died of a heart attack on 10 March 1966, before his case could be tried in state court.[57]

Liuzzo's killers did not escape justice entirely. The federal conspiracy charges remained, with trial scheduled for late November 1965. FBI memos reveal that Gary Rowe was "torn to pieces" after the first two trials in Hayneville and had to be "toned down a bit" by his handlers. A memo from Hoover, written on 24 November, admitted that Rowe had "no confidence in the attorneys of the [Justice] Department," but "leverage" to make him testify again was found in his "confidence in the FBI." Still, Rowe was shaky, and headquarters stubbornly refused to "furnish information to the

Department in writing concerning his status." All three defendants were convicted on 3 December 1965, receiving the maximum ten-year sentence for their crime. Eaton died while free on bond pending appeal, but Thomas and Wilkins ultimately served seven years in prison.[58]

Soon after their release in the summer of 1978, Thomas and Wilkins agreed to interviews with the ABC television program *20/20*. Both had "found Jesus" in prison, they said, and wished to share the truth about Liuzzo's murder. They named Gary Rowe as the killer and both passed polygraph tests in support of their story, but Rowe's test results indicated deception. That episode sparked a new grand jury hearing in Lowndes County, where Thomas and Wilkins repeated their story under oath. The panel indicted Rowe for Liuzzo's murder in September 1978. The governor of Georgia (where Rowe lived and served the federal government as U.S. marshal "Thomas Moore") approved extradition in February 1979, but the case was subsequently dropped. Meanwhile, Senator Edward Kennedy asked Justice to investigate any crimes Rowe may have committed as an informant, together with the bureau's role in hiding them. Deputy Attorney General Benjamin Civiletti launched the probe in 1978 and produced a 302-page report in February 1980. That document confirmed that G-men covered up Rowe's part in the 1961 Freedom Ride riots, and that the bureau knew of Rowe's "veto power" over Klan violence around Birmingham. Still, the investigators found no "credible evidence" that Rowe shot Viola Liuzzo.[59]

Liuzzo's children, naturally mistrustful of the government by that time, filed a claim of negligence against the FBI in 1977. Bureau headquarters refused to negotiate, so a formal lawsuit was filed in July 1979, seeking $2 million in damages. Howard Simon, executive director of the Michigan ACLU, described the FBI's relationship with Gary Rowe as follows: "They had a monster working for them. They took no effort to keep him on a leash. The FBI had a direct choice between preventing a crime and keeping him as an informant. They kept him as an informant." The trial opened on 21 March 1983, before federal judge Charles Joiner in Ann Arbor, Michigan. Liuzzo's family was hopeful, since the FBI had lost two other cases one month earlier and was forced to compensate plaintiffs Walter Bergman and James Peck for injuries suffered in the Freedom Rides. Attorney Dean Robb charged that G-men were negligent in recruiting, training and supervising Rowe, and thus were liable for Liuzzo's wrongful death. Thomas and Wilkins repeated their claim that Rowe shot Liuzzo with a pistol borrowed from Thomas. "After the shooting," Thomas testified, "I looked in the rearview mirror and saw her car veering off to the side of the road. And Rowe said, 'Well, I got 'em. Damn good shooting.'" Former attorney general Ramsey Clark told the court that many southern G-men in the 1960s shared the racist views of white police and Klansmen. Two Birmingham detectives said they had visited Rowe on the morning of 26 March 1965, whereupon he admitted the shooting.[60]

Justice attorney Ann Robertson, defending the bureau, dismissed the Birmingham policemen as pawns in a Ku Klux revenge plot against Gary Rowe. She also summoned Flossie Creel, ex-wife of Alabama's former grand dragon, to testify that Eugene Thomas had named Wilkins in her presence as Liuzzo's killer. FBI director William Webster visited the courtroom on the trial's last day in a show of support for his agents. The next morning, 27 May 1983, Judge Joiner rejected the plaintiffs' case, ordering Liuzzo's children to pay $80,000 in court costs for the FBI. They refused, preferring jail time for contempt, but the bill was cancelled in November 1983 after public outrage sparked a U.S. Senate resolution asking Justice to drop the vendetta. Gary Rowe returned to Atlanta, where he died in 1998.[61]

CAROLINA KLAN WARS

North Carolina was the Klan's strongest realm in 1964–65. Robert Shelton's UKA boasted 7,500 members in 192 klaverns, and James Venable's National Knights had an active chapter in Wilson County. Two knights were arrested for trying to burn a black church in Elm City in July 1964, and other terrorists proved more successful in their efforts. Bombers destroyed a civil rights worker's car in Charlotte in early January 1965, then visited New Bern on 24 January to damage a church used for NAACP meetings and a mortuary owned by a black activist. On 29 January, G-men arrested three knights, all members of a Klan front called the Craven County Improvement Association, who pled guilty in state court and received suspended sentences. Justice filed no federal charges in that case.[62]

Those arrests did not halt the mayhem in North Carolina. Klansmen beat 27 blacks in Plymouth during a voter-registration drive on 26 August 1965. The attacks resumed on 31 August, prompting Governor Dan Moore to ban all non-resident knights from the city, but G-men failed to act in the face of clear federal violations. Three months later, on 22 November, bombers struck the homes of four civil rights activists in Charlotte. Another bomb destroyed a black church in Ernul on 9 April 1966. On 30 June 1967, bombs damaged property owned by five members of the Anson County school board in Wadesboro. Finally, on 18 July 1967, FBI agents arrested 12 Klansmen for participating in a two-year reign of terror that spanned three counties. One of those charged, Wayne Dayvault, served as grand kligrapp (state secretary) of the UKA. Four cases were dropped before Dayvault and eight codefendants faced trial in January 1968. Dayvault and six others were acquitted on 19 January, jurors deadlocked on the eighth, and no further prosecution was pursued.[63]

The FBI batted zero in court, but its White Hate campaign proceeded apace. Agents in the Charlotte field office proposed asking the Rev. Billy Graham to preach an anti–Klan sermon in North Carolina. Although William Sullivan liked the idea, Hoover blocked it. Elsewhere, G-men used their fictional National Intelligence Committee to spark a feud between Grand Dragon J.R. Jones (briefly imprisoned for contempt of Congress) and his acting successor, George Dorsett. Their feud began with the previously mentioned letter reporting (falsely) that Jones and Robert Shelton had been exiled from the Klan for embezzling funds. Dorsett, himself an FBI informant, declared to reporters that the NIC was a secret Klan body organized "by the people to protect them from the leadership." Jones was paroled in 1967 and promptly expelled Dorsett from the UKA, whereupon Dorsett joined 1950s Klansman James "Catfish" Cole to organize a rival Klan, the Confederate Knights. Their initial recruiting letter was drafted with FBI assistance.[64]

Another informant active in the North Carolina realm, Edward Dawson, served the FBI for at least seven years. The $6,329.19 he earned in that period was a pittance compared to Gary Rowe's $22,000 (paid from 1960–65), but Dawson was a zealous bureau servant nonetheless. He joined the UKA soon after settling in Greensboro in the early 1960s and served nine months in jail during 1967 for shooting up black homes in Alamance County. A close friend of George Dorsett, Dawson remained in the UKA after Dorsett was banished, but G-men soon "turned" him with threats of further prosecution for his role in a July 1969 Klan riot in Swan Quarter, North Carolina. Traveling attorney Arthur Hanes received $15,000 from the UKA to defend Dawson and 13 other Klansmen in that case and arranged misdemeanor guilty pleas that placed them on probation after payment of $1,000 fines. Embittered despite escaping a potential ten-year sentence, Dawson signed up as an FBI informant in November 1969 and switched allegiance to the bureau-supported Confederate Knights.[65] Ten years later, Dawson's continuing involvement with the Klan would land him in the midst of a public mass murder.

AMERICAN FÜHRERS

Klansmen were not the only targets of Hoover's White Hate crusade. Various neo–Nazi groups associated with the KKK also suffered harassment, frequently based on their ties to the Klan. Ku Klux links to the NSRP were well known, dating from the party's creation — one leader complained in 1958 that "the only ones paying dues here are the FBI spies"—and similar ties bound the KKK to George Lincoln Rockwell's American Nazi Party (ANP). The UKA's grand dragon in Pennsylvania, Roy Frankhouser, joined the ANP and NSRP, as well as the heavily armed Minutemen. When Jerald Walraven, a UKA spokesman in Texas, was paid by check for a 1965 appearance on Houston radio station KTRH, the check was endorsed by Rockwell, with a swastika stamped beneath his signature. Dan Burros and William Hoff, successive king kleagles for the New York UKA in 1965–66, were both ANP members. Another UKA kleagle, Xavier Edwards of Maryland, resented criticism of his ANP connections so much that he defected to lead the competing Interstate Knights.[66]

The FBI reveled in such fertile prospects for disruption, especially where closet Jews were found among the Nazi–Ku Klux brotherhood. One, Dan Burros, shot himself at Roy Frankhouser's home on 31 October 1965 after *The New York Times* exposed his background. (G-men later denied that Burros's "outing" was a White Hate project; journalist Frank Donner disagrees.) Another Jewish Burros—Robert, no relation — was found in the National Renaissance Party, and Frank Collin was expelled in 1970 from the ANP's successor organization, the National Socialist White People's Party, after G-men sought to "demolish" him by leaking his true surname (Cohn). Undaunted, Collin founded his own National Socialist Party of America, graduating to violence where the ANP was satisfied with racist rhetoric. When no Jews could be found in Nazi ranks, the FBI resorted to snitch-jacketing, producing a bogus "informant report" that was "accidentally" addressed to NSRP headquarters, branding one active member as a spy for the Anti–Defamation League.[67]

The quality of FBI informants on the Nazi fringe is suggested by the bureau's recruitment of Roy Frankhouser. Dubbed "Riot Roy" after he lost an eye brawling with blacks in a Reading, Pennsylvania, tavern, Frankhouser won promotion that summer to serve as the Pennsylvania's grand dragon, simultaneously managing UKA affairs in Delaware. Some observers also suspected him of murder after Dan Burros took three shots to kill himself at Frankhouser's home in October 1965. A compulsive joiner, Frankhouser paid dues to more than 30 far-right groups in the 1960s, presumably reporting on all of them to the FBI or ATF, where his handlers deemed him "an excellent infiltrator and confidential informant." On 1 March 1974, a Philadelphia grand jury indicted Riot Roy and two associates for receiving and selling stolen explosives, including 240 pounds of TNT delivered to a friend of Michigan Klan leader Robert Miles. That arrest ended Frankhouser's career as an FBI informant, but he went down swinging, declaring himself a double-agent for the KKK, enlisted to determine what information the feds had collected on his fellow knights. A year later, CBS News reported that Frankhouser had also run errands for President Richard Nixon's National Security Council.[68]

FBI investigation of George Rockwell predated the White Hate crusade. G-men first scrutinized him in 1959, suspecting him of being an unregistered agent of Egypt. They returned in 1960 with unsubstantiated claims of illegal wiretapping, and a second "foreign agent" case was opened without result in 1962. Bureau headquarters branded the ANP a "dangerous organization," both "psychologically and physically" capable of violence, "though small in numbers." Agents feared that Rockwell's Nazis might "follow through with their obnoxious objectives of liquidating all whom they consider inferior," yet little violence sprang from the party before Rockwell himself was murdered by a rogue disciple in August 1967. Meanwhile, the party sought publicity primarily through means that bureau headquarters deemed "the shocking, the repulsive, and the horrifying."[69]

Under COINTELPRO, the Richmond, Virginia, field office proposed branding Rockwell's second-in-command, Matt Koehl, an ADL spy who had joined Dr. King's 1963 March on Washington, but Hoover vetoed the plan. Richmond was more successful with another plan in September 1965, sending Rockwell a letter from "a hopeful member from your best chapter" that branded Texas ANP supporter Alan Welch "a traitor to the Nazi Party" and "a damn queer." Rockwell complained to G-men that the "vicious" note had "cast a spell on one of his most trusted members." Headquarters memos gleefully reported that Rockwell was "wracking his brain" to locate the mythical "spy" in ANP-Dallas. Farther north, Chicago agents launched a two-pronged attack to "ruin the Chicago unit financially and disrupt its leadership." To that end, they collaborated with the ADL to pepper Frank Collin's ANP office with building code violations, prompting city officials to threaten eviction. G-men also forged a letter to Chicago's branch of the Jewish War Veterans, purportedly written by a Jew who resented insults from a Nazi cab driver.[70]

For Hoover, the ANP was a convenient weapon against Robert Shelton's United Klans. In August 1966, after California UKA leader William Fowler addressed a Nazi rally in San Francisco, G-men obtained photos of the rally from local police, then sent them to Rockwell and Klansmen across the country, with a letter that read:

The pictures you see are of interest to all who swear allegiance to the Ku Klux Klan. Recently the American Nazi Party held a rally in Northern California. Now the Klan has no beef because the Nazi Party holds a rally, but what should concern the Klan is the fact that the man speaking at the microphone is William Fowler, Chairman of the California Ku Klux Klan, United Klans of America....

The Klan stands for Christianity and decency, the Klan stands for this great country of ours, the Klan stands for the rights of the White Man ... but never should we be accused of needing the Nazi storm troopers to get our message across to the American people.

And what of these uniformed storm troopers who stand alongside our "Klan representative" at this rally, wearing the swastika of the American Nazi Party[?] Needless to say, fellow Klansmen, these are the followers of the crooked George Lincoln Rockwell, the psychopathic agnostic who laughs at the name of Christ. Rockwell is great when it comes to playing boyish tricks, but have you ever noticed that it is not Rockwell himself who performs these publicity seeking stunts[?] Oh no, it is always some poor lame-brained nut who performs for the "Commander" and who sits in jail while the "Commander" quietly counts his money and dreams of new worlds to conquer....

Be assured that our Imperial Wizard, Robert Shelton[,] will not tolerate the actions of Fowler in California. Fowler does not speak for the United Klans of America.[71]

Throughout the campaign of disruption, Rockwell usually cooperated with G-men, convinced that Hoover secretly sympathized with Nazi ideals. That misplaced camaraderie inspired another COINTELPRO plot, discussed in FBI memos between January and May 1965. That scheme, never realized, involved a plan to brand Robert Shelton a mixed-race imposter. As one memo suggested, "If Rockwell printed a report that Shelton had some Negro ancestors, it would [only] be necessary for us to know the names of certain ancestors who could, perhaps, have been an illegitimate child related to Shelton."[72]

The NSRP received equal attention from Hoover, including preparation of an anonymous letter — mailed on 27 January 1965 to 15 black churches and civil rights groups in Birmingham —"in an effort to expose the fact that [name deleted] is a member of the National Executive Committee of the National States Rights Party." On 19 February, the Birmingham field office sought Hoover's permission "to prepare a follow-up anonymous communication to the same Negro groups (15) to whom the original letter was sent."[73] That letter read:

It sure tickled me when I found out that [name deleted] wasn't [deleted] in Birmingham, Ala., any longer.... You are to be thanked if you helped get [deleted] transferred and maybe you can use your influence concerning his present job. It hurts to know he can manage a company which is dependent on Negro patronage for a very substantial portion of its business and also serve as [deleted] of the National Executive Committee of the National States Rights Party. Hope you can spread the word.[74]

Long on harassment but short on arrests, the FBI's White Hate campaign sent only one NSRP member to jail, and that for a matter of hours. James Robinson assaulted Dr. King at a Selma hotel on 15 January 1965, for which he was fined $100 and sentenced to 60 days in custody. Robinson was back on the street by 7 March, when he allegedly assaulted Agent Daniel Doyle on Highway 80 east of Selma. Doyle was watching a group of whites beat a black man, snapping photos of the scene for future reference, when Robinson and two others rushed Doyle, knocking him down and fleeing with his camera. Robinson was soon apprehended and fined $27 for that incident. Federal charges were filed in that case, including theft of government property (the missing camera), but none of the suspects were convicted.[75]

HUAC Lends a Hand

As it assisted Hoover in pursuing Reds and "fellow travelers," so HUAC did its part to undermine the KKK. Chairman Edwin Willis of Louisiana was a segregationist who scorned the Klan for soiling the "good name" of white supremacists. Still, he required a reason to stop hunting communists and turn his spotlight to the right. Klansmen unwittingly provided it with the Liuzzo murder. Five days later, on 30 March 1965, HUAC voted to conduct a full inquiry on the Ku Klux Klan.[76]

The familiar process began smoothly enough when FBI headquarters recommended a retired G-man to head HUAC's field investigation. HUAC hit a snag in May 1965, however, when Cartha Deloach complained that its agents were stepping on FBI toes in Alabama and Mississippi. After another conference, Willis agreed to withdraw his men from the field in return for greater access to FBI files. The bureau complied, "so that the Committee can intelligently question the individuals when they are on the witness stand," but Hoover privately complained that "[w]e will be doing all the digging and staff of House committee will take the bows."[77]

HUAC convened public hearings on 19 October 1965 and grilled a total of 187 witnesses before the show folded on 24 February 1966. Most of those summoned were Klansmen, and most of those refused to answer any substantive questions—a circumstance that let the FBI's bogus National Committee for Domestic Tranquility to chastise tight-lipped knights for "joining hands with communists who always hide behind the Fifth Amendment." The first round of hearings focused chiefly on Klan organization and alleged financial improprieties, and the latter phase revealed details of Ku Klux violence. Silent witnesses included Samuel Bowers, Byron De La Beckwith and Jesse Stoner, together with a host of others named as suspects in various crimes ranging from embezzlement to multiple murders. Robert Shelton and three of his grand dragons were cited for contempt of Congress because of their refusal to produce Klan records on demand. Convicted by future Watergate judge John Sirica in September 1966, Shelton received a one-year prison sentence and was fined $1,000. Dragons J.R. Jones (North Carolina) and Robert Scoggin (South Carolina) received identical terms and served nine months each, and Georgia's Calvin Craig escaped with only a fine.[78]

HUAC climaxed its inquiry with legislative hearings in July 1966 and released its final report on the Klan in December 1967. Meanwhile, Chairman Willis drafted an "Organizational Conspiracies Act" that imposed life sentences on members of vaguely-defined "clandestine organizations" who conspired in acts of violence. The bill, introduced on 19 September 1967, was so poorly drafted and so broad in scope that vocal adversaries ranged from the Klan to black activist groups and the ACLU. It died in committee as the show wound to a close.[79]

WHITE HATE—INFORMING JUSTICE

Hoover's anti–Klan COINTELPRO campaign accelerated during and after the HUAC inquiry. In 1967, while Robert Shelton appealed his federal conviction, G-men plotted to replace him with a paid informant, but FBI headquarters nixed the plan that year and again in 1971. Louisiana's grand dragon was falsely branded a spy, one more victim of bureau snitch-jacketing tactics, while Shelton proposed that all members of the UKA's imperial board be subjected to polygraph tests or "truth serum." When Ohio knights complained of anonymous mailings in their realm during May 1966, Cincinnati G-men publicly denied all knowledge of the postcards they printed and mailed.[80]

Despite its blanket coverage of the KKK, bureau headquarters was remarkably ill-informed about Klan membership. On 24 March 1966, William Sullivan issued a memo complaining that his division had insufficient manpower to mount surveillance on more than 71 of 152 klaverns nationwide. In fact, as HUAC demonstrated, there were 192 UKA klaverns in North Carolina alone, and some 714 overall. Sullivan's estimate of national Klan membership (14,000) also fell short of HUAC's (at 16,810), and both hood counts were far below the standard estimates of 40,000 to 50,000 Klansmen paying dues to 18 rival factions during 1964–66.[81]

Various attorneys general in the 1960s remained blissfully unaware of those FBI inadequacies. Nicholas Katzenbach opined that the bureau fought Klansmen "vigorously, actively, overtly and with outstanding success"—then admitted that he never asked for details of the illicit White Hate campaign. His successor, Ramsey Clark, questioned Cartha Deloach in December 1967 "concerning FBI coverage and penetration" of the KKK. Hoover responded to that query with a ten-page memorandum captioned "Ku Klux Klan investigation—FBI accomplishments." While noting that much of the bureau's "secret war" was public knowledge (thanks to deliberate press leaks), Hoover's memo also referred to "matters dealing with extremely sensitive operations of this Bureau and it is suggested that this be handled on a strict need-to-know basis." As an example, Hoover wrote, "We have found that by the removal of top Klan officers and provoking scandal within the state Klan organization through our informants, the Klan in a particular area can be rendered ineffective." A vague list of "special projects" included efforts to discredit and remove Klan leaders, reporting deputized Klansmen to state authorities, and selective interviews with knights designed to "cause disillusionment of the members and disruption of the organization."[82] "Special projects" in Virginia included the following:

> In the fall of 1965 the United Klans of America began an intensive organizational effort in the State of Virginia. We immediately began an all-out effort to penetrate the Virginia Klan, contain its growth, and deter violence. Working closely with local and state authorities we were able to disseminate information on contemplated cross-burnings. Several arrests were made....
> [In December 1966] We provided the Governor with information regarding Klan activities in his state. As a result, Governor [Mills] Godwin pressed for more effective enforcements of Virginia cross burning laws, and publically [sic] repudiated the Ku Klux Klan....
> In May, 1966, we learned of Klan plans to "arrange an accident" for [name

deleted] a civil rights worker working in the State of Virginia. We advised
[deleted] and local authorities of the plot against her life and alerted our informants to follow the plot closely. To this date, the Klan has taken no action against
[deleted]. This is just one of many examples of our notifying authorities and
intended victims of racial violence in order that they could take appropriate protective measures.[83]

Nearly two years later, on 17 September 1969, Hoover sent a similar memo to
Attorney General John Mitchell, captioned "Investigation of Klan organizations—
Racial Matters (Klan)." The report outlined "significant progress we have recently
made in our investigation of the Ku Klux Klan," while once again omitting crimes
committed by G-men during the White Hate operation. "During the last several
months," Hoover wrote, "while various national and state leaders of the United Klans
of America remain in prison, we have attempted to negate the activities of the temporary leaders of the Ku Klux Klan." The only "negation" activity specified was "careful use and instruction of selected racial informants" to "initiate a split within the
United Klans of America." Once that had been accomplished, Hoover vowed, the FBI
would devote "full attention to our responsibilities in an effort to accomplish the maximum possible neutralization of the Klan."[84]

In fact, White Hate had already expanded beyond the KKK and neo–Nazi groups.
In 1967 Hoover ordered all field agents to report "details concerning rallies [and]
demonstrations" held by any racist groups in the United States. In April 1968, he
demanded increased "informant coverage of the Klan, White Hate groups, and white
ghetto areas," regardless of their "potential for violence." New files were opened on
"unaffiliated white racial extremists" and "neighborhood groups" in suburbs
described as "white ghetto areas of the large cities which border on minority group
living areas," especially if "these groups are known to sponsor demonstrations against
integration and against the bussing [sic] of Negro students to white schools." G-men
were told to be "discreet," since "many of these organizations" acted "on principles
of fear rather than hate" and could not be "classified as hate groups." As new groups
formed, agents hired informants or used "established sources" to collect "background
data" and learn "the aims and purposes of the organization." In 1969 Hoover issued
another demand for "full details concerning the speeches made at the rallies and
demonstrations, as well as the identities of the speakers." Two years later, investigation spread to anyone "who in judgment of SAC [special agent in charge] should be
subject of investigation due to extremist activities." In short, Hoover granted himself authority to spy on all racial dissidents anywhere in the nation.[85]

WAR IN MISSISSIPPI

As the White Hate campaign began in Mississippi, so it continued there, with
violence and bloodshed. Crosses were burned in at least nine counties on 3 January
1966, and two G-men ducked bullets while observing one of the Klan demonstrations. Despite the presence of 15 lawmen, including two FBI agents, James Meredith
was shot and wounded on 6 June 1966 during a one-man "Walk Against Fear" through

Mississippi. The following month, when civil rights protests began in Grenada, members of the UKA's local klavern joined in violence against the demonstrators, escalating to full-scale riots when schools opened on an integrated basis in September. Mobs of 200 to 400 whites armed with chains, pipes and axe handles terrorized blacks in Grenada, beating 30 on 12 September alone, before Justice attorneys sued Grenada's top officials for "willful failure and refusal" to protect black children on their way to school. On 4 October 1966, a federal grand jury indicted six whites (including Grenada's justice of the peace) for conspiring to obstruct school integration, but the case was never tried.[86]

In Adams County, William Ferrell sought his second term as county sheriff in 1967, capping his campaign with a visit to a Klan rally held outside Natchez. Two weeks later, a pair of G-men visited Ferrell, informing him that they knew of his link to the Klan and saying that five of the 15 men present the night of his speech were informants. Ferrell won the election, and bureau surveillance continued. By 1968, agents had filled a dossier with evidence detailing his "receipt of kickbacks from gamblers and prostitution activities" in Natchez, but Ferrell was not prosecuted. Two years later, a black man complained to the bureau that liquor-running "hit men" were stalking him on orders from the sheriff. Agents dismissed that claim, citing the complainant's unspecified "mental problems," and no further action was taken. Ferrell consistently denied Klan membership, noting that he was a Catholic, but the prewar ban on "papists" had been dropped by many Klan groups in the 1950s.[87]

While the bureau's investigation of Ferrell was a fruitless sideshow, its pursuit of Sam Bowers's White Knights was a life-and-death struggle. Vernon Dahmer, an NAACP member active in voter-registration work around Hattiesburg, was marked for death by Bowers in December 1965. A month later, on 10 January 1966, nightriders attacked Dahmer's rural home and store, lobbing firebombs through the windows and trading shots with Dahmer while his family escaped through a rear exit. Dahmer suffered fatal burns in the assault, but his killers left numerous clues at the scene. Nervous knights shot up one of their own cars in the heat of battle, then abandoned it nearby, also dropping a gun, spent cartridges, and a Halloween mask as they fled. The day after Dahmer's murder, informants told G-men that Bowers was boasting. Members of his Jones County klavern had "scored a big one," Bowers said. The crime surpassed Neshoba County's triple murder, in his view, because "these men won't talk."[88]

In fact, one of them did. G-men soon traced the bullet-riddled car to Klansman Travis Giles, who had reported it stolen. Further investigation led agents to Klan "senator" Lawrence Byrd, who cracked under interrogation and confessed his part in the raid, naming Bowers and others as conspirators. The pistol found at Dahmer's home belonged to Klansman Billy Pitts, Byrd said. On 27 March 1966, the bureau filed conspiracy charges against Bowers and 13 other knights. All but Bowers were arrested the next day; he surrendered on 31 March with two lawyers, Charles Blackwell and Travis Buckley, who had represented Klansmen at the HUAC hearings. A federal grand jury indicted 15 suspects on 22 June 1966, but their attorneys challenged the racial composition of the all-white panel and the charges were dismissed. A second grand jury, including black members, indicted 12 of the 15 Klansmen once more on 27 February 1967. Byrd, as a potential prosecution witness, was among those dropped from the list.[89]

Six days later, G-men learned of a plot to discredit Byrd and the FBI's case. In a ploy that echoed rumors from the Medgar Evers slaying, ex-convict Jack Watkins told agents that he had been kidnapped by defendant Billy Pitts and lawyer Buckley and driven to the woods where they threatened him with death if he did not collaborate in defense of Buckley's clients. Specifically, they ordered Watkins to claim that FBI agents had hired him to beat Lawrence Byrd and extract his confession by force. State authorities indicted Pitts and Buckley for kidnapping and conspiracy. Pitts pled guilty and received a five-year prison term, and Buckley was convicted at trial and sentenced to ten years. That verdict was overturned on appeal by the state Supreme Court.[90]

In Dahmer's case, Sam Bowers twice faced murder charges, but two juries deadlocked and thereby set him free. Four other knights (including Billy Pitts) were convicted of murder and sentenced to life imprisonment, and Byrd received a lenient ten-year term as a reward for his cooperation. In federal court, one defendant saw his case dismissed, three more were acquitted, and a fifth's case was postponed indefinitely on grounds of poor health. Bowers and seven others were released when jurors found themselves unable to agree on verdicts. Only Billy Pitts was finally convicted of conspiracy, receiving another five-year sentence. Thirty years later, in May 1998, state authorities filed new murder indictments against Bowers. An integrated jury convicted him on 21 August 1998, and he was sentenced to life in prison.[91]

Before his first trial in the Dahmer case, Bowers launched a new terror campaign, this time including Mississippi Jews among his targets. At 10:40 P.M. on 18 September 1967, a powerful bomb damaged Jackson's Beth Israel synagogue. Two hours later, two G-men went to question notorious Klansmen Joe Denver Hawkins (also a director of the APWR) and his son Joe Daniel, commonly called Danny Joe (twice tried and released by hung juries on charges of assaulting civil rights workers). As the agents reached their home, the suspects leaped into a car with Klansman J.L. Harper and fled with the FBI in hot pursuit. Another car soon joined the chase and rammed the agents from behind. The three initial suspects were arrested in a nearby parking lot and were later indicted for assaulting federal agents, but the charges never went to trial.[92]

White Knights clearly were not intimidated by the FBI. Bombings continued, striking all-black Tougaloo College in Jackson on 6 October 1967, St. Paul's Church in Laurel on 15 November, the Jackson home of a liberal white family on 19 November, and the home of Rabbi Perry Nussbaum (also in Jackson) on 21 November 1961. Four days before Christmas, police in Collins stopped a car driven by Klansman Thomas Tarrants III; his passenger was Sam Bowers, traveling with a submachine gun in the backseat. Tarrants was charged with reckless driving, posted bail, and promptly went into hiding as a self-proclaimed "guerrilla for God." State authorities charged Bowers with weapons violations, but jurors acquitted him at trial. Although possession of machine guns is a federal crime, G-men ignored the incident.[93]

The terror increased in early 1968, with seven black churches burned around

Meridian. Gunmen fired into an NAACP leader's home in Hattiesburg in February, then strafed the Jackson home of Charles Evers (Medgar's brother) on 3 March 1968. Blackwell Realty, a Jackson firm that sold homes to blacks, was bombed four days later. On 10 April, a local grand jury indicted Bowers, Danny Joe Hawkins, L.E. Matthews and seven other Klansmen for that crime. Defendant James Harper, caught with 115 sticks of dynamite, escaped with a mistrial in July, and Hawkins won acquittal in August. Charges were dropped against two more defendants, and the rest were never tried. Meanwhile, black activist Kaley Duckworth was injured by a car bomb in Hattiesburg on 15 May 1968, and Meridian's Temple Beth Israel was bombed on 28 May. On 6 June 1968, another blast demolished the home of a rights worker's widow in Florence.[94]

By then, a sense of dread long familiar to black Mississippians had gripped the state's Jewish residents. In Jackson and Meridian, they huddled with police and FBI agents, plotting ways to halt the reign of terror. Meridian police chief Roy Gunn — who made his detectives wear wide-brimmed fedoras in homage to Hollywood G-men — was himself the target of Klan threats. Believing he possessed "almost a divine mandate" to break up the KKK, Gunn organized a "blackshirt squad" that "waged their own 'COINTELPRO' of anti–Klan harassment," setting off bombs at Klan homes and shooting into houses. That squad — led by Sgt. Lester "Gigolo" Joyner and nicknamed "Joyner's Gorillas"—collaborated with the FBI. On 30 May 1968, a memo from Jackson's field office to bureau headquarters identified Tom Tarrants as a prime suspect in the recent Meridian synagogue bombing. Three days later, when Chief Gunn and Mayor Algreene Key approached A.I. Botnick (regional director of the Anti-Defamation League) in New Orleans, they named the chief suspect as Alton Roberts, convicted in the MIBURN trial seven months earlier. Botnick had offered rewards for capture of the Mississippi terrorists. Now, Gunn and Key allegedly asked him whether the ADL "would be willing to purchase bodies and not testimony." Botnick says they asked "if he would make a contract somewhere in the North, such as Chicago, to have two Klansmen liquidated." The targets would be Alton Roberts and his brother Raymond. Gunn and Key reportedly "assured Botnick that if he could make the arrangements, there would be no investigation." Botnick says he rejected the murder contract (which Gunn and Key deny), but passed the message to his backers—who, he was chagrined to learn, "didn't give a Goddamn how the mess was cleared up, only that it was."[95]

Meridian police were pushed to that extremity, said Botnick, by a list of Klan assassination targets that included Gunn and Key, along with eight affluent Mississippi Jews. A memo from Meridian detective Luke Scarborough said that Raymond Roberts had "contacted Sam Bowers and wants to eliminate Chief Gunn and possibly two FBI agents." In response to that threat, Agent Frank Watts later told Jack Nelson, the bureau decided "to fight fire with fire." Specifically, G-men decided to procure the Roberts brothers as informants, acting on the premise that "[y]ou have to deal with the scum of the earth to catch the scum of the earth." Watts and Agent James Rucker held secret meetings with the brothers, climaxed on 10 June 1968, when the Robertses identified Tarrants and Danny Joe Hawkins as the knights responsible for a dozen bombings and an impending planned murder in Meridian. Jewish businessmen raised $20,000 for the brothers and attorney Tom Hendricks (a former G-man), but only $1,000 was paid on 11 June, when the Robertses demanded $150,000 for delivery of the suspects. They finally settled for half that amount and received $7,000 more in advance. On 19 June, Hawkins and Raymond Roberts agreed that the next bombing target should be Meridian businessman Meyer Davidson. Tarrants and Hawkins missed their first target date, eight days later, but Joyner's Gorillas and three carloads of G-men were waiting when the bombers arrived at 2:00 A.M. on 30 June 1968.[96]

Unknown to the police and FBI, a last-minute substitution had changed the cast of characters. Fearing that surveillance on Hawkins was too intense, Tarrants chose Klanswoman Kathryn Ainsworth to join him on the raid. Police opened fire on Tarrants as he approached Davidson's home with bomb in hand, then pursued him in a running battle that left Ainsworth dead. Tarrants, a policeman and a bystander were gravely wounded. Tarrants suffered 30 gunshot wounds, and Sgt. Joyner later told Jack Nelson, "We had in mind killing him, I don't mind telling you that." Instead, he would live to stand trial, convicted on 27 November 1968 and sentenced to 35 years in prison. Agent Watts later played a key role in converting inmate Tarrants to Christianity, all the while prodding him to inform on other Klansmen. Tarrants agreed to testify against Bowers and company "if the violence resumes," but he otherwise stood mute. In December 1976, at the urging of G-men and others, Governor Cliff Finch approved early release for Tarrants, allowing him to enroll at the state university. Tarrants served less than one-third of his sentence — four years less than the state's requirement for normal parole — and later wrote a book (*The Conversion of a Klansman*, 1979) that praised the bureau's COINTELPRO efforts. "Liberals and conservatives alike," he wrote, "should realize that their lives may one day depend on such a program."[97]

The Meridian ambush sent Mississippi Klansmen scurrying for cover. Danny Joe Hawkins, whose car Tarrants used on the raid, eluded arrest on conspiracy charges and remained at large until April 1981, when he was jailed with nine other knights for plotting the invasion of Grenada. (See Chapter 9.) The Roberts brothers, meanwhile, were outraged at being short-changed by the FBI. An additional payment of $21,850 failed to mollify them, as Raymond urged White Knights to retaliate for the shooting. On the day of Ainsworth's funeral, he and Hawkins were detained by state highway patrolmen who found them testing a submachine gun at a dump outside Jackson, but the officers released both men with their illegal weapon. Next, Ray Roberts told G-men of Danny Joe's plan to kill a black taxi driver. Agents stopped his car outside the governor's mansion, seizing three guns, 100 rounds of ammunition and a hangman's noose, but false charges linking Hawkins to a Memphis bank heist were dismissed and he fled once again. Two weeks after the ambush, the brothers received $20,000 more — still $25,150 short of what they were promised — but they refused bureau offers of $20,000 for testimony in open court.[98]

Klan violence declined in Mississippi after the Meridian ambush, but it did not end abruptly, as some sources say. G-men recorded 70 acts of terrorism between September 1969 and September 1970, including an attempt to kill Charles Evers in Fayette. Elected mayor in 1969, Evers took office that July and soon received death threats over his plan to erect a "freedom runner" statue in a local park. On 9 September 1969, police found Tupelo Klansman Dale Walton—founder of a splinter group, Knights of the Green Forest, and a friend of Byron De La Beckwith—circling Evers's office with three guns in his car. Two accomplices were caught in Natchez with a submachine gun, and a fourth conspirator was jailed in Hattiesburg. All four were charged with violations of the National Firearms Act, but Walton alone went to court. Upon conviction, he was fined $329 and sentenced to 45 days in jail.[99]

Reporter Jack Nelson broke the Meridian ambush story in 1970 after purchasing Detective Scarborough's file on the case for $1,000. (Scarborough later returned the check uncashed.) Hoover sought to have Nelson fired from the *Los Angeles Times*. He sent agents to badger his employers, and that failing, he spread false accusations about Nelson's private life. When a memo from Jackson to Washington noted the FBI's "excellent working relations with Jack Nelson," Hoover wrote in the margin: "It is obvious now that Nelson played [Agent Roy] Moore for a sucker." Another note from Hoover read: "I hope SAC Moore now realizes Nelson doesn't have a halo over his head." Headquarters denied any role in the ambush, contending, "This is a typical Jack Nelson article filled with lies and vicious innuendo." Finally, the defense fell back on nit-picking: "Nelson quotes SAC Moore as saying that a story disclosing the tactics used by the FBI and police would jeopardize their system of informants and hurt the cause of law enforcement. What Moore actually told Nelson was that if his story was slanted in any way it could hurt the cause of law enforcement."[100] The ADL also denied participating in the trap. Contradicting A.I. Botnick, another ADL spokesman said that:

> In an effort at the time to stem planned murders and the tide of actual bombings of Jewish houses and other communal establishments, the Jewish community of Mississippi raised funds to obtain information leading to the apprehension of the perpetrators of these acts of violence. Because human lives were in jeopardy, ADL's representative in the area recommended to Jewish leaders that they assist in this fund-raising as a matter of civic responsibility. This was the extent of ADL's involvement in the situation. We had no part in the disbursement of funds nor any contact with informants nor any participation in the police activity. So far as we know, there is no basis for criticism of the law enforcement authorities.[101]

Ex-agent Tom Hendricks was more forthright in his description of events. As he explained, "Scarborough brought a briefcase full of money to the trailer and told the Robertses it was a hundred thousand dollars and that was what they were supposed to get. But they double-crossed them. The FBI didn't live up to their word. When I was in the FBI, we kept our word."[102]

OTHER TARGETS

Founded by Missouri chemist Robert DePugh in 1959, the Minutemen was not a racist group per se, but its extreme right-wing philosophy and penchant for collecting military weapons naturally appealed to many Klansmen. Connie Lynch and Roy Frankhouser were early Minutemen recruits, followed by other knights and neo–Nazis. Frankhouser presumed to speak for both groups when he told reporters, "We work independently, but we also complement each other, and the lines of communication are always open between us. We've got the same enemies, the same friends, and the same goals." Dennis Mower, California's number-two Minuteman, was a friend of Sam Bowers; Thomas Tarrants carried Mower's business card to the Meridian shootout in June 1968. Other known crossover members included William Hoff, the UKA's king kleagle for New York, and Paul Dommer, active in the NSRP and the American Nazi Party. Hoff and Dommer were arrested on 26 August 1968 after they delivered explosives to an undercover policeman. Indicted for conspiracy to murder left-wing activists, the defendants pled guilty to reduced charges in 1969. Two years later, informants reported a merger of sorts between Louisiana Minutemen and the Universal Klans. "We won't need the National Guard if a race riot breaks out around here," one knight declared. "We'll wipe them out with the Minutemen."[103]

On 19 May 1965, Hoover told the House Appropriations Subcommittee, "We have long been aware of the Minutemen organization and our investigation is continuing." In fact, his comments—including a description of the Minutemen as "essentially a paper organization"—were lifted almost verbatim from a newspaper article by J. Harry Jones, published in *The Washington Post* six months earlier. The bureau's first known Minutemen informant was Michael Sadewhite (alias Desmond), who infiltrated the United Klans in 1966 and later served as Delaware's king kleagle under Roy Frankhouser. Riot Roy recruited Sadewhite for the Minutemen, and Sadewhite filed reports on both groups until August 1967, when he resigned in fear that his cover was blown. During Sadewhite's tenure, in August 1966 DePugh and two colleagues were held for federal firearms violations. Two months later, 20 Minutemen were charged with plotting to attack various left-wing targets in New York. Tons of weapons were seized in the raids, including 125 rifles, 25 pistols, 12 .30-caliber machine guns, five mortars with 50 rounds of ammunition, ten pipe bombs, six hand grenades, three grenade launchers, 20 brass knuckles and 220 knives.[104]

While Minutemen armed and trained to defend the U.S. against Red invaders, Klansmen devoted themselves to more traditional projects. Insurance salesman Robert Miles quit his job in 1970 to serve as Michigan grand dragon for the UKA and pastor of the Mountain Church of Jesus Christ. In April 1971, Miles led the Klan party that tarred and feathered Ypsilanti high school principal Wiley Brownlee. Four months later, bombs destroyed ten buses marked for use in school integration in Pontiac. Miles and four other knights were convicted of those crimes in federal court, and the dragon received a nine-year prison term. Miles won parole in 1979, based on promises to leave the KKK, but he remained a key figure in racist circles through the next decade.[105]

Roy Frankhouser's Pennsylvania realm of the UKA lost an estimated 300 members during 1970–71 because of "paranoia" over FBI informants. One who left was Steven White, who promptly organized a rival group—the White Christian Crusaders—and joined the mayoral campaign of Philadelphia police commissioner Frank Rizzo. In Texas, Houston's Pacifica radio station was bombed in May 1970 and again five months later. On 21 January 1971, an FBI tip sent Texas police after Klansman Jimmy Hutto, captured with weapons en route to raid a Pacifica radio outlet in California. Hutto and three fellow Klansman, including alleged ringleader Louis Beam, were charged with conspiracy in six Texas bombings and the California plot but none were convicted. Again, despite evidence of interstate plotting and federal crimes, the FBI declined further action.[106]

STATE-SPONSORED TERROR

The most shocking aspect of COINTELPRO was not the illegal harassment of racists, which even some civil libertarians illogically supported, but rather the FBI's direct sponsorship of far-right terrorist groups. Author Brian Glick contends that COINTEL-PRO—White Hate was a sham from the beginning:

> This unique "program" functioned largely as a component of the FBI's operations against the progressive activists who were COINTELPRO's main targets. Under the cover of being even-handed and going after violent right-wing groups, the FBI actually gave covert aid to the Ku Klux Klan, Minutemen, Nazis, and other racist vigilantes. These groups received substantial funds, information and protection — and suffered only token FBI harassment — so long as they directed their violence against COINTELPRO targets. They were not subjected to serious disruption unless they breached this tacit understanding and attacked established business and political leaders.[107]

That judgment seems harsh — some might say paranoid — yet FBI headquarters memos from July 1970 reveal that G-men furnished information on black activists to Jesse Stoner's violent NSRP, while bombarding civil rights workers with Klan publications and "any other literature that can be obtained from organizations having an extreme hatred for black people." By September 1965, an estimated 20 percent of all Klansmen were bureau informants, their number including at least two grand dragons. One informant told a Ku Klux audience that Klansmen would bring "peace and order in America" even "if we have to kill every Negro." Such inflammatory language might be explained as part of his "cover," but other hirelings—like Gary Rowe, "Nigger" Hall and the Roberts brothers—had long histories of violence, including murder.[108]

The bureau did not merely hire violent knights, but also created its own puppet Klans. One klavern, started with a handful of informants as its charter members, ultimately claimed 250 knights. Another FBI creation, the Confederate Knights of the KKK, was launched in 1967 with federal funds by informant George Dorsett and sidekick James Cole. (Cole had defected from the U.S. Klans a decade earlier to lead a rival faction of his own, then served time in prison for inciting a riot between Klansmen and Lumbee Indians in Robeson County, North Carolina.) Joseph Bryant, another ex-convict and 1950s Klansman, joined FBI informant Edward Dawson to create the North Carolina Knights in 1969. Ten years later, under new leadership, members of that bureau-sponsored Klan would murder five victims in Greensboro (see Chapter 9).[109]

Bureau apologists may argue that splinter Klans were created by FBI headquarters from pure motives, to divide and conquer the "real" KKK, but no such excuses apply to the Secret Army Organization (SAO), ostensibly created by members of the disintegrating Minutemen in February 1970. Based in San Diego, the SAO initially confined itself to paper battles, printing how-to manuals on bombing, burglary and booby traps, but its members ultimately tired of talk and turned to violence in autumn 1971. A primary target was Peter Bohmer, a professor at San Diego State College who offended SAO members by attending anti-war rallies on campus. The "patriot" guerrillas launched their campaign with threatening phone calls and letters, then firebombed a car outside Bohmer's home on 13 November 1971. In December, the SAO published Bohmer's address, telephone and auto license numbers for the benefit of "our readers who may care to look up this Red scum and say hello." On 6 January 1972, SAO callers warned Bohmer's friends to tell him good-bye. That night, drive-by gunmen fired into Bohmer's home, gravely wounding a visitor.[110]

The terror continued in San Diego until June 1972, when bombers wrecked the Guild Theater, a local porn house. Police were finally stirred to action, and after several false starts they arrested William Yakopec, a former member of the John Birch Society. Further investigation revealed that the SAO's membership included several San Diego firemen and police officers, some of them doubling as FBI informants. At Yakopec's bombing trial, defense attorneys were stunned to find one of the SAO's leaders, Howard Godfrey, listed as a prosecution witness. On the stand, Godfrey confessed that he had been an FBI informant since early 1967, drawing $250 a month for services rendered. He had begun his undercover journey with the Minutemen, then helped create the SAO when its parent group folded. From that day forward, he had played a key role in each of the SAO's crimes.[111]

Godfrey was not merely a watcher. While drawing a government paycheck, he also planned and participated in the SAO's terrorist activities. On one raid, he led a group of thugs who stole $4,000 worth of equipment from the *San Diego Street Journal*'s office, putting the newspaper out of business. Godfrey's FBI handlers had supplied him $60,000 worth of weapons and explosives, earmarked for the SAO. Some of those explosives were used on the Guild Theater — a crime planned by Godfrey himself, after meetings with Watergate conspirator Donald Segretti. Godfrey also drove the car from which SAO member George Hoover fired into Bohmer's home on 6 January 1972. After that shooting, Godfrey delivered the rifle and Hoover's jacket to G-man Steve Christiansen, who destroyed the jacket and hid the gun from local police for six months. Instead of prosecuting Christiansen, the bureau wished him well on retirement to Utah.[112]

Godfrey's public testimony prompted further revelations from another FBI informant, ex-policeman John Rasperry. After several failed efforts to entrap Peter Bohmer in criminal acts, Rasperry said his bureau handlers ordered him to "eliminate" and "get rid of" Bohmer as a threat to national security. Rasperry told reporters that he would have murdered Bohmer if his orders had been more specific. Howard Godfrey moved on from his FBI service to work as an explosives "specialist" for the state of California. His last case, in October 1989, involved a terrorist who left a bomb near Godfrey's home and telephoned police, saying, "I'm going to kill a trick-or-treater with a bomb." ATF agents arrested Godfrey on 15 November, charging that he built the bomb and made the call himself.[113]

COINTELPRO EXPOSED

On 8 March 1971, members of a self-styled Citizens' Commission to Investigate the FBI burglarized a bureau office in Media, Pennsylvania, escaping with hundreds of COINTELPRO files, including coverage of a Philadelphia UKA klavern. Copies were sent to reporters and members of Congress, some of whom made their contents public. The burglars were never identified, but exposure of his illicit activities drove J. Edgar Hoover to officially end COINTELPRO for "security reasons" on 28 April 1971. By July, he had closed 103 of the bureau's 538 resident agencies, while tightening security procedures at the rest.[114]

Though COINTELPRO was officially defunct, G-men continued their covert activities as if nothing had changed. FBI-sponsored SAO crimes continued for 14 months after Hoover's decree. Between 1972 and 1974, agents conducted at least 421 illicit wiretaps, planted 114 unauthorized bugs, and illegally opened 2,042 pieces of mail. On 26 November 1973 — nearly three years after COINTELPRO "ended"— Agent Richard W. Held wrote a memo to headquarters, urging that "Los Angeles and Minneapolis consider possible COINTELPRO measures to further disrupt [American Indian Movement] leadership." Klan informant Edward Dawson remained on the FBI payroll in North Carolina through August 1976.[115]

The Media burglary and the subsequent Watergate scandal prompted Congress to investigate U.S. intelligence abuses during 1975–76. The Senate's Church Committee — named for chairman Frank Church — conducted 800 interviews and held some 250 executive hearings, while compiling 110,000 pages of classified documents from the FBI and CIA. Gary Rowe wore a Klanlike mask for his appearance in Washington, reporting that his bureau handlers told him, "You can do anything to get your information.... [W]e don't want you to get involved in unnecessary violence, but the point is to get the information." Former Attorneys General Katzenbach and Clark were less forthcoming when they testified on 3 December 1975. Katzenbach denied any knowledge of the White Hate crusade, noting that bureau spokesmen frequently "used terms of art, or euphemisms, without informing the Attorney General that they were terms of art." Clark issued similar denials, then hedged in the face of a Hoover memo describing the illegal campaign. "I guess I think I didn't read this," Clark explained. "I think perhaps I had asked for it for someone else, and either bucked it on to them or I never saw it." In retrospect, Clark opined that the tactics Hoover's memo outlined "should be absolutely prohibited and subjected to criminal prosecution."[116]

The Church Committee's revelations sparked a rash of lawsuits in the late 1970s, filed by Klan victims and Klansmen alike. Most failed in court, including actions filed by Robert Shelton and six Birmingham knights who blamed G-men for disrupting their jobs and marriages. The UKA sought $50 million from the FBI for "fraud, continued harassment and intimidation" in the White Hate years, but that claim was also rejected. Veteran G-men defended the campaign, one telling author Kenneth O'Reilly, "In five years we blew them all to hell. We never got any credit for that." Agent Joseph Sullivan went further still, claiming credit for a veritable sea change in Dixie. "By the time I left the South in 1966," he told O'Reilly, "an entire society had resolved to suppress outlawry in racial matters." Charles Morgan, Jr., leader of the first ACLU chapter in Selma, Alabama, had a different take on the bureau's achievement. He told O'Reilly: "Years before those miserable, ignorant white men killed Viola Liuzzo, FBI agents surreptitiously peddled the lies which those killers believed and which Matt Murphy openly argued" at trial, in defense of killer Klansmen.[117]

8

"Open Season"

In May 1965, after an all-white jury failed to reach a verdict in the first trial resulting from Viola Liuzzo's murder, Alabama Klansmen decorated their cars with bumper stickers reading "Open Season." Blacks and others active in the civil rights movement immediately understood the threat and saw it carried out in other racist homicides throughout the South. Charles Evers contends that 41 blacks were murdered by terrorists in Mississippi alone during the four years following his brother's death in June 1963. No tabulation of those victims has been published, but information is available on several slayings fruitlessly investigated by the FBI during the 1960s.[1]

THE SILVER DOLLAR GROUP

Don Whitehead, working from FBI files still closed to the general public, reported in 1970 on the bureau's investigation of a Klan faction known to its members as the Silver Dollar Group. As described by Whitehead, the group was organized in late 1964, when Klansmen from Adams County, Mississippi, and neighboring Catahoula Parish, Louisiana, met at the Shamrock Hotel in Vidalia, Louisiana. The gathering included members of the UKA, White Knights and Original Knights, all angered by the "lack of guts" displayed by their respective Klans. White Knights who attended the meeting complained that Sam Bowers had ordered a 90-day moratorium on acts of violence in Mississippi, and others likewise lamented a recent decline in terrorism. One knight allegedly displayed a silver dollar minted in his birth year and proposed that such coins serve members of the new secret group as recognition symbols. Calling themselves the "toughest Klansmen in Mississippi or Louisiana," Silver Dollar knights prepared for action in a series of covert training sessions. Once, Whitehead reports, their wives served picnic lunches on a bayou farm while their menfolk practiced blowing stumps with dynamite and wiring bombs to a car's ignition switch.[2]

Practice paid off for the first time, Whitehead says, in the murder of Frank Morris, a black resident of Ferriday, Louisiana. Aside from running the town's only shoe repair shop, Morris also hosted a Sunday-morning radio program featuring gospel music and sermons from local clergymen. His life seemed blameless until Silver Dol-

lar knights heard rumors that Morris was "flirting" with white female patrons, perhaps taking some to the small apartment behind his shop. In the predawn hours of
10 December 1964, Morris woke to sounds of smashing glass and found a white man
pouring gasoline through a broken window. A second man, armed with a shotgun,
ordered Morris back inside as his companion struck a match and lit the fuel. Engulfed
in flames, Morris struggled to free himself. Across the street, a gas station attendant
watched a dark sedan speed off toward Vidalia before Morris staggered into the street.
Two FBI agents questioned Morris that morning, accompanied by Police Chief R.W.
Warren and Fire Chief Noland Mouelle. Morris told his visitors he recognized the
nightriders but did not know their names. "I think they might work at Johns Manville
or something like that over in Natchez," he said. Four days later, Morris died in
excruciating pain.[3]

Whitehead's description of events links the Silver Dollar Group to another pair
of heinous crimes in Natchez. Although he mentions no names, it is clear from Whitehead's text that the Klan's second victim was George Metcalfe, president of the
Natchez NAACP and chairman of a black voter-registration drive. On weekdays,
Metcalfe worked at the Armstrong Tire and Rubber Company's plant in Natchez,
where the best jobs were reserved for whites and many Klansmen drew their pay-
checks. On 27 August 1965, as Metcalfe left the plant for home, a bomb exploded in
his car, shattering both his legs and one arm and leaving him crippled for life. Whitehead reports that the bombing occurred "not long after" the Silver Dollar knights
enjoyed their picnic practice session in Louisiana.[4]

Wharlest Jackson, a black friend and fellow worker of Metcalfe's at the Armstrong plant, doubled as treasurer of the Natchez NAACP, defying Klan threats at
home and on the job. In early 1967 Jackson received a promotion to work as a chem-
ical mixer for Armstrong, a post formerly held by whites only. Although initially
afraid to take the job, Jackson decided that his family deserved the extra $6.80 a week
to make ends meet. Metcalfe advised Jackson to check beneath his pickup's hood for
bombs each time he used the vehicle, but caution failed Jackson in his third week on
the job. He left work at 8:01 P.M. on 27 February 1967, and died ten minutes later in
the blast of a time-delayed bomb attached to the pickup's chassis. The next morning, Charles Evers led 2,000 protesters to the Armstrong plant to "put ourselves before
all the Kluxers and say, 'You killed out brother, now kill all of us.'" Evers hinted darkly
that his patience was exhausted. "Once we learn to hate," he said, "they're through.
We can kill more people in a day than they've done in a hundred years."[5]

Governor Johnson called the Jackson bombing an "act of savagery which stains
the honor of our state," and although the Natchez Board of Aldermen offered a
$10,000 reward for arrest of the killers, Charles Evers insists to this day that local
police "never even investigated" the slaying. Whitehead says that G-men quickly
solved the bombing, along with Metcalfe's and the arson-murder of Frank Morris.
In 1970 he wrote, "The FBI is certain that it knows the klansmen responsible for the
murders and the attempted murder." Agents had collected "important bits and pieces
of information," but all in vain, since no witnesses agreed to testify in court. At four
decades and counting, the crimes remain officially unsolved.[6]

JAMES REEB

Viola Liuzzo was not the first casualty of the Selma voting rights campaign. After Al Lingo's state troopers and Sheriff Clark's mounted "posse" routed protest marchers on "Bloody Sunday"—7 March 1965—Dr. King issued a nationwide call for volunteers to join in the next demonstration. One of those who responded was the Rev. James Reeb, a Unitarian minister from Washington, D.C. Reeb flew to Montgomery on 8 March and reached Selma that night, in time to join a protest march the following day. Police stopped that demonstration as well, though without the customary beatings. Later on 9 March, Reeb joined fellow demonstrators for dinner at Walker's Café. Around 7:30 P.M., he left the restaurant with two other white Unitarian ministers, the Rev. Orloff Miller and the Rev. Clark Olsen. They became disoriented on the unfamiliar streets and walked mistakenly into a tough white neighborhood, soon passing a Klan hangout identified in various reports as the Blue Moon or Silver Moon Café. Across the street, four white men suddenly emerged from the C & C Novelty Company, rushing across the street and shouting, "Hey, you niggers!" One hammered Reeb's skull with a club, while the others assaulted Miller and Olsen with bare fists. In parting, they kicked the fallen ministers, one thug declaring, "Here's how it feels to be a nigger down here."[7]

The three victims hobbled to a black-owned business, where an ambulance was summoned for Reeb. He was initially examined at Selma's black hospital, where doctors lacked proper facilities to treat his fractured skull. The ambulance transported Reeb to Birmingham University Hospital, where he was diagnosed with a blood clot in his brain. Life support machinery kept Reeb alive for two days, and he died at 6:55 P.M. on 11 March. By that time, his presumed killers had already posted bond on an assault charge. They were identified as Elmer Cook (owner of C & C Novelty), R.B. Kelly, and brothers Namon and William Hoggle. Selma's city attorney released the four on modest bail over strenuous protests from Police Chief Wilson Baker, but their charges were upgraded with Reeb's death. A grand jury indicted Cook and the Hoggles for murder on 13 April, excusing Kelly after he provided evidence against the other three. Local journalists regarded the indictments as a minor miracle, since Judge James Hare had first treated the panel to a 50-minute lecture on the plague of civil rights, saying that U.S. leaders had,"selected Selma for assassination back in the fall of 1963." Hare opined that whites had shown "unbelievable restraint" in the face of "fantastic and terroristic" acts by blacks and "self-appointed saints" drawn from the Northern clergy. Still the panel recognized its duty. The indictments stood.[8]

Klan involvement in Reeb's murder was never widely publicized, but United Klans Imperial Wizard Robert Shelton took the lead in a posthumous propaganda campaign, declaring falsely on 27 March 1965 that Reeb "had been dying of cancer before he ever came to Alabama." Six weeks later, on 5 May, Grand Dragon Robert Creel told Klansmen gathered in Bladen Springs that Reeb's corpse had been cremated because it was "rotten with cancer and syphilis." One of Lingo's state troopers, Capt. Lionel Freeman, appeared to justify the killing when he said that he saw "two men dressed as priests and four young Negro girls cross U.S. 80" in Selma on 9 March. "The priests were holding hands with two Negro girls each," Freeman said. "The

Rev. Reeb was beaten about two or three hours later." FBI informant Gary Rowe provided another Klan link in his description of Viola Liuzzo's murder. Shortly before the shooting on 25 March, he said, his "wrecking crew" stopped at the Silver Moon Café for drinks. There, Eugene Thomas saw the Reeb defendants at a nearby table and allegedly introduced them to Rowe as brother Klansmen. In parting, Elmer Cook remarked, "God bless you boys. You boys go do your job. I already did mine."[9]

Cook and the Hoggles faced trial in Selma on 7 December 1965, before Judge L.S. Moore. Prosecutor Blanchard McLeod warned reporters in advance that "I don't have a very strong case," but it scarcely mattered. When McLeod questioned prospective jurors en masse, asking whether racial prejudice would hamper their impartial judgment, all but three stood mute. Judge Moore deemed their silence tantamount to a negative answer, and so they were seated, without any questions about their ties to the Klan or the Citizens' Council. One witness to the beating was absent from court, having fled the state for Mississippi, and Judge Moore barred another from testifying on grounds of "mental incompetence." Victims Miller and Olsen identified Elmer Cook as Reeb's club-wielding assailant, but defense attorneys contended that none of their clients were present at the assault. Furthermore, they said, Reeb's injuries as diagnosed in Selma were not lethal. By that theory, Reeb's death remained a mystery when jurors retired to deliberate on 10 December. Sheriff Clark dropped by the jury room while the deliberations were in progress, but no record of his comments was preserved. The panel returned after 90 minutes and was greeted with applause in court when all three defendants were acquitted.[10]

Harry and Bonaro Overstreet put a strange spin on the case in 1969, reporting that FBI agents arrested the Reeb defendants in Selma for conspiracy to violate their victim's civil rights under 18 USC Sec. 241. They note that "there were abundant precedents to justify the use of this law" but make no further mention of the case. There is no record of a federal arrest in Reeb's case. All published sources agree that his attackers were jailed and charged by Selma police, and their only trial — resulting in acquittal — occurred in local court. They never spent a night in jail. Officially, the crime remains unsolved.[11]

ONEAL MOORE AND CREED ROGERS

While Louisiana's Washington Parish seethed with Klan violence in the 1960s, Sheriff Dorman Crowe sought to alleviate part of the problem by appointing two black deputies. His candidates, sworn in on 2 June 1964, were Oneal Moore and Creed Rogers. They served for exactly one year before they were ambushed and shot by nightriding gunmen on the night of 2 June 1965 while driving together toward home in Vernado. A pickup truck with several white passengers overtook Moore's patrol car on a narrow country lane, riddling the cruiser with rifle and shotgun fire. Moore died instantly from a massive head wound. Rogers was hit in the shoulder and face. Though permanently blinded in one eye, Rogers survived to describe the pickup.[12]

Within an hour of the shooting, police in Tylertown, Mississippi, arrested Bogalusa resident Ernest McElveen at the wheel of a truck matching Rogers's description. Authorities found two pistols in the truck, one described by the Walthall County sheriff as having been recently fired. Media reports identified McElveen as a member of the Citizens' Council, the National States Rights Party, and the United Conservatives of Mississippi—a front group for United Klans Unit 702 in Poplarville. McElveen waived extradition on 4 June and was jailed in Bogalusa on a murder charge. He retained attorney Ossie Brown, who one month later would defend the Original Knights against a federal lawsuit filed by the Justice Department in Washington Parish. A relative, D.D. McElveen, was identified by HUAC as a member of the Original Knights and a participant in violent actions by that Klan's "wrecking crew."[13]

In custody, McElveen stonewalled authorities, refusing to submit a verifiable alibi. From Mississippi, members of the White Knights reportedly donated $500 to McElveen's defense fund. Governor John McKeithen offered $25,000 for apprehension of the gunmen. Terrorists struck again on 6 June, firing shots into the home of Doyle Holliday, a white deputy assigned to investigate the ambush. Legal maneuvers stalled the case until November, when McElveen's charges were dismissed for lack of evidence. No other suspects were identified, and the case remains open today. Despite their thorough infiltration of the Klan in Mississippi and Louisiana, G-men made no visible attempt to try the killers for conspiracy. Thirty-four years later, Moore's widow told ABC News, "I'm hoping that someway, somehow, somebody would come forward so this case could be solved." Creed Rogers, asked if he believed McElveen took part in the shooting, replied, "Yes, I do, because they caught him driving the truck. And that truck was the truck they was shooting from."[14]

JONATHAN DANIELS

Jonathan Myrick Daniels was enrolled at an Episcopal seminary in Cambridge, Massachusetts, when Dr. King issued his call for Selma volunteers on 7 March 1965. One day later, he landed in Montgomery aboard the same plane that carried James Reeb to his appointment with fate. Daniels lasted five months longer, working with the movement in "Bloody" Lowndes County, scene of the Liuzzo murder in March 1965. Four months later, on 14 August, Daniels was among demonstrators arrested for picketing segregated establishments in Fort Deposit. FBI agents warned the protesters in advance that a white mob had gathered downtown, urging them to cancel the march and reminding all present that G-men would observe any violence but would not protect them. The marchers dismissed that lecture as an effort to intimidate them, and they were not assaulted on 14 August. Sheriff's deputies transported them to jail in Hayneville. After six days in custody, they were abruptly released at 3 P.M. on 20 August by a jailer who refused them protection and ordered them all out of town. With other demonstrators, including several blacks and a white Catholic priest, the Rev. Richard Morrisroe, Daniels walked to a nearby grocery store that welcomed blacks as customers. Inside, they were confronted by a white man with a shotgun who ordered them to leave, then opened fire at close range, killing Daniels instantly and gravely wounding Morrisroe.[15]

The gunman, Thomas Coleman, was a well-connected engineer for the state highway department, son of Lowndes County's former school superintendent. His sister now held that job, and Coleman's son — Thomas Jr. — was a state trooper assigned as Al Lingo's personal chauffeur and bodyguard. Coleman Sr. was a member of the Citizens' Council, and although he publicly denied membership in the KKK, SNCC activists described him as "a known Klansman." Ten days before the shooting, Coleman had confronted state Attorney General Richmond Flowers in Hayneville, threatening, "If you don't get off the Klan investigation, we'll get you off." He was also a close friend of Selma sheriff Jim Clark and a heavy drinker familiar with violence. Six years earlier, in August 1959, guards at the Greenville prison camp had unaccountably summoned Coleman to help them subdue a rowdy black inmate in the camp's recreation room. Arriving with his shotgun, Coleman found the prisoner, Richard Jones, brandishing two broken soft-drink bottles. Although supported by a team of officers, civilian Coleman fired on Jones and killed him where he stood. On the day he shot Daniels and Morrisroe, Coleman carried a card identifying him as a "special deputy" for Lowndes County.[16]

After the shooting, Coleman left his shotgun at the grocery store and walked to the nearby courthouse, where he surrendered to a deputy. Sheriff Frank Ryals later told reporters he was out of town on 20 August. It was mere coincidence, he said, that Coleman answered the phone in his office when callers reported "a disturbance" at the store. From the courthouse, Coleman called Al Lingo and told him, "I just shot two preachers. You better get on down here." Rev. Morrisroe lay in the street for an hour before an ambulance arrived and drove him to Montgomery. He passed Lingo in transit, racing to Hayneville with Coleman's son at the wheel. Their other passenger was a bail bondsman described by Richmond Flowers as "a known Kluxer." Before he left Montgomery, Thomas Jr. telephoned attorney Robert Black (his father's nephew) to arrange for counsel in Lowndes County. Jim Clark beat Lingo to the scene, driving from Selma to console his friend in custody while Coleman waited for the first of his three lawyers to arrive. Prosecutor Carlton Perdue told reporters that Coleman was charged with first-degree murder, then cautioned, "We're not going to pre-try this man. We got our stomach full of that when the president tried to pre-try those other men [in the Liuzzo case]." Coleman and his family were "all good friends of ours," Perdue declared. As for the victims, "If they had been tending to their own business, like I was tending to mine, they'd be living and enjoying themselves." A local deputy was more forthright in speaking of Morrisroe. "I hope the son of a bitch dies," he said. "That'll give us two instead of just one."[17]

Coleman's arraignment on 21 August took all of ten minutes. Perdue conducted the proceedings in his office, setting bond at $10,000 on the murder charge and $2,500 for assault with intent to kill Morrisroe. Coleman's premier attorney, State Senator Vaughan Robison, condemned even that modest bond as "excessive," but Perdue stood firm. His description of the incident to journalists was brief. The victims had approached the grocery store "to do some picketing and singing, and the man just let them have it, so to speak." (In fact, there was no demonstration at the store.) Rumors quickly spread that Coleman had fired in self-defense after Daniels and Morrisroe threatened him with weapons. From Montgomery, Flowers called the case "another Ku Klux Klan murder," telling reporters, "Everything points to another Klan killing, as the accused is strongly believed to be a Ku Klux Klan member." He accused Lingo of whitewashing the case, and Lingo's public behavior supported that charge. When a newsman asked for information on the case, Lingo snapped at him, "It's none of your damned business." Investigators sent by Flowers fared no better. Lingo raged at them, "I'm not giving you or the damn attorney general or the damn FBI or anybody any information until I'm good and ready." He never did.[18]

With or without Lingo's help, G-men were on the case. Agents in Mobile learned of the shooting at 4:30 P.M. on 20 August and immediately telephoned the news to bureau headquarters. A short time later, the Justice Department's Civil Rights Division ordered Hoover to give the case "continuous and preferred investigative attention." Specifically, federal prosecutors wanted to know whether Coleman's status as a "special deputy" meant that he had acted "under color of law," thus violating 18 USC Sec. 242. Sheriff Ryals and Al Lingo supported that contention in their early statements referring to Coleman as a deputy, and the card in his pocket clearly stated that he was endowed with all the powers of a deputy sheriff. Ryals quickly changed his tune, however, after learning that official status might condemn his good friend to a federal prison cell. The card Coleman carried was nothing more than a common gun permit, Ryals now insisted, a privilege shared by numerous (white) citizens of Lowndes County. In fact, Ryals contended, Coleman had never in his life performed any official duties for the sheriff's office. G-men took the waffling sheriff at his word, reporting back to Washington that Coleman had not acted "under color of law" when he shot Daniels and Morrisroe. Neither could they find substantive evidence of a conspiracy or any proof that Coleman was a Klansman. Agents satisfied themselves that neither victim had been armed when Coleman shot them — yet strangely never shared that finding with the local prosecution.[19]

Alabama had suffered so much bad publicity by August 1965 that an ad hoc committee of Concerned White Citizens organized to press for justice in the latest atrocity. The group urged Richmond Flowers to relieve Carlton Perdue as prosecutor, charging that Perdue's public condemnation of the victims proved that he "could not possibly execute justice impartially." Committee spokesmen told Flowers, "There is no doubt about the immaturity and incapability of a county solicitor who implies that emotional outrage is justification for killing." And while Flowers agreed, he resisted the call on grounds that outside interference was the surest way to guarantee Coleman's acquittal. A murder charge had been filed, and justice must take its due course. Flowers changed his mind on 13 September 1965 after a local grand jury — influenced by "eyewitness" claims that both victims were armed — indicted Coleman on reduced charges of manslaughter (for Daniels) and assault and battery (for Morrisroe). Flowers was "shocked and amazed" by the charges, telling reporters, "If this is not murder, it is no case at all." On 15 September, Flowers moved to impanel a new grand jury. He told the press, "If this case was presented properly — and I have to assume that it was — the members of that grand jury are as guilty as the man who pulled the trigger." Despite that stinging criticism, Perdue refused to call a new hearing, so Flowers took charge of the case.[20]

Coleman's manslaughter trial opened on 27 September 1965, before Judge T.

Werth Thagard. Flowers arrived with an armed escort to request postponement of the case until his key witness—Morrisroe—was fit to leave the hospital. He also noted Al Lingo's obstructionist tactics, "heavily slanted" toward the defense, and said he had "strong evidence that several witnesses intend to commit perjury." Coleman's defenders opposed delay on such "frivolous grounds," insisting on their client's right to speedy trial, while openly questioning the attorney general's "sincerity" and "honesty with this court." Judge Thagard agreed, dismissing the state's motions and scheduling trial to begin the next day. Flowers stayed home in Montgomery on 28 September, reportedly fearing for his life, while assistant Joseph Gantt renewed objections to the case proceeding without Morrisroe. Judge Thagard promptly censured Gantt for "trifling with the court," returning control of the case to Perdue. Flowers announced that he had never seen "anything like this before," though he was "used to seeing strange things in the South." He somberly predicted that Coleman would "walk out of court a free man."[21]

And so it was, as Thagard's court upheld Alabama's tradition of exonerating racial terrorists. The dark comedy began when Coleman's name appeared on the prospective juror's list, followed by Perdue's inquiry as to whether any other jurors had a "fixed opinion" on the case. "I do," one venireman replied. "Not guilty!" He was removed from the panel, but those who remained were scarcely better. Viola Liuzzo's killers appeared as spectators in court on 28 September when an all-white jury was seated and testimony began. Deputy Joe Jackson testified under oath that Coleman had frequently aided the sheriff's department. On the day of the shooting, in fact, he was sent to retrieve riot gear from Montgomery "to maintain peace and order" in Hayneville. Jackson also said that he had seen Daniels kiss a "nigger" girl "right in the mouth" at his release from jail the day he died. (All demonstrators present fervently denied the charge.) If that was not bad enough, evidence displayed in court revealed that Daniels wore shoes "such as no man of God in Lowndes County ever wears," and carried a "subversive" paperback book—*The Fanatic* by Meyer Levin—in his pocket. Worst of all, the victim wore red underpants that "smelled of urine" after he was shot at point-blank range.[22]

Robert Shelton appeared in court on 29 September, accompanied by the chief of his Klan Bureau of Investigation. The defense produced three witnesses, all longtime friends of Coleman, who swore that Daniels was armed with a knife and that Morrisroe carried a pistol. Both weapons had vanished, presumably taken by blacks who were glimpsed by the same defense witnesses stuffing unknown objects into their pockets and fleeing the scene. Morrisroe's affidavit denying that either he or Daniels carried weapons was read to the court in his absence. Defense attorney Joseph Phelps, in his summation of the case, maintained that Coleman was "protecting all of us" when he fired on Daniels and Morrisroe, whom Phelps dubbed "false prophets." Lowndes County was the true victim, Phelps said, plagued by "agitators and terrorists" who "hide their evil motives behind the cloth of the church." Prosecutor Arthur Gamble Jr. told jurors that the defense "would have produced these weapons if they were actually there," then seemed to concede the case with repeated mention of "that knife" in Daniels's hand. "There is no evidence here at all," Gamble said, "that Jonathan Daniels was making any attempt to actually cut [Coleman] with that knife."

Vaughan Robison closed the proceedings with a classic line: "You can believe that knife was there or not. I believe it was there whether it was or not."[23]

The jurors recognized their duty. Leaving court to deliberate on 30 September, the last man out paused long enough to wink at Coleman. The panel returned in record time with a verdict of acquittal, and Coleman resumed his job with the state highway department. John Doar at Justice ordered G-men to renew their investigation under 18 USC Sec. 242, and to prepare "a complete background investigation of the subject." Despite sworn courtroom testimony that Coleman had served the sheriff's department on 20 August 1965 and many other occasions, bureau headquarters again denied any evidence of crimes committed "under color of law." Coleman's trial for assaulting Morrisroe was scheduled for 15 May 1966, but Judge Thagard postponed it to the court's fall term. In September 1966, Flowers asked a new grand jury—including seven whites and eleven blacks—to indict Coleman for assault with intent to kill Morrisroe. The priest testified in person, but the integrated panel needed only five minutes to reject the charge. As one native journalist explained, "Even illiterate Negroes in Lowndes County are speed readers of handwriting on the wall. They know the Klan is 'riding' in Alabama today." Flowers asked Judge Thagard to drop the assault charge on 26 September and thus enable some future grand jury to reconsider it, but Thagard filed a dismissal "with prejudice," thereby effectively prohibiting another trial. No federal charge was ever filed.[24]

DONALD THOMPSON

Two days after Jon Daniels died in Alabama, the Rev. Donald Thompson experienced a near-miss with death in Jackson, Mississippi. Like James Reeb, Thompson was a white Unitarian minister, serving as pastor of Jackson's racially integrated First Unitarian Church. He also had succeeded murder victim Medgar Evers as secretary of Mississippi's Council on Human Relations. On the night of Sunday, 22 August 1965, Thompson drove a black parishioner home from a church board meeting, then returned to his own apartment house. As he emerged from his car, he saw three white men slowly passing in another vehicle. One thrust a shotgun from the window and fired two blasts, striking Thompson in the back and shoulder with 12 buckshot pellets. The minister survived with a smashed shoulder blade, two broken ribs, a punctured lung, and a fractured joint between his left arm and the shoulder. Three months after the shooting, fresh death threats drove Thompson from the state. G-men, even then immersed in their "secret war" against Mississippi terrorists, failed to identify the shooters. The case remains unsolved today.[25]

LEE EDWARD CULBREATH

Fourteen-year-old Lee Culbreath, a black resident of Portland, Arkansas, was working his newspaper route when gunshots snuffed out his life on 5 December 1965. State troopers arrested two suspects in the case, brothers Ed and James Vail, and charged them with Culbreath's murder. Soon after their arrest, the brothers allegedly told officers that they were Klansmen, though both subsequently denied it in court. A 12-man jury, including one black, convicted Ed Vail of second-degree murder on 26 February 1966, deciding that his drunkenness ruled out premeditation. The panel recommended a sentence of 21 years in prison, subsequently imposed by Judge G.B. Colvin. James Vail, named as the driver of the murder car, was scheduled for trial at some unspecified future date, but charges against him were later dismissed.[26] Despite evidence of collusion between the two brothers — seemingly as obvious as any facts in the Penn or Liuzzo cases — G-men did not investigate the crime and no federal charges were filed.

BEN CHESTER WHITE

In April 1966, a handful of Klansmen in Adams County, Mississippi, organized a new splinter faction called the Cottonmouth Moccasin Gang. Their purpose was identical to that of the Silver Dollar Group — terrorism against blacks — although they lacked the older group's proficiency with dynamite. Instead, they planned to murder Dr. Martin Luther King, drawn to Mississippi in June 1966 after James Meredith was shot and wounded on his one-man "Walk Against Fear." King vowed to continue the march, and members of the Cottonmouth Moccasin Gang devised a scheme to lure him to Adams County and his death. Their bait was Ben White, an elderly black caretaker on the Carter Plantation near Natchez. On 10 June 1966, Klansmen Ernest Avants, Claude Fuller and James Jones lured White from home, promising payment if he helped them find a missing dog. They drove him into the Homochitto National Forest, then shot him at close range with an automatic rifle and a shotgun. In the process, Fuller shot so many holes in Jones's car that the killers decided to ditch it and set it on fire. Like Travis Giles in the Vernon Dahmer slaying exactly six months earlier, Jones told police that his car had been stolen.[27]

The clumsy ruse worked no better for Jones that it had for Giles. White's mangled, nearly headless corpse was pulled from Pretty Creek on 12 June, his many wounds prompting Sheriff Odell Anders to draw a connection with the burned-out, bullet-riddled car "stolen" from Jones. Questioned by deputies on 13 June, Jones failed a polygraph test and spent the night in jail, wracked by pangs of guilt that he was "deep in sin" for his role in the murder. Early next morning, he confessed and named the triggermen. Avants and Fuller were jailed on 14 June, and all three defendants were charged with first-degree murder. At a preliminary hearing on 17 June, Jones said that Fuller had told him White was active in the civil rights movement (a lie) and spoke of "orders from higher ups that the old darky had to go." Jones was first to face trial, but despite his confession the jury deadlocked on 10 April 1967, producing a mistrial. Avants was next, in December 1967. Defense attorney Travis Buckley granted that his client fired a shotgun blast into White's head, but argued that the victim was already dead from wounds inflicted by Claude Fuller. Jurors bought the argument and voted to acquit Avants. Fuller and Jones avoided further prosecution by pleading illness. A quarter-century after the fact, prosecutor Edwin Benoist recalled White's case as "the most atrocious murder and the greatest occurrence of injustice" he had ever seen.[28]

It need not have been so, however. Avants could not be tried a second time by state authorities, and Mississippi stubbornly refused to seek justice against his two accomplices, there was another avenue of prosecution. White was murdered in the Homochitto National Forest, on land owned by the U.S. government, and thus the charges could be tried in federal court without invoking rules of double jeopardy. That fact was obviously known to Hoover and his G-men, who had jailed many killers on identical charges since the 1920s. It was likewise known to Attorney General Katzenbach and his various successors, who ignored the case for nearly four decades. In the meantime, Jesse White filed suit against his father's killers and the White Knights of the KKK in federal court, seeking monetary damages for wrongful death. Judge Harold Cox ruled in White's favor on 13 November 1968, and a jury awarded the plaintiffs $1,021,500 which they would never collect from the bankrupt defendants.[29]

Federal prosecutors finally reopened the White murder case in November 1999, contending that they had no idea the crime had occurred on government land until they were alerted by a broadcast of ABC's popular *20/20* news program, describing unsolved murders from the civil rights era. Reporters accepted that incredible assertion as a new grand jury convened to review the case in February 2000. Klansmen Fuller and Jones were long dead by that time, but the panel indicted Avants on a fresh murder charge. Legal delays postponed his trial until February 2003, when Avants was finally convicted and sentenced to life imprisonment. He died in custody on 14 June 2004.[30] If not for a belated television story, White's murder would have remained officially unsolved.

CLARENCE TRIGGS

Clarence Triggs, a black bricklayer and military veteran, moved from Jackson, Mississippi, to Bogalusa, Louisiana one year after nightriders killed Oneal Moore and wounded Creed Rogers. Triggs joined his first civil rights protest in early July 1966, and among local racists it marked him for death. On 30 July, police found him shot in the head, slumped in a car parked outside Bogalusa. Officers barred black leaders from the crime scene and refused to let Triggs's widow identify his corpse where it was found. Local activists, suspecting a whitewash, called for nightly marches through town until the crime was solved. Thus motivated, authorities jailed two white suspects, John Copling, Jr., and Homer Seale. Detectives said their fingerprints were found inside the car with Triggs's body and on fragments of a broken whiskey bottle at the crime scene. Nonetheless, Copling was acquitted at trial, white jurors deliberating less than an hour before they released him, and Seale was never tried.[31] The case remains officially unsolved, apparently ignored by agents of the FBI.

LILLIAN BRILEY

On 30 January 1967, *The New York Times* ran a small story on page 16, beneath the headline "Wife of a Negro minister shot to death in Atlanta." No follow-up was published, but the basic facts are these: On 28 January, during services at the Rev. George Briley's all-black James Avenue Church of Christ, parishioners saw smoke rising beneath the door to Briley's office. Inside, they found a pile of burning cotton soaked in kerosene and doused the flames with fire extinguishers. Soon after midnight on 29 January, Lillian Briley answered the doorbell at her home in Atlanta, leaving husband George and their three-year-old grandson in bed. A shotgun blast rang out, and the Rev. Briley found his wife dying on the threshold, shot in the chest, according to communications from surviving members of the Briley family. The Klan-type crime remains unsolved today. If G-men bothered to investigate it, no record of their effort has been publicized.[32]

MARTIN LUTHER KING JR.

On 15 January 1963 — Dr. King's thirty-fourth birthday — FBI Associate Director Cartha Deloach wrote an internal memo branding King a "vicious liar" for his criticism of the bureau's civil rights performance. Deloach continued, "I see no further need to contacting [*sic*] Rev. King inasmuch as he obviously does not desire to be given the truth." Across the memo's bottom, J. Edgar Hoover wrote, "I concur." King biographer Taylor Branch contends that the FBI never again warned King of racist plots against his life, a statement flatly contradicting published claims that G-men rescued King from Klan conspirators on various occasions (twice in February 1965 alone).[33]

Hoover's hatred of Dr. King is legendary. The one-sided feud included countless illegal bugs and wiretaps, dozens of critical stories planted by G-men with "cooperative" journalists, and an anonymous letter mailed by the bureau in November 1964 urging King to commit suicide.[34] Some journalists and former agents say the FBI went further still, not only celebrating King's assassination but deliberately suppressing evidence of a conspiracy.

King was killed by a sniper's bullet at 6:01 P.M. on 4 April 1968 as he stood on a balcony of the Lorraine Motel in Memphis, Tennessee. The date marked King's second visit to Memphis, supporting a strike by black sanitation workers. King's first protest march in Memphis, conducted on 28 March 1968, had erupted into violence after members of a group called the Invaders — suspected as FBI *agents provocateur* — began smashing windows and stoning police. In the wake of that riot, anonymous FBI press releases appeared in newspapers nationwide, branding King a failure and condemning his "hypocrisy" for lodging at a Memphis hotel owned by whites. FBI ghostwriters chastised King for avoiding the Lorraine, "a first-rate Negro hotel in Memphis," and King booked rooms there for his scheduled return on 3 April 1968 to lead another march. On 2 April, a self-described "advance security man for Dr. King" arrived to inspect the Lorraine Motel, professing shock when he found King scheduled for a ground-floor suite. The stranger insisted that King be placed in a sec-ond-floor room at the rear, overlooking the motel's swimming pool. Coincidentally, the new room faced rear windows of a seedy rooming house across the street, from which police say King was shot on 4 April. Lorraine employees later learned that no such advance man was dispatched by King to Memphis. In retrospect, they opined that the unidentified visitor was a dark-skinned white man trying to pass for black.[35]

Security for King lay in the hands of Police Director Frank Holloman, who despite his title also controlled the Memphis Fire Department. Before accepting the post in Memphis, Holloman had spent 25 years in the FBI, including service as agent-in-charge of Memphis and eight years as supervisor of Hoover's personal office in Washington. Before King's arrival in Memphis on 3 April 1968, Holloman retired the normal ten-man detail assigned to protect King during his visits. Only two black officers remained on surveillance of King, watching the Lorraine from a nearby fire station, but even they were pulled out on 3 April after claims of a long-distance threat to their lives. So it was that King had no police protection on 4 April, when the fatal shot was fired. When King's alleged assassin fled the scene in a white Ford Mustang, described to police by multiple witnesses, no bulletin was broadcast for his appre-hension. Shelby County Sheriff William Morris later told reporters he knew nothing of the Mustang's flight on 4 April and thus failed to erect roadblocks that might have snared the killer within moments. In the wake of King's slaying, Director Holloman apparently forgot about the mortal threat to his black officers on King's security detail. He later said that threat was first reported to him by the U.S. Secret Service, yet spokesmen for that agency denied any knowledge of the incident.[36]

Friendly reporter Jeremiah O'Leary described the FBI's search for King's slayer as "the greatest manhunt in law enforcement history," but it proceeded at a strangely lackadaisical pace. Within 24 hours of the shooting, Attorney General Ramsey Clark told journalists "we are very close" to an arrest, and that the FBI had found no evi-dence of a conspiracy. Days later, Clark was forced to admit that "the trail has length-ened," while G-men chased leads from Memphis to Atlanta, Birmingham, Los Angeles, Mexico and Toronto. King's presumed slayer had left numerous personal items in Memphis, several bearing clear fingerprints, yet FBI headquarters took 15 days to identify their suspect as James Earl Ray, a convict who escaped from Mis-souri's state prison in 1967. Despite early claims that no conspiracy existed in King's murder, Ray was slapped with federal conspiracy charges on 20 April 1968. Seven more weeks elapsed before he was finally captured by British police at London's Heathrow Airport on 8 June. Hoover seized the opportunity to interrupt funeral services of another enemy, Robert Kennedy, with news of Ray's arrest.[37]

How zealous was the FBI's pursuit of Ray and any possible conspirators? Ex-agent Arthur Murtagh, assigned to the Atlanta field office when King was shot, reports that G-men cheered the news of his assassination, invoking King's FBI code-name as they crowed, "They got Zorro! They finally got the son of a bitch!" Later, Murtagh said, "We conducted a straight criminal investigation. We never even looked for a conspiracy." In fact, according to Murtagh, persuasive evidence of a murder plot was "washed out consistently and deliberately" in Atlanta and elsewhere. Another retired G-man, William Turner, reports that indications of conspiracy furnished to the bureau by Los Angeles police were flatly rejected. "We've got our man and that's it," a bureau spokesman told startled detectives. "The director didn't exactly light any candles after King was killed."[38]

On 13 June 1968, Ray's public defender in England contacted Arthur Hanes in Birmingham. The former G-man flew to London on 19 June and remained for three days, but court orders barred him from seeing his new client. Hanes met Ray for the first time in Memphis on 5 July and subsequently made a deal with Alabama author William Huie to finance the defense by selling story rights to Ray's case. Hanes rejected a parallel offer of cash from Jesse Stoner and the National States Rights Party, but FBI files reveal that Hanes met twice with UKA wizard Robert Shelton in June and August 1968. Their conversations were not recorded, but informants provided details. George Wilson, a Midwestern leader of the UKA, contended that the Klan contributed $10,000 to Ray's defense under the guise of supporting defendants in North Carolina. Grand Dragon Furman Williams allegedly mentioned the deal at a rally in South Carolina, and other informants confirmed it. One source said that Shelton had arranged with Hanes to preview a list of prospective jurors for Ray's trial. Another informant reported that Shelton solicited Klansmen for donations to Ray's cause in August 1968. In any case, whatever deals may have existed with the UKA, they were dissolved when Ray fired Hanes and hired a new attorney on 10 November 1968.[39]

The replacement was Percy Foreman, a Texas headliner who often boasted that his fee alone was punishment enough for any crime. Most of his clients were acquitted, although one who failed to benefit from Foreman's courtroom theatrics—Jack Ruby, the slayer of Lee Harvey Oswald—had still found his way to death row. Foreman preserved the book deal with Huie, then went to work on Ray, selling the prospect of a guilty plea. Between threats of execution and strategic loans to Ray's family, all contingent on a guilty plea with "no unseemly conduct" in court, Foreman achieved his goal after three months on the job. Ray pled guilty to murder in Memphis on 10 March 1969, accepting a ninety-nine-year prison term.[40]

Huie, meanwhile, was waffling in print on the subject of conspiracy. His first article on the case, published in Look magazine on 12 November 1968, was titled "The Story of James Earl Ray and the Plot to Assassinate Martin Luther King." Two weeks later, while vowing to "tell no more than should be told before the trial," Huie briefed Look readers on the case.[41] He wrote:

> The outline of the plot to murder Dr. King now begins to become visible to me. It may not be visible to my readers because, until Ray has been tried, I cannot reveal all that I have found to be true. But from what I know, from what I have learned from Ray, and from my investigative research some of the features of the plot were:
> * Dr. King was to be murdered for effect. His murder was planned, not by impulsive men who hated him personally, though they probably did hate him, but by calculating men who wanted to use his murder to trigger violent conflict between white and Negro citizens.
> * He was to be murdered in the election year of 1968.
> * Since he was to be murdered for maximum bloody effect, he was to be murdered, not while he was living quietly at home in Atlanta, but at some dramatic moment, at some dramatic place where controversy was raging. By March 15,

1968, the plotters clearly had begun aiming at murdering him at some point where he was forming or leading the Poor People's March [on Washington, D.C.]

    * He was to be murdered by a white man, or white men, who could be described as "Southerners" and "racists."

    * Preferably, he was to be murdered in Birmingham or Selma, since these cities were milestones in his career as an advocate of racial change.

    * There was no necessity, after the murder, for the murderer or murderers to be murdered to prevent a trial — because a trial could yield extra dividends of hatred and violence.

    Therefore, in this plot, Dr. King was the secondary, not the primary target. The primary target was the United States of America.[42]

Despite later disclaimers, Huie's devotion to the conspiracy theory lasted at least into December 1968, when he appeared as a guest on KNBC-TV in Los Angeles. During that interview, he stated flatly that "New Orleans is the place where the money came from to assassinate Dr. King," and he said he knew four men involved in the plot. "One or two of these men were wealthy and of the extreme right," Huie said, adding, "All the money, in my opinion, came from Louisiana." Despite his alleged personal knowledge of the guilty parties, Huie hedged, saying, "I can't tell their names because if the Justice Department can't arrest these people, I can't charge them with having paid money for the murder of Martin Luther King."[43]

Four months later, everything had changed. When Huie's third article appeared in *Look* on 15 April 1969, it presented a stark turnaround from his previous statements. He now denied the existence of any conspiracy, claiming that Ray alone shot King in hopes of achieving "criminal status." As Huie explained: "Month after month, I sought evidence to support this [conspiracy] account while I urged Ray to reveal more about the 'other man.' I found no supporting evidence I could believe. I had to conclude that, in all likelihood, the 'other man' wasn't there, that Ray went alone to the rooming house and shot Dr. King."[44]

Huie clearly recognized the weakness of his latest theory, hedging it with escape clauses. In regard to the murder weapon, he wrote that on or about 28 March 1968 "Ray *or someone else* decided he should buy a rifle."[45] (Emphasis added.) Finally, all but admitting the inadequacy of his published conclusions, Huie wrote:

> Well, there are large conspiracies and little conspiracies. In large conspiracies, rich and/or powerful men are involved. Small conspiracies involve only little men.... I believe that one or two men other than James Earl Ray may have had foreknowledge of this murder, and that makes it a little conspiracy. But if there was a conspiracy, I now believe that James Earl Ray was probably its leader, not its tool or dupe.[46]

The House Select Committee on Assassinations took a closer look at King's death in the late 1970s. Its investigators discovered that Vincent DePalma, a close associate of Robert DePugh in the Minutemen, had defected from that group in January 1968 and told ATF agents in Denver that the Minutemen had 19 strike teams nationwide, each armed with lists of prominent targets. King's name was on several of those lists, but the committee found "insufficient evidence to indicate that the Minutemen were involved in Dr. King's death." FBI files subpoenaed by Congress also revealed "approximately 25 Klan-related leads to potential conspiracies in the assassination of Dr. King," yet committee members deemed that only four "warranted the attention of the committee."[47]

The first emerged from testimony of an FBI informant in Mobile, Alabama, who advised G-men of a meeting held in Birmingham sometime before the BAPBOM blast of 15 September 1963. Participants included Sidney Barnes (known for his "close associates" in several Klans, including the White Knights); John Crommelin (an anti–Semite whose friends included Asa Carter and John Kasper); William Potter Gale (a closet Jew who led the California Rangers and the neo–Nazi Posse Comitatus); and Noah Carden (otherwise unidentified). Discussion at the meeting allegedly included plans to murder Dr. King, but agents failed to make a solid link in 1968.[48]

A second lead surfaced on 22 April 1968, when Myrtis Hendricks—a waitress at John's Restaurant in Laurel, Mississippi—reported conversations overheard at work. Her employer, Deavours Nix, was a notorious Klansman and chief of the White Knights' Klan Bureau of Investigation. On 2 April, Hendricks said, Nix had received "a call on King" from persons unknown. The next day, she saw two men remove a rifle with a telescopic sight from Nix's office and place it in a car parked outside. On 4 April, Nix allegedly received a call reporting King's death before it made national news. Sam Bowers stopped at John's on 5 April, she said, and made comments that "raised the possibility" of his involvement in the murder. Hendricks subsequently left her job, hiding out with a boyfriend in Texas before she called the FBI. Agents found "no corroboration" for her story at the time, and Hendricks refused to confirm it for the House committee.[49]

On 15 June 1968, one week after Ray's arrest in London, a long-distance telephone operator in Racine, Wisconsin, contacted G-men with information on the King assassination. Four days earlier, she had placed three calls for an unnamed Wisconsin resident to different numbers in North Carolina. Eavesdropping on one conversation, she heard the caller identify himself as "Robert," demanding money to finance a trip abroad. Robert alluded to payment from the KKK and voiced fears that Ray would "spill his guts" when he returned to the United States. Agents traced the phone numbers, assigned to three brothers in North Carolina. One was a used-car dealer, and local police identified another as a car thief and forger of checks. All were interviewed, and each denied involvement in the King assassination. House investigators later said the "operator" never actually worked for the telephone company — a fact strangely missing from FBI reports on the incident. Committee spokesmen decided that "the lead was not based on credible evidence and not worthy of further investigation."[50]

The committee's "most significant Klan-related lead" concerned attorney Arthur Hanes. The panel reviewed FBI files and questioned informants, collecting tales of sundry meetings between Hanes and leaders of the UKA. A bureau spy known only as "Source B" claimed knowledge of a meeting held in 1969 between Hanes and acting imperial wizard Melvin Sexton, where Klansmen approved paying Hanes $12,500 to defend knights charged with various crimes in North Carolina. After Hanes left the room, Sexton allegedly remarked that he had "a piece of paper for Hanes pertaining to the Ray case," but its significance is doubtful, since Ray had fired Hanes in November 1968. Before the committee, Hanes "vigorously denied" any Klan support of Ray's defense, a claim echoed under oath by Sexton, Robert Shelton, ex–Grand Dragon J.R. Jones and others. The committee noted that Hanes and Shelton "disagreed substantially regarding the duration of their friendship and whether Hanes helped establish the Klan's national defense fund," while both Hanes and the Klansmen "attempted to minimize their association." Those discrepancies were finally attributed to faulty memories or "an attempt by Hanes to minimize his relationship with Sexton and the legal work he did for him." Committee spokesmen left the matter unresolved, while finding "no indications of an agreement between the UKA and James Earl Ray prior to Dr. King's assassination."[51]

Before abandoning the KKK entirely, committee members also questioned FBI informant William Morris and longtime Klansman Jesse Stoner. G-men had eliminated Stoner as a suspect after King was killed, reporting that he addressed an NSRP rally in Meridian, Mississippi, on 4 April 1968. That alibi did not preclude involvement in the crime, however, and a link was forged in 1969 when Stoner replaced Percy Foreman as counsel of record for Ray and Ray's brothers. Stoner himself blamed the FBI for King's murder, contending that Morris approached him in the 1950s with a $25,000 contract on King's life. Convinced even then that Morris served the bureau, Stoner admitted offering to bomb King for $5,000, but he contended that Morris had been adamant: The contract's sponsors wanted King shot with a rifle. Stoner then declined the job, while saying that Morris had tried to solicit Ace Carter. Morris "vehemently denied" such discussions with Stoner, Carter, or anyone else, but the committee found an FBI report from 1961 in which Morris told fellow Klansmen that King's death would solve all the South's racial problems. He knew a mobster in New Orleans, Morris said, who would be glad to do the job. Morris denied that claim as well, professing total innocence.[52]

The House committee finally announced a "likelihood" that King was slain "as a result of a conspiracy," then ruled out every racist group in the U.S. as active plotters. In that scenario, Ray was the lone gunman, assisted and financed at times by his brothers, John and Jerry. The Rays allegedly acted in hope of collecting a five-figure "bounty" on King, offered by St. Louis businessmen John Kauffmann and John Sutherland. Both were dead when the committee held its hearings, but other testimony indicated that the pair had sponsored an "open" contract on King, with a blanket offer of payment to anyone who killed him. No link to the Rays was established, though John Ray lived in St. Louis.[53] The verdict was, in effect, a new version of Huie's "little conspiracy" from 1969.

There is no solid evidence, as some have charged, that G-men themselves planned or carried out King's assassination. Nonetheless, Hoover and company were plainly glad to see him go, and the director's malice followed King beyond the grave. From 1969 until his own death three years later, Hoover fought all moves to name a federal holiday for Dr. King. In the process, he carried out a posthumous campaign of slander, leaking facts and innuendoes from FBI files to various allies in Congress and the media. One who served him eagerly was John Rarick, a Louisiana representative who led the House attack on King in June 1969. At that time, Hoover knew — or should have known — that before his election, while a district judge in West Feliciana Parish, Rarick had doubled as exalted cyclops of the local Ku Klux Klan.[54]

9

"Yesterday, Today, Forever"

When J. Edgar Hoover died at home on 2 May 1972, he left the FBI much as he had found it in 1924 — stronger and more respected, to be sure, but snared in mounting scandal nonetheless. Over the next four years, congressional investigations and journalistic exposés revealed most of the COINTELPRO-era abuses and some of Hoover's personal corruption, while leaving enough secrets to enthrall writers and readers through the turn of a new millennium. Watergate added a fresh layer of grime to the bureau's once-pristine image, and while illegal domestic spying would continue on various fronts through the 1980s (at least), bureau priorities had definitely changed.[1]

New leaders focused increasingly on organized crime (long dismissed by Hoover as "baloney"), and while COINTELPRO-style harassment was still employed against various leftists and minority activists across America, the FBI reportedly abandoned Klan-watching entirely. David Bumble, retiring as agent-in-charge of Jacksonville, Florida, in November 1980 told the *Florida Times-Union* that surveillance of Klansmen and Nazis had been discontinued by the bureau and "has not been taken up by anybody." That claim was not strictly true, however. In Greensboro, North Carolina, Klansman Ed Dawson drew his last paycheck as an FBI informant in 1976, after Attorney General Edward Levi imposed new guidelines restricting infiltration and disruption of domestic groups, but he soon found employment as a spy for the Greensboro Police Department.[2]

Deliberate confusion surrounds the FBI's Klan-watching activities throughout the 1970s. In 1976, an unnamed bureau contact assured author Patsy Sims that the FBI no longer conducted anti–Klan surveillance, but that denial collided with public announcements that the Justice Department was "concerned about a possible resurgence of Klan-type activity." At the same time, a police intelligence officer told Sims that FBI headquarters was "trying to make a decision to actively investigate the Klan." Such indecision may explain the bureau's glaring ignorance of KKK activities throughout the decade, including a public claim that all Klans combined had a national membership below two thousand. The Anti-Defamation League, meanwhile, published reports pegging Klan membership at 5,000 in 1973, 6,500 in 1975, and 8,000 to 10,500 in 1979. Ignoring all such contradictions, the bureau maintained its tradition of deception. When Sims hand-delivered a Freedom of Information Act request to FBI headquarters in 1976, requesting criminal records for 83 publicly recognized Klansmen (identified by attached newspaper clippings), bureau spokesmen first denied receiving her package, then "found" it five months later — with the news clippings removed.[3]

Violence by Klansmen and their neo–Nazi allies continued through the 1970s, and while local authorities in Dixie were more likely to prosecute terrorists, the FBI maintained a hands-off attitude toward right-wing violence. This was especially surprising, since passage of a new Federal Bombing Statute in 1972 gave the bureau even broader jurisdiction to investigate the very crimes long practiced by white knights in "Bombingham" and elsewhere. The catch lay in the statute's wording, which allowed G-men to shift responsibility for cases they wished to avoid. Specifically, postal inspectors were charged with investigating any mail bombs or bombings of post offices, and FBI agents were assigned to solve any bombings on federal property (other than postal facilities or property owned by the Treasury Department). Treasury's Bureau of Alcohol, Tobacco and Firearms (ATF) was detailed to investigate all other blasts— unless the crimes were designated acts of "terrorism," in which case the FBI assumed primary jurisdiction. Unfortunately, since bureau leaders defined terrorism on their own terms, accommodating personal prejudice and political Powers That Be, the FBI was free to sidestep any case that did not suit its fancy. So it was that ATF inherited a list of "un-terrorists," including many Klansmen, whom the FBI refused to touch.[4]

One local law enforcement agency that followed the FBI's example was the Los Angeles Police Department. While chief Edward Davis constantly requested more funds and equipment to suppress terrorism, L.A. led the nation in bombings—152 blasts during a 12-month period in 1974–75. Within the first five months of 1975, the city suffered 18 bombings traceable to the KKK, the National Socialist Liberation Front, the American National Socialist Party, and various far-right Cuban exile groups. Only one case was solved, with the arrest of a Jewish Defense League member, prompting some critics to say that LAPD maintained a see-no-evil attitude where neo-fascist bombers were concerned. It came as no surprise, then, that the targets rocked by right-wing bombs included various Jewish facilities, the Progressive Labor Party and the Socialist Workers Party (long a target of illegal FBI harassment). The FBI's Los Angeles field office likewise failed to investigate the bombing epidemic, preferring to turn a blind eye.[5]

"GREENKILL"

FBI inaction, coupled with police negligence or worse, paid a bloody dividend at Greensboro, North Carolina, in November 1979. Members of a small biracial labor group, the Workers Viewpoint Organization, had enjoyed little success in organizing Greensboro's textile mill workers in 1978–79, prompting leaders of the group to seek a new, more militant image and thus reap free publicity. In summer 1979 they renamed their group the Communist Workers Party (CWP), waving a literal red flag before Greensboro's ultra-conservative establishment. Where proselytizing of workers had failed, the CWP switched to public confrontation with the local Klan.[6]

Joe Grady's White Knights of the KKK ignored taunts from the CWP, but the North Carolina Knights proved more accommodating. Organized by informant Ed Dawson with FBI backing in 1969, the North Carolina Knights was led a decade later by mill worker Virgil Griffin. Griffin had recently closed ranks with the National Socialist Party of America (NSPA)—formed by Frank Collin after COINTELPRO tactics drove him from the National Socialist White People's Party, led after 1975 by globe-trotting Nazi Harold Covington — to create a new United Racist Front (URF). On 8 July 1979, CWP members disrupted a Klan rally in China Grove, North Carolina, and publicly burned the KKK's banner. Griffin and company were hungry for payback three months later when the CWP announced a "Death to the Klan" rally in Greensboro. On 19 October, civic leaders granted the CWP a parade permit for 3 November, contingent on the promise that marchers would carry no weapons "open or concealed." Two days before the demonstration, Ed Dawson — still an active Klansman and police informant — requested and received a copy of the CWP's parade permit, including the assembly point, starting time and route of the march. Later, the same police who paid his secret salary would say they mistook Dawson for a CWP member. When that excuse failed, they explained that the parade permit was a matter of public record, readily available to anyone.[7]

With the permit in hand, Dawson embarked on a campaign of agitation to ensure that Klansmen would be out in force to meet the unarmed marchers. Incessantly, he urged them to avenge the China Grove insult. One knight who joined the rush to combat later told the *Greensboro Daily News,* "We'd never have come to Greensboro if it wasn't for Ed Dawson berating us." Another informant, Cleveland ATF agent Bernard Butkovich, worked within the NSPA in Winston-Salem, playing a key role in formation of the URF and its violent response to the CWP. Aside from urging Nazis to meet the Red marchers head-on, Butkovich offered illegal explosives (including hand grenades) and special kits that would convert semiautomatic weapons into illegal machine guns. Both Dawson and Butkovich attended planning sessions for the URF-CWP confrontation on 3 November 1979. Dawson twice warned Greensboro police (on 31 October and 3 November) that Klansmen would be heavily armed when they met the parade. Butkovich allegedly issued a similar warning to his ATF superiors on 3 November. The FBI, meanwhile, denied any advance knowledge of the impending massacre.[8]

Greensboro police were strangely lethargic on 3 November 1979. Despite plans to cover the parade with a crack tactical unit — the equivalent of a SWAT team — local officers began assembling at 11:30 A.M., a full hour *after* the starting time clearly printed on the CWP's parade permit. Department spokesmen called it a "logistical error," but critics accused them of acting in concert with Klansmen and Nazis. In either case, the result was tragedy. Ed Dawson admits leading a motorcade of armed URF members to intercept the CWP march but says he fled the scene before mayhem erupted. The racists opened fire on their defenseless targets at 11:23 A.M., killing five persons and wounding nine or ten (reports vary). The murdered victims—four white men and one black woman — were a stark contrast to their semiliterate killers: their number included three physicians, a computer operator from Duke University, and the student body president of Bennett College. Dawson recovered his composure in time to help Virgil Griffin's entourage escape from Greensboro, while police floundered in the wake of bloodshed.[9]

President Jimmy Carter ordered a federal investigation of the massacre (code-named "GREENKILL" by the FBI, for "*Green*sboro *Kill*ings"), while local authorities tried to restore some semblance of order. Investigation was facilitated by the fact that video cameras had captured the killers in action, and a city patrolman had followed the Klan motorcade. Ed Dawson met with G-men on 9 November, to blame his police employers for the fiasco. "I think it was handled stinky," he complained. "With all the advance notice they had — and I told them about some of the people — I expected when I turned that corner to see nothing but helmets, just a wall of city police." (CWP spokesmen agreed, accusing police of complicity in the murders.) At the same time, however, Dawson denied any advance plans for heckling or violence against the marchers, thus refuting his own prior warnings to police.[10]

Of forty URF gunmen present at the murder scene, only 16 were arrested, and only six of those (four Klansmen and two NSPA members) were charged by state authorities with any criminal offense. No charges were filed against Dawson, Virgil Griffin, or kleagle Mark Sherer (who admitted firing shots "into the air" during the murders). Both Griffin and Sherer were ex-convicts, banned by law from owning firearms, but state prosecutors ignored their possession of weapons on 3 November and during their flight from Greensboro. Neither Dawson nor ATF agent Butkovich would be called to testify at trial, prosecutors explaining that the informants "didn't witness anything that would have helped us." They *could* have described the URF conspiracy to murder CWP members, a fact corroborated by one Nazi who admitted that photos of the five slain victims were passed out to racists a week in advance, but District Attorney Michael Schlosser dismissed all conspiracy counts before trial. The killers caught on film would not be tried for plotting their crime, merely for pulling the triggers. As CWP member Nelson Johnson told author Elizabeth Wheaton, "By dismissing the possibility of a planned assault with a flippant observation such as 'The Klan always carries guns,' Schlosser gave the defense attorneys the opening they needed: self-defense."[11]

And so it was at trial in autumn 1980. The state called 2,200 prospective jurors, some of whom were frankly sympathetic toward the killers. One told the court, "The only thing the Klan is guilty of is poor shooting." Another said, "I don't think we are out a lot because those people aren't with us anymore. I think we are better off without them." Those veniremen were dismissed, but the final all-white panel proved little better. They were seemingly blind to videotapes of the murders in progress, deaf to testimony from eyewitnesses. Ed Boyd, a reporter for WTVD in Durham, described the massacre: "It wasn't any shootout. It was a military execution. It was like in the cowboy movies when they corner you in a box canyon." The accused claimed self-defense, pretending they were "threatened" by the unarmed marchers bearing picket signs. One defense attorney told the jury that if Griffin's knights "had taken a machine gun and mowed the crowd down, it would have been justified," since the marchers "were attacking the very society that gives them the right to be out on the street." Jurors accepted the strange logic that those with rights should be killed for exercising them, and all defendants were acquitted on 17 November 1980. Defendant Jerry

Smith announced plans to run for Lincoln County sheriff in 1982, and Virgil Griffin eyed a gubernatorial race in 1984.[12]

The Greensboro verdict, strongly reminiscent of Ku Klux trials from the mid-1960s, provoked a groundswell of national outrage. Americans who thought there had been "progress" in the South since 1965 were swiftly disabused of that idea. It was small consolation when six Nazis were convicted in September 1981 of plotting to detonate bombs throughout Greensboro if their comrades were convicted. In May 1982 the ACLU helped survivors of the massacre draft a complaint against Dawson, Butkovich and other defendants, including the Justice Department, for negligence in failing to prevent the murders. According to that lawsuit: "A plan was mutually agreed upon by the Klan and Nazi defendants and agents of defendants Greensboro Police Department, BATF, and FBI, including Dawson and Butkovich.... This was a plan by which an attack on plaintiffs and other members of the targeted classes would be made, the police defendants would not prevent or provide protection from the attack, and the informant-defendants Dawson and Butkovich would facilitate and participate in the attack."[13]

That lawsuit prompted federal prosecutors to move against the URF. On 21 April 1983 nine racists were indicted on charges of conspiracy to violate their victims' civil rights and conspiracy to violate federal statutes, plus interference with interstate commerce (for wounding a television photographer). This time, the defendants included Dawson and Griffin. Klansmen Chris Bensen and Max Hayes were granted immunity in return for testimony against their fellow knights. Another witness, Mark Sherer, escaped indictment for the second time, despite his sworn admission of firing shots at the crime scene and later lying to FBI agents (a federal crime in itself). The trial opened on 9 January 1984 before another all-white Carolina jury. The defendants repeated their self-defense plea, contradicting statements from Agent Butkovich that he warned police of violent plans including manufacture of pipe bombs for use against the CWP marchers. As before, the jury found all nine defendants not guilty. Ed Dawson, stunned, told journalists, "For once in my life, I can't think of anything to say." A smiling Virgil Griffin said, "I feel like I died and went to heaven. Now I can go to a Klan rally again."[14]

Nothing remained of GREENKILL but the civil lawsuit filed in 1982, lumping Klansmen and Nazis together with Greensboro police, the FBI and ATF. Plaintiffs sought $48 million in damages for their injuries or loss of loved ones, while the Klan joined ranks with civic leaders and federal agents in denial of any wrongdoing. The courtroom tableau presented a study in contrast, with supporters of the plaintiffs ranged on one side, while G-men, ATF agents and local police sat shoulder-to-shoulder with Klansmen and Nazis across the aisle. Defendant Wayne Wood amused his comrades by appearing in court with T-shirts bearing messages: "Eat Lead You Lousy Red" and "Kill a Commie for Mommie." Witness Butkovich testified that one of his ATF superiors, Agent Robert Dukes, purchased a Nazi uniform for Butkovich when he went undercover in the NSPA, but he denied any role as an *agent provocateur*. Jurors dismissed all claims of conspiracy but found eight defendants (Ed Dawson, five shooters and two Greensboro policemen) liable for various injuries. Damages were fixed at $394,959.55 — including $351,500 for the death of victim Michael

Nathan,$3,600 for assault and battery on Nathan, $38,359.55 for assault and battery on survivor Paul Bermanzhon, and $1,500 for assault and battery on survivor Tom Clark. Spokesmen for the city of Greensboro announced plans to appeal the verdict, then settled the case with a payment of $351,500 to Michael Nathan's estate. None of the killers spent a day in prison for their crimes; no law enforcement agents were dismissed, suspended or reprimanded for their handling of the incident.[15]

TERROR IN THE REAGAN ERA

President Ronald Reagan, inaugurated in January 1981, made no secret of his far-right sympathies. An FBI informant in the 1930s (code-named "T-10"), Reagan had surrounded himself with members of the John Birch Society as governor of California (1967–1975), and his presidential campaign drew support in equal measures from ultra-fundamentalist religious groups and leaders of the Mafia-infested Teamsters' union. Both factions were well represented in Reagan's administration, thereby explaining both the ineffective White House "war on drugs" and a pervasive blindness toward right-wing terrorism.[16]

Reagan's first move was dismissal of terrorist charges against various bands of anti–Castro Cuban exiles who had plagued the western hemisphere since 1960. Members of such groups as Alpha 66 and Omega 7 proudly claimed responsibility for 14 bombings that killed 94 victims between 1973 and 1979, but Reagan's Justice Department had no interest in such trifles. Where they had not already done so, G-men followed Reagan's lead and gave up any pretense of investigating Klansmen, Nazis and the like. The handful of federal Klan prosecutions during 1981-82 were invariably initiated by ATF agents pursuing bomb and firearms violations against such groups as the Adamic Knights of the KKK (in Maryland and Pennsylvania), the Confederate Vigilantes of the KKK (in Tennessee), and the Death Knights of the KKK (in Kentucky). ATF agents also arrested and convicted the Nazis who planned to bomb Greensboro targets in 1981. For their efforts, President Reagan slashed ATF's funding, then made unsuccessful efforts to disband the unit altogether.[17]

The most peculiar case of 1981 involved a plot to invade and conquer the tiny Caribbean island of Dominica. Deposed Prime Minister Patrick John sought mercenary warriors to depose successor Mary Charles, for which service he offered $150,000 and future economic concessions to the victors. Ex-convict Michael Perdue took the bait, recruiting KKK imperial wizard Stephen Black to furnish men, weapons and explosives. Canadian Klansman and smuggler Wolfgang Droege signed on in hopes that "free" Dominica might become his new base of operations. Soldiers recruited for the putsch included an ex-police chief from Kansas and various Klansmen or neo–Nazis, Mississippi fugitive Joe Daniel Hawkins among them. Their plan, fueled by visions of slavery and limitless wealth, involved a ten-man amphibious invasion and conquest of the capital (Roseau), where Klan shock troops would defeat local police and clear the way for John's triumphant return. To that end, Black and Perdue chartered a boat from Mike Howell of New Orleans and prepared to launch their strike from a marina on Lake Ponchartrain.[18]

The plan hit a snag when Howell blew the whistle and welcomed two ATF agents aboard, disguised as merchant seamen. On 27 April 1981, as Black and company prepared to set sail for Dominica, they were surrounded by agents and relieved of a small arsenal that included machine guns and explosives. All ten plotters were arrested, charged with federal weapons offenses and violation of the Neutrality Act. Seven defendants pled guilty, and Black and Hawkins stood trial and were convicted on 20 June 1981. Jurors acquitted Alabama Klansman Michael Norris, accepting his claim that he believed he had been working for the CIA. Those found guilty received three-year prison terms, augmented in Droege's case by 13 years on weapons, drug and immigration charges. Bemused ATF agents christened their adventure the "Bayou of Pigs."[19]

FBI agents provided only marginal assistance in the Dominica affair — though bureau headquarters later claimed sole credit for cracking the case — and they were generally nowhere to be seen in Klan investigations nationwide. One glaring exception was the case of Elbert "Bill" Wilkinson, a Louisiana native who defected from David Duke's Knights of the KKK to create his own Invisible Empire Knights in August 1975. By 1979 Wilkinson's faction was the second-largest in America, claiming 2,500 of 10,000 knights nationwide. Wilkinson's followers attacked black demonstrators in Decatur, Alabama, and Tupelo, Mississippi, during 1979, and were linked to other violent crimes. The wizard himself brandished weapons at every opportunity, declaring, "These guns ain't for rabbit hunting; they're to waste people." The end came for Wilkinson in January 1982 when newspaper stories identified him as a longtime FBI informant. Angry Klansmen defected en masse from the Invisible Empire Knights, and the faction was bankrupt by January 1983. Strangely, though Wilkinson admitted spying for the FBI from the time he formed his Klan in 1975, reporters failed to draw a link between his bureau paymasters and the mayhem perpetrated by Wilkinson's knights. Despite his open advocacy of criminal violence and his presence at various riot scenes, no charges were filed against Wilkinson.[20]

Another Klansman who slipped through the FBI's net was Louis Beam, Texas grand dragon for David Duke's Knights of the KKK. In January 1981, Beam opened an illegal paramilitary training camp for racists on federal land outside Dallas. One month later, he led 300 Klansmen in armed protests against Vietnamese fishermen around Galveston, exhorting white vigilantes to reclaim the nation "by blood." Beam was indicted and convicted of practicing guerrilla warfare on government property without permission, but his conviction was overturned on appeal and he went unpunished. It required a private organization, the Southern Poverty Law Center (SPLC), to halt his harassment of Asians in Texas. It obtained a civil injunction against Beam on 14 May 1981. Two months later, Beam left the Klan to become a self-styled "ambassador at large" for the neo–Nazi Aryan Nations.[21]

Overall, Southern state authorities proved more successful than FBI agents in bringing Klansmen to justice during the 1970s and early 1980s. Alabama Attorney General Bill Baxley persevered, despite bureau obstructionism, to convict Robert Chambliss in the Birmingham BAPBOMB case in 1977. Three years later, still with no help from the FBI, he convicted Jesse Stoner of bombing another Birmingham church in 1958. Stoner skipped bail and went into hiding on 27 January 1983, then surrendered four months later, ultimately serving three and a half years in prison.[22]

The KKK's most heinous crime since Greensboro was the abduction and lynching of 19-year-old Michael Donald on 21 March 1981. Donald, a black youth, was kidnapped, beaten and hanged from a tree in downtown Mobile, Alabama, one-half mile from the spot where black prisoner Glenn Diamond suffered a "mock lynching" in 1976 at the hands of Mobile policemen. The officers in that case sought to force a robbery confession from their innocent prisoner. No federal charges were filed in that case, and two policemen were acquitted of assault at trial, though the city later settled a civil lawsuit out of court for $40,000. Five years later, after the mistrial of another black defendant charged with killing a policeman in Mobile, agitated members of the United Klans decided to "show Klan strength in Alabama" with a random act of murder. Plucking their victim off the street, Klansmen questioned Donald about his supposed knowledge of the Atlanta child murders, then beat, strangled and hanged him, leaving their victim with a boot print on his forehead. A cross was burned at Mobile's courthouse the same night as a Klan "signature" for the lynching.[23]

The crime went unsolved for two years while local police ignored the Klan and pursued innocent black suspects. Next, District Attorney Chris Galanos sought FBI assistance, but G-men spent their time retracing the same false leads and produced no arrests. Finally, in early 1983, U.S. Attorney Thomas Figueres ordered a new FBI investigation, and agents belatedly noticed the obvious: Donald had been hanged directly opposite a house owned by Bennie Hays, a convicted cattle rustler and grand titan for the UKA in southern Alabama. The tenant was his son, Henry Hays, kligrapp (secretary) of the local klavern. That "coincidence" led G-men to investigate the Mobile Klan, and so the case was broken at long last. Klansman James "Tiger" Knowles pled guilty in federal court to violating Donald's civil rights, while Hays denied any knowledge of the crime. Both were charged with murder on 16 June 1983, and Justice dismissed the federal charge against Hays. Both were convicted, Knowles receiving a sentence of ten years to life for cooperating with the prosecution. Jurors voted life imprisonment for Hays, but Judge Braxton Kittrell Jr. took the unusual step of ignoring that recommendation when he sentenced Hays to die. In August 1987, Bennie Hays and Klansman Benjamin Cox were indicted as accomplices in Donald's murder. Poor health spared Bennie Hays from trial, but Cox was convicted and sentenced to life in May 1989. With his appeals exhausted, Henry Hays was executed on 7 June 1997.[24]

The case might have ended there, but leaders of the Southern Poverty Law Center filed a wrongful-death lawsuit against the UKA on behalf of grieving mother Beulah Mae Donald. The trial convened on 9 February 1987, with retired FBI informant Gary Rowe on hand to describe the UKA's violent history. Imperial Wizard Robert Shelton and his UKA hierarchy branded the Mobile klavern a violent rogue faction, but SPLC lead attorney Morris Dees produced a 1979 issue of the *Fiery Cross* including a cartoon of a white man advising the reader: "It's terrible the way blacks are being treated! All whites should work to give the blacks what they deserve!" The next page bore a drawing of a black man dangling with a rope around his neck, just as

Donald had died. Shelton denied foreknowledge of the cartoon, blaming the magazine's Louisiana editor, then admitted under oath that he had never ordered a retrac-
tion. An all-white jury found the UKA responsible for Donald's murder and awarded
his mother $7 million in damages. Unable to pay the tab, Shelton surrendered his
national headquarters building in lieu of cash.[25]

"ATKID"

It may have been no accident that Michael Donald's killers questioned him about
the ongoing Atlanta "child murders" in March 1981. That rash of slayings in and
around Georgia's capital city began in July 1979, when a woman hunting empty bottles found the corpses of two teenage boys, one shot to death, the other "probably"
asphyxiated. Two more victims, aged nine and 14, were discovered in October and
November. The first officially recognized victim of 1980 was also the first female, 12-
year-old Angel Lenair, found raped and bound to a tree with someone else's panties
jammed in her throat.[26]

From that point onward, the relentless pace of deaths and disappearances sparked
panic in Atlanta's black community. Police were helpless in the face of the onslaught,
fumbling clues and bickering over which dead or missing children should be posted
to Atlanta's victim list. Thirty cases ultimately made the roster, although the selection process defied all logic. Murder victim Faye Yearby was barred from the list in
January 1981, although she was tied to a tree (like Angel Lenair) and stabbed to death
(like four other victims on the list). When questioned on those points, police
explained that they discounted Yearby because she was female (like Lenair and
another acknowledged "list" victim), and that her age (22) disqualified her as a child-
killer's target. The latter argument collapsed in April 1981 when detectives added
Michael McIntosh — a 23-year-old ex-convict — to the list. Four other men ranging
in age from 20 to 27 finally made the list of murdered "children," but Faye Yearby
remained ostracized. In fact, as authors Chet Dettlinger and Jeff Prugh revealed in
1983, a total of 38 black victims whose death fit the broad profile were excluded from
official victim status during 1979-1981. Their deaths remain unsolved today.[27]

Atlanta FBI agents provoked a storm of outrage in April 1981 with their
announcement that several of the murders were "substantially solved." Specifically,
they claimed that certain unnamed victims had been killed by their own parents,
then admitted that no evidence existed to support indictments in those cases. While
that storm was raging, CORE leader Roy Innis produced a female witness who
described Atlanta's murders as the actions of a cult involved in drugs, pornography
and Satanism. Innis led searchers to an apparent ritual site, complete with large
inverted crosses and mutilated animals, and his witness passed two successive polygraph tests. By that time, however, Atlanta police had focused their attention on
another suspect, narrowing their focus to the exclusion of all other possibilities.[28]

By spring 1981 several bodies had been pulled from local rivers, and police staked
out the waterways by night. In the predawn hours of 22 May a rookie officer stationed beneath a bridge spanning the Chattahoochee River heard a splash in the water

nearby. Above him, a car rumbled past, and officers manning the bridge were alerted. Police and FBI agents stopped a vehicle driven by Wayne Bertram Williams, a black man, and spent the next two hours searching his car, grilling Williams intensely before they released him. Two days later, the corpse of another ex-convict, 27-year-old Nathaniel Cater, was hauled from the river downstream. Authorities illogically concluded that Williams must have thrown the 149-pound victim from his car while crossing the bridge (presumably one-handed, through a window, since he never stopped), and from that moment onward evidence favorable to Williams was consistently ignored, if not illegally suppressed.[29]

From the start, Williams made an unlikely suspect. The only child of two Atlanta teachers, he still lived with his parents at age 23. Williams quit college to pursue a career as a music promoter, but thus far had missed the big time. In younger days, he had constructed a functional radio station in the basement of his family home. He had no history of "kinky" sex or conflict with the law. Nonetheless, Williams was arrested on 21 June and charged with killing Nathaniel Cater — this despite testimony on record from two witnesses who saw Cater alive on 22 and 23 May, hours *after* the infamous Chattahoochee "splash." On 17 July, Williams was formally indicted on two counts of murder, including victims Cater and 21-year-old Jimmy Payne, another ex-convict. Reported missing on 21 April, Payne was found suffocated six days later, the cause of death alone sufficient to place him on Atlanta's list of murdered "children."[30]

FBI agents John Douglas and Roy Hazelwood were pleased with the apparent solution of their "ATKID" case (bureau code for *At*lanta *kid*s). As members of the federal "mindhunter" team in Quantico, Virginia, they had profiled the Atlanta suspect as:

> [A] black male, single, between the ages of twenty-five and twenty-nine. He would be a police buff, drive a police-type vehicle, and somewhere along the way he would insinuate himself into the investigation. He would have a police-type dog, either a German shepherd or a Doberman. He would not have a girlfriend, he would be sexually attracted to young boys, but we weren't seeing any signs of rape or sexual abuse. This ... spoke to his sexual inadequacy. He would have some kind of ruse or con to use with these kids.... He would have a good line, but he couldn't produce. At some point early in each relationship, the kid would reject him, or he would at least perceive it that way, and he would feel compelled to kill.[31]

G-men stand by that profile today as proof of their skill in tracking serial offenders. They note the suspect's age, unmarried status, and the fact that his family owned a German shepherd. Some sources also contend that Williams joined in a civilian search for one of Atlanta's missing children. In contrast, neither the Williams family's 1970 Chevrolet station wagon nor their 1979 Ford sedan bore any resemblance to police cars, and a former girlfriend testified in court to having "normal" sex with Williams while they dated. The rest of the profile was broad-stroke guesswork, drawn from common crime statistics in America. On average, 90 percent of all convicted murderers (and eighty-seven percent of identified serial killers) are male; most serial murderers kill for the first time in their early twenties; and 95 percent kill victims of their own race (except where the murders are racist in nature). It is thus no great feat to profile a killer of young black victims as a young black male. Despite those glaring inconsistencies, however, Agent Douglas later called the Williams case "a major triumph for the art of profiling and criminal investigative analysis."[32]

On its face, the Williams indictment did not suggest a child killer. He was charged with overpowering and killing two adult ex-convicts, both larger and stronger than himself, who bore no resemblance to the FBI's hypothetical star-struck children. No evidence immediately linked Williams to either adult victim, whereas two eyewitnesses reported Nathaniel Cater alive and well a full day after Williams allegedly dropped his corpse into the river. How, then, was Williams finally convicted in those cases and then, after trial, publicly branded the slayer of 21 others whose deaths were never legally charged against him?

At trial, beginning in December 1981, the prosecution painted Williams as a violent homosexual and bigot, so disgusted with his own race that he hoped to wipe out future generations by killing black children before they could breed. That motive never surfaced in the FBI profile, but in Atlanta's lynch-law atmosphere the discrepancy proved irrelevant. One witness testified that he saw Williams holding hands with Nathaniel Cater on 21 May, a few hours before the river "splash." Another, 15 years old, claimed that Williams had paid him two dollars for the privilege of fondling his genitals. Defense attorneys tried to offset that testimony with the ex-girlfriend who found Williams "normal" in bed, but prosecutors won a crucial point when Judge Clarence Cooper admitted testimony on ten other deaths from the "child murders" list, designed to prove a pattern in the slayings. Though Williams was charged with none of those crimes, the jury was given details involving victims Alfred Evans (July 1979), Eric Middlebrooks (May 1980), Charles Stephens (October 1980), Terry Pue (January 1981), Lubie Geter (January 1981), Patrick Baltazar (February 1981), Joseph Bell (March 1981), Larry Rogers (March 1981), John Porter (April 1981), and William Barrett (May 1981).[33] The murder "pattern," as described in court, included fifteen separate elements:

1. All victims were black males.
2. All came from poor families.
3. All were raised in broken homes.
4. None owned a car.
5. All were branded "street hustlers."
6. None were forcibly abducted.
7. All were strangled or asphyxiated.
8. All were transported after death.
9. All were dumped near "major arteries" of travel.
10. Bodies were disposed of in "unusual" ways.
11. Clothing was absent from the crime scenes.
12. No valuables were found with any victim.
13. Similar fibers were found on several bodies.
14. No motive was apparent in the crimes.
15. Williams denied contact with the victims.[34]

Discounting the last two points (which are equally consistent with the suspect's claim of innocence) and number 12 (for its contradictory suggestion of robbery in gay-racist murders), prosecutors still had glaring problems with their "pattern." Seven of the ten victims were too young to drive, so their lack of cars was superfluous, and victim Middlebrooks vanished while riding a bicycle. Middlebrooks and Rogers were beaten to death, not strangled or asphyxiated, and the "pattern" list excluded Alfred Evans, a gunshot victim whose corpse was found with that of Evans. Prosecutors likewise ignored phone calls received after Joseph Bell's abduction (referring to multiple kidnappers) and their own alleged discovery (reported in the media) of still-unidentified fingerprints found on Terry Pue's corpse.[35]

Those omissions were part of an insidious pattern, which included perjured testimony at trial. Prosecution witness Darrell Davis described glancing out the window of his workplace, seeing Williams and victim Lubie Geter together in a car on the same day Geter disappeared. Later, Davis's employer signed an affidavit that Davis had not come to work on the day in question, and thus had seen nothing. A second witness, Ruth Warren, initially told police that she saw Geter with a scar-faced white man on the day he vanished. At trial, while prosecutors concealed her original statement from the defense, she described a black suspect "resembling" Wayne Williams. Robert Henry testified in court to seeing Williams with Nathaniel Cater on 22 May 1980, but in a post–trial affidavit he recanted that claim, contending that police and prosecutors pressured him to lie.[36]

The most impressive evidence of guilt was offered by a team of scientific experts who described assorted hairs and fibers found on certain "pattern" victims. They testified that fibers from a brand of carpet found inside the Williams home (and countless other homes, as well) had been retrieved from several bodies. Furthermore, fibers from the trunk liner of a 1979 Ford sedan (owned in common by the Williams family and many other drivers) were found on victims Cater, Middlebrooks and Stephens, as well as on the corpses of two others strangely omitted from the "pattern" list, Aaron Wyche (June 1980) and Earl Terrell (July 1980). If that was not confusing enough, investigators also said they found carpet fibers from a 1970 Ford station wagon on Charles Stephens.[37]

Jurors were *not* advised of a critical gap in the state's fiber case. Specifically, Wayne Williams had no access to the cars in question when three of the five "fiber" victims were killed. His father took the Ford in for repairs at 9:00 A.M. on July 30, 1980—five hours before Earl Terrell disappeared that afternoon. Terrell was long dead before Williams retrieved the car on 7 August, and it was returned to the shop on 8 August, still refusing to start. A new estimate of repair costs ran so high that Wayne's father refused to pay, and the family never again used that vehicle. As for Charles Stephens, killed on 9 October 1980, Wayne's family did not purchase the Chevrolet station wagon until twelve days later, on 21 October. Prosecutors also concealed the fact that two Caucasian hairs were found on Stephens's underclothes.[38]

Jurors, thus deprived of vital exculpatory evidence, convicted Williams of two murder counts in January 1982, and Judge Cooper sentenced him to a double life term on 27 February. Two days later, the Atlanta "child murders" task force disbanded, announcing that 23 of its 30 official "list" cases were solved, with Williams named as the killer. That lumping of untried cases included another glaring discrepancy in the August 1980 slaying of Clifford Jones. Soon after Jones was found dead, witness Freddie Cosby told police he had seen two white men, Jamie Brooks and Calvin Smith, rape Jones in a backroom at the laundromat Brooks managed. After the rape, said Cosby, Brooks had strangled Jones and carried his body to a nearby garbage bin (an act confirmed by other witnesses). Defense attorneys never saw those statements, nor were they presented to jurors in the trial where Jones was carefully omitted from the list of "pattern" victims. Jamie Brooks, meanwhile, was convicted and imprisoned for sodomizing another young boy.[39]

The Williams verdict and subsequent task force announcement left seven "list" cases unsolved. They remain so today, ignored by Atlanta police and the FBI. In December 1982, parents of twelve Atlanta victims filed suit in federal court, demanding either that Williams be charged with the murders of their children, or that the cases be officially reopened. District Attorney Lewis Slaton refused to "waste" time or money on another trial, and the lawsuit was later dismissed. Georgia's Supreme Court reviewed the Williams verdict in 1983, with Justice Richard Bell assigned to draft the majority opinion. His initial statement was a shocker: "We find it necessary to reverse." That unpublished draft decision, later obtained by *The Washington Post,* chastised Judge Cooper for admitting "pattern" evidence with respect to victims Baltazar, Evans, Middlebrooks, Porter and Stephens.[40] Specifically, Bell wrote:

> There was no evidence placing Williams with these five victims before their murders, and as in all the murders linked to Williams, there were no eyewitnesses, no confession, no murder weapons and no established motive. Also, the five deaths, while somewhat similar to each other in technique, were unlike the two for which Williams was tried.[41]

That judgment, if published, would have demanded a new trial for Williams, excluding the spurious "pattern" cases. Instead, however, six judges changed their minds within hours of the court's scheduled adjournment, ruling to *uphold* the Williams verdict by a vote of six to one. Justice George Smith cast the lone dissenting vote, writing: "The only thing similar about these cases is that they're all dead." Today, those involved refuse to discuss the court's strange turnabout, and all subsequent appeals in the case have been denied.[42]

More than a guilty verdict was required to make the case against Wayne Williams, though. Conviction and appellate judgments meant nothing if the murders in Atlanta continued—and they did. Despite insistent claims from the press, Atlanta's police, and various FBI profilers basking in the glory of their "triumph," authors Dettlinger and Prugh list 25 similar murders in Atlanta between the date of Williams's arrest and early 1983. Even John Douglas, while insisting on Wayne's guilt in 11 murders, dismisses the other cases and says that "[d]espite what some people would like to believe, young black and white children continue to die mysteriously in Atlanta."[43]

The key to finally solving Atlanta's child murders may lie with victim Charles Stephens. Years after the fact, defense attorneys learned that the Georgia Bureau of Investigation — once led and staffed by Klansmen under the Talmadge regime — had investigated KKK involvement in the slayings. That investigation (code-named

"8100") was initiated in 1980 after an informant in the Klan told GBI agents that Klansmen were "killing the children" in Atlanta, hoping to ignite a race war that would turn into a statewide purge of blacks. One knight in particular, 30-year-old Charles Sanders, had publicly threatened victim Lubie Geter in December 1980 after Geter crashed a go-cart into Sanders's car. The GBI informant reported Sanders raging, "See that little black bastard? I'm gonna kill him. I'm gonna choke that black bastard to death." Geter vanished three weeks later, on 3 January 1981; when his corpse was found on 5 February, pathologists attributed his death to strangulation. Carlton Sanders, father of Charles and subject of 35 arrests since 1951 (including one for molestation, case dismissed), matched Ruth Warren's original description of the scar-faced white man seen with Geter on the day he vanished.[44]

GBI agents ordered a polygraph test for their key informant, which he passed. Aided by a second spy, authorities intensified surveillance on Charles Sanders and six other members of his family, conducting wiretaps and persuading one informant to wear a microphone in meetings with the Klansmen.[45] One phone tap recorded the following conversation between brothers Don and Terry Sanders:

Don: Is Ricky around?
Terry: Well, he just left with Kenneth.
Don: Did he?
Terry: Yeah.
Don: Where's he headed?
Terry: To his apartment or something.
Don: Do you think he'll be back?
Terry: Oh, yeah.
Don: After a while.
Terry: Yeah.
Don: I'll give a buzz back, and I might get out and ride around a little bit, and I might come by there.
Terry: Go find you another little kid?
Don: Yeah, scope out some places. We'll see you later.[46]

GBI informants also reported another conversation with the Sanders brothers in 1981, warning that "after twenty black-child killings they, the Klan, were going to start killing black women." And in fact, Atlanta police records reveal the unsolved murders of 27 black women in Atlanta during 1980–81, with most of the victims strangled. While reporting on the murder plots, informants also purchased various illegal weapons from the Sanders brood, including bazookas and machine guns, but no state or federal charges were filed.[47]

The GBI's "8100" probe became public knowledge in 1985, forming the basis for another unsuccessful appeal by the Williams defense team, but FBI agents knew of it from the beginning. Ex-agent Douglas summarized their reaction in 1995:

> The Georgia Bureau of Investigation had received several tips about Ku Klux Klan involvement, but we discounted them. If you study hate crimes going all the way back to the early days of the nation, you find that they tend to be highly public,

highly symbolic acts. A lynching is intended to make a public statement and create a public display. Such a crime or other racial murder is an act of terrorism,
and for it to have an effect, it must be highly visible. Ku Klux Klansmen don't
wear white sheets to fade into the woodwork. If a hate group targeted black children throughout the Atlanta area, it wouldn't have been content to let months go
by before the police and the public figured out something was going on. We would
have expected bodies strung up on Main Street, USA, and the message would have
been none too subtle. We didn't see any of that type of behavior in these cases.[48]

That assessment, while accurate enough with respect to Klan bombings and
lynchings, is also misleading in several respects. First, the GBI's information did not
consist merely of "tips": It included statements from informants in the Klan, supported by recordings of the suspects themselves discussing abduction of children. That
evidence included a specific victim and a threat to kill him, three weeks in advance,
using the method that eventually took his life. Douglas errs, furthermore, in suggesting that all Klan crimes are public spectacles. In 1964 alone, the White Knights of Mississippi killed five victims whose bodies were hidden for months, and a sixth murder
(in 1965) is listed to this day as an accidental death. Motive determines method, in
hate crimes as in any other, and Douglas has ignored the KKK's purported goal of
sparking race war in Atlanta with a series of murders targeting women and children.

While the notion of race war in modern America may seems fantastic, it remains
an obsession with certain white supremacists. Chapter 10 details efforts by The Order,
a small collection of Klansmen and neo–Nazis, to topple the U.S. government in
1983. Two years later, five members of the United Klans were jailed in Florida for
trying to foment racial warfare in St. Petersburg by means of serial assaults on blacks,
Jews and gays. Three Jacksonville, Florida, knights with similar aims were arrested
in November 1990, for stealing military weapons and explosives from a military arsenal. One Klan-allied fascist cult, the World Church of the Creator (WCC) uses
RAHOWA!—*Racial Holy War*—as its motto. In July 2002, racist (and alleged WCC
associate) Leo Felton was arrested in Boston for plotting to bomb prominent black
and Jewish targets, including Jesse Jackson, Al Sharpton, Steven Spielberg and the
Holocaust Museum. His goal: to ignite a wave of ethnic cleansing in America, driving Jews and nonwhite "mud people" from the country.[49]

Preposterous? Of course. But to extremists of the Klan and allied groups, absurd
conspiracies are day-to-day reality, and no less deadly to innocent victims because
they spring from addled minds. More to the point, Atlanta harbored brooding fears
of race war during the "child killer's" reign of terror. On 28 June 1979, exactly one
month before the slayer's first two victims were found in Atlanta, a young white
physician was killed by black muggers while attending a medical convention. Four
months later, a white legal secretary was murdered on her birthday by a mentally
unbalanced black assailant. Atlanta's black mayor and police commissioner heard
the calls for a crackdown on street crime, coupled with rumors that a white conspiracy lay behind the murders of young blacks. Indictment of a white suspect, much
less an outspoken racist with ties to militant terrorist groups, risked igniting the
powder keg. Official Atlanta *needed* a black child-killer, both to defuse the conspiracy talk and to demonstrate for the record that black officials were doing their job
without fear or favor.[50]

Would FBI agents collaborate in the frame-up of an innocent defendant? Sadly, the answer to that question, based on revelations spanning more than eight decades, must be affirmative. From the Sacco-Vanzetti case of 1920, wherein G-men recorded (but did not protest) introduction of false evidence by Massachusetts prosecutors, through the 1990 case of Earth First! activists Judi Bari and Darryl Cherney (framed for bombing their own car in an attack that nearly killed them), bureau agents have collaborated with local law enforcement agencies to convict — and in some cases execute — innocent defendants. In the 1930s, FBI gangbusters framed bootlegger Roger Touhy for a kidnapping that never occurred, and sent him to prison for life. Thirty years later, Boston agents acting in league with organized crime framed four men for a murder they did not commit; two of those defendants died in prison, and the others were exonerated after serving some 35 years behind bars. (Agent John Connolly was convicted for his role in that case, receiving a ten-year prison term in September 2002). Elmer "Geronimo" Pratt, a member of the militant Black Panther Party, served 27 years on a fraudulent murder conviction after he was framed by G-men and Los Angeles police. Grave doubts linger in many other cases, ranging from the Lindbergh kidnapping of 1932 to the murder conviction of Native American activist Leonard Peltier in 1977.[51]

We may never know the full truth of what happened in Atlanta during 1979–82, but sufficient evidence exists to make it obvious that justice was not served. And once again, where FBI agents joined state and local officers to mask the truth, the Ku Klux Klan was a primary beneficiary. Despite its many crimes, the KKK has reason to boast that it will endure "yesterday, today and forever — as long as the white man liveth."[52]

10

Defending "ZOG"

Klan doctrine and propaganda underwent a radical change after 1980. Previously, the hooded knights proclaimed themselves defenders of a U.S. government besieged and infiltrated by sinister enemies— Catholics, Communists, Jews, and "liberals." In the last years of the twentieth century, however, American government itself was cast as the enemy, christened "ZOG"— the Zionist Occupational Government.[1] To Klansmen and their allies on the rabid right, Washington and the federal system at large had been lost. Armed resistance or outright revolution were the only remedies remaining. And the FBI, still reviled among white knights as the "Federal Bureau of Integration," was seen as part of the problem, its agents front-line defenders of a hostile regime.

Such attitudes did not spring into being overnight. They were derived, instead, from individuals and groups that mingled with the Klans over a period of years, expounding messages that catered to Ku Klux bigotry while raising the ante, pressing toward the day when Klansmen and neo–Nazis would write formal declarations of war against the U.S. government in Washington. First and foremost among those organizations, ironically, was a group of militant racists founded and led by a Jew.

POSSE COMITATUS

William Potter Gale, born in November 1916, was the son of Jewish refugees who fled anti–Semitic persecution in their Eastern European homeland in the 1880s. He served with the U.S. Army in 1934–37 and again in 1941-50, retiring as a major. Gale's military records reveal frequent complaints of illness, but they fail to document his claims of combat wounds suffered in the Philippines. Back in civilian life, driven by private demons yet unknown, Gale fell under the sway of "Christian Identity," a racist cult that teaches that white Europeans are the true lost tribes of Israel, while Jews are the literal children of Satan (who later created nonwhite "mud people" through weird experiments). Gale's mentors in the creed were two California Klansmen, Wesley Swift and San Jacinto Capt.[2]

Gale organized his first armed racist group, the California Rangers, in 1960. Four years later, he diversified, founding the Ministry of Christ Church with a paramilitary arm called the Christian Defense League. That same year, 1964, Gale's son reported finding a Klan robe in his father's closet. In 1972 Gale launched his ultimate vehicle, the United Christian Posse Association, based on a garbled misinterpretation of the 1878 Posse Comitatus Act. That federal statute bars civilian authorities from using military units to enforce domestic laws, but Gale and his disciples viewed it as a sweeping indictment of the whole U.S. government. Fixated on the Latin term *posse comitatus* ("power of the county"), Gale decreed that county sheriffs constitute the highest law enforcement authority in the United States, empowered to deputize all able-bodied men over 18 years of age.[3] Ignoring the fact that his troops had never been deputized, Gale proclaimed himself a posse leader. Over time, his followers and other Posse Comitatus members nationwide would threaten and attack local sheriffs, just as they did federal agents.

Another contender for the rank of Posse pioneer was Henry Beach, a veteran of the 1930s Silver Shirt Legion who also espoused Identity theology. Some accounts say that Beach organized his posse in 1969, but his first publication on the subject— the Posse *Blue Book*— was plagiarized verbatim from Gale's *Guide to Volunteer Christian Posses* and a series of articles Gale published in the newsletter *IDENTITY* between June 1971 and July 1972. From that time forward, despite their mutual hatred for Jews and nonwhites, Gale and Beach would be ardent competitors and bitter enemies.[4]

Regardless of its origins and fractured leadership, the Posse Comitatus struck a chord with racists nationwide. It won early endorsement from the National Association to Keep and Bear Arms (NAKB), an extremist pro-gun lobby organized in 1974 by Minutemen founder and ex-convict Robert DePugh. The NAKB, in turn, was closely allied with DePugh's Patriots Organizational Communications Center, a far-right clearinghouse that welcomed Imperial Wizard Robert Shelton as a founding member. The NAKB's newsletter also ran ads for the Klan, thus confirming DePugh's affinity for white-supremacist organizations. Klan wizard David Duke, meanwhile, told reporters, "We work with the Posses wherever we can.... We get their material and funnel it to our groups." Articles published in the *Christian Posse Comitatus Newsletter* featured titles such as "Jewish Ritual Murder" and "Scientists Say Negro Still in Ape Stage."[5]

FBI response to the Posse — described in bureau files as a "loose-knit, nationwide organization"—was muddled at best. Surveillance of sorts began in April 1973 when the Portland, Oregon, field office first reported to headquarters an "organization calling itself Identity, or alternatively the Portland Posse Comitatus.... [A]n association of longtime Right Wing extremists ... preaching hate against the Negroes and the Jews, and calling for the repudiation and overthrow of the existing law enforcement and judicial systems of this nation." Director Clarence Kelley ordered a nationwide investigation, which found six active chapters in Oregon and others scattered across eight states, from Alaska to Ohio, Arkansas and Virginia. Bureau headquarters warned field agents to consider Posse members "armed and dangerous," but the FBI's final report of June 1974 was strangely anticlimactic. Despite a nonstop outpouring of racist bile from Posse propagandists, FBI analysts concluded that the Posse was not "anti-semitic [*sic*] or anti–black in its pronouncements." Posse demands for overthrow of the IRS and federal government at large were deemed "unusual," but headquarters said that "[g]roup members [are] not considered threat[s] to [the] community."[6]

Bureau investigation of the Posse was doubtless retarded by external events in 1973–74, including exposure of illegal COINTELPRO campaigns against other domestic groups and anxiety over impending congressional probes of FBI abuses. At the same time, western bureau field offices seemed bent on actively subverting orders from Washington. San Francisco's agent-in-charge earned a formal reprimand for his defiant refusal to interview Posse leaders or cultivate informants in the group. A similar wrist-slap was dealt to the agent-in-charge in Butte, Montana, for identical negligence. Oregon G-men were hopelessly confused, first describing Dean Kennedy's Portland Posse as the nation's most active, then saying that chapters in their state had "never established themselves as functional organizations."[7] On balance, it is difficult not to conclude that some high-ranking agents, conditioned by careers spent hounding leftists and racial minorities, shared at least some of the Posse's prejudice and paranoia.

As in the past, where G-men turned a blind eye to right-wing extremist activity, violence soon followed. Sixteen months after the bureau's all-clear report on the Posses on 25 August 1976, seven armed Posse members occupied a farm in Umatilla County, Oregon, staging a tense 11-hour standoff with police. The FBI's response on 5 October 1977 was yet another report claiming "a marked decline of [Posse] chapters and membership and illegal activity." In fact, the opposite was true, as Posse recruiters enlisted new recruits from coast to coast, graduating from angry rhetoric to training classes in guerrilla warfare. Nonetheless, at the recommendation of his Portland agent-in-charge, Director Kelley formally closed the FBI's Posse investigation.[8]

In spring 1981, ignored by bureau agents, the Posse Comitatus held joint paramilitary training exercises with Klansmen and Minutemen remnants in California's Sierra Nevada mountains. Another training camp was established in Wisconsin around the same time. A year later, in March 1982, William Gale himself offered knife-fighting classes to Posse stalwarts and members of the anti–Semitic American Agriculture Movement in Weskan, Kansas. Also in attendance at that session was James Wickstrom from Wisconsin, self-appointed national director of counterinsurgency for the Posse. The Weskan gathering was organized by Wesley White, who three weeks later delivered a consignment of illegal explosives to fellow Posse member Charles Howarth in Colorado. Howarth, dissatisfied with the Posse program, soon defected to revive the United Klans realm in Colorado, then found himself jailed for selling pipe bombs to undercover policemen. A search of his home revealed KKK paraphernalia and a list of 50 Klan/Posse members statewide. Howarth and White pled guilty to explosives charges, receiving prison terms of two years and one year, respectively.[9]

After years of threat and bluster, the Posse Comitatus claimed its first fatalities in early 1983. In North Dakota, Posse member Gordon Kahl had avoided prison in a June 1977 federal tax-evasion case, then violated his probation with further extremist activities. U.S. marshals and local sheriff's deputies tried to arrest him on 13 February 1983, but they found Kahl armed and supported by 17 more Posse members. When the gunsmoke cleared moments later, two federal marshals and Kahl's son were dead, and three other lawmen and two Posse members were wounded. Kahl fled to Smithville, Arkansas, where he died in a second shootout on 3 June 1983, after killing Sheriff Gene Matthews. Posse members spread rumors that Kahl was tortured and executed by FBI agents, who murdered Sheriff Matthews when he tried to intervene.[10]

More Posse-related murders were recorded in August 1985 when police exhumed the corpses of a five-year-old boy and a 26-year-old man at a rural compound near Rulo, Nebraska. The commune was run by sadistic "survivalist" Michael Wayne Ryan, a self-styled messenger of God whom Posse member Donald Zabawa identified as "Jim Wickstrom's main man" in the Kansas-Nebraska region. Kansas authorities, who began investigating Ryan's cult in March 1983, complained that FBI agents dismissed their reports of stockpiled arms and other violations as "a joke."[11]

Between the North Dakota and Nebraska murders, William Gale's two-year-old Committee of the States issued a 15-point "Declaration of Alteration and Reform," demanding immediate repeal of the federal income tax, to be followed by resignation en masse of all U.S. senators and representatives. Gale's committee would assume "all functions of the Department of Justice [and] the Department of Defense." Gale declined to sign his own declaration but put his name on other documents identifying him as "chief of staff" of the committee's "unorganized militia." The document's 41 signatories included William Butler, head of the Aryan Nations, and several members of the far-right Arizona Patriots. Two weeks later, Gale promoted his Committee of the States at Butler's Aryan Nations compound in Idaho.[12]

Dramatic pronouncements were one thing, but direct actions often have consequences. On 23 October 1986, Gale and seven other defendants were jailed on a ten-count federal indictment charging them with conspiracy, attempts to interfere with U.S. tax laws, and mailing death threats to IRS agents. Spurred by those arrests, David Moran—"National Education Chairman" for the Committee of States—committed five armed robberies in northern California on 1 December 1996. A written explanation of his crimes declared: "The arrests of William P. Gale and others by the agents of ZOG is the proverbial straw that broke the camel's back. Thus I, like the members of the Brüder Schweigen [see below], have declared war." Moran died in a shootout with police on 8 December, but other Possemen carried on the crusade. On 2 March 1987, explosive rounds from nine homemade mortars were fired at a federal courthouse in Laguna Niguel, California. Gale's court case was anticlimactic by comparison. Three defendants pled guilty and turned state's evidence against their comrades, and Gale and four others were convicted at trial on 2 October 1987. Gale received three concurrent one-year sentences and died in custody on 28 April 1988. His colleagues received prison terms ranging from 30 months to seven years, each with a $5,000 fine.[13]

Other Posse factions continued the fight without Gale. On 15 December 1986, FBI agents arrested eight members of the Arizona Patriots, confiscating large quantities of arms, ammunition and explosives. Four defendants were charged with plotting to rob an armored car in the name of patriotism, followed by bombings of a Phoenix synagogue, an IRS office in Utah, three dams, the Anti-Defamation League and the Simon Wiesenthal Center. Four other Posse members were jailed in North Carolina on 23 October 1989 for their participation in a $3 million real estate fraud.

Gale's successor as chief of the Posse, James Wickstrom, was convicted on 14 June 1990 of conspiracy to distribute counterfeit money. He received a three-year prison term.[14]

THE ORDER

If William Gale's guerrilla war against America seemed half-hearted and scatterbrained, the same could not be said of Texas native Robert Jay Mathews. A longtime anti–Semite associated with the John Birch Society, Aryan Nations and National Alliance, Mathews developed an obsession for *The Turner Diaries*, a racist novel published in 1978 by National Alliance leader William Pierce. *The Turner Diaries* describes America enslaved by ZOG, wherein white patriots of "The Order" struggle to reclaim their native land, at one point blasting FBI headquarters with a massive truck bomb.[15] In summer 1983, Mathews decided it was time for the fictional war to begin in real life.

Surrounded by like-minded fanatics at the Aryan Nations compound in July 1983, Mathews recruited would-be guerrillas for his version of the Order, also known within its ranks as *Brüder Schweigen* ("Silent Brotherhood" in German). Members were drawn from the Aryan Nations, the National Alliance and other neo–Nazi groups, with a contingent of Klansmen including James Dye (of Philadelphia), Randy Evans (California), Mark Jones (Alabama), David Lane (Denver kleagle, Knights of the KKK), Thomas Martinez (Philadelphia), Michael Norris (Alabama) and Frank Silva (exalted cyclops of California's New Order Knights of the KKK). As part of the Order's program, Mathews adopted a point system for prospective "Aryan warriors," established by Texas racist Louis Beam in his *Essays of a Klansman*. As outlined by Beam, would-be saviors of the race scored escalating points for homicides, with targets ranging from "street niggers" to the President of the United States. In their spare time, Order members often relaxed by watching *The Birth of a Nation* on videotape.[16]

For all its murderous ambition, the Order started small with a counterfeiting scheme. Its efforts were inept, producing $50 bills of such poor quality that member Bruce Pierce (no relation to William) was jailed on his first attempt to pass them. A bungled bank robbery in December 1983 was followed by the bombing of an adult theater four months later. Mathews finally found his niche with armored cars, bagging $534,000 in a Seattle heist on 23 April 1984. The group's first murder victim was Walter West, a loose-lipped Aryan Nations member whom Mathews rejected as an early recruit. The rebuff set West's alcoholic tongue wagging until Mathews ordered his execution. On 27 May 1984 a group of Order members bludgeoned West with a sledgehammer, shot him in the head, and left him in a shallow grave.[17]

The group's next murder was conceived as a military operation. Mathews selected Alan Berg, a Jewish talk-show host in Denver who frequently attacked right-wing extremists in general and neo–Nazis in particular. Colorado Klansman Fred Wilkins had publicly threatened Berg's life on 6 November 1979, a move that got him suspended from the Lakewood Fire Department, but Berg was still talking, still heaping scorn on white supremacists and Christian Identity cultists. David Lane drove the getaway car on 18 June 1984, when an Order hit team machine-gunned Berg at home in Denver, leaving him dead in his driveway.[18]

One month after Berg's murder, on 16 July 1984, Order members stopped a Brinks truck near Ukiah, California, and took $3.6 million. Mathews kept $100,000 of the money for himself, while placing some three-quarters of the loot in the Order's war chest. Several witnesses swore under oath that Mathews also donated cash to several of his racist heroes, including Louis Beam ($100,000), Richard Butler of Aryan Nations ($40,000), Michigan Klansman Robert Miles ($15,500), Frazier Glenn Miller of the Carolina Knights ($200,000), Tom Metzger of White Aryan Resistance ($260,000 to $300,000), and William Pierce ($50,000). All but Miller denied the allegations, and none were convicted of receiving stolen money.[19]

Despite its apparent success, the Ukiah holdup was Mathews's undoing. FBI agents traced a pistol, dropped at the robbery scene, to Order member Andrew Barnhill and began collecting information on his known associates. Their big break came when Klansman Tom Martinez was jailed for passing more substandard counterfeit bills. To avoid trial, on 1 October 1984 Martinez agreed to betray his fellow "warriors" to the bureau. Still, G-men had trouble pinning down the fugitives. Gary Yarbrough escaped in a flurry of gunshots when agents raided his Idaho home on 18 October. On 23 November Martinez led G-men to a rendezvous with Mathews at a Portland, Oregon, motel. It was another fiasco. Gary Yarbrough was captured, but Mathews escaped with shotgun pellets in one hand, leaving an FBI agent and the motel's manager wounded.[20]

By 26 November 1984 FBI agents knew that several Order fugitives had gathered on Whidbey Island, off the coast of Washington. Instead of closing in immediately. G-men bided their time, enabling Mathews to complete a "declaration of war on ZOG" that read:

> We, the following, being of sound mind and under no duress, do hereby sign this document of our own free will, stating forthrightly and without fear that we declare ourselves to be in full and unrelenting state of war with those forces seeking and consciously promoting the destruction of our faith and race. Therefore, for Blood, Soil, and Honor, for the future of our children, and for our King, Jesus Christ, we commit ourselves to battle. Amen.[21]

Mathews signed the declaration first, followed by Bruce Pierce, Randy Duey, Richard Scutari, Randy Evans, Robert Merki and his wife. Over the next few days, signatures accumulated from Ian Stewart, Mark Jones and Michael Norris, all using pseudonyms. A raid during that time would have netted most of the Order's top gunmen, but FBI agents delayed their attack, thus permitting two of Alan Berg's killers (Pierce and Scutari) to escape. Another who fled the island unobstructed by G-men, David Tate, murdered one Missouri policeman and wounded another before he was finally captured in April 1985. Meanwhile, FBI agents obtained warrants for a Whidbey Island raid on 4 December, then delayed three days more before making their move. G-men arrested Duey and the Merkis without incident on 7 December, but Mathews stood his ground and fought to the death, incinerated in the ruins of his hideout on 8 December 1984.[22]

Mopping up the rest of the Order required four more months and cost the life of Missouri state trooper Jimmie Linegar, shot by David Tate near Ridgedale on 15 April 1985. That crime earned Tate a prison term of life without parole, sparing him from trial for crimes committed with the Order. Fifteen other defendants pled guilty on various charges, receiving sentences that ranged from six months to 60 years (for Richard Scutari). Klansmen James Dye and Randy Evans drew terms of 20 and 40 years, respectively. Eleven Order defendants were convicted at trial, their prison terms ranging from three years to 190 years (David Lane) and 250 years (Bruce Pierce). Commemorative medals depicting Robert Mathews were sold for seven dollars each at Richard Butler's 1986 Aryan World Congress. They read: "Should you fall my friend, another friend will emerge from the shadows to take your place."[23]

WHITE PATRIOT PARTY

The threat of an Order revival was realized before that medallion was cast, even before Mathews's disciples faced their days in court. In spring 1985, emboldened by his share of the Ukiah loot, Klansman Glenn Miller renamed his Carolina Knights the White Patriot Party, which he dubbed "a citizens' militia." Members shed their robes in favor of camouflage army fatigues, berets and combat boots, symbolizing a new aggressive militancy. Their goal was nothing less than the creation of a "White Republic within the geographical bounds of the Southern United States." Stockpiles of weapons and training sessions led by active-duty soldiers from Fort Bragg, North Carolina, prompted Morris Dees and his Southern Poverty Law Center to sue Miller, demanding a federal investigation of WPP ties to Army personnel. That case produced a court order banning further paramilitary exercises and drove Miller to write his own declaration of war.[24] It read:

> Dear White Patriots:
> I warned the S.O.B.s ... the federal dogs, to leave me alone. All 5,000 White Patriots are now honor bound and duty bound to pick up the sword and do battle against the forces of evil. Swear you'll not put down your sword until total victory is ours. Yahweh will fill your hearts with courage and strength and confidence.... Let the blood of our enemies flood the streets, rivers, and fields of the nation, in Holy vengeance and justice.... The Jews are our main and most formidable enemies.... They are truly the children of Satan. Throw off the chains which bind us to the satanic, Jewish controlled and ruled federal government. The following point system for Aryan warriors of The Order: Niggers (1), White race traitors (10), Jews (10), Judges (50), Morris Seligman Dees (888). Let the battle axes swing smoothly and the bullets whiz true.
> Glenn Miller, loyal member of "The Order"[25]

All things considered, Miller's "war" was a tempest in a teapot. He plotted to kill Dees but never followed through on the plan. Nine WPP members were jailed at Belle Glade, Florida, in June 1985, for a series of racial assaults and vandalism incidents. (All pled guilty and received probation.) Miller and a comrade were found guilty of contempt on 25 July 1986 for resuming their paramilitary exercises. Two months later, several party members were charged with plotting to rob a restaurant in Fayetteville, North Carolina. Five more White Patriots were indicted on 8 January 1987 on federal charges of conspiring to steal weapons from Fort Bragg. (Two pled guilty, two were convicted at trial, and one was acquitted.) Nine days later, party members raided an adult bookstore in Shelby, North Carolina, leaving three men dead and two wounded in a blaze of gunfire. Miller fled underground in March 1987, but he was captured on 30 April and slapped with a nine-count conspiracy indictment. He pled guilty to reduced charges on 4 January 1988 and received five years in prison on reduced charges. Two codefendants took their chances with a jury and received 20-year terms. In the wake of Miller's sentencing, the WPP dissolved, some of its members drifting off to join the Maryland-based National Democratic Front.[26]

SEDITION

Part of Miller's plea bargain was an agreement to testify against fellow racist leaders at their impending sedition trial.[27] That case arose in equal parts from crimes committed by the Order and another Christian Identity cult, the Missouri-based Covenant, Sword and Arm of the Lord (CSA).

Founded as a religious order in 1971, the CSA established a fortified compound near the Missouri-Arkansas line five years later after leader James Ellison claimed that "God spoke to me" and ordered the move. A veteran racist and anti–Semite, Ellison was ready to practice what he preached by summer 1983. On 9 August, Ellison and CSA member William Thomas torched a church in Springfield, Missouri, whose congregation supported gay rights. Six days later, while casing bank jobs in Bloomington, Indiana, Ellison, Thomas and an accomplice firebombed a synagogue. That autumn, stung by demands that he pay income tax, CSA member Richard Snell hatched a plot to bomb the Alfred P. Murrah Federal Building in Oklahoma City. Snell and Ellison sketched the target, but Snell was soon distracted by other campaigns. On 2 November 1983, with William Thomas and Stephen Scott, he bombed a natural gas pipeline outside Fulton, Arkansas. Nine days later, Snell and Thomas robbed a pawnshop in Texarkana; Snell murdered proprietor William Strumpp in the mistaken belief that Strumpp was a Jew. On 26 December 1983, Ellison, Snell and four others set off toward Fort Smith, Arkansas, planning to kill an FBI agent and a federal judge whom they blamed for Gordon Kahl's death, but a car wreck derailed that conspiracy. On 30 June 1984 Snell murdered a black policeman who stopped him for speeding near Broken Bow, Oklahoma. He was subsequently captured and sentenced to die, executed on 19 April 1995. Ellison received a five-year prison term in August 1985, after he and five others pled guilty to manufacturing illegal weapons for the Order.[28]

Ellison was tired of prison by 1987, when he offered testimony against others in exchange for early release. Aside from his own group's activities, he revealed further details of the Order's crimes and distribution of its Brinks loot to racist leaders across the country. Those charged with sedition as a result included Louis Beam, Richard Butler and Robert Miles; CSA members Snell, David McGuire, Lambert Miller, William Wade and his son Ivan; Order members Andrew Barnhill, David Lane, Ardie McBreatry, Bruce Pierce and Richard Scutari; and Arkansas gun dealer Robert Smalley, earlier convicted of falsifying records of his sales to Order members. Indictments were issued on 24 April 1987, and Beam promptly fled to Mexico, recaptured there after his wife shot and wounded a Mexican policeman. In addition to the known crimes of the Order and the CSA, defendants charged in the indictment were accused of buying stolen weapons and explosives in Missouri and Oklahoma; planning demolition of federal buildings in Denver, Kansas City, Minneapolis, New Orleans, New York City and St. Louis; plotting to poison the municipal water supplies of Chicago, New York, and Washington, D.C.; and to sabotage sundry railroads, utilities and sewer lines.[29]

Trial on the charges began in February 1988 before Judge Morris Arnold at Fort Smith, Arkansas. Over the next seven weeks, more than 100 witnesses testified, and prosecutors presented some 1,200 pieces of physical evidence. James Ellison described secret meetings in which Robert Mathews allegedly planned illegal acts with defendants Beam and Butler. In a separate incident, Ellison said that Robert Miles delivered a 30-gallon barrel of the deadly poison ricin, slated for use on water supplies in the nation's capital. Glenn Miller detailed his receipt of stolen cash from Mathews and his girlfriend, Zillah Craig. Craig confirmed the story, and Order turncoat William Soderquist described a similar payment to Robert Miles. Tom Martinez outlined the Order's bungled counterfeiting operation. Another ex–Aryan warrior, Denver Parmenter, walked jurors through the Brinks holdup. After both sides had rested their cases, Judge Arnold entered a directed verdict of acquittal for Robert Smalley. On 7 April 1988 jurors acquitted the other 13 defendants on all counts. Louis Beam, emerging from the courthouse, bowed to a nearby Confederate monument and proclaimed, "The Zionist Occupation Government has suffered a terrible blow."[30]

Why were the Fort Smith defendants acquitted? Peacetime sedition charges have never fared well in U.S. courts, and federal prosecutors might have been wise to frame their case in terms of racketeering or conspiracy. Witnesses Ellison, Miller and Parmenter were all serving time in state or federal prisons, a circumstance that made their testimony suspect in some jurors' eyes. Ellison's credibility was further damaged by a proclamation from the witness stand that he received personal messages from God. Defense attorneys stressed that half the defendants had already been tried, convicted and sentenced for crimes charged in the federal indictment, thus constituting double jeopardy. Finally, it cannot be ruled out that the all-white Arkansas jury shared certain racist or anti-government sentiments espoused by the defendants. After the trial, two female jurors openly declared that they had fallen in love with two of those accused.[31]

DEFINING TERRORISM

In 1983, at the urging of President Ronald Reagan, FBI headquarters elevated domestic terrorism from third to first place on its public priorities list. Over the next five years, 500 of the bureau's 9,000 full-time agents were assigned to investigate and prevent terrorist acts within the United States. As defined by FBI spokesmen, domestic terrorism comprised "[t]he unlawful use of force or violence, committed by a group(s) or two or more individuals, against persons or property to intimidate or coerce a government, the civilian population, or any segment thereof, in furtherance of political or social objectives."[32]

While that definition was broad enough to cover most acts of sociopolitical violence, bureau analysts still wore blinders where right-wing terrorism was concerned. A headquarters survey of terrorist acts investigated by the FBI during 1982–92 found 79 percent allegedly committed by leftist or militant nonwhite groups. A second bureau survey of the 1990s listed only two cases of right-wing terrorism during 1992–94. Only a single case of terrorism, the Oklahoma City bombing (see below), was identified for all of 1995. As noted by author Beau Grossup, publication of those statistics "meant ignoring the fact that several major personalities and organizations who came to dominate the new and violent right-wing Patriot Movement of the 1990s had been active in FBI-documented terrorism from the 1970s through the mid-1980s. More importantly, it required ignoring or 'defining away' numerous domestic terrorist incidents."[33]

Henceforth, private watchdog groups such as the Anti-Defamation League and the Southern Poverty Law Center would be left to monitor right-wing and white-supremacist mayhem, while the FBI remained aloof. When those groups were attacked, as with the arson fire that destroyed SPLC headquarters in Alabama, G-men left solution of the crimes to agents of the Treasury Department's Bureau of Alcohol, Tobacco and Firearms.[34] Retired ATF agent James Moore describes the FBI's contribution to fighting domestic terrorism:

> FBI "achievements" in the field of terrorism generally fall into two categories: cases they "adopt" without disclosing that the most critical aspects of the case were actually accomplished by other agencies; and instances where the "accomplishment" is described as "preventing a terrorist act." The latter, translated into what the FBI actually *did,* consists of having received a tip and interviewing the alleged would-be terrorists—informing them that "we know what you're planning" and warning of the consequences, should they choose to carry out the reported plot. Receiving tips is no accomplishment—considering the $3.5 million the FBI paid to informers in 1975 and their mandate, which makes it every police agency's duty to report such rumors to the FBI. "Resolving" the situation through aggressive questioning and dire warning is something any officer could do. Result: No one knows whether there really was a plot, so no one goes to jail.[35]

The FBI's failure to curb domestic terrorism is nowhere more obvious than in the realm of violence against U.S. abortion clinics. Between 1977 and 2000, the following acts of "pro-life" violence were recorded nationwide: seven murders; 17 attempted murders; 40 bombings; 163 arsons; 80 attempted bombing or arson attacks; 526 bomb threats; 368 clinic invasions; 115 incidents of assault and battery; 332 death threats; three kidnappings; 60 burglaries; 420 stalking incidents; and 8,246 incidents involving hate mail or telephone harassment. In 1994 alone the "pro-life" toll was 159 violent acts, including four murders, eight bombings, three arsons and four arson attempts—yet the FBI listed no acts of domestic terrorism anywhere in the United States that year.[36]

FBI negligence in the field of clinic terrorism was a matter of established policy, preceding the inauguration of "pro-life" President Reagan by three full years. The bureau shirked its first case of a clinic firebombing in February 1978, handing off the Cleveland incident to ATF agents while declaring it could find "no basis for an FBI investigation in this matter under the Federal Bombing Statute." G-men likewise ignored the August 1982 kidnapping of Dr. Hector Zevallos and his wife, held for eight days by zealots representing the self-styled Army of God. Local police were left to solve that case and send the kidnappers to prison. In August 1983 the FBI was informed of bomb threats made against the Hillcrest Clinic in Norfolk, Virginia. Although the bureau has clear jurisdiction in such cases, the Norfolk field office disposed of the case with a one-page report stamped "Open and close." Bombers struck the clinic on 17 February 1984, leaving a note from the Army of God at the scene. Local G-men filed a memo stating that their "Terrorism Section does not consider the 'Army of God' as a terrorist group, and therefore, no FBI investigation appears warranted at this time." (ATF agents arrested the bombers and sent them to prison, as they had three other AOG terrorists in 1982.) On 4 December 1984, days after bombers destroyed a clinic in Wheatland, Maryland, FBI Director William Webster repeated the bureau's contention that "pro-life" violence did not qualify for FBI investigation as domestic terrorism.[37] The *Minneapolis Star Tribune* replied to Webster with an editorial that read:

> The nation's leading law enforcement agency seems to be policing the cabbage patch with a blind eye to clinic bombings.... Webster says bombings and arsons at abortion and family planning clinics across the country are not terrorism.... He says the FBI gives investigations of these attacks low priority.... Webster's words conveyed the wrong message. Another Webster — Noah — defines terrorism as acts of violence or force to intimidate or coerce. [The] bombings at abortion and family planning clinics this year fit the definition. The apparent motive — to frighten people away — qualifies as intimidation. Because their number is increasing, the chance of injury to patients, clinic workers and passers-by is increasing, too. Every reasonable effort by law enforcement agencies must be devoted to curbing this violence. If the FBI isn't investigating whether an organized group or conspiracy is involved, it should be.... The president has decried terrorism overseas, but he has been silent about the bombings and arson at home. Reagan should speak out against this ugly domestic terrorism. And he should be sure that all federal law enforcement agencies get the message.[38]

Indeed, Webster's contention about pro-life violence flew in the face of the FBI's own "terrorism" definition. Clinic bombings and other attacks involved unlawful force and violence; they commonly included two or more offenders acting in concert; they patently aimed at intimidating both civilian targets and the U.S. government itself, pledged to upholding legal abortions since the *Roe v. Wade* decision of January 1973; and finally, the stated religious goals of the terrorists clearly announced their "political or social objectives." Only by denying its own staff-written definition of domestic terrorism could the FBI maintain a hands-off attitude toward clinic violence, but the glaring contradiction was ignored in Washington.

In January 1985 the president of Planned Parenthood asked Webster to investigate Joseph Scheidler, whose Pro-Life Action League encouraged criminal violence and praised those responsible for clinic attacks. Again, Webster refused to act. In June 1986 a consortium of pro-choice organizations filed a federal racketeering lawsuit against Scheidler, Operation Rescue, and a mixed bag of individuals known to encourage or participate in crimes against women's clinics. The case dragged on in federal court for 13 years until a jury found the defendants guilty of extortion, intimidation and other criminal acts on 20 April 1998, awarding the plaintiffs $257,780 in damages. (Thus far, the losers have not paid a penny of their debt.) Once more, the FBI left private watchdog groups to do its job.[39]

For FBI headquarters, ignoring clinic violence also meant ignoring the Ku Klux Klan once again. From the early 1980s onward, Klansmen and their neo–Nazi allies railed against *Roe v. Wade* as part of a vast Jewish conspiracy to destroy the Aryan race. In 1985 Glenn Miller's White Patriot Party pioneered the use of "Wanted" posters targeting abortion providers, including their photos and home addresses for the benefit of would-be assassins. Tom Metzger, once grand dragon of the California Klan before he launched his independent White Aryan Resistance, told reporters: "Almost all abortion doctors are Jews. Abortion makes money for Jews. Almost all abortion nurses are lesbians. Abortion gives thrills to lesbians.... Jews must be punished for this holocaust and murder of white children along with their perverted lesbian nurses." Spokesmen for the Confederate Knights of the KKK agreed, saying that "[m]ore than ten million white babies have been murdered through Jewish-engineered legalized abortion since 1973 here in America and more than a million per year are being slaughtered this way.... The Klan understands that this is just one of many tools used to destroy the white race and we know who it is." When Florida's Templar Knights of the KKK rallied in defense of a convicted clinic murderer, Klan leaders said, "It's part of our Holy War for the pure Aryan race."[40]

No individual epitomized the KKK–"pro-life" connection more clearly than John Burt, an anti-abortion crusader who described himself as an ex–Klansman, reformed alcoholic and ex-drug addict. Burt discovered "pro–life" activism soon after settling in Pensacola, Florida, in the early 1980s. He purchased a strip of land next-door to the Ladies Center and erected "pro-life" billboards and led abusive chanting choruses of congregants drawn from his fundamentalist church, the Whitfield Assembly of God. Burt joined Joseph Scheidler's network and billed himself as the Florida spokesman for Rescue America. On the side, Burt also ran Our Father's House, a home for wayward girls endowed with state permission to inflict corporal punishment and compel Sunday church attendance by its teenage inmates. In public, he was fond of carrying a pickled fetus that he dubbed "Baby Charlie." About the KKK, Burt told reporters, "Fundamentalist Christians and those people [Klansmen] are pretty close, scary close, fighting for God and country. Some day we may all be in the trenches together in the fight against the slaughter of unborn children."[41]

Rhetoric soon gave way to action where Burt was concerned. Pensacola suffered its first clinic bombing on 25 June 1984, followed by three more on Christmas Day. (ATF agents jailed the Christmas bombers six days later, with no help from the FBI.) No evidence links Burt to the explosions, but he milked the incidents for free publicity, and members of his congregation had already crossed the line from lawful protest into violence. On 20 December 1984, a female resident of Our Father's House invaded the Ladies Center, disrupting its procedures forcefully enough to earn a 60-day jail term for trespassing. On 26 March 1986 Burt led three female accomplices on another clinic raid, vandalizing equipment and menacing employees. Burt and two of his companions pled guilty in that case and received probation; a third female defendant claimed her right to trial by jury and received a five-year prison term in July 1986. On 6 May 1988 "pro-life" terrorist John Brockhoeft spent the evening with Burt at Our Father's House, departing once with Burt to drive past the Ladies Center. Next morning, ATF agents trailed Brockhoeft from Burt's home and nabbed him en route to the clinic with a bomb in his car. In custody, Brockhoeft confessed to burning another clinic in Cincinnati. He received a seven-year term for that crime and 26 months for the Pensacola bomb plot, but Burt avoided charges in that case.[42]

In December 1992 Burt acquired a new disciple and part-time employee, Michael Griffin. Griffin started as a handyman, working around Our Father's House to please his wife, and viewed his first "pro-life" video there on 9 January 1993. Twelve days later, he took a firearms training course offered to civilians by the Pensacola Police Department. The same week, Griffin attended Burt's memorial service for two alleged fetuses, and he soon joined the chanting picket line outside the Ladies Center. On 7 March 1993 Griffin stood in Burt's church to lead prayers for the "redemption" of Dr. David Gunn, a physician at the Ladies Clinic who was featured on Klan-type "Wanted" posters published by Burt and Rescue America. Three days later, Griffin ambushed Dr. Gunn outside the clinic and shot him to death. While Griffin sat in jail, awaiting trial and his eventual sentence of life imprisonment without parole, Burt and activist Paul Hill joined forces to identify Gunn's successor. They traced Dr. Lawrence Britton's license plate and tracked him to his home near Jacksonville, leaving a pamphlet on his doorstep titled *What Would You Do If You Had Five Minutes Left to Live?* Another "Wanted" poster followed, listing Britton's home address.[43]

Dr. Gunn's murder in Florida, coupled with the rising tide of clinic violence nationwide, at last prompted Congress to act against "pro-life" terrorism in early 1994. Forewarned, the FBI bestirred itself that February, announcing for the first time that it would investigate death threats against clinic staffers in Florida, Indiana, Kansas and Wisconsin. Bureau leaders also promised to collect information from local police, but they still denied any jurisdiction in cases of clinic mayhem, urging state and city law enforcement agencies to cope with the problem themselves. A headquarters memo urging all field offices to stay alert for any criminal activities by John Burt and colleague John Brockhoeft was generally ignored. Senator Edward Kennedy introduced the Free Access to Clinic Entrances (FACE) Act on 23 March 1994, providing both civil and criminal sanctions for interfering with legal abortions; Congress swiftly passed the act, and President Bill Clinton signed it into law on 26 May 1994. FBI headquarters could no longer deny jurisdiction in cases of clinic terrorism, but getting G-men to act was something else entirely.[44]

Paul Hill reacted to the FACE Act's passage with a series of hysterical performances outside the Pensacola Ladies Center. FBI agents were summoned on 10 June 1994, and while they briefly interviewed Hill in police custody, they told clinic staffers (incorrectly) that any charges filed must be local. A spokesman for the bureau's civil rights division later told clinic administrators, "We know about Paul Hill and we know about your clinic, but this is not the time to make an arrest. We don't want to test the law in Florida." Thus encouraged, Hill returned to the clinic with a shotgun on 29 July 1994, killing Dr. Britton and a bodyguard and severely wounding Britton's wife. While Hill awaited trial on multiple state and federal charges, Florida's Templar Knights of the KKK held a rally in his honor. Tried for violations of the FACE Act in October 1994, Hill received two terms of life imprisonment. Florida later tried and condemned him on murder charges, leading to his execution on 3 September 2003.[45]

On 30 September 1994 the Feminist Majority Foundation sent a letter to its members across the U.S. assessing federal enforcement of the FACE Act in its first four months. That letter read:

> With the exception of the charges against Paul Hill and the clinic blockades in Milwaukee in June, the Department of Justice has moved at a snail's pace in enforcement. Too many incidents of terrorism, violence and obstruction at the clinics since FACE was passed have not been prosecuted. To date, no charges have been brought against extremists for threats and intimidation against doctors. In Jackson, Mississippi, Dr. Joseph Booker reported to the FBI that he was threatened the day of the Pensacola murders in a face-to-face encounter with a leading anti-abortion extremist and signer of Hill's Justifiable Homicide petition. Although Booker continues to receive federal Marshals' protection, the alleged threat has not been prosecuted.... In Des Moines, Iowa two staff members were physically blocked as they were attempting to leave the clinic by a known anti-abortion extremist. The U.S. Attorney declined to press charges, mistakenly claiming that only physicians and nurses are covered under the FACE law. Other clinic administrators and doctors around the country have received death threats and have been stalked. Even in Ohio, where an anti-abortion extremist was arrested by local police for stalking a physician from the clinic to his home and attempting to force the physician's car off the road, no federal charges have been filed.[46]

Late in 1994 a federal grand jury in Virginia finally opened hearings on possible evidence of a conspiracy behind "pro-life" terrorism nationwide. John Burt was one of the first witnesses forced to testify under subpoena, producing on demand his copy of a guerrilla warfare manual published by the Army of God. The investigation continued into 1995, resulting in no indictments and apparently ignoring reams of evidence before concluding that no proof existed of coordinated violence, encouragement of terrorism, or support for "pro-life" felons charged with crimes. Meanwhile, the wave of violence grew, with reported clinic arsons doubling from 1994 to 1995. It remained for Morris Dees and the SPLC to sue John Burt privately in March 1995, charging him with wrongful death in the case of Dr. Gunn. Burt settled the case in July 1996, surrendering possession of his land beside the Ladies Center. Nine years later, Pensacola police charged Burt with molesting a 15-year-old tenant of Our Father's House. In April 2004 Burt was convicted on five felony counts in that case, receiving an 18-year prison term.[47]

DIXIE BURNS AGAIN (1990–1996)

Abortion clinics were not the only targets of far-right terrorism in the 1990s, nor the only ones ignored by agents of the FBI. Between 1990 and 1996, 57 black churches were burned by arsonists in Southern states, with 32 of those fires recorded in 1995–96. None were listed by the FBI as acts of domestic terrorism; indeed, G-men ran true to form in the handful of cases they investigated, demanding church records and polygraph tests for church leaders, suggesting that the victims themselves were guilty of arson. Congress belatedly convened a one-day hearing on the problem, and while President Clinton demanded a federal investigation, his National Church Arson Task Force reported in June 1997 that it could find "no evidence of a national conspiracy" to burn black churches.[48]

That finding may have been technically accurate, but there was nonetheless ample evidence of conspiracy in individual cases. A report from the Anti-Defamation League, published on 20 June 1996, identified 14 Klan factions active in nine states where churches were burned; other militant racist groups organized in the same region included the Aryan Nations, the Christian Defense League, the National Alliance, and David Duke's National Association for the Advancement of White People. In South Carolina, two members of the Christian Knights of the KKK faced state arson charges for burning black churches at Bloomville and Greeleyville on consecutive nights in June 1995. Federal charges were filed against the two suspects, Gary Cox and Timothy Welch, in July 1996. Both pled guilty the following month and agreed to help ATF agents with their ongoing investigation of various church fires. (They also confessed to a separate nonfatal stabbing.)[49]

On 16 August 1996, two days after Cox and Welch entered their guilty pleas, federal prosecutors indicted Christian Knights leader Arthur Haley and Klansman Hubert Rowell on 20 felony counts, including conspiracy to instigate the South Carolina church fires. Other charges were that members of the Klan plotted to burn a black man's car and to destroy a Hispanic migrant labor camp. From Washington, Deval Patrick, assistant attorney general for civil rights, told CNN, "We believe that we have proof of a conspiracy here. We have admissions by two of the defendants … about a conspiracy that seems to be in furtherance of this particular Klan group." Defendant Rowell not only burned one of the churches in question, prosecutors alleged, but also threatened to "burn the son of a bitch down" again if it was rebuilt. Haley and Rowell eventually pled guilty as charged, earning prison terms of 21 and 15 years, respectively; Cox and Welch received sentences of 19 and 18 years, each reduced by five years for their cooperation with the government. In July 1998 jurors in a civil lawsuit filed against the Christian Knights by the Southern Poverty Law Center awarded Klan victims $37.8 million dollars in damages.[50]

Yet another arson case was solved in July 1997 when FBI agents arrested five white teenagers for burning one black church and vandalizing a second near Little River, Alabama, on 30 June. The attacks followed a public rally held by the White Knights of Alabama in Tenesaw, ten miles from the scene of the attacks, on 28 June 1997. Three defendants were convicted at trial, including Alan Odom (sentenced to 180 months in prison on three felony counts), and Brandy Boone and Kenneth Cumbie (41 months each on charges of conspiracy). No actual Klansmen were charged in that case, which marked the FBI's only arrests in the 1990s spate of church arsons in Dixie.[51]

THE MILITIA MOVEMENT

The twentieth century's last great upheaval of far-right conspiratorial violence sprang ironically from the FBI's mishandling of two siege situations in 1992–93. The first involved a single family in Idaho, the second a religious sect in Texas. Both resulted in unnecessary loss of life and prompted the formation of extremist paramilitary groups from coast to coast.

The first case involved Randall Weaver, an ex–Green Beret whose dreams of becoming an FBI agent were spoiled when he dropped out of high school. With wife Vicki, Weaver converted to Christian Identity in the late 1970s and lived for a time at the Aryan Nations compound before he was expelled for drinking. In 1983 the Weaver family settled on remote Ruby Ridge, Idaho, where Randall ran for sheriff (unsuccessfully) and sold illegal weapons on the side. In October 1989 he sold two sawed-off shotguns to an ATF informant. Prosecutors indicted Weaver in December 1990 after several failed attempts to recruit him as a spy inside the Aryan Nations, and he was arrested on 17 January 1991. Released without bond, Weaver missed his scheduled court date on 20 February. Evidence suggests that he believed the trial was set for March, based on errors in a letter he received from the court clerk, but it made no difference. A fugitive warrant was issued for Weaver on 14 March 1991. Though authorities knew where he was—at home on Ruby Ridge—they made no effort to arrest him for a year. At last, on 8 March 1992, a local newspaper publicly questioned the reasons for that inordinate delay.[52]

Thus motivated, six U.S. marshals infiltrated Ruby Ridge on 21 August 1992. Discovered first by Weaver's dog, they shot the yapping animal, then fought a brief skirmish that claimed the lives of Marshal William Deegan and Weaver's 14-year-old son. By 22 August, 50 members of the FBI's elite Hostage Rescue Team had Weaver's home surrounded, acting under orders that any armed adult seen on the property "could and should be the subject of deadly force." That afternoon, bureau sniper Lon Horiuchi fired on Randall Weaver and friend Kevin Harris outside Weaver's cabin, wounding both men and killing Vicki Weaver as she stood nearby, unarmed and holding her 10-month-old daughter. Weaver and Harris surrendered nine days later, facing murder charges for the death of Marshal Deegan, but both were acquitted of that charge and other felony counts on 8 July 1993. (Jurors convicted Weaver on two minor counts, including failure to appear in court on his original indictment, and he served four months in jail.) Outrage over the FBI's mishandling of the siege prompted multiple investigations. Agent Michael Kahoe, heading the bureau's internal probe, later confessed to destroying embarrassing files and received an 18-month jail term for obstructing justice in October 1997. Idaho authorities indicted Agent Horiuchi for manslaughter, but a federal judge dismissed that charge in May 1998. Weaver sued the U.S. government for wrongful death of his wife and son, winning a judgment of $3.1 million in 1995.[53]

Even before the FBI's cover-up was exposed, the Ruby Ridge episode agitated far-right activists with a zeal one author has dubbed "Weaver fever." Two months after the Idaho siege, on 23–25 October 1992, Identity preacher Pete Peters convened a "Rocky Mountain Rendezvous" at Estes Park, Colorado. An estimated 160 extremists, including Klansmen, neo–Nazis and "pro-life" crusaders, filled the local YMCA building to cheer strident messages from speakers who included Peters, Louis Beam, Richard Butler and Larry Pratt (Gun Owners of America). Invoking Patrick Henry's call for liberty or death, Beam told his audience, "The federal government in north Idaho has demonstrated brutally, horribly, and with great terror how it will enforce its claim that we are religious fanatics and enemies of the state. We must, in one voice, cry out that we will not tolerate their stinking, murdering, lying, corrupt government." Several speakers called for the creation of private "patriot militias," and Beam followed the Estes Park meeting with a "special report" that reprinted an earlier essay on "leaderless resistance" conducted by militant "phantom cells."[54] Klansman and Order member David Lane expanded on that thesis in April 1993, writing from prison on behalf of an Aryan warrior he dubbed "Wotan."

> The goal of Wotan is clear. He must hasten the demise of the system before it totally destroys our gene pool. Some of his weapons are fire, bombs, guns, terror, disruption and destruction. Weak points in the infrastructure of an industrialized society are primary targets. Individuals who perform valuable service for the system are primary targets. Special attention and merciless terror is [sic] visited upon those white men who commit race treason. Wotan has a totally revolutionary mentality. He has no loyalty to anyone or anything except his cause. Those who do not share his cause are expendable and those who oppose his cause are targets. Wotan is mature, capable, ruthless, self-motivated, silent, deadly, and able to blend into the masses. Wotan receives no recognition for his labors for if the folk knows his identity then soon the enemy will also. Wotan are small autonomous cells, one man cells if possible. No one, not wife, brother, parent or friend, knows the identity or actions of Wotan.[55]

Eva Lamb, a neighbor of the Aryan Nations compound, had already launched the Idaho Organized Militia in May 1992, and others formed after the Rocky Mountain Rendezvous. In May 1993, at a Wisconsin gathering of the U.S. Taxpayers Party, "pro-life" crusader Matthew Trewhella urged all fundamentalist Christian churches to organize militia units. John Trochmann, a frequent visitor to the Aryan Nations compound who met Randall Weaver there in 1990, used the mailing list from a Weaver support group — United Citizens for Justice — to advertise his new Militia of Montana, founded on 1 January 1994. Trochmann later split with Richard Butler, earning Butler's condemnation as an "anti–Christ," but literature from the Aryan Nations, the KKK, the National Alliance, the John Birch Society and other fringe groups circulated widely among militia groups nationwide. From Florida to the Pacific Northwest, militia leadership frequently overlapped with that of the Klan and other white-supremacist groups.[56]

Five months after the Estes Park conclave, on 28 February 1993, ATF agents staged a disastrous raid on the Branch Davidian religious sect at a rural compound outside Waco, Texas. The ensuing firefight killed four agents and six cult members, leaving 26 other persons wounded. Once again, FBI agents took charge of the siege, which continued for nearly six weeks. On 19 April, spurred by rumors of mass suicide, G-men in armored vehicles advanced to spray the camp's fortified barracks with tear gas. Six hours into the protracted assault, the buildings caught fire and burned to the ground. Charred corpses of 76 cult members were found in the rubble, including at least 17 children (some accounts say 25). Nineteen of the dead had been shot before flames reached their bodies, and a two-year-old boy had been stabbed. Eleven surviving Davidians were charged with murder and conspiracy to murder federal agents. All were acquitted on those counts at trial, but five were convicted of manslaughter and received 40-year prison terms. Four others drew terms of ranging from three to 20 years for lesser crimes.[57]

Militia spokesmen instantly proclaimed the Waco deaths an FBI massacre committed to suppress religious freedom. A leading proponent of that view was Linda Thompson, an Indianapolis lawyer and self-proclaimed "acting adjutant general" of the Unorganized Militia of the United States. Her website advertised that illusory group as "a network of doers, not whiners or fakers." Thompson produced and marketed two videotapes on the Branch Davidian tragedy, *Waco: The Big Lie* and *Waco: The Big Lie Continues*. On 19 April 1994 she issued a sweeping "indictment" of Congress titled *Ultimatum*, which was largely plagiarized from William Gale's 1984 "Declaration of Alteration and Reform." Mailed to all members of Congress, Thompson's *Ultimatum* demanded repeal of the federal income tax, gun control legislation, and various constitutional amendments including the Fourteenth (black citizenship), Sixteenth (income tax) and Seventeenth (selection of senators and electors). Thompson also demanded official repudiation of the United Nations, revocation of the North American Free Trade Agreement, and nullification of all debts owed to the Federal Reserve. "If you do not personally and publicly attend to these demands," Thompson warned federal lawmakers, "you will be identified as a Traitor, and you will be brought up on charges for Treason before a Court of the Citizens of this Country." She called for all militia groups to gather in Washington, D.C., "armed and in uniform" on 19 September 1994, to enforce her demands. When they failed to appear, Thompson backpedaled, describing her *Ultimatum* as a mere recruiting ploy.[58]

As in the case of "pro-life" violence, FBI analysts denied any terrorist conspiracy among the leaders or members of various militias. Any criminal activity, the bureau said, was carried out by disaffected and mentally unbalanced loners. In reaching that conclusion, G-men doggedly ignored a wealth of contrary evidence including:

1. Repeated gatherings that produced calls for militant action against the U.S. government, including explicit declarations of war. From the Rocky Mountain Rendezvous onward, self-styled "patriots" made their criminal intentions known in no uncertain terms. At the 1995 Aryan World Congress, assembled white supremacists launched a surveillance campaign against ZOG and various civil rights groups, employing "SALUTE" reports to document the size, activity, location, unit, time and equipment of their chosen targets. Soon after the Idaho meeting, SALUTE forms were distributed among 200 zealots at the Tri-State Militia Conference in South Dakota. In April 1996, 500 Christian Identity cultists gathered for "Jubilation '96" at Lake Tahoe, Nevada, where they declared war on Washington. One week later, the third annual Identity "Super Conference" at Branson, Missouri, trained 400 fanatics for "spiritual warfare" against the elected government.[59]

2. A massive outpouring of literature that began with *The Turner Diaries* and included a blueprint for the Oklahoma City bombing of April 1995 (see below). The

propaganda wave included 85 "patriot" newsletters, countless individual books and pamphlets, military training manuals, hundreds of Internet websites, plus various radio and television programs.[60]

3. Open calls by group leaders for their members to adopt Beam's plan of "leaderless resistance," thus using "phantom cells" or "lone wolf" terrorists to frustrate state and federal surveillance of criminal activities.[61]

4. Public statements encouraging illegal violence against minorities and government officials, including Beam's point system capped by murder of the U.S. president. Some groups maintained hit lists of federal officials marked for assassination. Threatening the president is a felony in itself, yet no far-rightists were arrested for that crime.[62]

5. Ongoing links, financial and otherwise, between groups that FBI spokesmen branded as terroristic in the 1980s, only to reverse that designation ten years later. The federal retreat is inexplicable, since the groups in question had become *more* violent over time, in both rhetoric and actions.[63]

6. Creation or expansion of illegal private armies and paramilitary training facilities across the country, in clear violation of a federal court order banning civilian groups that include a "command structure, training, and discipline so as to function as a combat or combat support unit." Indeed, a federal statute from 1903 — the Dick Act, ignored by G-men to this day — had established the National Guard as the only legitimate successor to individual state militias, placing it under U.S. jurisdiction.[64]

7. Recruitment of active-duty military personnel whose involvement with various extremist groups included leadership of illegal paramilitary training exercises and delivery of stolen weapons to their comrades. A report issued in 1996 revealed 70 hard-core hate groups with headquarters located near U.S. military bases.[65]

In 1997 the SPLC counted 523 active "patriot" groups in the United States, including 221 armed militias. Distressed by the FBI's inaction in that area, and recalling the bureau's long covert war against militant minorities, Morris Dees told *Newsweek* magazine, "I seriously doubt if black militia units training with assault weapons, distributing recipes for building bombs, and preaching hatred of the government would be tolerated." Author Kenneth Stern agreed, concluding that "[t]he FBI was not overly concerned with the militias because they looked too much like mainstream America — and like the FBI."[66]

"PATRIOTIC" TERROR

Historically, FBI agents have not shown much regard for the civil rights of those they wish to investigate. Exposure of illegal COINTELPRO tactics in the 1970s briefly curbed such abuses, but they expanded again under Presidents Reagan and George H.W. Bush until the Ruby Ridge fiasco turned another unwelcome spotlight on bureau misdeeds. Henceforth, the hands-off attitude toward armed and belligerent "patriots" was broadly justified as respect for First Amendment freedoms, but the roster of 1990s right-wing violence makes it clear that G-men could have acted, had they wished to. A partial list of those cases includes the following:

22 October 1990: Jurors in Portland, Oregon found Tom Metzger and his White Aryan Resistance liable for the 1988 skinhead murder of an Ethiopian immigrant, declaring that Metzger's disciples urged local neo–Nazi skinheads to commit acts of violence and supplied baseball bats used in the murder. The civil lawsuit, filed by SPLC attorneys, cost Metzger and WAR $12.5 million.[67]

23 January 1991: Two active-duty Green Berets, a U.S. Postal Service employee and a fourth defendant — all members of the white-supremacist Knights of the New Order — were indicted for stealing weapons and explosives from Fort Bragg.[68]

15 May 1991: A "minister" of the neo–Nazi World Church of the Creator shot and killed a black naval veteran of the Gulf War in Florida. The gunman was convicted of murder by local prosecutors, and the SPLC filed a civil suit against the "church," winning a $1 million default judgment. National Alliance leader William Pierce was fined $85,000 for conspiring to hide cult assets after the lawsuit was filed.[69]

29 August 1991: Bandits robbed a Muskogee, Oklahoma, thrift store for the second time in six weeks. Suspect Walter Thody later confessed that the stolen money ($52,000 in the first holdup alone) was earmarked for the Phineas Priests, a militant racist group whose adherents included homicidal Klansman Byron De La Beckwith.[70]

4 August 1994: Two members of the Minnesota Patriots Council were arrested for manufacturing ricin, a deadly poison. In March 1995 they and two other defendants were convicted of plotting to poison law enforcement officers.[71]

8 September 1994: Three Michigan Militia members were stopped by police in Fowlerville, found with a carload of illegal weapons and notes indicating surveillance of local authorities.[72]

12 September 1995: "Patriot" Charles Polk was indicted for plotting to bomb the IRS office in Austin, Texas. He was convicted at trial and received a 20-year prison term in 1996.[73]

9 November 1995: Oklahoma Constitutional Militia leader Willie Lampley was arrested with his wife and another follower as they prepared bombs for use against the SPLC, abortion clinics, welfare offices and gay bars. Lampley had previously told his disciples, "God won't be mad at us if we drop four or five buildings. He will probably reward us." Jurors convicted all three defendants on 24 April 1996.[74]

15 March 1996: Federal authorities in Tampa, Florida accused the Constitutional Common-Law Court, led by Emilio Ippolito and his daughter, of plotting to kidnap and hang federal judges, mailing threats to various authorities, and obstructing justice. Both were convicted in 1997, receiving prison terms of 11 and ten years, respectively.[75]

25 March 1996: A group of self-styled "Freemen" launched an 81-day standoff with the FBI in Jordan, Montana after two of their leaders were charged with participation in a multimillion-dollar real estate fraud. Upon surrendering, several group members received prison terms up to 22 years for various crimes.[76]

26 April 1996: ATF agents jailed two members of the Militia-at-Large for the Republic of Georgia [*sic*], captured with enough materials to build 40 pipe bombs.

The defendants were convicted of conspiracy to manufacture and distribute illegal explosive devices. A third militia member was convicted of conspiracy for training a hit team to kill politicians.[77]

1 July 1996: FBI agents arrested 12 members of an Arizona "patriot" group, the Viper Team, on weapons charges and multiple counts of conspiracy to bomb government buildings in Phoenix. Ten defendants pled guilty, drawing prison terms up to ten years; another was convicted at trial, and the twelfth was acquitted.[78]

30 July 1996: Eight members of the Washington State Militia were jailed for conspiracy to make and possess illegal destructive devices. They had also conducted classes in bomb-making.[79]

8 October 1996: Three Phineas Priests were charged with detonating bombs in Spokane, Washington, as a prelude to a $108,000 bank robbery. Bombing targets included banks, a newspaper office and Planned Parenthood. The stolen money was not recovered, but the defendants received life prison terms. A fourth accomplice was later sentenced to 55 years.[80]

11 October 1996: G-men arrested seven members of the Mountaineer Militia, charged with plotting to bomb the FBI's new $200 million Criminal Justice Information Services Center at Clarksburg, West Virginia. The conspirators had a floor plan of the building, obtained from a member who doubled as a lieutenant in a local fire department. Militia leader Floyd Looker received an 18-year prison term in that case, and three other defendants faced shorter sentences.[81]

26 March 1997: Militia activist Brendon Blasz was jailed in Kalamazoo, Michigan, charged with plotting to bomb a Battle Creek federal building, the IRS office in Portage, a Kalamazoo TV station and various federal armories. He received a three-year prison term after turning state's evidence against accomplices.[82]

22 April 1997: Police jailed three Texas Klansmen for conspiracy to bomb a natural gas plant near Fort Worth. The three knights and a fourth defendant later pled guilty, receiving 20-year prison terms.[83]

23 April 1997: Todd Vanbiber, a member of the National Alliance and League of the Silent Soldier, suffered wounds when a homemade bomb exploded on his workbench in Tampa, Florida. He received a six-year sentence on weapons charges at a trial in which colleagues said Vanbiber had robbed banks and given at least $2,000 of his stolen loot to William Pierce.[84]

23 February 1998: Authorities in East St. Louis, Illinois, jailed members of a Klan spin-off group, the New Order, on wide-ranging conspiracy charges. Indictments said the three planned to bomb various state capital buildings, post offices, communications centers and the SPLC's Alabama headquarters. The plotters also hoped to poison major urban water sources, murder Morris Dees and assassinate a federal judge. Six defendants pled guilty to weapons and conspiracy charges.[85]

18 March 1998: Three North American Militia members were arrested in Michigan, charged with plotting to bomb federal buildings, an interstate highway and a Kalamazoo TV station. Group leader Ken Carter, also a member of Aryan Nations, confessed to a master plan to spark nationwide uprisings in 1999. All three defendants were convicted, drawing prison terms up to 55 years.[86]

4 December 1999: Police seized two San Joaquin County Militia members in California, accused of planning to launch a race war by bombing two Sacramento propane tanks that contained 23 million gallons of volatile gas.[87]

8 December 1999: A violent decade closed with the Florida arrest of Don Beauregard, ex-leader of a militia umbrella group dubbed the Southeastern States Alliance, on charges of conspiracy to steal explosives and attack various targets, including a nuclear power plant.[88]

OKLAHOMA CITY

At 9:02 A.M. on 19 April 1995 a truck loaded with 4,800 pounds of homemade explosives detonated outside the Alfred P. Murrah Federal Building in Oklahoma City. It demolished the building, killing at least 168 persons (some reports say 169) and injuring 850. More than a thousand FBI and ATF agents were assigned to investigate the crime, which most Americans initially assumed to be the work of Islamic extremists. The FBI team included explosives analysts flown into Oklahoma City from the bureau's laboratory division in Washington, D.C.[89]

The crime scene investigation was curious in some respects, later described by critics as fatally flawed. FBI explosives expert David Williams reportedly ordered his team to ignore small pieces of evidence, telling them, "If you can't see it at rake's length, it's not worth picking up." Hours later he called off the search entirely, with the announcement: "We've got thousands of pieces. We don't need to pick up any more." G-man Ed Kelso was "shocked" by that order (and later called Williams a "laughingstock" in the Washington lab), but he obeyed the command. Two other colleagues from the FBI Explosives Unit, Jim Lyons and Wallace Higgins, reportedly left the scene disgusted by Williams's mishandling of evidence.[90]

While the search was still in progress, some 90 minutes after the blast an Oklahoma highway patrolman made a routine traffic stop in Noble County, 60 miles north of Oklahoma City. The car he stopped had no license plates, and its driver carried a poorly-concealed pistol. In custody at Perry, Oklahoma, the driver identified himself as 26-year-old Timothy McVeigh. His name meant nothing at the time, and a scan of the FBI's national computer system showed no outstanding warrants, but McVeigh was held pending arraignment on criminal charges.[91]

Meanwhile, searchers in Oklahoma City found a truck axle and bumper marked with vehicle identification numbers, which led G-men to a Ryder rental agency in Junction City, Kansas. The truck had been rented to one "Robert Kling," whose name proved to be false. Agents obtained descriptions of Kling and an unnamed male companion, then scoured local motels. At one establishment, they found that "Kling's" description matched that of tenant Timothy McVeigh, who rented a room on 14 April. When his name was checked through Washington, McVeigh's arrest was noted and police in Perry were instructed to detain him. McVeigh's "home address" on the motel registration led G-men to a Michigan farm owned by James Nichols, whose brother Terry was a friend of McVeigh's from the U.S. Army. Agents searched the Nichols farm on 21-22 April, seizing "components of improvised explosive devices" that included fuse, blasting caps, blue plastic barrels similar to those used in the

Oklahoma bomb, a receipt for 2,000 pounds of ammonium nitrate, fuel oil and other chemicals (also used in the bomb). James Nichols, in his defense, argued that all the items confiscated had normal applications to farming.[92]

G-men quickly learned that Timothy McVeigh was not an angry Muslim, but rather a ZOG-hating zealot who had joined the KKK while still an active-duty soldier (in 1990–91) and wore "White Power" T-shirts at Fort Riley, Kansas. He later left the Klan, branding its literature "manipulative to young people," and gravitated toward "patriot" groups including the Michigan Militia and the Arizona Patriots. McVeigh was "very upset" when he failed Green Beret training on psychological grounds in April 1991, and afterward became "fanatical and loved to collect guns, and … always had a gun with him." Upon leaving the Army, McVeigh became a fixture at gun shows nationwide, where he bought and sold weapons, hawking countless copies of *The Turner Diaries* on the side. (As previously noted, that book included a scene in which patriots use a truck bomb including a "little under 5,000 pounds" of fuel oil and ammonium nitrate to blast FBI headquarters.) McVeigh telephoned National Alliance headquarters at least seven times, and shortly before the Oklahoma City bombing he conducted a long conversation with someone at author William Pierce's unlisted phone number in West Virginia. Michigan Militia leaders said they had expelled McVeigh from one group meeting, but Florida militiamen told police that a man matching McVeigh's description had toured Florida with Michigan activist Mark Koernke on a recruiting mission.[93]

On 1 May 1995 a federal grand jury in Michigan indicted James Nichols on four counts of building and detonating homemade bombs, possessing bomb components and storing hand grenades. An unnamed witness told G-men of a 1989 conversation with Nichols in which Nichols spoke of making bombs and sketched a target closely resembling the Murrah Building. (That witness reportedly passed an FBI polygraph test.) Nichols made bail on 22 May, after a federal judge decreed that no solid evidence linked him to the Oklahoma bombing, and all charges filed against him were dismissed on 10 August 1995. One day later, a second federal grand jury indicted McVeigh and Terry Nichols for conspiracy and for the murder of eight federal agents killed in the April blast. Massive publicity prompted Judge Richard Matsch to grant a change of venue in February 1996, moving the trial to Denver, Colorado. Eight months later, Matsch granted a motion that McVeigh and Nichols should be tried separately.[94]

Before either of those trials convened, however, prosecutors had to deal with serious problems at the FBI laboratory, where technician Frederic Whitehurst had gone public with a series of complaints about mishandling of evidence and deliberate skewing of test results to convict accused suspects. The Justice Department's inspector general launched a full-scale investigation and, while hampered by a campaign of obstruction at the lab, corroborated most of Whitehurst's charges. Agent Roger Martz, assigned to explosives analysis despite his total lack of chemistry training, told inspectors who questioned his methods that "[n]o protocol in the Chemistry/Toxicology Unit requires any examiner to perform a certain type of analysis." In fact, there *was* a protocol (withheld from inspectors by Martz) which detailed specific steps for the analysis of explosives residue. As for David Williams, the inspector general found that he had "tilted" evidence against defendants and based some findings on speculation rather than scientific analysis. The report noted that Williams lacked the "objectivity, judgment and scientific knowledge" to analyze explosives, further stating that he "failed to present an objective, unbiased and competent report." Authors John Kelly and Phillip Wearne were more plainspoken in their book *Tainting Evidence* (1998), reporting that Williams's September 1995 report on the Oklahoma bombing "showed all the hallmarks of his tendency to work backward, draw unscientific conclusions, and overstate results, all in aid of the incrimination of the only suspects."[95]

McVeigh's trial opened on 24 April 1997, two days after his twenty-ninth birthday. Prosecutors presented 137 witnesses and reviewed 7,000 pounds of physical evidence over 18 days. FBI lab technicians were excluded from the proceedings to avoid further embarrassment, but some of the remaining witnesses were even worse. Michael and Lori Fortier, called as key witnesses for the government, were habitual drug users who had lied repeatedly to FBI agents after the bombing. In media interviews, they denied any knowledge of the crime and proclaimed McVeigh innocent. Their story changed only after Michael was charged with transporting stolen weapons and with failure to report the bomb plot in advance. A plea bargain on those counts (and a grant of full immunity for Lori) turned the Fortiers into cooperative witnesses against McVeigh, who had served as best man at their wedding. Michael told his brother, recorded for posterity on an FBI wiretap, "I can tell a fable. I can tell stories all day long.... The less I say now, the bigger the price will be later."[96]

McVeigh's battery of 14 court-appointed lawyers presented a more modest case, calling 25 witnesses in four days. Jurors convicted McVeigh on 2 June 1997 and on 13 June recommended a death sentence. Terry Nichols faced trial in Denver on 3 November 1997, but prosecutors failed to place him at the crime scene, prompting a compromise verdict. Nichols was convicted of conspiracy and eight counts of involuntary manslaughter (reduced from murder), and acquitted on charges of destruction by explosives and using a weapon of mass destruction. Jurors deadlocked on penalty deliberations, and Judge Matsch settled the matter by imposing a life prison term on 4 June 1998. (Subsequent trial for Nichols on state murder charges produced 161 additional terms of life without parole in August 2004.)[97]

On 10 May 2001, six days before McVeigh's scheduled execution, FBI headquarters announced that certain files on his case had been "inadvertently" withheld from defense attorneys. The dribble soon became a flood, with 4,500 documents retrieved from 46 bureau field offices. Agent Danny Defenbaugh, lead investigator on the case, blamed the problem on "archaic" FBI computers, then admitted knowing of the "misplaced" files for several months before headquarters broke the news. The announcement was delayed, Defenbaugh said, because he "wanted to ascertain the magnitude of the problem." Attorney General John Ashcroft granted McVeigh a 30-day stay of execution, but the documents were soon deemed immaterial to his defense and McVeigh was executed by lethal injection on 11 June 2001. Justice released another report by the inspector general on 19 March 2002, this one concerning mishandling of documents in McVeigh's case.[98] That report recommended disciplinary action against two FBI supervisors and reported the following errors:

* Nine bureau field offices destroyed documents that should have been delivered to McVeigh's defense team.
* At least two field offices began destroying files before permission was granted by records archive officials in late 2000.
* The FBI's Oklahoma City bombing task force "lost" various documents and pieces of physical evidence between 1995 and 2000.
* There was "confusion and differing interpretations" within the bureau concerning which documents should be delivered to defense attorneys.
* FBI supervisors waited five months to warn Justice officials of the problem, then delayed two more days before informing the court and defense attorneys.[99]

Assuming that McVeigh and Terry Nichols were guilty as charged, a nagging question remains: Do any other conspirators in the Oklahoma City bombing remain at large and unpunished? McVeigh reportedly failed a polygraph test, administered by his defense team, in which he said that he and Terry Nichols were alone in the conspiracy. All sides agree that a still-unknown man, the elusive "John Doe No. 2," accompanied McVeigh to rent the Ryder truck in Kansas, but no further efforts have been made to locate him. Still, it is apparent from the evidence available that G-men may have missed — or willfully ignored — a broader plot.[100]

On 12 October 1993 Timothy McVeigh received a speeding ticket on Oklahoma County Route 220, near the state's border with Arkansas. Route 220 is the only access road to Elohim City, a Christian Identity compound located ten miles from the point where McVeigh was stopped by police. Given proximity and his political leanings, it is reasonable to assume that McVeigh may have visited Elohim City — but indeed, no such speculation is necessary. McVeigh told his attorneys that he wrote a letter to Robert Millar, a colleague of James Ellison and convicted murderer Richard Snell, at Elohim City in March 1995. On 5 April 1995, two weeks before the bombing, McVeigh telephoned Elohim City and left a message for someone named "Andy." His links to the compound and its residents are thus well established.[101]

The "Andy" in question, some authors suggest, may have been German native Andreas Strassmeir, alias "Andy the German." Strassmeir, the grandson of a high-ranking Third Reich Nazi, came to Texas in the late 1980s, spending time with the KKK and a proto-militia group, the Texas Light Infantry. From there, he migrated to Elohim City, where he took charge of security and weapons training. Oklahoma police arrested Strassmeir in 1992 for driving without a license and carrying false identification; the arresting officers also found bomb-making manuals in his car. Despite the expiration of his tourist visa, Strassmeir was soon released without penalties, a lapse in vigilance that prompted rumors of his service as a federal informant or *agent provocateur*. Strassmeir's attorney was Kirk Lyons, also Louis Beam's defender at the 1988 sedition trial, whose legal practice is essentially restricted to white "patriots." (Lyons or someone in his office allegedly received a 15-minute call from Timothy McVeigh a month after his arrest, on 18 May 1995.) In 1993, on a visit to Germany, FBI Director Louis Freeh faced questions by state security agents about Strassmeir's activities in the United States. Freeh assured them that the bureau was "monitoring" Strassmeir, but the nature and extent of that surveillance is unknown.

Strassmeir left Elohim City soon after the Oklahoma City bombing and resurfaced in Germany before year's end.[102]

While residing in Oklahoma, Strassmeir spent much of his time with Klansman Dennis Mahon, a member of the White Knights of the KKK and third-in-command of Tom Metzger's White Aryan Resistance. Mahon divided his time between Tulsa and Elohim City, where multiple informants said he drew a monthly stipend from Iraq in gratitude for anti–U.S. protest demonstrations he led during the Gulf War. A widely-traveled bigot, Mahon had established Klan cells in Germany, while facing travel bans in Canada and England for his racist statements. In regard to Strassmeir, Mahon told McVeigh defense attorney Stephen Jones, "I've gotten drunk with him. I've partied with him. We've screwed the same women." Carol Howe, an ATF informant at Elohim City, told federal agents that McVeigh visited Strassmeir several times at Elohim City. She also claimed that Strassmeir and Mahon made three trips to Oklahoma City between November 1994 and February 1995; that she accompanied them on one trip to scout the Murrah Building; that she videotaped them discussing plans to bomb a federal building; and that published sketches of "John Doe No. 2" strongly resembled Michael Brescia, Strassmeir's roommate at Elohim City. ATF agents fired Howe for "instability" three weeks before the Oklahoma bombing, then unaccountably rehired her on 20 April 1995. (She subsequently passed several polygraph tests.) Despite her statements, the FBI never interviewed Dennis Mahon, and Justice Department spokesperson Beth Wilkinson told Stephen Jones in February 1997, "At no time did the FBI consider Andreas Strassmeir or Dennis Mahon a subject of the Oklahoma City bombing investigation." Strangely, in spite of that denial, the U.S. State Department circulated Strassmeir's photo to its counterterrorism section, identifying him as a suspected terrorist. That leaflet bore a code number for the Oklahoma City bombing case.[103]

Another trail of conspiracy — or perhaps a different branch of the same one — is traceable through Michael Brescia, identified by Carol Howe as Oklahoma City's "John Doe No. 2" and Andreas Strassmeir's roommate at Elohim City. Between 1993 and 1996, Brescia was also a member of the Aryan Republican Army, which robbed 22 Midwestern banks to finance an Order-style war against ZOG and various ethnic minorities. With fellow fascists Peter Langan, Richard Guthrie, Jr., Scott Stedeford, Kevin McCarthy and Mark Thomas, Brescia stole at least $250,000 (some accounts say $500,000) for use in the ARA's jihad. In action, armed with automatic weapons, smoke grenades and pipe bombs, the ARA bandits wore Halloween masks of U.S. presidents, an idea lifted from the 1991 movie *Point Break*.[104]

Aside from their ties to Elohim City, the ARA commandos had much in common with Timothy McVeigh. All members were required to read *The Turner Diaries,* and they shared author William Pierce's views on violent revolution against ZOG. Richard Guthrie, like McVeigh, had washed out of training for an elite military corps— in his case, the U.S. Navy SEALS. Obsessed with firearms and explosives, the ARA collected an arsenal of illegal weapons that were used in their holdups across the Midwest. Before the Oklahoma City bombing, Timothy McVeigh gave his sister three $100 bills, which he described as loot from a bank heist that he helped to plan. McVeigh's sister subsequently told reporters that her brother had robbed several banks. After one holdup in 1995, the ARA bandits left a newspaper clipping about McVeigh's arrest in their abandoned getaway car (rented in the name of an FBI agent). FBI documents on McVeigh's case, belatedly released on 10 May 2001, included reports that he was an ARA member — and yet, to this day, no other ARA defendants have been questioned as possible suspects in the Oklahoma City bombing.[105]

The ARA had a curious history. Founder and leader Peter Langan, dubbed "Commander Pedro" by his troops, was a CIA agent's son who lived in Vietnam until age six. Imprisoned for a Georgia Pizza Hut holdup in 1989, Langan was released in 1993 at the behest of U.S. Secret Service agents who persuaded him to infiltrate the far-right underground. Specifically, they wanted Langan to locate and spy on his friend Richard Guthrie, Jr., who threatened former President George H.W. Bush in 1991. Once on the street and reunited with Guthrie, however, Langan reneged on the deal and "went to ether," fleeing underground to organize the ARA. In January 1995 Langan made a drunken recruiting video, railing against ZOG and promoting *The Turner Diaries* and another racist book, *Vigilantes of Christendom,* which describes the Phineas Priesthood. Investigative journalist J.D. Cash suggests that the ARA was in fact a strike team of Phineas Priests, three of whom were full-time residents of Elohim City. On the side, Langan was also a cross-dressing "preoperative transsexual" who called himself "Donna," though that side of his existence was presumably unknown to his fellow Aryan warriors.[106]

The ARA's crime spree ended after a young recruit, Aryan Nations member Shawn Kenney, backed out of his first scheduled heist and betrayed his comrades to authorities. Guthrie was captured in January 1996 and fingered Langan in Columbus, Ohio. G-men pumped 30 bullets into Langan's van, but he emerged with only minor injuries, denying that he ever fired a shot in the encounter. Still, he was prepared for war, his mobile armory including assault weapons, 3,400 rounds of ammunition, 11 pipe bombs, blasting caps and five grenades. Peripheral gear included police uniforms, fake IDs, the 1995 recruiting video, and a U.S. marshal's badge. In February 1996 St. Louis police stopped a car driven by Richard Guthrie's brother Nicholas. A search of the vehicle revealed weapons and another copy of the ARA recruiting video. That arrest led police to a storage facility in Joplin, where they seized more weapons, ammunition and explosives. Richard Guthrie, Jr., pled guilty to 19 bank holdups in seven states, then hanged himself in a Kentucky jail cell on 12 July 1996. In February 1998, Peter Langdon was convicted of two Ohio bank robberies, plus weapons charges and possession of a bomb by a convicted felon. A second conviction in October 1998, on assault, weapons and explosives charges, earned him a sentence of life without parole plus 35 years. Other ARA members received commensurate sentences, but as of press time for this book, none had been questioned as suspects in the Oklahoma City bombing.[107]

WHAT NEXT?

The FBI remains tight-lipped about paramilitary "patriot" and racist groups in the United States. Such information as is now available comes once again from private watchdog groups, led by the Southern Poverty Law Center. Though the number of active militias declined from 221 in 1997 to 72 in 2000, white-supremacist groups in the United States have demonstrated fierce resilience in the new millennium. The SPLC counted 436 white hate groups nationwide in 2000. That number increased to 625 in 2001, then to 626 in 2002, and dipped slightly to 615 in 2003. Besides recognized Klan units—up from 138 in 2000 to 158 in 2003—the mix included neo–Nazi groups, skinhead gangs, Christian Identity cults, and a motley group of "other" organizations including David Duke's National Association for the Advancement of White People.[108]

Many of the groups thus tabulated have documented histories of violence. Nearly all communicate in quasi-military rhetoric, admonishing their members and supporters to arm and train in resistance to ZOG. The "war on terror" declared by President George W. Bush in 2001 ignores these home-grown revolutionaries, while obsessing over threats from adversaries in the Middle East. If the FBI has taken any steps to monitor such groups or to curtail their illegal activities, those steps remain "classified" by a regime devoted to secrecy. And while the FBI delays, it seems inevitable that its dedicated enemies on the far right will plan and execute more terrorist attacks. Once again, those who fail to learn from the mistakes of history are destined to repeat them.

Notes

Introduction

1. Trelease, pp. 3–4; Wade, pp. 31–32.
2. Trelease, pp. 4–5; Wade, pp. 33–36, 41.
3. Wade, pp. 14–20.
4. Bennett, pp. 224–225, 477; Wade, pp. 21–22.
5. Bennett, pp. 478–479; Wade, pp. 27–28.
6. Bennett, pp. 225, 478; Trelease, p. xliv; Wade, pp. 24–25.
7. Wade, p. 38.
8. Trelease, pp. 13–18; Wade, pp. 37–38, 409, 418.
9. Bennett, p. 201; Trelease, pp. 19–20; Wade, p. 41.
10. Trelease, pp. 49, 57, 65, 68, 70–71, 73, 79, 81–82, 88–90, 92–93, 98, 101, 103–104, 108–109, 211–212.
11. Trelease, pp. 20, 28–29, 74–75, 83, 117, 120, 246, 252; Wade, p. 58.
12. Trelease, pp. 20, 67, 100–102, 119–120, 135, 156–157, 165, 242–245, 290–293, 310–312; Wade, pp. 58, 79, 84, 88.
13. Trelease, pp. 91, 124–125, 216–218, 224, 282, 351–352, 357–358, 365, 373; Wade, pp. 23, 79.
14. Trelease, pp. 119, 136, 176, 273, 281–282, 224, 415.
15. Bennett, pp. 489–492.
16. *Report of the Joint Select Committee to Inquire into the Condition of Affairs in the Late Insurrectionary States*; Wade, p. 106.
17. Bennett, p. 492; Trelease, pp. 279, 399–418; Wade, pp. 100, 103.
18. Trelease, pp. 67, 136, 173, 179, 242, 247, 308.
19. Bennett, pp. 494–499; Wade, p. 110.
20. Bennett, p. 260.
21. 18 USC Sec. 241.
22. 18 USC Sec. 242.
23. Bennett, pp. 262, 267, 494; Woodward, p. 71; *Slaughter-House Cases*, 16 Wall. 83 U.S. 36; *Minor v. Happersett*, 21 Wall. 178; *United States v. Cruikshank*, 92 U.S. 542, 555–556; *Unites States v. Rees et al.*, 92 U.S. 214, 217–218; *James v. Bowman*, 190 U.S. 127.

24. Bennett, pp. 502, 506, 509–510, 513; Van Woodward, pp. 84–85, 97.
25. Chalmers, p. 23; Woodward, p. 94; Wade, pp. 122–123.
26. Bennett, pp. 503–514; NAACP, p. 29.
27. Cook, *FBI Nobody Knows*, pp. 53–54; Lowenthal, pp. 3–5; Powers, pp. 132–133.
28. Cook, *FBI Nobody Knows*, pp. 54–58; Lowenthal, pp. 5–12.
29. Lowenthal, pp. 12–14; Powers, p. 134.
30. Lowenthal, pp. 14–21; Powers, p. 134.
31. Ron Flatter, "Johnson boxed, lived on own terms," ESPN.com; Theoharis, *FBI*, p. 46.
32. Bennett, pp. 515–520; NAACP, pp. 337, 341, 342, 351.
33. Newton, *Ku Klux Klan*, pp. 335, 358, 359.
34. Chalmers, pp. 22–27; Wade, pp. 119–139.
35. Wade, pp. 143–144.
36. U.S. Congress, *The Ku Klux Klan Hearings*. 67 Cong., 1 Sess., House Committee on Rules (1921): 114–126.
37. Bennett, p. 519; Chalmers, pp. 28–31; Wade, pp. 140–148.
38. NAACP, pp. 29, 62.
39. Chalmers, p. 31; Cook, *FBI Nobody Knows*, pp. 64–65; Powers, p. 45; Theoharis, *FBI*, p. 361; Wade, p. 149.
40. Gentry, p. 71; Lowenthal, p. 24; Theoharis, *FBI*, pp. 48, 361.
41. Messick, p. 9; Powers, pp. 41–54.
42. Cook, *FBI Nobody Knows*, pp. 66–71; Gentry, pp. 71–72; Lowenthal, pp. 22–35; Theoharis, *FBI*, p. 362.
43. Bennett, pp. 521–522; Kornweibel, pp. 17–18; NAACP, p. 29.
44. Blum, p. 450.
45. Cook, *FBI Nobody Knows*, pp. 81–89; Powers, pp. 58–63.
46. Cook, *FBI Nobody Knows*, pp. 81–89; Gentry, pp. 75–76.
47. Lowenthal, pp. 67–79.
48. Gentry, pp. 78–79; Lowenthal, pp. 147–148; Powers, pp. 63–64.

49. Cook, *FBI Nobody Knows,* pp. 96–97; Powers, pp. 86–89.

50. Cook, *FBI Nobody Knows,* pp. 97–114; Gentry, pp. 83–103; Lowenthal, p. 156–172, 184, 262; Powers, pp. 86–116; Whitehead, *FBI Story,* p. 50.

51. Gentry, pp. 98–102; Lowenthal, pp. 199–236; Whitehead, *FBI Story,* . 51.

52. Cook, *FBI Nobody Knows,* pp. 102–105; Overstreet, pp. 43–46; de Toledano, pp. 62–64; Whitehead, *FBI Story,* pp. 46–53.

53. Cook, *FBI Nobody Knows,* pp. 102–105; Gentry, pp. 79, 95; Lowenthal, p. 260; Powers, p. 124–126.

54. Kornweibel, pp. 21, 60, 67, 165; Lowenthal, pp. 120–129.

55. Bennett, pp. 522–524; Kornweibel, pp. 22, 44.

56. Chalmers, p. 31; Jackson, pp. 7–8; Wade, p. 157.

57. Chalmers, pp. 31–34; Wade, pp. 153–155.

58. Chalmers, pp. 109–111; Wade, pp. 148, 151–152.

59. Chalmers, pp. 34–35; Wade, pp. 155–161.

60. Bennett, pp. 524–525; Gannon, p. 300; Newton, pp. 374–376, 378; Wade, p. 160.

61. Chalmers, pp. 14, 35–39, 49, 56, 59, 66, 78–79, 85, 92, 98; Wade, pp. 160, 162

62. Theoharis, *FBI,* pp. 4, 362–363.

Chapter 1

1. "Burns gets orders to trail Ku Klux." *New York Times* (25 September 1921), p. 14; Overstreet, p. 301; Whitehead, *FBI Story,* p. 61.

2. Kornweibel, pp. 28, 47, 67, 97–98.

3. Whitehead, *FBI Story,* p. 61; Overstreet, p. 301; de Toledano, p. 68.

4. De Toledano, p 68; Overstreet, p 301; Whitehead, *FBI Story,* p. 61.

5. Whitehead, *FBI Story,* p. 61.

6. Overstreet, pp. 301–302.

7. Alexander, p. 71; Chalmers, p. 62; "Secret Service men still track Klan." *New York Times* (29 January 1923), p. 17.

8. Alexander, pp. 68–71; Chalmers, pp. 60–63.

9. Alexander, pp. 71–75; Chalmers, pp. 62–64.

10. De Toledano, p. 69; Overstreet, pp. 301–301; Whitehead, *FBI Story,* p. 62.

11. Gentry, pp. 109, 117; Overstreet, p. 46; Whitehead, *FBI Story,* p. 55.

12. De Toledano, p. 66.

13. Cook, *FBI Nobody Knows,* p. 116; Gentry, p. 109; Whitehead, *FBI Story,* p. 56.

14. De Toledano, p. 67; Gentry, p. 109.

15. Overstreet, p. 46.

16. Gentry, pp. 109–110.

17. Cook, *FBI Nobody Knows,* pp. 131–141; Gentry, pp. 118–121; Theoharis, *The FBI,* pp. 110–111; Whitehead, *FBI Story,* pp. 63–65.

18. Cook, *FBI Nobody Knows,* pp. 131–141.

19. Chalmers, pp. 220–221.

20. de Toledano, p. 71; Whitehead, *FBI Story,* p. 67;

21. Whitehead, p. 68.

22. Theoharis and Cox, p. 92.

23. Overstreet, p. 105.

24. Alexander, pp. 59, 64, 67, 76; Chalmers, pp. 41, 51, 56, 73, 76, 78–79, 158–159, 177, 228, 237–239, 271–273, 298; Feldman, pp. 133–134; Jackson, pp. 67–68; Newton, *Racial and Religious Violence,* p. 387; Wade, p. 160.

25. Alexander, p. 64; Chalmers, pp. 51, 73, 78–79, 197; Feldman, pp. 66, 73, 346; Gillette and Tillinger, p. 57; Jackson, p. 241; Newton, *Invisible Empire* pp. 51–52, 54–56; Newton, *Ku Klux Klan,* p. 37.

26. Chalmers, pp. 76, 186–188, 237–239, 259, 299; Gillette and Tillinger, p. 45; Newton, *Racial and Religious Violence,* p. 390.

27. Alexander, pp. 68, 72, 78; Chalmers, p. 41, 119; Feldman, pp. 30, 44–45, 85; Jackson, pp. 68–69, 190–191, 208–209, 212.

28. Alexander, p. 77; Chalmers, pp. 3, 94, 120, 122, 259; Feldman, pp. 41–42, 44–45; Newton, *Invisible Empire,* pp. 51–52; Newton, *Racial and Religious Violence,* p. 373–394; "Police chief charged with whipping women." *New York Times* (26 April 1923), p. 8.

29. Jackson, pp. 12–13, 259; Chalmers, p. 36; Rice, p. 11; "Clarke quits Klan, and Mrs. Tyler, too." *New York Times* (25 September 1921), p 14; "Clarke resignation stirs Ku Klux Klan." *New York Times* (26 September 1921), p. 5.

30. Chalmers, pp. 100–104; Rice, p. 11; Wade, pp. 186–191.

31. Chalmers, pp. 104, 199; Rice, p. 11; Theoharis, *FBI,* p. 47; Wade, p. 191; Whitehead, *FBI Story,* p. 62.

32. O'Reilly, p. 16; FBI Internet website, "FBI History," http://www.fbi.gov/libref/historic/history/lawless.htm (accessed 7 April 2004).

33. Jackson, p. 237; Overstreet, p. 303; *Washington Post* (2 November 1930), p. 14; Whitehead, *FBI Story,* p. 62.

34. Chalmers, p. 198; Rice, p. 59; Wade, pp. 165, 477.

35. Chalmers, pp. 3, 71–72, 80, 89, 127, 133, 139, 170, 173, 178, 184, 200; Feldman, p. 89; Newton, *Ku Klux Klan,* pp. 237, 374, 483; Rice, pp. 60–61, 65–67; Wade, pp. 196–197.

36. Chalmers, pp. 4, 290; Gillette and Tillinger, pp. 56, 61; Newton, *Invisible Empire,* p. 73; Wade, p. 247.

37. Chalmers, pp. 291–299; Wade, pp. 248–254.

38. Chalmers, pp. 162–174; Wade, pp. 248–256.

39. Chalmers, pp. 241–242, 298–299; Gillette and Tillinger, pp. 57–60; Myers, pp. 230–234.

40. *Knights of the Ku Klux Klan v. Strayer et al.* 26F (2d) Federal Reporter, pp. 727–729.

41. Alix, pp. 67–104; Theoharis, *FBI*, pp. 13–14; Whitehead, *FBI Story*, pp. 92–103.

42. Gentry, pp. 169–177; Theoharis, *FBI*, pp. 15–16; Whitehead, *FBI Story*, p. 92.

43. Theoharis, *FBI*, p. 17.

44. Dray, pp. 304–305; Newton, *Invisible Empire*, pp. 88–99; Newton, *Racial and Religious Violence*, pp. 395–415.

45. Dray, pp. 344–354; McGovern, pp. 121–123.

46. McGovern, pp. 121–123.

47. Chalmers, pp. 308–310; Donner, *Protectors of Privilege*, pp. 56–57.

48. Chalmers, pp. 308–310; Donner, *Protectors of Privilege*, pp. 56–57; Wade, p. 262; "Many deaths laid to 'Black Legion'; Klan link charged." *New York Times* (24 May 1936), p. 1.

49. Theoharis and Cox, p. 11; Wade, p 265–6, 271–2; Whitehead, *FBI Story*, p. 111.

50. Jenkins, pp. 87–88; Newton, *Invisible Empire*, pp. 103–104; Wade, pp. 268–72.

51. Clegg, pp. 84–87, 90–98; Jenkins, pp. 184–185, 216–217.

52. Chalmers, pp. 321–322; Newton, *Ku Klux Klan*, pp. 551–552; Newton, *Racial and Religious Violence*, pp. 415–420; Rice, p. 94; Wade, pp. 263–264.

53. Carlson, *Under Cover*, pp. 48–49; Newton, *Ku Klux Klan*, pp. 492, 584.

54. Dray, pp. 440–441; Newton, *Racial and Religious Violence,* pp. 415–417; Whitehead, *FBI Story*, pp. 254–258.

55. Chalmers, pp. 323–324; Wade, p. 275.

Chapter 2

1. Chalmers, pp. 325–327; Feldman, p. 290; House Committee on Un-American Activities (hereafter HUAC), *The Present-Day Ku Klux Klan Movement*, p. 9; Kirkham, p. 362.

2. Rice, pp. 112–114.

3. Dray, pp. 377–382; Newton, *Racial and Religious Violence*, pp. 420–425; Rice, p. 109; Carlson, *The Plotters*, pp. 49–50; "Klan is accused of a revolt plot." *New York Times* (21 June 1946), p. 46; "Klan terrorists linked to killing." *New York Times* (8 June 1946), p. 28.

4. Newton, *Ku Klux Klan*, pp. 376–377; Newton, *Racial and Religious Violence*, pp. 420–425; Rice, p. 109; Wade, pp. 283, 294.

5. Chalmers, pp. 330–331; Rice, p. 109; Wade, p. 283.

6. Carlson, *The Plotters*, pp. 50–51; Mendelsohn, p. 65; Newton, *Racial and Religious Violence*, p. 423.

7. Gillette and Tillinger, pp. 69–70; Kirkham, p. 363; McWhorter, pp. 57–59, 75; Newton, *Racial and Religious Violence*, p. 422; Nunnelley, p. 3.

8. Green, p. 59; Newton, *Racial and Religious Violence*, pp. 420–421.

9. Sullivan, p. 38.

10. Dray, pp. 382–383; Green, pp. 55–58, 69–70; Newton, *Racial and Religious Violence*, p. 423.

11. Dray, pp. 374–376; Green, p. 71; Newton, *Racial and Religious Violence*, pp. 420–423; Whitehead, *FBI Story*, p 258.

12. Dray, p. 433.

13. *Ibid.*, pp. 383, 433.

14. Green, p. 94; O'Reilly, p. 28; Wade, pp. 287–288.

15. O'Reilly, p. 28; Wade, p. 288.

16. Gentry, pp. 356–359.

17. *Ibid.*, pp. 360–434.

18. O'Reilly, p. 27; Parenti, pp. 195–196; Russo, pp. 240–242, 380.

19. Newton, *Ku Klux Klan*, p. 240; Newton, *Racial and Religious Violence*, pp. 425–434; Wade, p. 287; "Federal aide threatened." *New York Times* (30 August 1949), p. 28.

20. Chalmers, pp. 336–337; Feldman, pp. 314–315; Gillette and Tillinger, p. 91; Nunnelley, p. 3; Wade, pp. 289–290.

21. Chalmers, pp. 335–336; Newton, *Racial and Religious Violence*, pp. 425–434.

22. Wade, pp. 296–297; Whitehead, *FBI Story,* p. 262.

23. Newton, *Ku Klux Klan*, pp. 361–362; "Flogging victim says sheriff ignored plea." *New York Times* (30 November 1949), p. 56; "Federal case rests in Georgia flogging." *New York Times* (2 December 1949), p. 27; "Sheriff says Klan took prisoners." *New York Times* (10 December 1949), p. 28.

24. Newton, *The Ku Klux Klan*, p. 362; Overstreet, pp. 311–312; Whitehead, *FBI Story*, p. 263; "Klan flogging trial frees 2 of accused." *New York Times* (3 December 1949), p. 28; "Georgia civil rights trial ended with jury in 48-hour deadlock." *New York Times* (18 December 1949), pp, 1, 58; "Jailed in Negro beatings." *New York Times* (18 March 1950), p. 30; "Georgia Klan case is hailed in South." *New York Times* (19 March 1950), p. E10.

25. Chalmers, pp. 337–339; Newton, *Ku Klux Klan*, p. 27; Newton, *Racial and Religious Violence*, pp. 427–433; "Judge in Klan robe killed in gun battle." *New York Times* (29 August 1950), p. 28.

26. Chalmers, pp. 337–339; Newton, *Ku Klux Klan*, pp. 65, 74; Carter, *Voices of Fear*, pp. 159–163; Newton, *Racial and Religious Violence*, pp. 427–433; "Klan chief arrested in killing of officer." *New York Times* (1 September 1950), p. 14.

27. Carter, *Voices of Fear*, pp. 127–129.

28. Carter, *Voices of Fear*, pp. 135–136, 139–141, 145–150, 159–163; Newton, *Ku Klux Klan*, p. 74, 198–199, 203; Newton, *Racial and Religious Violence*, pp. 427–433.

29. Carter, *Voices of Fear*, pp. 145–150, 165–168, 177–78.

30. *Ibid.*, pp. 189–190, 193–194; "Former Klan

leader paroled." *New York Times* (23 February 1954), p. 47.

31. Newton, *Invisible Empire*, pp. 106–118.
32. Green, pp. 95–98; Newton, *Invisible Empire*, pp. 111–112, 119–124.
33. Green, pp. 106–107, 115–116, Newton, *Invisible Empire*, pp. 124–126.
34. Green, pp. 148–149, 152–153; Kennedy, pp. 240–254; Newton, *Invisible Empire*, pp. 124–126.
35. Kennedy, pp. 229–230; Newton, *Invisible Empire*, pp. 129–130; Newton, *Racial and Religious Violence*, pp. 426–434.
36. Green, pp. 173–174, 182–186; Newton, *Invisible Empire*, pp. 130–132.
37. Green, pp. 229–245; Newton, *Invisible Empire*, pp. 130–132.
38. Green, pp. 193–196; Newton, *Invisible Empire*, pp. 137–139; Overstreet, pp. 312–313.
39. Green, pp. 193–196; Newton, *Invisible Empire*, pp. 132–135, 137–139.
40. Milan, pp. 1, 161.
41. *Ibid.*, pp. 164–165.
42. *Ibid.*, pp. 165–173, 177–182.
43. *Ibid.*, p. 183.

Chapter 3

1. Bartley, pp. 58–60; Rice, p. 118.
2. Chalmers, pp. 349–350; McMillen, pp. 11, 17; Newton, *The Ku Klux Klan*, pp. 54–55; Whitfield, p. 35.
3. O'Reilly, pp. 41, 46.
4. McMillen, pp. 18–19, 22–24, 43, 59–61, 82, 100, 104.
5. McMillen, pp. 54–55, 71, 78, 89; McWhorter, pp. 98, 201; Newton, *The Ku Klux Klan*, pp. 114–115.
6. McMillen, pp. 22–24.
7. Newton, *The Ku Klux Klan*, p. 114.
8. Mendelsohn, pp. 3–6, 9–10, 14–17, 19.
9. Manchester, p. 738; O'Reilly, pp. 41–42; Whitehead, p. 258; Whitfield, pp. 31, 73–74, 76–78.
10. McMillen, pp. 54, 108, 283–284, 289; McWhorter, pp. 98–99.
11. McMillen, pp. 224–225.
12. Gentry, pp. 441–442; McWhorter, p. 104; Ungar, pp. 407–409.
13. Gentry, pp. 441–442; O'Reilly, pp. 41–42; Ungar, pp. 407–409.
14. O'Reilly, pp. 41–42; Whitehead, *FBI Story*, p. 263.
15. Whitehead, *FBI Story*, p. 263.
16. Gentry, p. 442; McWhorter, p. 104; Overstreet, p. 327; Ungar, p. 409.
17. O'Reilly, p. 37.
18. Bartley, pp. 202–203; Forster and Epstein, p. 19; AC, p. 12; Rice, p. 118.
19. McWhorter, p. 129; Newton, *The Ku Klux Klan*, pp. 181–183; Newton, *Racial and Religious Violence*, pp. 435–457; Whitehead, *FBI Story*, p. 262; Cook, *The Segregationists*, pp. 119–120, 140–144; Parker, pp. 6–7.
20. Cook, *The Segregationists*, pp. 119–120; Newton, *Racial and Religious Violence*, pp. 435–457; Parker, p. 16.
21. Dray, pp. 436–443; Parker, pp. 11–12.
22. Newton, *Racial and Religious Violence*, p. 435; Barbara Patterson, "Defiance and dynamite." *New South* 18 (May 1963): 8–11.
23. McWhorter, p. 121; Newton, *Racial and Religious Violence*, pp. 435–457; Rose, p. 190.
24. Newton, *Ku Klux Klan*, pp. 400–401; Newton, *Racial and Religious Violence*, pp. 435–457; Nunnelley, pp. 77–79; Parker, pp. 18.
25. Cook, *The Segregationists* p. 119; McWhorter, pp. 114–115; Parker, pp. 7, 9–10.
26. McWhorter, p. 132; Newton, *The Ku Klux Klan*, p. 533; Nunnelley, p. 79; Parker, p. 9.
27. Greene, p. 230; McWhorter, pp. 132–135; House Select Committee on Assassinations (hereafter, HSCA), pp. 501–502.
28. Greene, pp. 230–231.
29. Greene, pp. 272–273; HSCA, pp. 501–502; McWhorter, pp. 132–135; Nunnelley, p. 79.
30. Chalmers, p. 531; Greene, pp. 272–273, 280, 288–289, 297–298, 300, 305, 316–317, 322, 333, 369–370; McWhorter, p. 200; Parker, pp. 10–11.
31. Greene, p. 369.
32. McMillen, pp. 283–284.
33. Overstreet, p. 327.
34. McMillen, p. 284; Parker, pp. 16–17; Tully, pp. 231–233.
35. McMillen, p. 284; Tully, pp. 231–233.
36. Cook, *The Segregationists*, pp. 3–4; Forster and Epstein, pp. 21–22; Parker, p. 25.
37. Branch, pp. 524–561; Newton, *Racial and Religious Violence*, pp. 445, 456.
38. Forster and Epstein, p. 22; Newton, *Racial and Religious Violence*, pp. 456–457; Parker, pp. 27–28; Tully, p. 224.
39. Parker, pp. 27–28; Tully, pp. 222–224; Zinn, p. 31; "Dr. King says FBI in Albany, Ga., favors segregationists." *New York Times* (19 November 1962), p. 21.
40. Branch, pp. 866–870, 874–875, 895, 916, 921; Garrow, *FBI and Martin Luther King*, pp. 54–135; O'Reilly, pp. 118–121; Ungar, p. 411.

Chapter 4

1. Feldman, pp. 15–20; McWhorter, pp. 58, 63–64, 170; Nunnelley, p. 3; Woodward, p. 118.
2. Carter, *Politics of Rage*, pp. 94–95; Cook, *The Segregationists*, pp. 129–130.
3. McWhorter, pp. 153–154; Newton, *Racial and Religious Violence*, pp. 444–452.

4. McWhorter, pp. 160–163, 166–168, 177–178; Rowe, pp. 6–8.

5. McWhorter, pp. 166–168, 190–194.

6. Donner, *Protectors of Privilege,* p. 308; McWhorter, pp. 192–194.

7. McWhorter, pp. 180–282, 187–188, 190–192, 196; Rowe, p. 38.

8. Bennett, pp. 543–544; McWhorter, p. 195; Parker, p. 19; Woodward, p. 140.

9. Donner, *Protectors of Privilege,* p. 309; McWhorter, pp. 194, 197–198.

10. Gentry, p. 483; McWhorter, pp. 198, 213; Nunnelley, p. 98; O'Reilly, pp. 83, 88.

11. McWhorter, pp. 201, 203–204; Nunnelley, pp. 94–96; Parker, p. 19.

12. Gentry, p. 483; McWhorter, p. 204; Nunnelley, pp. 94–96; O'Reilly, pp. 84, 87; Parker, p. 19.

13. McWhorter, p. 201, 205–209, 211; Nunnelley, pp. 96–97; Rowe, p. 40.

14. McWhorter, p. 211; Rowe, pp. 44–46.

15. Gentry, p. 484; McWhorter, pp. 212–213.

16. Donner, *Protectors of Privilege,* pp. 310–311; Nunnelley, pp. 101–102; Parker, p. 19.

17. Gentry, p. 485; McWhorter, pp. 228–229; Nunnelley, p. 103; Parker, pp. 20–21.

18. O'Reilly, p. 91.

19. Newton, *Racial and Religious Violence,* pp. 453–454; O'Reilly, p. 92; Parker, pp. 21–22.

20. McWhorter, pp. 218–219, 225, 239–240; Newton, *Ku Klux Klan,* p. 214; O'Reilly, p. 85; Parker, p. 20.

21. Branch, pp. 468–469; McWhorter, pp. 205, 239–240, 242–243; Nunnelley, pp. 104–105.

22. McWhorter, pp. 239–240.

23. McWhorter, pp. 205, 242–243; Nunnelley, pp. 104–106.

24. Newton, *Ku Klux Klan,* p. 616; O'Reilly, pp. 94–95.

25. Gentry, p. 485; O'Reilly, pp. 85–87, 93–94.

26. Newton, *Ku Klux Klan,* pp. 47, 457; Nunnelley, pp. 106–107.

27. McWhorter, p. 259; Newton, *Racial and Religious Violence,* pp. 453–457.

28. Nunnelley, pp. 110–111.

29. McWhorter, pp. 275–277.

30. Carter, *Politics of Rage,* pp. 96, 106–107, 125; Flowers, pp. 40, 44; McWhorter, pp. 268–269, 303–304, 311, 473, 490–491.

31. McWhorter, p. 341, 425–429, 434; Parker, pp. 42–44.

32. McWhorter, pp. 433–434; Parker, pp. 42–44.

33. McWhorter, pp. 435, 443–444, 512; Nunnelley, p. 104.

34. Carter, *Politics of Rage,* p. 139; McWhorter, pp. 455–459.

35. McWhorter, pp. 455–459; Rowe, pp. 81–81, 84, 91.

36. McWhorter, pp. 473, 477–478; Newton, *Racial and Religious Violence,* pp. 460–462.

37. McWhorter, p. 581; "Army feared King, secretly watched him." Memphis (Tenn.) *Commercial-Appeal* (21 March 1993).

38. McWhorter, pp. 479–480, 482–483, 485, 567.

39. McWhorter, pp. 490, 498–501, 505–504.

40. McWhorter, pp. 23, 58–59.

41. McWhorter, p. 531, 535; Parker, pp. 47–48.

42. McWhorter, p. 561; O'Reilly, pp. 111, 113–114.

43. Gentry, p. 484; McWhorter, pp. 483–485, 523, 537, 539, 546–547, 558.

44. McWhorter, pp. 509–511, 514–515, 524, 528, 529,

45. McWhorter, pp. 532–534, 536, 539, 540–541.

46. McWhorter, pp. 542–543, 546; Parker, p. 48.

47. McWhorter, pp. 516–517, 546–549.

48. Kessler, p. 382; McWhorter, pp. 550–554.

49. McWhorter, pp. 551, 555–556, 558, 565; O'Reilly, p. 112.

50. Chalmers, p. 403; Kessler, p. 382; McWhorter, pp. 559–560, 574; Wade, p. 324.

51. HUAC, *Activities of Ku Klux Klan Organizations in the United States, Part 2,* pp. 2215–2216, 2222–2225, 2229–2230; George McMillan, "New bombing terrorists in the South call themselves Nacirema ... American spelled backward." *Life* (11 October 1963).

52. McWhorter, p. 567.

53. Chalmers, pp. 402–403; Kessler, p. 379; McWhorter, pp. 573–575; Newton, *The Ku Klux Klan,* p. 40; O'Reilly, p. 114.

54. Kessler, pp. 380–381; Newton, *FBI Encyclopedia,* p. 28.

55. Kessler, p. 379; Newton, *FBI Encyclopedia,* p. 28.

56. Kessler, p. 384; Newton, *FBI Encyclopedia,* p. 28.

Chapter 5

1. Massengill, p. 222; O'Reilly, p. 41; Silver, p 153.

2. HUAC, *The Present-Day Ku Klux Klan Movement,* p. 29; Newton, *The Ku Klux Klan,* p. 397.

3. Cook, *The Segregationists,* p. 20; Newton, *Racial and Religious Violence,* pp. 450–452.

4. Mendelsohn, pp. 22–28.

5. Branch, p. 511; Bullard, p. 48; Mendelsohn, pp. 29–31.

6. Bullard, pp. 48, 50–51; Cagin and Dray, p. 183; Newton, *Racial and Religious Violence,* pp. 454–457.

7. Parker, pp. 30–34.

8. Doyle, pp. 81, 92, 96.

9. Doyle, pp. 13–15, 96–97; Walker, pp. 30–34.

10. *Ibid.*, pp. 96–100, 129, 218; Hendrickson, pp. 52–53; Newton, *The Ku Klux Klan*, p. 242.

11. Doyle, pp. 96–97, 129, 147–148; Parker, pp. 30–34; Sherrill, p. 281.

12. Doyle, pp. 186–187.

13. Bullard, pp. 52–53; Doyle, pp. 162–166, 211–216; Parker, pp. 30–34.

14. Bullard, pp. 52–53; Doyle, pp. 278, 280–281, 283–284, 287; Parker, pp. 30–34.

15. Doyle, p. 309; Newton, *Ku Klux Klan*, pp. 78–79, 449; Parker, pp. 30–34.

16. Doyle, pp. 281–282; Hendrickson, pp. 14, 52–53, 62, 64, 157–158; Newton, *The Ku Klux Klan*, pp. 22, 295–296; Parker, p. 34.

17. Doyle, p. 309; Epstein and Forster, p. 15.

18. Newton, *Racial and Religious Violence*, pp. 457–460.

19. Newton, *Racial and Religious Violence*, p. 460; Vollers, pp. 74–77, 122–123.

20. Overstreet, p. 167; Parker, p. 39.

21. Massengill, pp. 139–140, 143–145.

22. *Ibid.*, 143–145, 148, 151–154.

23. Gentry, pp. 566–567; Massengill, p. 370; Nossiter, pp. 130–132; Villano and Astor, pp. 90–94.

24. Massengill, p. 155; Mendelsohn, pp. 83–84; Nossiter, pp. 130–132; Parker, p. 40; Vollers, pp. 151, 154.

25. DeLaughter, p. 46; O'Reilly, pp. 109–110.

26. McMillen, p. 360; Nossiter, p. 119; Vollers, pp. 52–53, 241.

27. Massengill, p. 190; McMillen, p. 360; Mendelsohn, pp. 83–84; Nossiter, pp. 130–132; Parker, p. 40; Vollers, pp. 160–161, 163–164.

28. Massengill, p. 223.

29. DeLaughter, pp. 82, 149–150, 161–162; Massengill, pp. 145, 149–150, 174; Nossiter, p. 136.

30. DeLaughter, pp. 50, 82; Massengill, p. 175; HUAC, *Activities of Ku Klux Klan Organizations in the United States, Part 3*, pp. 2667–2682, 2698–2701.

31. DeLaughter, pp. 149–150; Massengill, pp. 174, 227–228; McIlhaney, p. 38; Newton, *Ku Klux Klan*, p. 44; Vollers, pp. 221–222.

32. Massengill, pp. 243–244; Vollers, pp. 225–226.

33. Massengill, pp. 243–244; Vollers, pp. 225–226.

34. Nossiter, pp. 8–9, 138–139; Vollers, p. 227.

35. Newton, *Ku Klux Klan*, p. 44; Nossiter, pp. 139–141; Vollers, pp. 232–233, 240–241.

36. Nossiter, p. 140; Vollers, pp. 237–239, 240–242.

37. DeLaughter, pp. 89, 117, 136, 143–144; Nossiter, pp. 139, 142.

38. DeLaughter, pp. 143–144.

39. *Ibid.*, pp. 149–150, 161–163, 179–181, 207–208.

40. DeLaughter, p. 211; Nossiter, pp. 250–251, 254; Vollers, p. 360.

41. Massengill, pp. 317–318; Vollers, p. 377; "Beckwith, assassin of Medgar Evers, dies serving life term." *Washington Post* (22 January 2001).

Chapter 6

1. Bullard, p. 64; Chalmers, p. 387; Deloach, p. 164; Forster and Epstein, pp. 7–10; Hendrickson, p. 268.

2. Garrow, *St. Augustine,* pp. 30–31.

3. Garrow, *St. Augustine,* pp. 31, 127–129, 204, 210–211; HUAC, *The Present-Day Ku Klux Klan Movement,* p. 149; Newton, *Invisible Empire,* pp. 163–164.

4. Garrow, *St. Augustine,* pp. 112, 129–130, 189; Newton, *Invisible Empire,* p. 169.

5. Garrow, *St. Augustine,* pp. 127, 183–184, 225; Newton, *Invisible Empire,* p. 164; Newton, *Racial and Religious Violence,* pp. 464–476.

6. Garrow, *St. Augustine,* p. 111; Newton, *Invisible Empire,* pp. 161, 172; Parker, p. 59.

7. Garrow, *St. Augustine,* p. 111; Newton, *Invisible Empire,* pp. 172–173; Parker, p. 59.

8. Cagin and Dray, pp. 180, 229; Newton, *Ku Klux Klan,* p. 299.

9. DeLaughter, p. 168; HUAC, pp. 29, 44, 169–170; Newton, *Ku Klux Klan,* pp. 16, 397, 607–608.

10. Cagin and Dray, p. 386; Newton, *Ku Klux Klan,* p. 215.

11. Cagin and Dray, pp. 228–229; Mendelsohn, pp. 33–34, 36–37; Vollers, p. 173.

12. Cagin and Dray, pp. 391–393; Marsh, p. 57; Moody, pp. 356–357, 361–362; Sims, p. 245.

13. Bullard, pp. 64–65; Parker, p. 65; Whitehead, *Attack on Terror,* pp. 98–100; Jerry Mitchell, "'66 Klan slaying not only killing on federal property." Jackson (MS) *Clarion-Ledger* (14 January 2000); Jerry Mitchell, "'64 suspect in Klan murders scoffs at reinvestigation talk." Jackson *Clarion-Ledger* (23 January 2000).

14. O'Reilly, pp. 178–179.

15. Deloach, p. 167; O'Reilly, p. 163; Wade, pp. 336–339; Whitehead, *Attack on Terror,* pp. 51, 131.

16. Cagin and Dray, p. 333; O'Neil, pp. 163–165.

17. Cagin and Dray, pp. 355–357, 361–362; Gillette and Tillinger, p. 142; O'Reilly, p. 165; Whitehead, *Attack on Terror,* pp. 65, 76; Ungar p. 412.

18. Cagin and Dray, pp. 327–328.

19. Cagin and Dray, pp. 369; Sims, p. 245; Whitehead, *Attack on Terror,* p. 91.

20. Cagin and Dray, p. 370; Gentry, pp. 562–563; O'Reilly, pp. 169, 172; Whitehead, *Attack on Terror,* pp. 92–94; Ungar, pp. 413–414.

21. Deloach, pp. 177–178; O'Reilly, p. 169; Ungar, pp. 413–414, 417; Whitehead, *Attack on Terror,* pp. 100–101, 104–108.

22. Cagin and Dray, p. 394.

23. Deloach, pp. 185, 190; Gentry, p. 563; O'Reilly, p. 174; Parker, p. 63.

24. Deloach, p. 9; O'Reilly, pp. 185–189; Theoharis, *FBI*, pp. 322–323.

25. Newton, *Racial and Religious Violence,* pp. 473–476; O'Reilly, pp. 174, 190.

26. Cagin and Dray, p. 435; Deloach, pp. 194–195.

27. Cagin and Dray, pp. 432–434; Deloach, pp. 196–197; Parker, pp. 63–64, 67; Vollers, p. 220; Whitehead, *Attack on Terror,* pp. 126, 174.

28. Cagin and Dray, pp. 436–437, 443; Deloach, p. 196; Gillette and Tillinger, p. 146; Parker, pp. 65–66; Whitehead, pp. 196–197, 218–219, 258–259.

29. Cagin and Dray, p. 452; Whitehead, *Attack on Terror,* pp. 260, 264, 268, 276, 282–283, 304.

30. Cagin and Dray, pp. 407–408.

31. Cagin and Dray, p. 452.

32. Bullard, pp. 70–71; Gillette and Tillinger, pp. 127–128; Wade, p. 345; Whitehead, *Attack on Terror,* pp. 310–312.

33. HUAC, pp. 89–90, 119–120; Newton, *Racial and Religious Violence,* pp. 464–476.

34. Gillette and Tillinger, pp. 128–130; Parker, pp. 69–70; Whitehead, *Attack on Terror,* pp. 310–312.

35. Bullard, pp. 70–71; Gillette and Tillinger, p. 129, 130–132; HUAC, *Present-Day Ku Klux Klan,* p. 119; Tully, p. 217.

36. HUAC, *Present-Day Ku Klux Klan,* pp. 27, 39, 119–120.

37. Gillette and Tillinger, pp. 133–138; HUAC, p. 73; Overstreet, pp. 308, 310; Parker, p. 70; Tully, p. 215–216, 219.

38. Gillette and Tillinger, p. 138; HUAC, pp. 27, 52, 120, 140; Newton, *Ku Klux Klan,* pp. 410, 521; Overstreet, pp. 310–311; Parker, p. 70; Tully, pp. 213–214.

39. Bullard, p. 71; HUAC, *Present-Day Ku Klux Klan,* p. 120; Overstreet, p. 311; Parker, pp. 70–71.

Chapter 7

1. Theoharis, *FBI,* p. 182; Churchill and Vander Wall, pp. 33, 42–45, 50, 67, 177, 304.

2. Gentry, p. 563; Overstreet, p. 208; Theoharis, *Spying on Americans,* p. 168.

3. Theoharis, *Spying on Americans,* pp. 141–142; Ungar, pp. 300–301.

4. Gentry, p. 564; Nelson, p. 94; O'Reilly, p. 201.

5. O'Reilly, pp. 195, 198, 209, 214.

6. Nelson, p 91; Overstreet, p. 304; Tully, p. 228.

7. Donner, *Age of Surveillance,* p. 207; Lee, p. 334; O'Reilly, pp. 215–216.

8. Donner, *Age of Surveillance,* p. 208; Gentry, p. 564; Nelson, pp. 91, 94; O'Reilly, pp. 203–204; Sims, p. 120.

9. Donner, *Age of Surveillance,* p. 209; O'Reilly, p. 203.

10. Donner, *Age of Surveillance,* p. 210; Sims, pp. 122–123; Theoharis, *Spying on Americans,* pp. 143–144.

11. Donner, *Age of Surveillance,* p. 208; O'Reilly, pp. 202–203; Sims, p. 123.

12. HTML Index of cointelpro Documents, http://www.derechos.net/paulwolf/cointelpro/cointelindex.htm#WhiteHate.

13. *Ibid.*

14. Chalmers, p. 433; Gentry, pp. 564–565.

15. Gentry, pp. 564–565.

16. Sims, p. 121.

17. *Ibid.*

18. Donner, *Age of Surveillance,* p. 209.

19. *Ibid.,* p. 207.

20. Theoharis, *Spying on Americans,* p. 142.

21. *Ibid.*

22. Gillette and Tillinger, p. 148.

23. Deloach, p. 176.

24. Churchill and Vander Wall, p. 169.

25. HUAC, *Present-Day Ku Klux Klan,* p. 18; O'Reilly, p. 223.

26. Hoffman, p. 69.

27. HUAC, *Present-Day Ku Klux Klan,* pp. 103–109, 154; Parker, pp. 73–74; Whitehead, *Attack on Terror,* pp. 166–169.

28. HUAC, *Activities of Ku Klux Klan Organizations in the United States, Part 3,* p. 2810; Newton, *Racial and Religious Violence,* pp. 479–490.

29. Donner, *Age of Surveillance,* p. 209; O'Reilly, p. 202.

30. Newton, *Ku Klux Klan,* pp. 58–59; Newton, *Racial and Religious Violence,* pp. 464–496.

31. HUAC, *Present-Day Ku Klux Klan,* pp. 106–107; Overstreet, pp. 285–297.

32. Newton, *Ku Klux Klan,* p. 156; O'Reilly, p. 394.

33. Chalmers, pp. 388–389; Mendelsohn, pp. 176–183.

34. O'Reilly, p. 196.

35. Stanton, p. 197.

36. Mendelsohn, p. 185, Overstreet, p. 303; Whitehead, p. 305.

37. Stanton, pp. 193, 198.

38. McWhorter, p. 573; Stanton, p. 192–194, 197.

39. Gentry, p. 585; O'Reilly, pp. 197, 218–219.

40. Gentry, p. 585; Stanton, pp. 53, 127.

41. Mendelsohn, p. 191; Rowe, pp. 165, 175–176; Stanton, pp. 44, 52, 193; Whitehead, *Attack on Terror,* p. 305.

42. Gillette and Tillinger, pp. 15–17; O'Reilly, p. 197; Stanton, p. 45.

43. Mendelsohn, p. 190; O'Reilly, p. 220.

44. Mendelsohn, p. 190; Stanton, pp. 53–54.

45. Mendelsohn, pp. 179–180; Stanton, p. 55.

46. Gentry, p. 586; Stanton, pp. 100–101.

47. O'Reilly, pp. 219–220, 224; Wade, p. 352,

48. McWhorter, p. 550; O'Reilly, p. 220; Parker, pp. 99–100; Stanton, p. 45.

49. Lowe, pp. 86–87; Mendelsohn, p. 192; Parker p. 99; O'Reilly, p. 221; Rowe, p. 172; Stanton, pp. 123, 199; Wade, p. 353.

50. Stanton, pp. 94.

51. *Ibid.*, pp. 97–100.

52. O'Reilly, pp. 219–220; Stanton, p. 59.

53. O'Reilly, pp. 201–202.

54. HTML Index of cointelpro Documents, http://www.derechos.net/paulwolf/cointelpro/cointelindex.htm#WhiteHate.

55. Mendelsohn, p. 193; O'Reilly, p. 221.

56. Flowers, pp. 40, 44; Wade, p. 353.

57. Parker, p. 99; Stanton, pp. 123, 127.

58. O'Reilly, p 222; Parker, p. 99; Stanton, p. 188.

59. McWhorter, p. 573; Newton, *Ku Klux Klan,* p. 495; Stanton, pp. 188–189.

60. Stanton, pp. 204–206; Wade, p. 354.

61. McWhorter, p. 573; Stanton, pp. 206–210.

62. HUAC, *Present-Day Ku Klux Klan,* pp. 27, 147, 155–159; Newton, *Ku Klux Klan,* p. 169; Newton, *Racial and Religious Violence,* pp. 470, 479.

63. Newton, *Ku Klux Klan,* p. 156; Newton, *Racial and Religious Violence,* pp. 487, 490–491; Parker, p. 120.

64. O'Reilly, p. 202–203; Sims, pp. 43, 122–123.

65. Gentry, p. 484; Wheaton, pp. 11–12, 40, 42.

66. Greene, p. 226; HUAC, *Present-Day Ku Klux Klan,* pp. 18, 3334, 36; Lowe, pp. 68–69.

67. Donner, pp. 208–209; Lee, pp. 163–164; Schmaltz, p. 264; Wheaton, pp. 12, 46.

68. Lee, pp. 163–164; Newton, *Ku Klux Klan,* pp. 209–210.

69. Schmaltz, pp. 44, 68–69, 150–151; Simonelli, pp. 2, 33.

70. Schmaltz, pp. 226–227, 243–245, 248–250, 258–259.

71. *Ibid.*, pp. 295–296.

72. O'Reilly, p. 204; Simonelli, p. 87.

73. HTML Index of cointelpro Documents, http://www.derechos.net/paulwolf/cointelpro/cointelindex.htm#WhiteHate.

74. *Ibid.*

75. Newton, *Ku Klux Klan,* p. 488; Tully, pp. 221–222.

76. Goodman, pp. 465–467; Parker, p. 99.

77. O'Reilly, p. 204.

78. Donner, *Age of Surveillance,* p. 209; Goodman, p. 465; HUAC, *Present-Day Ku Klux Klan,* pp. 1–2; Newton, *Ku Klux Klan,* pp. 142, 304, 507, 514.

79. Goodman, pp. 470–471; HUAC, *Present-Day Ku Klux Klan,* p. 2.

80. Donner, *Age of Surveillance,* p. 28; Gentry, pp. 565–566.

81. Chalmers, p. 387; Forster and Epstein, p. 7; HUAC, pp. 19, 27; O'Reilly, p. 223.

82. Gentry, p. 565; O'Reilly, p. 202; Theoharis, *Spying on Americans,* pp. 144–145.

83. Theoharis, *Spying on Americans,* pp. 144–145.

84. *Ibid.*, p. 145.

85. O'Reilly, p. 225; Theoharis, *Spying on Americans,* p. 145.

86. Parker, pp. 167, 169–171.

87. Hendrickson, pp. 239–241, 256–257.

88. Whitehead, *Attack on Terror,* pp. 234, 238–239.

89. Whitehead, *Attack on Terror,* pp. 238–239, 249, 251.

90. *Ibid.*, pp. 251–252.

91. *Ibid.*, pp. 304–305; "Klan leader faces new trial in 1966 firebombing." CNN News (28 May 1998); "Former KKK leader convicted of 1966 murder." CNN News (21 August 1998).

92. Newton, *Racial and Religious Violence,* p. 508; Whitehead, *Attack on Terror,* pp. 285–287.

93. Newton, *Racial and Religious Violence,* pp. 508–510; Whitehead, *Attack on Terror,* p. 286.

94. Newton, *The Ku Klux Klan,* p. 57; Newton, *Racial and Religious Violence,* pp. 511, 513, 532–533; Whitehead, *Attack on Terror,* p. 288.

95. Nelson, pp. 22, 133–134, 137–139; Whitehead, *Attack on Terror,* pp. 289–290.

96. Nelson, pp. 11, 20, 139, 147–148, 153, 155, 166–167, 170–171, 264.

97. *Ibid.*, pp. 173–187, 205, 208, 246–247, 255–257.

98. *Ibid.*, pp. 188–189, 195, 198–199, 200–201 *Ku Klux Klan,* p. 260.

99. Ungar, p. 415; Evers and Szanton, pp. 244–245, 261–265.

100. Nelson, pp. 227, 238–241, 264; Ungar, p. 380.

101. Nelson, p. 241.

102. *Ibid.*, p. 264.

103. Newton, *The Ku Klux Klan,* pp. 167, 270, 395–396.

104. Jones, pp. 131–133, 295, 298, 358–364, 372–375, 378–379; Parker, pp. 153–154.

105. Newton, *Ku Klux Klan,* pp. 78, 389; Smith, p. 55.

106. Newton, *Ku Klux Klan,* pp. 41, 279, 451–452; 603–604.

107. Glick, pp. 12–13.

108. O'Reilly, pp. 180, 217–218.

109. Newton, *Ku Klux Klan,* pp. 80, 122–123, 131; O'Reilly, p. 217.

110. Blackstock, pp. 15–16; Popkin, pp. 36, 58.

111. Popkin, p. 58.

112. Churchill and Vander Wall, pp. 194–195, 201–203, 224–225; Popkin, p. 58.

113. Blackstock, pp. 15–16; Moore, pp. 126, 337.

114. Theoharis, *FBI,* pp. 126, 181–182; Ungar, p. 139.

115. Churchill and Vander Wall, p. 304; Newton, *FBI Encyclopedia,* p. 72; Wheaton, p. 40.

116. Donner, *Age of Surveillance*, pp. 207–208; Gentry, p. 565; Theoharis, *FBI*, pp. 127–130; Theoharis, *Spying on Americans*, pp. 143, 145.

117. O'Reilly, pp. 222–223, 225; Sims, pp. 119–122.

Chapter 8

1. Evers and Szanton, p. 191; Mendelsohn, p. 206.

2. Whitehead, *Attack on Terror*, pp. 225–226, 229–230.

3. *Ibid.*, pp. 226–229.

4. Parker, pp. 119–120; Whitehead, *Attack on Terror*, p. 230.

5. Bullard, pp. 90–91; Parker, pp. 199–200.

6. Evers and Szanton, p. 190; Whitehead, *Attack on Terror*, p. 230.

7. Bullard, pp. 74–75; Mendelsohn, pp. 168–169; Rowe, p. 169.

8. Bullard, pp. 75; Mendelsohn, pp. 169–171; Newton, *Ku Klux Klan*, pp. 479–480; Parker, p. 91.

9. Mendelsohn, pp. 190–191; Newton, *Ku Klux Klan*, p. 479; Rowe, p. 169; Stanton, pp. 47, 122, 146.

10. Mendelsohn, pp. 172–173; Parker, p. 91.

11. Overstreet, p. 317; Parker, p. 91.

12. Bullard, pp. 78–79; "Justice delayed," *20/20* (29 November 1999).

13. HUAC, *Activities of Ku Klux Klan Organizations in the United States, Part 2*, p. 2449; HUAC, *Present-Day Ku Klux Klan*, p. 154; Newton, *Ku Klux Klan*, pp. 402–403; Parker, p. 115.

14. Bullard, pp. 78–79; "Justice delayed," *20/20* (29 November 1999); Newton, *Ku Klux Klan*, pp. 402–403; Parker, p. 115; "McElveen is granted hearing." Baton Rouge *Morning Advocate* (11 August 1965); "First hearing for McElveen is postponed." *Morning Advocate* (17 August 1965); "McElveen hearing request withdrawn." *Bogalusa Daily News* (17 September 1965); "Jury to mull McElveen case today." *Morning Advocate* (5 November 1965).

15. Bullard, pp. 82–83; Eagles, pp. 169–170, 209; Mendelsohn, pp. 196, 204, 206–207.

16. Eagles, pp. 190–192, 194; Flowers, p. 44.

17. Eagles, pp. 194–196; Flowers, p. 44; Mendelsohn, pp. 210–212; Parker, p. 102.

18. Eagles, pp. 195–196; Flowers, p. 44; Mendelsohn, p. 211.

19. Eagles, pp. 195, 201–202.

20. Bullard, pp. 82–83; Eagles, pp. 200, 202–205.

21. Eagles, pp. 206, 210; Mendelsohn, pp. 214–215.

22. Eagles, pp. 214, 218–223.

23. *Ibid.*, pp. 226–227, 235–238, 240, 242; Newton, *Ku Klux Klan*, p. 152.

24. Eagles, pp. 243, 251–252; Parker, p. 102.

25. Mendelsohn, pp. 212–213; Newton, *Ku Klux Klan*, p. 561.

26. "Suspect in murder called a Klansman." *New York Times* (26 February 1966), p. 43; "Mechanic is guilty in death of Negro." *New York Times* (27 February 1966), p. 44; personal communication with David Moyers, publisher of the *Ashley County Ledger* (29 June 2004).

27. Jerry Mitchell, "The last days of Ben Chester White." Jackson (MS) *Clarion-Ledger* (23 February 2003).

28. Bullard, p. 88; Mitchell, 23 February 2003; Newton, *Ku Klux Klan*, pp. 602–603; Parker, pp. 173–174.

29. Bullard, p. 88; Newton, *Ku Klux Klan*, p. 603.

30. Jerry Mitchell, "Grand jury examining evidence in '66 death." *Clarion-Ledger* (8 February 2000); Manuel Roig-Franzia, "After nearly 40 years, a guilty verdict." *Washington Post* (1 March 2003); "Avants dies in federal prison." WLOX-TV Channel 13, Biloxi, MS (16 June 2004).

31. Bullard, p. 89.

32. "Wife of a Negro minister shot to death in Atlanta." *New York Times* (30 January 1967), p. 16.

33. Branch, p. 362; Gillette and Tillinger, p. 148.

34. Garrow, *FBI vs. Martin Luther King*, pp. 125–126.

35. Newton, *King Conspiracy*, pp. 28–36.

36. Melanson, pp. 68–69; Newton, *King Conspiracy*, pp. 36–42, 64–65.

37. Newton, *King Conspiracy*, pp. 76–77, 88–89, 100–101, 111–112.

38. *Ibid.*, pp. 136–137.

39. HSCA, pp. 496–499; Newton, *King Conspiracy*, pp. 175–178, 182; Newton, *Ku Klux Klan*, p. 523.

40. Newton, *King Conspiracy*, pp. 188–194.

41. *Ibid.*, pp. 207–208.

42. *Ibid.*, pp. 208–209.

43. *Ibid.*, p. 209.

44. *Ibid.*, pp. 209–210.

45. *Ibid.*, p. 210.

46. *Ibid.*

47. HSCA, pp. 492–493.

48. Cook, *The Segregationists*, pp. 155–166; HSCA, pp. 493–494; Levitas, pp. 1–23.

49. HSCA, pp. 494–495.

50. *Ibid.*, pp. 495–496.

51. *Ibid.*, pp. 496–499.

52. *Ibid.*, pp. 499–502.

53. *Ibid.*, pp. 470–485.

54. Newton, *FBI Encyclopedia*, p. 284; Newton, *Ku Klux Klan*, pp. 477–478.

Chapter 9

1. Theoharis, *FBI*, pp. 127–135.
2. Kennedy, p. 284; Wheaton, p. 40.
3. Sims, pp. 5, 124, 185; *Hate Groups in America* (New York: Anti-Defamation League, n.d.), p. 4.
4. Moore, pp. 106–107, 218–233, 244–277.
5. Donner, *Protectors of Privilege,* p. 269.
6. Chalmers, pp. 419–420.
7. Chalmers, pp. 419–420; Wade, pp. 378–380; Wheaton, pp. 46, 171.
8. Wade, p. 380; Wheaton, pp. 208, 265.
9. Chalmers, p. 418; Wheaton, pp. 3, 188, 241.
10. Chalmers, p. 422; Wheaton, pp. 3, 186.
11. Wade, pp. 381–382; Wheaton, pp. 106, 186, 241–242.
12. Wade, pp. 381–382, 388–389; *Klanwatch Intelligence Report* 47 (December 1989), p. 3.
13. Wheaton, pp. 245–246.
14. Wheaton, pp. 252–254, 256, 260–261, 265, 272–276, 279–280.
15. *Ibid.,* pp. 4, 281–282, 284.
16. Newton, *FBI Encyclopedia*, pp. 284–285.
17. Grossup, pp. 100–101; Moore, pp. 218–220, 223–225, 231–232; Newton, *FBI Encyclopedia*, p. 52.
18. Moore, pp. 227–228; Flynn and Gerhardt, p. 352.
19. Flynn and Gerhardt, pp. 351–352; Moore, pp. 227–228; Newton, *Ku Klux Klan*, pp. 166–167, 171.
20. Moore, p. 365; *ADL Facts* 25 (November 1979): 3; *Klanwatch Intelligence Report* 47 (December 1989), p. 6; Newton, *FBI Encyclopedia*, p. 368; *Extremism on the Right* (New York: Anti-Defamation League, 1983), pp. 16–17, 153–156.
21. *Klanwatch Intelligence Report* 47 (December 1989), pp. 3–5.
22. *Klanwatch Intelligence Report* 47 (December 1989), p. 2.
23. Stanton, *Klanwatch*, pp. 87–88, 193–195, 197–198.
24. *Ibid.,* pp. 192, 195–196, 199, 203–204, 248.
25. *Ibid.,* pp. 201, 221–222, 232–235, 244–247.
26. Newton, *Encyclopedia of Serial Killers,* pp. 7–8.
27. *Ibid.,* p. 8; Dettlinger and Prugh, pp. 21–22.
28. Newton, *Encyclopedia of Serial Killers,* p. 8.
29. *Ibid.*
30. *Ibid.*
31. Douglas and Olshaker, p. 204.
32. *Ibid.,* pp. 198–204, 215; Newton, *Serial Slaughter,* pp. 47–62, 94–98.
33. Dettlinger and Prugh, p. 21; Michael Newton, "Suitable for framing," in *Abuse Your Illusions* (St. Paul, MN: The Disinformation Co., 2002), p. 110.
34. Newton, "Suitable for framing," p. 110.
35. *Ibid.*
36. *Ibid.*; Mary Fischer, "Was Wayne Williams framed?" *GQ* (April 1991), p. 235.
37. Newton, "Suitable for framing," p. 110.
38. *Ibid.,* pp. 110–111.
39. Fischer, p. 233; Newton, "Suitable for framing," p. 111.
40. Newton, "Suitable for framing," p. 111.
41. *Ibid.*
42. Fischer, pp. 232–233.
43. Dettlinger and Prugh, pp. 22–23; Douglas and Olshaker, p. 223.
44. Fischer, p. 234; Newton, "Suitable for framing," p. 111.
45. Fischer, p. 234.
46. Newton, "Suitable for framing," p. 111.
47. *Ibid.*
48. Douglas and Olshaker, p. 202.
49. Newton, "Suitable for framing," p. 112; Newton, *Invisible Empire,* pp. 205–205.
50. Newton, "Suitable for framing," p. 113.
51. Newton, *FBI Encyclopedia*, pp. 123–125.
52. Chalmers, p. 438.

Chapter 10

1. Lee, p. 339.
2. Levitas, pp. 16–31.
3. *Ibid.,* pp. 50–51, 66, 93–94, 109; Ridgeway, p. 129.
4. Levitas, pp. 114, 439–440.
5. *Ibid.,* pp. 116, 135–136; *Klanwatch Intelligence Report* 47 (December 1989), p. 4; Stern, p. 52.
6. Levitas, pp. 119–120, 132.
7. *Ibid.,* pp. 134, 137.
8. *Ibid.,* pp. 137, 167.
9. *Ibid.,* pp. 183–185, 462.
10. *Ibid.,* pp. 5, 195–200, 372.
11. *Ibid.,* pp. 232–233, 228–239.
12. *Ibid.,* pp. 286, 288.
13. *Ibid.,* pp. 284–285, 296–298.
14. Levitas, p. 289; Stern, p. 191; *Klanwatch Intelligence Report* 47 (December 1989), pp. 17, 20, 22; *Klanwatch Intelligence Report* 97 (Winter 2000), p. 18.
15. Smith, pp. 67–68.
16. Flynn and Gerhardt, pp. 135, 141, 196, 201–202; Lee, p. 340; Smith, pp. 68, 71; Dees and Corcoran, p. 42.
17. Flynn and Gerhardt, pp. 203–208; Smith, pp. 68–69.
18. Flynn and Gerhardt, pp. 209–250.
19. Dees and Corcoran, p. 45; Flynn and Gerhardt, pp. 251–290, 318–325, 331.
20. Flynn and Gerhardt, pp. 354–355, 369–375, 393–406; Smith, pp. 71–72.
21. Flynn and Gerhardt, p. 419.
22. *Ibid.,* pp. 407–447; Smith, pp. 72–73.
23. Flynn and Gerhardt, pp. 451, 464; Hamm, p. 14; Smith, pp. 66, 74–77.

24. Dees and Corcoran, pp. 98–99; Smith, pp. 84–86.

25. Dees and Corcoran, pp. 100–101.

26. *Klanwatch Intelligence Report* 47 (December 1989), pp. 14, 16, 18; Smith, pp. 86–87; Lutz, p. 66.

27. Smith, p. 87.

28. *Extremism on the Right,* p. 7; Hamm, pp. 5–6; Smith, pp. 62–68.

29. Dees and Corcoran, p. 43; Flynn and Gerhardt, p. 471; Hamm, pp. 15–16; Smith, pp. 56, 88.

30. Dees and Corcoran, pp. 44, 46; Smith, pp. 55–56, 88–89.

31. Dees and Corcoran, p. 46; Flynn and Gerhardt, pp. 461–473.

32. Grossup, pp. 89, 104–105.

33. *Ibid.,* pp. 104–107, 116–117.

34. *Ibid.,* p. 117; Moore, p. 249.

35. Moore, p. 359.

36. Grossup, p. 111; Baird-Windle and Bader, p. 354.

37. Baird-Windle and Bader, pp. 55, 64–66, 78, 83; Moore, pp. 248–250.

38. Baird-Windle and Bader, pp. 83–84.

39. *Ibid.,* pp. 100–102; Risen and Thomas, pp. 115–116.

40. Newton, *Invisible Empire,* p. 196; Tom Burghardt, "Neo-Nazis salute the anti-abortion zealots." *Covert Action Quarterly* (Spring 1995), p. 27.

41. Baird-Windle and Bader, pp. 78–79; Burghardt, p. 32; Risen and Thomas, pp, 194–197, 199.

42. Baird-Windle and Bader, pp. 78–79, 84, 110–111; Risen and Thomas, pp. 199, 200–202.

43. Baird-Windle and Bader, pp. 206–208; Risen and Thomas, pp. 339, 341–342, 348.

44. Baird-Windle and Bader, pp. 142, 210, 225–226, 263; Risen and Thomas, p. 359.

45. Baird-Windle and Bader, pp. 229–234; Burghardt, p. 27.

46. Baird-Windle and Bader, p. 239.

47. *Ibid.,* p. 263, 367–369; *Klanwatch Intelligence Report* No. 111 (Fall 2003), p. 4; Feminist Daily News Wire (12 May 2004), http://www.feminist.org/news/newsbyte/uswirestory.asp?id=843.

48. Grossup, pp. 114, 117; William Booth, "In church fires, a pattern but no conspiracy." *Washington Post* (19 June 1996), p. A1.

49. ADL press release, "Hate Groups and Black Church Arsons—State by State" (20 June 1996); "Volunteer firefighter, KKK members charged in separate black church burnings." CNN (9 July 1996); "Former Klansmen plead guilty in church fires." CNN (14 August 1996).

50. "Two more ex-Klansmen charged in black church fire." CNN (16 August 1996); "Former KKK member allegedly vowed to burn church again." CNN (20 August 1996); Leslie Feinberg, "Klan members confess." *Workers World* (29 August 1996); Wendy Brinker, "Macedonia Baptist has their day in court." *South Carolina Black News* (23 July 1998); Wendy Brinker, "KKK, King and conspirators ordered to pay \$37.8 million." *South Carolina Black News* (30 July 1998).

51. "Five teens arrested in Alabama church fire." CNN (6 July 1997); *U.S. v. Alan Odom and Brandy Nicole Boone* No. 98-6241-BB, http://www.usdoj.gov/crt/briefs/odom.htm.

52. Newton, *FBI Encyclopedia,* p. 362; Stern, pp. 21–22; Snow, pp. 3–5.

53. Newton, *FBI Encyclopedia,* pp. 362–363; Snow, pp. 8, 11–12; Stern, p. 23.

54. Dees and Corcoran, pp. 1–3; Stern, pp. 35–36.

55. Jeffrey Kaplan, "Leaderless resistance." *Terrorism and Political Violence* 9 (Autumn 1997): 89–90.

56. Stern, pp. 36, 41, 45, 68–71; *Klanwatch Intelligence Report* No. 97 (Winter 2000), pp. 18–19.

57. Levitas, pp. 303–305; Newton, *FBI Encyclopedia,* pp. 43–44.

58. Levitas, p. 305; Snow, pp. 66, 68–69, 148.

59. Grossup, p. 118.

60. *Ibid.,* p. 119.

61. *Ibid.*

62. *Ibid.*

63. *Ibid.*

64. *Ibid.,* p. 120; Levitas, pp. 320–321; *Vietnamese Fisherman's Association v. The Knights of the Ku Klux Klan,* 543 F. Supp. 198, 210 (S.D. Texas 1982).

65. Grossup, p. 120.

66. Snow, pp. 117–118; Stern, p. 232; "Extremism in the ranks." *Newsweek* (25 March 1996), pp. 34, 36.

67. *Klanwatch Intelligence Report* 97 (Winter 2000), p. 11.

68. *Ibid.,* pp. 12, 15.

69. *Ibid.,* p. 12.

70. *Ibid.;* Massengill, pp. 10–12, 302–306.

71. *Klanwatch Intelligence Report* 97 (Winter 2000), p. 18.

72. *Ibid.*

73. *Ibid.,* p. 21.

74. *Ibid.;* Dees and Corcoran, p. 9.

75. *Klanwatch Intelligence Report* 97 (Winter 2000), p. 22; *Klanwatch Intelligence Report* 102 (Summer 2001), p. 18.

76. *Klanwatch Intelligence Report* 97 (Winter 2000), p. 23.

77. Dees and Corcoran, pp. 8–9; *Klanwatch Intelligence Report* 97 (Winter 2000), p. 22.

78. Dees and Corcoran, p. 9; *Klanwatch Intelligence Report* 97 (Winter 2000), PP. 22–23.

79. Dees and Corcoran, p. 9.

80. *Klanwatch Intelligence Report* 97 (Winter 2000), p. 23.

81. Dees and Corcoran, p. 9; *Klanwatch Intelligence Report* 97 (Winter 2000), p. 23.

82. *Klanwatch Intelligence Report* 97 (Winter 2000), p. 24.

83. *Ibid.*

84. *Ibid.*, pp. 24–25.

85. *Ibid.*, p. 26.

86. *Ibid.*, p. 27.

87. *Ibid.*, p. 29.

88. *Ibid.*

89. Newton, *FBI Encyclopedia,* p. 219.

90. *Ibid.*, pp. 219–220; John Kelly and Phillip Wearne, *Tainting Evidence* (New York: The Free Press, 1998), pp. 198–201.

91. Newton, *FBI Encyclopedia,* p. 220.

92. Jones and Israel, pp. 74–75; Michel and Herbeck, pp. 250–275; Newton, *FBI Encyclopedia,* p. 220.

93. Dees and Corcoran, pp. 162–165; Jones and Israel, p. 149; Stern, pp. 189–192.

94. Jones and Israel, pp. 74–77; Newton, *FBI Encyclopedia,* p. 220.

95. Kelly and Wearne, pp. 195–230; Michel and Herbeck, pp. 317–318.

96. Kelly and Wearne, pp. 208–209.

97. Newton, *FBI Encyclopedia,* p. 220; "Terry Nichols." *Wikipedia,* http://en.wikipedia.org/wiki/Terry_Nichols.

98. Newton, *FBI Encyclopedia,* pp. 220–221.

99. *Ibid.*, p. 221.

100. Max McCoy, "White noise." *Fortean Times* 189 (December 2004), pp. 47–48.

101. Dees and Corcoran, p. 165; Jones and Israel, p. 149; McCoy, p. 47.

102. Jones and Israel, pp. 151–153, 156–157; Lee, pp. 352–353.

103. Jones and Israel, pp. 148–149, 156–157, 159, 191–193, 290; Lee, pp. 352–353.

104. Lee, p. 353; McCoy, p. 47; "The Aryan Republican Army." http://eyeonhate.com/mcveigh/mcveigh7.html.

105. Lee, p. 354; McCoy, p. 47; James Ridgeway, "McVeigh papers: What did the government know?" *Village Voice* (11 May 2001).

106. McCoy, pp. 45–48; "The Aryan Republican Army." http://eyeonhate.com/mcveigh/mcveigh7.html.

107. Lee, p. 354; McCoy, p. 48.

108. *Klanwatch Intelligence Report* 97 (Winter 2000), p. 30; *Klanwatch Intelligence Report* 102 (Summer 2001), p. 34; *Klanwatch Intelligence Report* 105 (Spring 2002), p. 34; *Klanwatch Intelligence Report* 109 (Spring 2003), p. 38; *Klanwatch Intelligence Report* 113 (Spring 2004), p. 38; Snow, pp. 17–18.

Bibliography

Alexander, Charles. *The Ku Klux Klan in the Southwest*. Norman: University of Oklahoma Press, 1965.

Alix, Ernest. *Ransom Kidnapping in America, 1874–1974*. Carbondale: Southern Illinois University Press, 1978.

Baird-Windle, Patricia, and Eleanor Bader. *Targets of Hatred*. New York: Palgrave, 2001.

Bartley, Numan. *The Rise of Massive Resistance*. Baton Rouge: Louisiana State University Press, 1997.

Bennett, Lerone, Jr. *Before the Mayflower: A History of Black America*. 6th edition. New York: Penguin Books, 1988.

Blackstock, Nelson. *COINTELPRO: The FBI's Secret War on Political Freedom*. New York: Vintage Books, 1975.

Blum, William. *Killing Hope: U.S. Military and CIA Interventions Since World War II*. Monroe, ME: Common Courage Press, 1995.

Branch, Taylor. *Parting the Waters*. New York: Simon & Schuster, 1988.

Bullard, Sara (ed.). *Free at Last*. Montgomery, AL: Southern Poverty Law Center, n.d.

Cagin, Seth, and Philip Dray. *We Are Not Afraid*. New York: Bantam Books, 1988.

Carlson, John. *The Plotters*. New York: E.P. Dutton, 1946.

_____. *Under Cover*. New York: E.P. Dutton, 1943.

Carter, Dan. *The Politics of Rage*. Baton Rouge: Louisiana State University Press, 2000.

Carter, W. Horace. *Voices of Fear*. Tabor City, NC: The Author, 1991.

Chalmers, David. *Hooded Americanism: The History of the Ku Klux Klan*. 3rd edition. Durham, NC: Duke University Press, 1981.

Churchill, Ward, and Jim Vander Wall. *The COINTELPRO Papers*. Boston: South End Press, 1990.

Clegg, Claude III. *An Original Man: The Life and Times of Elijah Muhammad*. New York: St. Martin's, 1997.

Cook, Fred. *The FBI Nobody Knows*. New York: Pyramid Books, 1964.

Cook, James. *The Segregationists*. New York: Appleton-Century-Crofts, 1962.

Dees, Morris, and James Corcoran. *Gathering Storm*. New York: HarperPerennial, 1996.

DeLaughter, Bobby. *Never Too Late*. New York: Scribner, 2001.

Deloach, Cartha. *Hoover's FBI*. Washington, D.C.: Regnery Publishing, 1995.

de Toledano, Ralph. *J. Edgar Hoover: The Man in His Time*. New York: Manor Books, 1974.

Dettlinger, Chet, and Jeff Prugh. *The List*. Atlanta: Philmay Enterprises, 1983.

Donner, Frank. *The Age of Surveillance*. New York: Alfred A. Knopf, 1980.

_____. *Protectors of Privilege: Red Squads and Police Repression in Urban America*. Berkeley: University of California Press, 1990.

Douglas, John, and Mark Olshaker. *Mindhunter*. New York: Pocket Books, 1995.

Doyle, William. *An American Insurrection*. New York: Anchor Books, 2001.

Dray, Philip. *At the Hands of Persons Unknown: The Lynching of Black America*. New York: Modern Library, 2002.

Eagles, Charles. *Outside Agitator: Jon Daniels and the Civil Rights Movement in Alabama*. Chapel Hill: University of North Carolina Press, 1993.

Epstein, Benjamin, and Arnold Forster. *Report on the John Birch Society 1966*. New York: Random House, 1966.

Evers, Charles, and Andrew Szanton. *Have No Fear.* New York: John Wiley & Sons, 1997.

Feldman, Glenn. *Politics, Society, and the Klan in Alabama, 1915–1949.* Tuscaloosa: University of Alabama Press, 1999.

Flowers, Richmond. "Southern plain talk about the Ku Klux Klan." *Look* (3 May 1966).

Flynn, Kevin, and Gary Gerhardt. *The Silent Brotherhood.* New York: Signet, 1995.

Forster, Arnold, and Benjamin Epstein. *Report on the Ku Klux Klan.* New York: Anti-Defamation League, 1966.

Gannon, Michael. *The New History of Florida.* Gainesville: University Press of Florida, 1996.

Garrow, David. *The FBI and Martin Luther King, Jr.* New York: W.W. Norton, 1981.

_____ (ed.). *St. Augustine, Florida, 1963–1964.* New York: Carlson, 1989.

Gentry, Curt. *J. Edgar Hoover: The Man and the Secrets.* New York: 1992.

Gillette, Paul, and Eugene Tillinger. *Inside Ku Klux Klan.* New York: Pyramid Books, 1965.

Glick, Brian. *War at Home: Covert Action Against U.S. Activists and What We Can Do About It.* Boston: South End Press, 1989.

Goodman, Walter. *The Committee.* Baltimore: Penguin, 1969.

Green, Ben. *Before His Time.* New York: Free Press, 1999.

Greene, Melissa. *The Temple Bombing.* New York: Fawcett Columbine, 1996.

Grossup, Beau. *The Newest Explosions of Terrorism.* Far Hills, NJ: New Horizons Press, 1988.

Hamm, Mark. *Apocalypse in Oklahoma.* Boston: Northeastern University Press, 1997.

Hendrickson, Paul. *Sons of Mississippi.* New York: Alfred A. Knopf, 2003.

Hoffman, Abbie. *Soon to Be a Major Motion Picture.* New York: G.P. Putnam's Sons, 1980.

House Committee on Un-American Activities, *Activities of Ku Klux Klan Organizations in the United States.* Washington, DC: U.S. Government Printing Office, 1966.

_____. *The Present-Day Ku Klux Klan Movement.* Washington, DC: U.S. Government Printing Office, 1967.

House Select Committee on Assassinations, *The Final Assassinations Report.* New York: Bantam, 1979.

Jackson, Kenneth. *The Ku Klux Klan in the City, 1915–1930.* New York: Oxford University Press, 1967.

Jenkins, Philip. *Hoods and Shirts: The Extreme Right in Pennsylvania, 1925–1950.* Chapel Hill: University of North Carolina Press, 1997.

Jones, J. Harry Jr. *The Minutemen.* Garden City, NY: Doubleday, 1968.

Jones, Stephen, and Peter Israel. *Others Unknown.* New York: BBS Publications, 1998.

Kennedy, Stetson. *The Klan Unmasked.* Boca Raton: Florida Atlantic University Press, 1990.

Kessler, Ronald. *The Bureau: The Secret History of the FBI.* New York: St. Martin's Press, 2002.

Kirkham, James. *Assassination and Political Violence.* New York: Bantam, 1970.

Kornweibel, Theodore Jr. *Seeing Red: Federal Campaigns Against Black Militancy, 1919-1925.* Bloomington: Indiana University Press, 1998.

Lee, Martin. *The Beast Reawakens.* Boston: Little, Brown and Co., 1997.

Levitas, Daniel. *The Terrorist Next Door.* New York: Thomas Dunne Books, 2002.

Lowe, David. *KKK: The Invisible Empire.* New York: W.W. Norton, 1967.

Lowenthal, Max. *The Federal Bureau of Investigation.* New York: Harcourt Brace Jovanovich, 1950.

Lutz, Chris. *They Don't All Wear Sheets.* Atlanta: Center for Democratic Renewal, 1987.

Manchester, William. *The Glory and the Dream.* Boston: Little, Brown, 1974.

Marsh, Charles. *God's Long Summer.* Princeton, NJ: Princeton University Press, 1997.

Massengill, Reed. *Portrait of a Racist.* New York: St. Martin's Griffin, 1996.

McGovern, James. *Anatomy of a Lynching: The Killing of Claude Neal.* Baton Rouge: Louisiana State University Press, 1982.

McIlhaney, William II. *Klandestine: The Untold Story of Delmar Dennis and His Role in the FBI's War Against the Ku Klux Klan.* New York: Arlington House, 1975.

McMillen, Neil. *The Citizens' Council.* Urbana: University of Illinois Press, 1971.

McWhorter, Diane. *Carry Me Home.* New York: Simon & Schuster, 2001.

Melanson, Philip. *The MURKIN Conspiracy.* New York: Praeger, 1989.

Mendelsohn, Jack. *The Martyrs: Sixteen Who Gave Their Lives for Racial Justice.* New York: Harper & Row, 1966.

Messick, Hank. *John Edgar Hoover.* New York: David McKay Co., 1972.

Michel, Lou, and Dan Herbeck. *American Terrorist.* New York: Regan Books, 2001.

Milan, Michael. *The Squad*. New York: Berkley Books, 1989.

Moody, Anne. *Coming of Age in Mississippi*. New York: Dell, 1968.

Moore, James. *Very Special Agents*. New York: Pocket Books, 1997.

Myers, Gustavus. *History of Bigotry in the United States*. New York: Capricorn Books, 1960.

National Association for the Advancement of Colored People. *Thirty Years of Lynching in the United States, 1889-1918*. New York: Negro Universities Press, 1919.

Nelson, Jack. *Terror in the Night: The Klan's Campaign Against the Jews*. Jackson: University of Mississippi Press, 1993.

Newton, Michael. *The Encyclopedia of Serial Killers*. New York: Facts on File, 2000.

_____. *The FBI Encyclopedia*. Jefferson, NC: McFarland, 2003.

_____. *The Invisible Empire*. Gainesville: University Press of Florida, 2001.

_____. *The King Conspiracy*. Los Angeles: Holloway House, 1987.

_____. *Serial Slaughter*. Port Townsend, WA: Loompanics, 1993.

Newton, Michael, and Newton, Judy. *The Ku Klux Klan: An Encyclopedia*. New York: Garland, 1991.

_____. *Racial and Religious Violence in America*. New York: Garland, 1991.

Nossiter, Adam. *Of Long Memory*. Reading, MA: Addison-Wesley, 1994.

Nunnelley, William. *Bull Connor*. Tuscaloosa: University of Alabama Press, 1991.

O'Reilly, Kenneth. *"Racial Matters": The FBI's Secret File on Black America, 1960–1972*. New York: The Free Press, 1989.

Overstreet, Harry, and Overstreet, Bonaro. *The FBI in Our Open Society*. New York: W.W. Norton, 1969.

Parenti, Michael. *Dirty Truths*. San Francisco: City Light Books, 1996.

Parker, Thomas (ed.). *Violence in the U.S.: Volume 1, 1956–67*. New York: Facts on File, 1974.

Popkin, Richard. "The strange case of the Secret Army Organization (USA)." *Ramparts* (October 1973).

Powers, Richard. *Secrecy and Power: The Life of J. Edgar Hoover*. New York: The Free Press, 1987.

Report of the Joint Select Committee to Inquire into the Condition of Affairs in the Late Insurrectionary States, 13 vols. Washington, DC: U.S. Government Printing Office, 1872.

Rice, Arnold. *The Ku Klux Klan in American Politics*. Washington, D.C.: Public Affairs Press, 1962.

Ridgeway, James. *Blood in the Face*. 2nd edition. New York: Thunder's Mouth Press, 1995.

Risen, James, and Judy Thomas. *Wrath of Angels*. New York: Basic Books, 1998.

Rowe, Gary. *My Undercover Years with the Ku Klux Klan*. New York: Bantam, 1976.

Russo, Gus. *The Outfit*. New York: Bloomsbury, 2001.

Schmaltz, William. *Hate: George Lincoln Rockwell and the American Nazi Party*. Washington, DC: Brassey's, 1999.

Sherrill, Robert. *Gothic Politics in the Deep South*. New York: Grossman, 1968.

Silver, James. *Mississippi: The Closed Society*. New York: Harcourt, Brace & World, 1963.

Simonelli, Frederick. *American Fuehrer*. Urbana: University of Illinois Press, 1999.

Sims, Patsy. *The Klan*. New York: Stein and Day, 1978.

Smith, Brent. *Terrorism in America: Pipe Bombs and Pipe Dreams*. Albany: State University of New York Press, 1994.

Snow, Robert. *The Militia Threat*. New York: Plenum Trade, 1999.

Stanton, Bill. *Klanwatch*. New York: Grove Weidenfeld, 1991.

Stanton, Mary. *From Selma to Sorrow*. Athens, GA: University of Georgia Press, 1998.

Stern, Kenneth. *A Force Upon the Plain*. New York: Simon & Schuster, 1996.

Sullivan, William. *The Bureau: My Thirty Years in Hoover's FBI*. New York: W.W. Norton, 1979.

Theoharis, Athan (ed.). *The FBI: A Comprehensive Reference Guide*. New York: Checkmark Books, 2000.

_____. *Spying on Americans*. Philadelphia: Temple University Press, 1978.

Theoharis, Athan, and John Cox. *The Boss: J. Edgar Hoover and the Great American Inquisition*. Philadelphia: Temple University Press, 1988.

Trelease, Allen. *White Terror: The Ku Klux Klan Conspiracy and Southern Reconstruction*. New York: Harper & Row, 1971.

Tully, Andrew. *The FBI's Most Famous Cases*. New York: Dell, 1965.

Ungar, Sanford. *FBI*. Boston: Atlantic-Little, Brown, 1976.

Villano, Anthony, and Gerald Astor. *Brick Agent: Inside the Mafia for the FBI*. New York: Quadrangle, 1977.

Vollers, Maryanne. *Ghosts of Mississippi*. Boston: Little, Brown, 1995.

Wade, Wyn. *The Fiery Cross: The Ku Klux Klan in America*. New York: Oxford University Press, 1987.

Wheaton, Elizabeth. *Codename GREENKILL: The 1979 Greensboro Killings*. Athens: University of Georgia Press, 1987.

Whitehead, Don. *Attack on Terror: The FBI Against the Ku Klux Klan in Mississippi*. New York: Funk & Wagnalls, 1970.

_____. *The FBI Story: A Report to the People*. New York: Random House, 1956.

Whitfield, Stephen. *A Death in the Delta*. Baltimore: Johns Hopkins University Press, 1988.

Woodward, C. Vann. *The Strange Career of Jim Crow*. 3rd edition. New York: Oxford University Press, 1974.

Zinn, Howard. *Albany: A Study in National Responsibility*. Atlanta: Southern Regional Council, 1962.

Index

www.ingramcontent.com/pod-product-compliance
Lightning Source LLC
Chambersburg PA
CBHW080552270326
41929CB00019B/3270